# Email

**Other titles available from Law Society Publishing:**

**Drafting Confidentiality Agreements (2nd Edition)**
Mark Anderson and Simon Keevey-Kothari

**Entertainment Law Handbook**
Richard Verow, Nick Kanaar, Estelle Overs and Vincent Scheurer

**Execution of Documents (2nd Edition)**
Mark Anderson and Victor Warner

**Intellectual Property Law Handbook**
Bird & Bird, Edited by Lorna Brazell

All books from Law Society Publishing can be ordered from all good bookshops or direct (telephone 0870 850 1422, email **law.society@prolog.uk.com** or visit our online shop at **www.lawsociety.org.uk/bookshop**).

# EMAIL

## Law, Practice and Compliance

**Stewart Room**

ISBN 978-1-85328-594-3



Published in 2009 by the Law Society
113 Chancery Lane, London WC2A 1PL

Typeset by J&L Composition Ltd, Filey, North Yorkshire
Printed by Hobbs the Printers Ltd, Totton, Hants

The paper used for the text pages of this book is FSC certified. FSC (The Forest Stewardship Council) is an international network to promote responsible management of the world's forests.

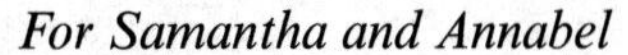

*For Samantha and Annabel*

# Contents

# About the author

Stewart Room, a partner in Field Fisher Waterhouse's Technology Law Group, is a dual qualified barrister and a solicitor with considerable expertise and reputation in privacy, data protection and data security law matters. He is rated as a leading individual in the field of data protection by the legal directory Chambers UK.

His contentious experience in the field of data protection covers both civil and criminal cases. In 2007 he successfully defended private investigators in landmark criminal proceedings brought by the Information Commissioner about theft of electronic data from a government department; this case was the one that the Information Commissioner relied upon in a report to Parliament in May 2006, *What price privacy?*, to support his call for amendment of the Data Protection Act 1998 to introduce custodial penalties for data theft. In 2008 he successfully represented a leading national retailer in Data Protection Act appeal proceedings which resulted in the cancellation of a regulatory enforcement notice issued by the Information Commissioner following the theft of an unencrypted laptop computer.

His non-contentious experience covers all aspect of data protection, including risk assessments, advice on compliance strategies, and creation and development of internal policy documents. His clients include Marks & Spencer, BBC, BP, Nestlé and UNICEF.

He also advises IT companies on Privacy Enhancing Technologies and on how technology generally can help organisations meet their legal obligations. His clients include EMC, Computer Associates, Hitachi Data Systems, RSA, IBM, Hewlett Packard, Symantec, Computer Associates, Mimecast and GWAVA.

He is the author of *Data Protection and Compliance in Context* (2006) and author and editor of the data protection chapter in *Goode: Consumer Credit Law and Practice* (since 2005).

He is a member of the Middle Temple and of the Law Society and is the elected President of the National Association of Data Protection and Freedom of Information Officers. He is in great demand as a conference speaker and frequently quoted in the national press.

In October 2008 he was named as the winner of the *Financial Times* 'Legal Innovator of the Year' Award.

# Preface

This is a book about email law; or rather, a book about core laws and practice rules that impact upon the use of email, and about how organisations can structure and manage themselves so as to be compliant with these laws and rules. However, at the outset it is important to manage expectations: this book does not and cannot seek to claim that it is about all of the laws and rules that impact on email. To say otherwise would be an idle boast that would not persuade even an idiot. In fact, if we are to be truly honest it might be possible for a much more creative and brainier author than this one to 'retro-fit' the entire laws of England and Wales into a book on email law. For example, I would not be at all surprised if there was some obscure area of ecclesiastical law that could be legitimately housed in a work of this title! Thus, at the outset I wish to make it clear that this book can only scratch the surface of the body of laws and practice rules that might be engaged by the use of email.

The approach taken in this book is a thematic one, which is aimed at bringing a kind of structure to the 'thinking process' that would lead an organisation, whether assisted by a lawyer or not, to a state of legal compliance in its email use that it would feel comfortable with. For this reason the book tackles, admittedly in a somewhat loose manner, a connected chain of core themes that would apply in the hypothetical 'average' email-enabled organisation (if such an organisation were ever to exist), heavily supported by extracts from statutes and case law.

**Chapter 1** begins with a brief examination of the character and technology of email, to equip the non-geek with a basic level of understanding of what email does, why and how. **Chapter 2** then moves on to examine a group of laws that have deliberately addressed the worlds of technology and electronic communications and the at-a-distance commercial relationships that technology and electronic communications have either spawned or supported, with the central proposition being that in one way or another they have encouraged the take-up, use and acceptance or email, either directly or indirectly. In **Chapter 3** the theme turns to privacy and data protection law, which is fundamental to any analysis of email. In fact, data protection is so important within the world of email, that the discussion continues in **Chapter 4**, at Mimecast; Laurence O'Brien and Mitch Lauer at GWAVA; Ed Gibson at Microsoft; Charlie McAlister at Sensage; Mark Saville at Smartways; James Kirkland at Computer Associates; Debra Ames at MTI; Malcolm Marshall and George Thompson at KMPG; Theresa Pa at Accenture and Ian Lockhart and Simon Gay; you have all contributed to this book in one way or another.

Finally, a special word of thanks to Mike Pritchard at EMC, who was the person who introduced me to the delights of email archiving and storage technologies and became my first client at a major IT company; heartfelt thanks Mike for all of the work and for all of the introductions.

# Table of cases

# Table of statutes

# Table of statutory instruments

# Table of European legislation

## Treaties and conventions



## Directives

## Regulations

# Abbreviations

| | |
|---|---|
| ATCSA 2001 | Anti-Terrorism, Crime and Security Act 2001 |
| B2B | business-to-business |
| B2C | business-to-consumer |
| CDPA 1988 | Copyright, Designs and Patents Act 1988 |
| CDRD | Communications Data Retention Directive 2006 |
| CEA 1968 | Civil Evidence Act 1968 |
| CEA 1995 | Civil Evidence Act 1995 |
| CJA 2003 | Criminal Justice Act 2003 |
| CJPA 2001 | Criminal Justice and Police Act 2001 |
| CMA 1990 | Computer Misuse Act 1990 |
| CPIA 1996 | Criminal Procedure and Investigations Act 1996 |
| CPR | Civil Procedure Rules 1998 |
| CrimPR | Criminal Procedure Rules 2005 |
| DNS | Domain Name System |
| DPA 1998 | Data Protection Act 1998 |
| ECHR | European Convention on Human Rights |
| EE(A)R 2006 | Employment Equality (Age) Regulations 2006 |
| FSA | Financial Services Authority |
| HRA 1998 | Human Rights Act 1998 |
| HTTP | Hypertext Transfer Protocol |
| IETF | Internet Engineering Task Force |
| IMAP | Internet Message Access Protocol |
| IP | Internet Protocol |
| ISMS | Information Security Management System |
| ISP | Internet Service Provider |
| MiFID | Market in Financial Instruments Directive |
| MIME | Multipart Internet Mail Extensions |
| MoReq | Model Requirements for the Management of Electronic Records |
| P2P | peer-to-peer |
| PACE | Police and Criminal Evidence Act 1984 |
| PECD | Privacy and Electronic Communications Directive 2002 |
| PETs | Privacy Enhancing Technologies |

| | |
|---|---|
| PHA 1997 | Protection from Harassment Act 1997 |
| PII | Public Interest Immunity |
| POP3 | Post Office Protocol version 3 |
| RIPA 2000 | Regulation of Investigatory Powers Act 2000 |
| RRA 1976 | Race Relations Act 1976 |
| SDA 1975 | Sex Discrimination Act 1975 |
| SMTP | Simple Mail Transfer Protocol |
| SOCPA 2005 | Serious Organised Crime and Police Act 2005 |
| SSL | Secure Socket Layer |
| SYSC | Senior Management Arrangements, Systems and Controls |
| TCP | Transmission Control Protocol |
| UDP | User Datagram Protocol |
| URL | Uniform Resource Locator |
| WWW | World Wide Web |

CHAPTER 1

# The character and technology of email

## 1.1 INTRODUCTION

While at the date of publication of this book it would not be accurate to say that everyone uses email, email is nonetheless ubiquitous. However, understanding of the true character of email and the technologies underpinning its use and operation is less widespread. From the lawyer's perspective this cannot be acceptable, as email pervades every aspect of legal practice.

This chapter seeks to shed some light on the murkier, technical aspects of email, with two reasons in mind. First, the lawyer as a user of email might be influenced in the design and creation of internal usage policies for their practice once equipped with a basic knowledge of how email works; indeed, in two of the most infamous examples of email mishaps, City law firms were embarrassed. Second, the lawyer as an adviser to and representative of email users may attract a charge of failure of duty if they are unable to provide a basic level of competent advice on email. Thus, it is hoped that once equipped with an understanding of the basic technical aspects of email the lawyer can become a better lawyer, both in terms of the administration of their own practice and in the delivery of their professional services.

Furthermore, for lawyers engaged in contentious business an understanding of the basic technical aspects might be integral to the discharge of their duties owed to the court (for example, see Rule 1.01 of the Solicitors' Code of Conduct 2007 concerning the proper administration of justice: **www.sra.org.uk/rule1**). Consider the situation of the litigator: the case in which they are acting might result from improper use of email and/or emails might form part of the documentary evidence in the case. Consequently, disclosure obligations will arise relating to email[1] and there might also be a need for expert evidence, perhaps concerning the provenance of certain emails. In such a case the litigator will be under a duty to provide positive assistance to the court to ensure effective case management, but a breach of duty is probable where the lawyer is ignorant of the basic technical aspects of email.

## 1.2 WHAT IS EMAIL?

A helpful definition of email is 'a store and forward method of composing, sending, storing, and receiving messages over electronic communication systems'.[2] Within this definition are two terms – 'messages' and 'electronic communications systems' – that have important legal implications.

The reference to messages tells us that, first and foremost, email is a system for communications. Communications are at the very heart of the human experience, fundamental to every single aspect of private and public life. As such there is an immense corpus of law relating to communications. For example, as a form of expression freedom to communicate is protected as a human right (European Convention on Human Rights, Article 10), as is privacy within communications (Article 8). Communications can sometimes be defamatory (see Defamation Act 1996), harassing (see Protection from Harassment Act 1997) or discriminatory. Communications that are hateful (Public Order Act 1986, ss.17–29, discussed at **Chapter 6**), malicious (see Malicious Communications Act 1988, discussed at **Chapter 6**), dishonest (see Fraud Act 2006, s.2) and even merely annoying (see Communications Act 2003, s.127, discussed at **Chapter 6**) can all attract criminal liability. Contracts are always made by a process of communications. Other obligations may result from innocent and negligent communications.

As a system for communications, email can act as a substitute for both the spoken word and the written word. This bridging of forms of communications carries with it special perils for the email user; while email displays some of the instantaneous characteristics of conversation, it also displays the permanent characteristics of the written word. Implicit within all of the email mishap stories is the probability that the sender used a permanent medium to convey messages that they would usually only dare speak.

Communicating over electronic communications systems carries with it other forms of risk. For example, these systems operate in a manner that can expose the communication to more people than the intended recipient. They also involve a significantly greater risk of surveillance than is likely with face-to-face or postal communications: they permit comprehensive real-time[3] monitoring of activity and they generate considerable, detailed information about the communication distinct from its content[4] that also permits comprehensive post-event analysis of activity. They also easily cross international borders, raising jurisdictional problems.

From a more technical perspective, email is a service that is available over the internet. Other services available over the internet include the World Wide Web, online chat and file transfers.[5]

## 1.3 HOW EMAIL WORKS

The beauty of email is its apparent simplicity. In the real world of traditional mail, a writer, John, would set down his thoughts with pen and ink, seal the letter in an envelope, address that envelope to his friend Sarah on the other side of the world, apply a stamp (or frank it), and then find a postbox or other point of despatch. The Royal Mail (or other service provider) would then take the letter to a sorting office, interpret the address, and ship or fly it to the destination country where the local postal service would again interpret the address at one or more sorting offices before ultimately delivering it to Sarah's letterbox.

Should John wish instead to send Sarah an email, all he needs to do is to use his computer to type the message into the body of the email, and add Sarah's address to the To: field (together with a subject line, out of courtesy rather than necessity) before he clicks Send. From John's point of view, and all being well, the message will reach Sarah's inbox within seconds. There are no postal workers, no sorting offices, no intercontinental flights or ocean journeys and no stamp or franking to pay for.

It all sounds so simple and we can easily forget that what goes on behind the scenes is quite different from what happens to a traditional letter. However, and continuing with the traditional mail analogy, John might be quite upset to find that before it reached Sarah his letter had been rewritten in code and ripped into small pieces (packets) before being reassembled and decoded at the end of its journey!

### 1.3.1 The technology

When considering how the law might apply to modern communications, it is important to understand exactly what happens when John clicks Send. Unfortunately, achieving understanding requires the ingestion of much jargon, but a glossary can be found at page 374.

There are certain things on which email relies. Each of the sender and recipient has a device which at once functions as postbox and letterbox, allowing them to send and receive messages. This is of course the computer or, more precisely, a piece of software known as an email client. The email client can be a standalone application or it might be an internet browser accessing a remote web mail service.

When John wants to communicate with Sarah he opens his email client, types his message ('Sarah, when do you arrive in the UK? John'). He then addresses it to the recipient using her email address, 'sarah@example.com' ('example.com' denotes the second-level domain name registered to Sarah's company or other email provider (such as a web mail service), while 'sarah' specifies the mailbox at example.com which should receive the message). In comparison, John's email address is john@example.net (a different domain, in the .net top-level domain). John might add the subject line 'Holiday plans' to his email, but this isn't essential. He then clicks Send.

When John clicks the Send command in his email client, a number of things happen. First, the client formats the message according to a number of standards, together described as Multipurpose Internet Mail Extensions, or MIME. John's email client is configured to use his mail server 'smtp.example.net' and so it sends his message to that mail server in MIME format and using the Simple Mail Transfer Protocol (SMTP). As John's email client has told it to send the message to 'sarah@example.com', the next thing John's mail server does is to find out how to reach that domain. It does this by making a Domain Name System (DNS) request; Sarah's domain, like every other, will have a name server holding information about that domain, in this case the name server 'ns.example.com'. John's mail server asks ns.example.com for the IP address of the mail server for the domain example.com; in reply ns.example.com tells it the Internet Protocol (IP) address of Sarah's mail server 'smtp.example.com'.

Sarah's mail server, like John's, will be configured to listen for communications on certain Transmission Control Protocol (TCP) ports, and in particular port 25. Once John's mail server connects to Sarah's, it will again use the SMTP to relay the email to Sarah's mail server in the same way that John's email client gave it the message to begin with.

Once the email arrives at Sarah's SMTP server, it will recognise that the email is intended for the 'sarah' mailbox at example.com and will relay it to the Post Office Protocol version 3 (POP3) server at that domain. In practice the SMTP and POP3 servers for a domain are likely to be programs running on the same machine. Sarah's POP3 server allocates the email to Sarah's inbox, and it is then retrieved to her own email client, using the POP3 protocol, when she logs on to check her mail.

The email is usually then deleted from the POP3 server as part of the retrieval process; sometimes a copy may be stored but a key feature of the POP3 protocol is that the copy of a message held by the email client is the authoritative version. This distinguishes POP3 from the other commonly used mail retrieval protocol, the Internet Message Access Protocol (IMAP); where IMAP is used, the authoritative copy of a message is held in a store on the server rather than by a user's email client. This allows emails to be accessed by multiple clients (which will create their own local copies of the message) and is the way in which Sarah would read John's email if she were using a web mail client.

Mail servers may also use proprietary protocols (such as those used when the Microsoft Outlook client communicates with a Microsoft Exchange Server, as might be used in a corporate email system) but they will also support the standard protocols of SMTP, POP3 and IMAP. Emails held by a machine running Microsoft Exchange Server can also be accessed through a web browser interface, using Microsoft's Outlook Web Access (OWA).

One last, and increasingly common, technology is 'push email'. Push email is the technology by which email is routed to 'always on' devices, mainly smartphones and RIM's BlackBerry and Apple's iPhone. Whereas a corporate email client such as Microsoft Outlook might poll its mail server at regular intervals to retrieve any email which may have arrived in the user's mailbox, a push system, such as one running a BlackBerry Enterprise Server, will 'push' a message to the ultimate email client (the software application running on the BlackBerry handset) as soon as it arrives in the mailbox, without the need for a request from the client.

Although this book does not intend to give a comprehensive technical assessment of the email protocols, it is worth remembering that the different protocols will affect where copies of an email are stored (whether 'permanently' or in a temporary cache). When considering forensic recovery of evidence, for example, it is possible that copies of John's email will exist on the hard drive of his computer (running his email client), his and Sarah's mail servers (or those of their Internet Service Providers (ISPs)) and Sarah's computer running her email client. If she has read and displayed the email from a number of different machines using a web mail interface, cached copies may exist on the hard drives of each of those machines. Although they will often have been deleted, in certain circumstances where the relevant disk sectors have not been overwritten it may be possible for specialists to recover the 'deleted' email.

In practical use, email is a little more complicated than that described above. Because SMTP only really supports the transmission of plain text messages using a very limited character set, it cannot immediately process any message written using more complex characters (such as those with diacritics not found in English), let alone messages with JPEG image or mp3 audio attachments. When John's email client formats his email according to the MIME definition, it will also encode the message and its attachments using one of several forms of MIME content transfer encoding and making it suitable for relay by SMTP. The MIME headers (i.e. supplemental data placed at the beginning of a block of data being stored or transmitted) will tell the email clients which encoding has been used, such as MIME Base64.

Another complication of email is that, like any other data transmitted across the internet, a single message may be split into a number of 'packets' of data which are sent separately and reconstituted when they arrive. This is a feature of the TCP which underpins much of the working of the internet; while I have discussed how the SMTP is used to direct an email, it is primarily concerned with the recipients and therefore provides in general terms only the message body and meta-information such as the recipient address. The actual transmission of the data is achieved by TCP, which is designed to address the integrity of the data. Each data packet will consist of information, in 'headers', which describe it to the machines which receive it, together with the 'payload' of the user information it carries (i.e. the actual data being sent). Because the internet is a network of networks, each connected by backbone fibre-optic cables and routers functioning as network access points, each packet may travel any one of myriad pathways between John and Sarah's mail servers. One of the great advantages of this system is the concept of redundancy: should one backbone connection, or even several routers, fail, there are always other paths by which a packet can be transported between two computers connected to the internet. It is important to note two consequences of the structure of the internet and the way that data are transferred across the internet in packets. First, the number of relays involved increases the chance that poor connection quality (such as signal degradation over a wireless link) or hardware errors (such as a problem with a router not properly directing the packet) could cause the loss of one or more data packets and risk the integrity of the email at its destination (although TCP, in comparison to another transfer protocol, User Datagram Protocol (UDP), is designed to minimise if not eliminate the practical effect of packet loss and corruption). Second, the number of stages by which an email is relayed means that there is more opportunity for it to be intercepted and read or tampered with along the way. These 'man in the middle' attacks are generally prevented by the use of cryptographic protocols; for example, the Secure Socket Layer (SSL) protocol used to encrypt internet shopping transactions using the Hypertext Transfer Protocol (HTTP) works by verifying the data recipient against an independent source. Email can also be protected with various implementations of public key encryption to provide confidentiality, and digital signatures, based on a private encryption key, to provide authentication of origin.

## CHAPTER NOTES

1 See Civil Procedure Rules 1998, Part 31 and Practice Direction 31 (**www.justice.gov.uk**).
2 See Wikipedia: **http://en.wikipedia.org/wiki/Email**.
3 See the Regulation of Investigatory Powers (Maintenance of Interception Capability) Order 2002, which gives the Secretary of State the power to require providers of public telecommunication services to maintain a real-time interception capability, discussed at **Chapter 7**.
4 See Directive 2006/24/EC of the European Parliament and of the Council of 15 March 2006 on the retention of data generated or processed in connection with the provision of publicly available electronic communications services or of public communications networks and amending Directive 2002/58/EC. Article 5 identifies some of the information that is created by electronic communications systems during the course of a communication.
5 There is considerable confusion as to the distinction between the internet and the World Wide Web – these terms are not synonymous. The internet consists of a series of interconnected computer networks that are publicly available. As such, the internet is often described as being a 'network of networks'. Providers of these networks include public bodies, businesses, academic institutions and domestic

users. Data are transmitted in packets between these networks, using a series of standard protocols. The World Wide Web consists of a series of interlinked files, connected by hyperlinks, which is accessible through the internet. It is widely accepted that the World Wide Web was invented by Sir Tim Berners-Lee in 1989. The date of invention of the internet is less easy to pinpoint, but it certainly pre-dates the invention of the World Wide Web and its developmental history is traceable back to at least the late 1960s when the US Department of Defense Advanced Research Projects Agency commenced work on the development of the ARPANET, the forerunner to today's internet.

CHAPTER 2

# Lawmaking that encourages email

## 2.1 INTRODUCTION

The focus of this chapter is laws that have encouraged the take-up, use and acceptance of email. The essence of these laws is that they have all contributed to the creation of an environment that has enabled email as a medium for communications to flourish.

To understand this point it is worth recalling one of the key points made in the previous chapter, that email is a service available through the internet. Although the internet now seems to be unstoppable, there was a time, not all that long ago (and certainly within the span of the author's memory and career as a lawyer), when the world coped very well without the internet, thank you very much! Although it might not seem so now, the internet's rise to global prominence was not always an inevitability; as well as requiring the inventive skills of technologists and scientists, the internet also required supportive lawmaking and it might be fair to say that without supportive lawmaking the internet – and, therefore, email – would have remained a nascent technology, with its use being confined, perhaps, to certain governments, public authorities and academic institutions. However, as we know, things panned out differently and the internet is now one of the essential components of modern society.

The laws discussed in this chapter have collectively contributed to the creation of the right environment for email, in that they have encouraged its take-up, use and acceptance. For example, data protection laws have tackled two core concerns at the heart of data processing – the protection of fundamental rights and the free movement of data – and are connected to email in a direct sense, in that email's very essence is data processing (**2.2**). Telecommunications liberalisation laws have operated differently: they have created an environment which has led to the opening-up and renewal of the physical infrastructures upon which the internet's very existence is dependent – telecommunications networks – and have introduced competition in the supply of internet services, thereby lowering the barriers to the take-up and use of email (**2.2**). The group of laws that have been gathered together under the badge of dotcom fever and the information society operate differently again: they have acted to support email in a variety of ways, all of which have deliberately fostered take-up, acceptance and use (**2.3**). They have made email a viable substitute for older forms of communication, by guaranteeing the legal effect of electronic data and electronic contracts, while at the same time protecting the interests of consumers and users during their use of email.

## 2.2 DATA PROTECTION LAWS AND TELECOMMUNICATIONS LIBERALISATION

During the 1970s and 1980s, lawmakers in Europe embraced two concepts that have had a truly profound effect on email: data protection and telecommunications liberalisation. Laws that were designed to promote data protection and telecommunications liberalisation have operated to encourage the take-up, acceptance and use of email.

In summary, data protection laws have helped to encourage acceptance, take-up and use of email in two key ways:

- First, they have ensured a high level of protection across Europe for personal information that undergoes processing by computers and over communications networks. These protections have acted to instil confidence in the users of email that their interests will be protected. This confidence has encouraged demand for email services, which has led to a thriving and successful email economy.
- Second, they have helped to maintain the flow of personal information across Europe – it will be appreciated that the movement of information from one place to another is the very essence of email communications.

Data protection laws are discussed in more depth in subsequent chapters.

Similarly, it would be no exaggeration to say that without the telecommunications liberalisation agenda email services as we now know them would not have been possible. Prior to liberalisation, the telecommunications industry in Europe consisted of a handful of national incumbent monopolistic providers who had little incentive to modernise their industry. Networks were decrepit, voice telephony services were patchy and data services were virtually non-existent. Indeed, most people under the age of 40 would be aghast to learn just how poor the pre-liberalised telecommunications service actually was; in the writer's youth, 'party lines' were still the norm, which enabled one to listen-in on neighbours' conversations until they cottoned-on and told you where to go!

The telecommunications liberalisation agenda in Europe commenced properly in 1981, within the United Kingdom, with the passing of the British Telecommunications Act 1981. This Act introduced a minor level of competition into the UK industry, through the limited licensing of Mercury Communications. Subsequently, the liberalisation agenda spread to mainland Europe and over a period of about 10 years laws were passed allowing competition in the provision of telecommunications equipment, then services and then networks. This concerted effort has resulted in the modern, electronic communications industry with which we are now all familiar. Email is one of the most successful fruits of this labour.

## 2.3 DOTCOM FEVER AND THE INFORMATION SOCIETY

In the late 1990s the world – perhaps, more accurately, the Western world – was gripped by dotcom fever. The internet bubble had yet to burst.[1]

'Clicks and mortar' companies that had turned hardly a penny in profit were being valued in excess of long-standing stock market 'bricks and mortar' stalwarts, sometimes by considerable orders of magnitude. It seemed that anyone could be an internet entrepreneur, if they could take advantage of venture capital, personal savings, bank loans or contributions from friends, colleagues and relatives, and many people seriously expected to make millions overnight, if only on paper. Almost-forgotten buzzwords of the time, which are now uttered with a vague sense of embarrassment, included 'information superhighway' and 'knowledge economy'.

Looking back at those heady days with the benefit of hindsight we might wonder with incredulity how so many people were taken in by the hype and hyperbole of dotcom, but many otherwise-sensible people became victims of its siren allure. Even the European Community remodelled itself as an 'information society' and national governments were just as excited. This interest resulted in significant new lawmaking for the internet, particularly with the aim of encouraging e-commerce activities and, as a direct by-product, e-government.

Of course, the internet has survived the crazy days of dotcom; e-commerce is thriving and so is e-government; there are many successful 'pure' online businesses and still many fortunes to be made. The laws of the dotcom era are still with us too, continuing to help shape the internet for the present and for the future. These laws have made an indelible impact: being designed to encourage acceptance, take-up and use of the internet and new technologies, they have helped to create an environment in which the internet and all its constituent services, such as email, can thrive. While these laws adopt a myriad different phrases and terminology, they serve a surprisingly small number of key objectives, in particular:

- They seek to foster confidence in the new environment: users of the internet – whether they are service providers, recipients of services, investors or infrastructure providers – need to feel confident that their interests are protected. For this reason legislation has focused on the legal recognition of electronic contracting, the protection of the consumer's interests and data protection.

- They seek to create a favourable environment for market entry for new online service providers and for infrastructure providers: removal of barriers to entry has been a key objective. This is represented by 'light touch' regulation for the internet,[2] the doing-away with most requirements to obtain licences and regulatory approvals prior to commencing service provision and exclusions from key areas of liability. Monopolistic structures, environments in which monopolistic structures can develop and other anti-competitive behaviour have been tackled head-on.
- They seek to protect the intellectual property rights of online service providers.

## 2.4 DISTANCE SELLING DIRECTIVES – PROTECTING CONSUMERS IN DISTANCE CONTRACTS

One of the great benefits of communications technologies is that they allow people to contract over very large distances and on a global scale. This increases competition and empowers the consumer. However, there are downsides; for example, the consumer can be exploited when transactions are at a distance.

Although the issue of consumer protection in the field of e-commerce has been addressed by the E-Commerce Directive, the EC's Distance Selling Directive of 1997 represented the first step towards increased protections in this area, in the sense that the Distance Selling Directive extends to some facets of B2C (business-to-consumer) e-commerce. The Distance Selling Directive has not been superseded or replaced by the E-Commerce Directive either; it stands as a complementary legal regime, particularly notable for the fact that it actually covers a wider span of distance contracting than e-commerce.

### 2.4.1 Distance Selling Directive 1997

The focus of the Distance Selling Directive (Directive 97/7/EC of the European Parliament and of the Council of 20 May 1997 on the protection of consumers in respect of distance contracts), the first substantive EC legal instrument to impact on e-commerce, is not e-commerce but distance contracting between suppliers of goods and services and consumers. Of course, e-commerce is very often a subset of distance contracting, although B2B (business-to-business) e-commerce cannot fall within the scope of the Distance Selling Directive.

Article 2(1) defines a distance contract in the following terms:

> 'distance contract' means any contract concerning goods or services concluded between a supplier and a consumer under an organized distance sales or service-provision scheme run by the supplier, who, for the purpose of the contract, makes exclusive use of one or more means of distance communication up to and including the moment at which the contract is concluded.

This definition identifies the essential feature of a distance contract as being the making use of a means of distance communication. This concept is defined in Article 2(4) in the following terms:

> 'means of distance communication' means any means which, without the simultaneous physical presence of the supplier and the consumer, may be used for the conclusion of a contract between those parties. An indicative list of the means covered by this Directive is contained in Annex I.

The indicative list of distance communications set out in Annex I includes email.

The overriding purpose of the Directive is consumer protection. As such it can be said to encourage the acceptance, take-up and use of email. Its core components are concerned with:

- transparency;
- cancellation of distance contracts;
- performance of contracts;
- prevention of payment card fraud;
- restricting certain types of distance communication; and
- judicial and administrative redress.

However, the Directive does not apply to all contracts concluded through the means of a distance communication. Excluded are contracts for financial services covered by the Financial Services Distance Selling Directive (Directive 2002/65/EC); contracts concluded through automatic vending machines or automated commercial premises; contracts concluded with telecommunications operators through the use of public payphones; contracts concluded for the construction and sale of immovable property; and contracts relating to other immovable property rights except for rental and contracts concluded at auction (Article 3(1)).

### *Transparency in service provision – the supply of pre- and post-contractual information*

The Directive's transparency provisions are contained in Articles 4 and 5. They do not apply to the excluded contracts identified immediately above, nor do they apply to contracts for the supply of certain consumables or certain services which have an expiry date.[3]

Article 4 identifies key pieces of information that must be provided to the consumer by the supplier prior to the conclusion of the contract. This information must state the supplier's commercial purpose, it must be provided in a 'clear and comprehensible manner', it must have regard to the principles of good faith in commercial transactions and in providing this information the supplier must also have regard to any national laws governing the protection of those who are unable to give consent, such as minors. The information which is to be provided is:

(a) the identity of the supplier and, in the case of contracts requiring payment in advance, their address;
(b) the main characteristics of the goods or services;
(c) the price of the goods or services, including all taxes;
(d) delivery costs, where appropriate;
(e) the arrangements for payment, delivery or performance;
(f) the existence of a right of withdrawal;
(g) the cost of using the means of distance communication, where it is calculated other than at the basic rate;
(h) the period for which the offer or the price remains valid;
(i) where appropriate, the minimum duration of the contract in the case of contracts for the supply of products or services to be performed permanently or recurrently.

While the information should be provided in a clear and comprehensible manner, there is no requirement that the information should be provided in writing. Thus, where the means of distance communication is the telephone it will be lawful for the supplier to provide the information orally, whether by a person reading from a script or by a pre-recorded message. This distinguishes Article 4 from Article 5, which is concerned with the provision of written information or information in 'another durable medium', which, of course, covers email.

Article 5 applies after a contract has been concluded, i.e. after a contract has been made. Therefore, during the performance of the contract and prior to the delivery of goods to the consumer (if, that is, the contract is for goods) the supplier is required to provide the customer with written confirmation of the information identified above at points (a) to (d) inclusive (or, if not written, in some other durable medium, such as within an email[4]) plus:

(a) information about cancellation rights and procedures;
(b) the geographical address of the place of business of the supplier to which the consumer may address complaints;
(c) information on any after-sales service and guarantees which exist;
(d) the procedure for cancelling the contract where it is of unspecified duration or will last for more than one year.

These provisions do not apply (save for the requirement to give the information identified at 2 above) if:

- the contract is for services; and
- the services are to be performed through the use of a means of distance communication; and
- they are supplied on only one occasion; and
- they are invoiced by the operator of the means of distance communication.

### *Withdrawal – the 'cooling-off', or cancellation, provision*

Perhaps the most important innovation of the Distance Selling Directive is the right of withdrawal, which gives the consumer a minimum seven working-day cooling-off period during which time they may withdraw from, or cancel, the contract. The consumer cannot be penalised for withdrawal and is not required to provide reasons. The right of cancellation does not apply to all distance contracts, however (see Article 3).[5]

Where the right of cancellation applies, the cooling-off period will commence from the date of receipt of goods or from the date of conclusion of a services contract, provided that the information required by Article 5 has been provided. If the required information is not supplied in accordance with Article 5, the cooling-off period will be three months, but if the information is supplied within that three-month period the cooling-off period will be seven working days from the date it is provided.

In addition to the exemptions previously mentioned (see Article 3),[6] the right of cancellation will not apply in the following kinds of distance contracts without the parties' prior agreement:

- in service contracts if performance has begun, with the consumer's agreement, before the end of the cooling-off period;
- in contracts for the supply of goods or services where the price is dependent on fluctuations in the financial markets which cannot be controlled by the supplier;
- in contracts for the supply of goods that are made to the consumer's specifications or that are clearly personalised or that, by reason of their nature, cannot be returned or are liable to deteriorate or expire rapidly;
- in contracts for the supply of audio or video recordings or computer software which were unsealed by the consumer;
- in contracts for the supply of newspapers, periodicals and magazines; and
- in contracts for gaming and lottery services.

### *Performance of contracts*

Article 7 of the Directive sets a maximum period of 30 days for performance of a contract, unless the parties agree a different period. This period commences with the day following that on which the consumer forwarded their order to the supplier. If the supplier is unable to perform the contract within the maximum period (or within the agreed period, if different) and this is due to the goods or services being unavailable, the supplier must inform the consumer of this fact and must offer a refund. The refund must be made as soon as possible, and in any case within 30 days.

These rules are subject to a power that allows Member States to provide that the supplier may perform by providing goods or services of equivalent quality and price, provided that the consumer is informed of this possibility in a clear and comprehensible manner prior to conclusion of the contract.

### *Prevention of payment card fraud*

Payment card fraud is a continuing and real risk in distance contracts. Therefore, Article 8 requires Member States to ensure appropriate measures to allow a consumer to request cancellation of a payment that has been made through fraudulent use of their card. In such cases the consumer is entitled to have their cards re-credited.

### *Unsolicited communications – restrictions on the use of automated calling systems and fax*

Article 10 prevents suppliers from using automated calling systems and faxes without the prior consent of the consumer, which covers unsolicited commercial communications. These restrictions echo those for direct marketing within the Directive on Privacy and Electronic Communications (Directive 2002/58/EC).

### *Judicial and administrative redress*

Article 11 requires Member States to implement measures to allow various interested bodies to take legal action to protect the interests of consumers. Article 11 says:

> 1. Member States shall ensure that adequate and effective means exist to ensure compliance with this Directive in the interests of consumers.
> 2. The means referred to in paragraph 1 shall include provisions whereby one or more of the following bodies, as determined by national law, may take action under national law before the courts or before the competent administrative bodies to ensure that the national provisions for the implementation of this Directive are applied:

(a) public bodies or their representatives;
(b) consumer organizations having a legitimate interest in protecting consumers;
(c) professional organizations having a legitimate interest in acting.

3.

(a) Member States may stipulate that the burden of proof concerning the existence of prior information, written confirmation, compliance with time-limits or consumer consent can be placed on the supplier.
(b) Member States shall take the measures needed to ensure that suppliers and operators of means of communication, where they are able to do so, cease practices which do not comply with measures adopted pursuant to this Directive.

4. Member States may provide for voluntary supervision by self-regulatory bodies of compliance with the provisions of this Directive and recourse to such bodies for the settlement of disputes to be added to the means which Member States must provided to ensure compliance with the provisions of this Directive.

### 2.4.2 Financial Services Distance Selling Directive 2002

The Financial Services Distance Selling Directive (Directive 2002/65/EC of the European Parliament and of the Council of 23 September 2002 concerning the distance marketing of consumer financial services and amending Council Directive 90/619/EEC and Directives 97/7/EC and 98/27/EC) applies provisions equivalent to the Distance Selling Directive to financial service. 'Financial service' is defined in Article 2(b) as 'any service of a banking, credit, insurance, personal pension, investment or payment nature'.

#### *Transparency – pre- and post-contractual information*

Articles 3 to 5 are the equivalent of Articles 4 and 5 of the Distance Selling Directive. Article 3 identifies the pre-contractual information that should be supplied and is considerably more detailed than Article 3 of the Distance Selling Directive. Article 3(1) divides the pre-contractual information into three categories, namely information about the supplier, information about the financial service and information about redress. Article 3(3) prescribes added detail for voice telephony communications. Article 4 allows Member States to require the supply of enhanced information under their national laws for financial services. Article 5 (which is the equivalent of Article 5 of the Distance Selling Directive) gives the consumer the right to request a paper version of the contractual information, which is an advance.

### *Withdrawal*

The right to withdraw is contained in Article 6. The withdrawal period is 14 days, except for distance contracts relating to life insurance and personal pensions, where it is 30 days. The cooling-off period commences from the conclusion of the contract or, from the date when the consumer is informed that a contract for life insurance has been concluded, provided that the supplier has provided the contractual information required by Article 5. If the supplier has not provided that information the cooling-off period will only start when it is provided. This is another advance.

Article 6(2) contains the exemptions from the right of withdrawal. These fall into three broad categories, namely:

- financial services whose price depends on fluctuations in the financial markets outside the supplier's control, which may occur during the withdrawal period;[7]
- travel and baggage insurance policies or similar short-term insurance policies of less than one month's duration;
- contracts whose performance has been fully completed by both parties at the consumer's express request before the consumer exercises their right of withdrawal.

In addition to these exemptions the Member States are allowed to make exemptions for:

- any credit intended primarily for the purpose of acquiring or retaining property rights in land or in an existing or projected building, or for the purpose of renovating or improving a building;
- any credit secured either by mortgage on immovable property or by a right related to immovable property;
- declarations by consumers using the services of an official, provided that the official confirms that the consumer is guaranteed the rights under Article 5(1).

### *Payment for services provided*

Article 7 allows suppliers to charge for any services that are used prior to withdrawal, but this cannot amount to a penalty. The amount charged must also be proportionate, judged by reference to the contract price as a whole.

### *Payment card fraud*

Article 8 contains provisions equivalent to those within Article 8 of the Distance Selling Directive.

*Prohibition against unsolicited services*

Article 9 prohibits the supply of financial services without the consumer's prior approval.

*Unsolicited communications*

Article 10 repeats the effect of Article 10 of the Distance Selling Directive for the use of automated calling systems and faxes. It also extends its concern to other forms of distance communication, allowing Member States to choose between 'opt-in' and 'opt-out' consent. Again, this reflects the framework within the Privacy and Electronic Communications Directive.

*Sanctions, judicial and administrative redress and out of court redress*

Article 11 requires Member States to implement appropriate sanctions to deal with non-compliance by a supplier; such sanctions must be 'effective, proportional and dissuasive'. This is an advance. Article 13 deals with judicial and administrative redress and is equivalent to Article 11 of the Distance Selling Directive. Article 14 encourages the promotion of alternative dispute resolution procedures.

### 2.4.3 UK implementation of the Distance Selling Directives

The UK implementation of the Distance Selling Directives is represented by:

- Consumer Protection (Distance Selling) Regulations 2000 ('Distance Selling Regulations 2000'), SI 2000/2334 (as amended by the Consumer Protection (Distance Selling) Amendment Regulations 2005, SI 2005/689); and
- Financial Services (Distance Marketing) Regulations 2004, SI 2004/2095 (these also made some minor amendments to SI 2000/2334).

*Distance Selling Regulations 2000*

The Distance Selling Regulations 2000 adhere closely to the general framework and phraseology of the Distance Selling Directive. The definition of distance contract, which is contained in reg.3, is the same as the definition in Article 2(1) of the Directive. Schedule 1 to the regulations contains an indicative list of various means of distance communications, repeating the approach within Annex I of the Directive, and email appears at para.11.

Again echoing the Directive, not all kinds of distance contracts are within scope. Those out of scope are called 'excepted contracts' and are identified at reg.5. They accord with those at Article 3(1) of the Directive.[8] Likewise, there is also a series of contracts to which the regulations have only limited application, which are identified at reg.6. These contracts are exempted from the key information requirements and the right of cancellation. Again, the regulations follow the pattern of the Distance Selling Directive, thereby exempting contracts for consumables and leisure, etc.[9]

The pre-contractual information that is to be supplied is identified at reg.7.[10] This is the same as the information required by Article 4 of the Directive, although reg.7 also requires the supplier to include a notice if they propose to provide substitute goods in the event of the goods or services ordered by the consumer being unavailable (any substitutes must be of equivalent quality and price) and a notice that the cost of returning any substitute goods in the event of cancellation will be met by the supplier. Again, this information is to be provided in a 'clear and comprehensible manner appropriate to the means of distance communication used, with due regard in particular to the principles of good faith in commercial transactions and the principles governing the protection of those who are unable to give their consent such as minors' and the supplier should make their commercial purpose clear.

The contractual information that is to be supplied is identified at reg.8,[11] which marries up with Article 5 of the Directive. This information must be in writing or in another durable medium.

The right of cancellation is contained in reg.10. Once exercised, the contract is treated as if it has not been made. In order to exercise their right to cancel, the customer must indicate their intention to cancel in writing or in another durable medium. This can be done by posting a letter to or leaving a letter at the supplier's last known business address, by sending a fax to the supplier's fax number or by sending an email to the business email address last known to the customer.

The cancellation period for contracts for the supply of goods is contained in reg.11. It is calculated as follows:

- If the supplier has provided the contractual information prior to the conclusion of the contract, the cancellation period is seven working days commencing the day after the day on which the goods are received.
- If the supplier supplies the contractual information in the three-month period commencing the day after the day on which the goods are received, the cancellation period is seven working days commencing the day after the day on which the information is supplied.
- If the supplier fails to supply the contractual information, the cancellation period is three months and seven working days commencing the day after the day on which the goods are received.

The cancellation periods for service contracts are contained in reg.12. They are outlined below.

- If the supplier has provided the contractual information prior to the conclusion of the contract, the cancellation period is seven working days commencing the day after the day on which the contract is concluded.
- If the supplier supplies the contractual information within three months beginning the day after the day on which the contract is concluded, the cancellation period is seven working days commencing the day after the day on which the information is supplied.
- If performance of the contract has commenced by agreement before the expiry of seven working days from the day after the day on which the contract is concluded, and the contractual information is supplied in good time during performance, the cancellation period is either seven working days commencing the day after the day on which the contract is concluded, or, if the performance is completed prior to then, the date of completion.
- In any other case, the cancellation period is three months and seven working days commencing the day after the day on which the contract is concluded.

Regulation 13 echoes Article 6(3) of the Distance Selling Directive, concerning contracts to which the right of cancellation will not apply.

The remainder of the regulations continue in the same vein as the Distance Selling Directive. Notable additional points are:

- Regulation 15 concerns the automatic cancellation of related credit agreements.
- Regulation 16 concerns the payment of credit interest on cancelled agreements.
- Regulation 18 concerns the restoration of goods given in part exchange.
- Regulation 19 says that the performance period is 30 days, commencing with the day after the day on which the consumer places their order.

### *Financial Services (Distance Marketing) Regulations 2004*

The purpose of these regulations is to fill the gaps left by the Financial Services and Markets Act (FSMA) 2000 and regulations made thereunder. For this reason the information requirements and the cancellation provisions do not apply to an 'authorised person' (para.4(2)). An authorised person is one authorised by the Financial Services Authority under the FSMA 2000. Consequently, most distance selling of financial services will not fall within the scope of the regulations.

The regulations basically follow the pattern of the Directive and reference to the regulations should be made for the details.

## 2.5 THE E-SIGNATURES DIRECTIVE 1999 – GUARANTEEING LEGAL RECOGNITION OF ELECTRONIC DATA

A major concern within the use of electronic communications systems is related to the issue of data authenticity: with paper communications it is relatively easy to determine when a document is authentic as it can be 'held up to the light' and subjected to scrutiny, if necessary with the assistance of expert evidence, but with electronic data the issue is fundamentally different. The essence of electronic data is binary code (a series of 0s and 1s) and it is generally impossible to draw any meaningful conclusions about the authenticity of an electronic communication just by viewing a hard copy of the information. From a legal perspective, this can be very troubling; for example, in the event of a dispute about the authenticity of electronic information, how can a judge be expected to decide the case?

The authenticity issue is tackled head-on by the E-Signatures Directive (Directive 1999/93/EC of the European Parliament and of the Council of 13 December 1999 on a Community framework for electronic signatures), for reasons that are stated with total clarity within Recital 4:

> Electronic communication and commerce necessitate 'electronic signatures' and related services allowing data authentication; divergent rules with respect to legal recognition of electronic signatures and the accreditation of certification-service providers in the Member States may create a significant barrier to the use of electronic communications and electronic commerce; on the other hand, a clear Community framework regarding the conditions applying to electronic signatures will strengthen confidence in, and general acceptance of, the new technologies; legislation in the Member States should not hinder the free movement of goods and services in the internal market.

The scope of the Directive is contained within Article 1, which says:

> The purpose of this Directive is to facilitate the use of electronic signatures and to contribute to their legal recognition. It establishes a legal framework for electronic signatures and certain certification-services in order to ensure the proper functioning of the internal market.
>
> It does not cover aspects related to the conclusion and validity of contracts or other legal obligations where there are requirements as regards form prescribed by national or Community law nor does it affect rules and limits, contained in national or Community law, governing the use of documents.

### 2.5.1 The nature of electronic signatures

The Directive identifies three forms of electronic signatures. The first is called, simply, an 'electronic signature', which is defined in Article 2(1) as meaning 'data in electronic form which are attached to or logically associated with other electronic data and which serve as a method of authentication'.

The second is called an 'advanced electronic signature', which is defined in Article 2(2) in the following terms:

> 2. 'advanced electronic signature' means an electronic signature which meets the following requirements:
>
>    (a) it is uniquely linked to the signatory;
>    (b) it is capable of identifying the signatory;
>    (c) it is created using means that the signatory can maintain under his sole control; and
>    (d) it is linked to the data to which it relates in such a manner that any subsequent change of the data is detectable;

As its name rightly implies, an advanced electronic signature is a considerably more sophisticated device than a 'mere' electronic signature. It is the product of a 'signature-creation device', which is configured software or hardware that is used to create 'signature-creation data'. Signature-creation data is 'unique data, such as codes or private cryptographic keys, which are used by the signatory to create an electronic signature'. Thus, advanced electronic signatures are generally encrypted.

The third form is an advanced electronic signature that is based on a 'qualified certificate' and which is created by a 'secure-signature-creation device'. This form of advanced electronic signature has special legal effect, as is discussed below. A qualified certificate is defined at Article 2(10) as a certificate 'which meets the requirements laid down in Annex I and is provided by a certification-service-provider who fulfils the requirements laid down in Annex II'. A certification-service-provider is an entity or a legal or natural person who 'issues certificates or provides other services related to electronic signatures' (see Article 2(11)).[12]

The requirements of Annex I are:

> **Requirements for qualified certificates**
>
> Qualified certificates must contain:
>
> (a) an indication that the certificate is issued as a qualified certificate;
> (b) the identification of the certification-service-provider and the State in which it is established;
> (c) the name of the signatory or a pseudonym, which shall be identified as such;
> (d) provision for a specific attribute of the signatory to be included if relevant, depending on the purpose for which the certificate is intended;
> (e) signature-verification data which correspond to signature-creation data under the control of the signatory;
> (f) an indication of the beginning and end of the period of validity of the certificate;
> (g) the identity code of the certificate;
> (h) the advanced electronic signature of the certification-service-provider issuing it;

(i) limitations on the scope of use of the certificate, if applicable; and
(j) limits on the value of transactions for which the certificate can be used, if applicable.

A 'secure-signature-creation device' is one that meets the requirements contained in Annex III, which are:

**Requirements for secure signature-creation devices**

1. Secure signature-creation devices must, by appropriate technical and procedural means, ensure at the least that:
   (a) the signature-creation-data used for signature generation can practically occur only once, and that their secrecy is reasonably assured;
   (b) the signature-creation-data used for signature generation cannot, with reasonable assurance, be derived and the signature is protected against forgery using currently available technology;
   (c) the signature-creation-data used for signature generation can be reliably protected by the legitimate signatory against the use of others.
2. Secure signature-creation devices must not alter the data to be signed or prevent such data from being presented to the signatory prior to the signature process.

### 2.5.2 The legal effects of electronic signatures

Article 5 identifies the legal effects of electronic signatures:

**Legal effects of electronic signatures**

1. Member States shall ensure that advanced electronic signatures which are based on a qualified certificate and which are created by a secure-signature-creation device:
   (a) satisfy the legal requirements of a signature in relation to data in electronic form in the same manner as a handwritten signature satisfies those requirements in relation to paper-based data; and
   (b) are admissible as evidence in legal proceedings.
2. Member States shall ensure that an electronic signature is not denied legal effectiveness and admissibility as evidence in legal proceedings solely on the grounds that it is:
   - in electronic form, or
   - not based upon a qualified certificate, or
   - not based upon a qualified certificate issued by an accredited certification-service-provider, or
   - not created by a secure signature-creation device.

Article 5(1) has the effect of granting advanced electronic signatures the same legal status as handwritten signatures on paper documents, provided that the signature is one based on a qualified certificate and is created by a secure-signature-creation device; this is the third type of electronic signature identified earlier. So, for example, if a signature is required to conclude a contract or create a deed, an advanced electronic signature will satisfy those requirements. Article 5(2) is designed to ensure that electronic signatures not meeting the strict requirements of those identified in Article 5(1) are still afforded legal recognition.

### 2.5.3 Other provisions

Article 3 is concerned with market access. Among other things, it prevents Member States from making the provision of certification services subject to prior authorisation and requires them to establish appropriate systems for the supervision of certification-service-providers.

Article 6 is concerned with liability. In general terms it requires Member States to ensure that certification-service-providers are held liable to persons suffering damage through reliance upon an inaccurate certificate.

Article 8 is concerned with data protection. Certificate-service-providers are required to comply with the Data Protection Directive.

## 2.6 UK IMPLEMENTATION OF THE E-SIGNATURES DIRECTIVE

The UK implementation of the E-Signatures Directive is spread across the Electronic Communications Act 2000 and the Electronic Signatures Regulations 2002, SI 2002/318. The Act deals generally with the issue of legal effect of electronic signatures, while the regulations implement the definitions and annexes of the Directive and the provisions on market access, liability and data protection.

Electronic Communications Act 2000, s.7 implements Article 5(2) of the Directive, saying:

> **7. Electronic signatures and related certificates**
>
> (1) In any legal proceedings –
>
> (a) an electronic signature incorporated into or logically associated with a particular electronic communication or particular electronic data, and
> (b) the certification by any person of such a signature,
>
> shall each be admissible in evidence in relation to any question as to the authenticity of the communication or data or as to the integrity of the communication or data.
>
> (2) For the purposes of this section an electronic signature is so much of anything in electronic form as –

(a) is incorporated into or otherwise logically associated with any electronic communication or electronic data; and
(b) purports to be so incorporated or associated for the purpose of being used in establishing the authenticity of the communication or data, the integrity of the communication or data, or both.

(3) For the purposes of this section an electronic signature incorporated into or associated with a particular electronic communication or particular electronic data is certified by any person if that person (whether before or after the making of the communication) has made a statement confirming that –

(a) the signature,
(b) a means of producing, communicating or verifying the signature, or
(c) a procedure applied to the signature,

is (either alone or in combination with other factors) a valid means of establishing the authenticity of the communication or data, the integrity of the communication or data, or both.

Section 8(1) of the Act implements Article 5(1) by giving the appropriate minister the power to modify legislation and any related schemes 'for the purpose of authorising or facilitating the use of electronic communications or electronic storage (instead of other forms of communication or storage) for any purpose mentioned in' s.8(2). The purposes in s.8(2) are:

(a) the doing of anything which under any such provisions is required to be or may be done or evidenced in writing or otherwise using a document, notice or instrument;
(b) the doing of anything which under any such provisions is required to be or may be done by post or other specified means of delivery;
(c) the doing of anything which under any such provisions is required to be or may be authorised by a person's signature or seal, or is required to be delivered as a deed or witnessed;
(d) the making of any statement or declaration which under any such provisions is required to be made under oath or to be contained in a statutory declaration;
(e) the keeping, maintenance or preservation, for the purposes or in pursuance of any such provisions, of any account, record, notice, instrument or other document;
(f) the provision, production or publication under any such provisions of any information or other matter;
(g) the making of any payment that is required to be or may be made under any such provisions.

So far more than 30 orders have been made under s.8.

## 2.7 THE E-COMMERCE DIRECTIVE – ENCOURAGING B2B AND B2C INFORMATION SOCIETY SERVICES

As mentioned earlier, it is possible to regard some forms of e-commerce as being subsets of distance selling within the means of the Distance Selling Directives, but while the Distance Selling Directives' focus is consumer protection, the focus of the E-Commerce Directive (Directive 2000/31/EC of the European Parliament and of the Council of 8 June 2000 on certain legal aspects of information society services, in particular electronic commerce, in the internal market ('Directive on electronic commerce')) is considerably wider; it regulates both B2B and B2C e-commerce. Its overriding intention is to encourage the acceptance, take-up and use of information society services, and as such, the Directive promotes email. It achieves these things by lowering the barriers to entry into the e-commerce market space for information society service providers; by imposing overarching transparency provisions on them; through specific measures to protect the interests of consumers; and by guaranteeing the legal validity of e-commerce contracts.

### 2.7.1 E-commerce and information society services

While the Directive refers to e-commerce (or, rather, electronic commerce) in both its title and its recitals, its articles talk about 'information society services'. For example, Article 1, which is titled 'Objective and scope', says that the Directive 'seeks to contribute to the proper functioning of the internal market by ensuring the free movement of information society services between the Member States'. However, for the purposes of the Directive and the following analysis, information society services and e-commerce are synonymous.

### 2.7.2 Economic activities and services that are normally remunerated

The recitals explain that information society services 'span a wide range of economic activities which take place on-line' and they give various examples of them: information society services include 'services consisting of the transmission of information via a communication network', the selling of goods online and the provision of commercial communications by email (see Recital 18). However, the scope of regulation of information society services extends to cover any service that is normally provided for remuneration, at a distance by means of electronic equipment and at the individual request of a recipient of a service.[13] This means, of course, that the Directive can capture future developments in e-commerce.

The requirement that the service be one that is normally provided for remuneration seems to inject the necessary commercial element into information society services to justify the commerce tag, but the Directive does require information society services to be remunerated – Recital 18 observes that:

> information society services are not solely restricted to services giving rise to on-line contracting but also, in so far as they represent an economic activity, extend to services which are not remunerated by those who receive them, such as those offering on-line information or commercial communications, or those providing tools allowing for search, access and retrieval of data.

This formulation clearly captures the nature of search engines provided by the likes of Google: users of search engines do not pay for the service, but the providers of search engines are engaged in economic activity nonetheless, enabling it to be said that the search engine service represents an economic activity. Likewise, the senders of spam email are engaged in economic activity; they do not charge the recipient for their blight, yet their purpose is fundamentally economic.

### 2.7.3 Lowering the barriers to entry for e-commerce service providers

The provisions discussed below act to lower the barriers to entry into the e-commerce marketplace in many different ways. In particular, they reduce the administrative, bureaucratic and legal headaches for the new entrant, as well as cost, which in turn reduces the lead-time to market. The lowering of the barriers to entry is represented by four key elements, which are:

- The introduction of 'home country regulation' of information society services (see Article 3(1)). Thus, if an information society service is lawful in one Member State it will be lawful in every other Member State, so receiving States cannot block or restrict the service (see Article 3(2)). (However, Article 3(4) allows Member States to derogate from this rule on the grounds of public policy, the protection of public health, public security and the protection of consumers.)
- Prohibition on Member States requiring service providers to be licensed as a condition of commencing the provision of service (see Article 4; however, this does not extend to licensing schemes which are not specifically and exclusively targeted at information society services or to the licensing framework for telecommunications networks and services).
- Exclusion of 'intermediary service providers' from liability for the information they transmit and store. In other words, the Directive excludes service providers from liability for third party content and communications.
- Exemption of intermediary service providers from an obligation to monitor third party content.

### *Exclusion of liability*

The exclusion of liability provisions are contained in Articles 12–15 and they apply where the information society service consists of 'the transmission in a communication network of information provided by a recipient of a service' (see Articles 12(1) and 13(1)) and any associated 'automatic, intermediate and transient storage of the information transmitted' (Article 12(2)), where the service consists of the provision of 'access to a communication network' (Article 12(1)) and where the service consists of the 'storage of information provided by a recipient of a service' (Article 14(1)). An intermediary service provider that also provides content cannot avail itself of the benefit of the exclusions for any offending content that it generates.

This range of intermediary services covers a multitude of activities, ranging from the classic services of the internet service provider (ISP) (e.g. internet access, email, instant messaging, etc.), the provision of social networking websites like MySpace and Facebook, the provision of user-generated content websites like YouTube, the provision of 'virtual world' websites like Second Life and the provision of the many varieties of online forums, chatrooms, blogs and newsgroups.

Article 12 excludes service providers from liability for the transmission of information and any associated automatic, immediate and transient storage of the information, provided that they act as 'mere conduits'. The kinds of service providers benefiting from this exclusion include those providing internet access, communications services such as email and the core networks and infrastructure over which information travels. Service providers will only be 'mere conduits' if they do not initiate the transmission, do not select the receiver of it and do not select or modify the information transmitted (Article 12), or, where storage of transmitted information is concerned, the information is stored for the sole purpose of carrying out the transmission and only for as long as is reasonably necessary to effect the transmission.

Article 13 deals with the 'caching' of information being transmitted. Caching means the 'automatic, intermediate and temporary storage' of information being transmitted where that is 'performed for the sole purpose of making more efficient the information's onward transmission to other recipients of the service upon their request' (Article 13(1)). Again, conditions need to be satisfied for this exclusion to apply: the service provider must not modify the cached information; it must comply with conditions on access to the information; it must comply with industry-recognised rules on the updating of the information; it must not misuse technology to obtain data on the use of the information; and it must remove the information or disable access to it upon obtaining actual knowledge of the fact that the information at the initial source of the transmission has been removed from the network, or access to it has been disabled or a court or administrative body has ordered the removal or disablement of it; see Article 13(1).

Article 14 deals with the 'hosting' of illegal information and information about illegal activity, and it provides exclusion from both criminal and civil liability. Hosting means 'the storage of information provided by a recipient of the service' (Article 14(1)). The conditions applying to the application of this exclusion focus upon the service provider's knowledge and its actions upon acquiring knowledge. For the exclusion to apply, the service provider should not have actual knowledge of the illegal information or illegal activity and, as regards damages claims, it should not be aware of facts or circumstances from which the illegal activity or information is apparent. Once the service provider obtains knowledge or awareness, it will only be able to rely upon the exclusion if it acts expeditiously to remove or disable access to the information.

Article 15 exempts the intermediary from any obligations to monitor third party content that it transmits or stores during the provision of the services covered by Article 12–14 and actively to search for information indicating illegal activity. Thus, intermediaries do not have to filter or censor information, or exercise any editorial functions.

### 2.7.4 Transparency in service provision

The Directive contains a range of provisions that foster transparency in the provision of information society services by requiring service providers to supply recipients of services with key pieces of information. These provisions build upon the transparency provisions within the Distance Selling Directive.

Many of these requirements apply equally to consumer and non-consumer recipients of services, but some are only mandatory in consumer cases. Furthermore, in places the rules are modified when parties contract by email. The key provisions are:

- Article 5 contains a general information requirement, which applies to both consumer and non-consumer cases, whenever an information society service is used. The information to be provided includes details of the service provider's name, geographic address and their contact details. In addition, if the service provider is registered in a trade or public register they must provide their registration number; if their activities are subject to licensing they must provide details of their regulator; if they are a member of a regulated profession they must name their professional body, their professional title and their professional rules and if they are liable to pay VAT they must give their VAT number. As regards prices, they must state whether these are inclusive of tax and delivery charges. Information must be rendered 'easily, directly and permanently accessible to the recipient of the services and competent authorities' and pricing information must be stated 'clearly and unambiguously'.

- Articles 6, 7 and 8 concern commercial communications. A commercial communication is defined as 'any form of communication designed to promote, directly or indirectly, the goods, services or image of a company, organisation or person pursuing a commercial, industrial or craft activity or exercising a regulated profession' (Article 2). These must be 'clearly identifiable at such'; they must identify the person upon whose behalf they are made and they must clearly identify if a promotional offer or a promotional competition is involved and any conditions that apply (see Article 6). Unsolicited commercial communications shall be 'identifiable clearly and unambiguously as such' and service providers shall consult opt-out registers for natural persons (see Article 7). Regulated professions may only send commercial communications if these comply with their professional rules (see Article 8).
- Articles 10 and 11 concern electronic contracting. The information that is to be provided by service providers is compulsory in the case of consumer contracts, whereas in non-consumer contracts two exempting provision apply: first, the parties can contract out from these requirements; and second, the service provider is not required to supply the information in any case where the contract is 'concluded exclusively by exchange of electronic mail or equivalent individual communications' (see Articles 10(4) and 11(3)). Article 10 says that before a contract is concluded the service provider must provide the customer with clear information about the different technical steps that are required to conclude the contract; must state whether the concluded contract will be filed and whether it will be accessible; must identify the technical means for identifying and correcting inputting errors prior to the placing of an order; and list the languages offered for conclusion of the contract. This information must be provided 'clearly, comprehensibly and unambiguously' (Article 10(1)). Article 11 states that service providers must acknowledge receipt of orders electronically and without undue delay.

All of these provisions are clearly aimed at boosting the confidence of users of information society services, particularly consumers, which should lead to further acceptance, take-up and use.

### 2.7.5 Guaranteeing legal recognition of e-commerce contracts and the technical facilities for contract-making

One of the most important provisions within the E-Commerce Directive is contained in Article 9, which is titled 'Treatment of contracts'. Article 9(1) says:

> Member States shall ensure that their legal system allows contracts to be concluded by electronic means. Member states shall in particular ensure that the legal requirements applicable to the contractual process neither create obstacles for

> the use of electronic contracts nor result in such contracts being deprived of legal effectiveness and validity on account of their having been made by electronic means.

Article 9(2) allows for exemptions for contracts creating or transferring rights in real estate (apart from rental rights); contracts requiring by law the involvement of courts, public authorities or professions exercising public authority; contracts requiring by law the involvement of courts, public authorities or professions exercising public authority; contracts of suretyship granted and on collateral securities furnished by persons acting for purposes outside their trade, business or profession; and contracts governed by family law or by the law of succession.

Article 9(1) underpins the entire process of electronic contracting, for it is fundamental to the acceptance, take-up and use of e-commerce that concluded contracts will be enforced by the courts in the event of dispute – thus, contracts made by email have legal effect. However, it is important to note that the Directive does not address the issue of contract formation, leaving national rules unaffected.

Articles 10 and 11 also contain provisions about the technical facilities that service providers must make available for electronic contracting. Article 10(3) says that 'contract terms and general conditions to be provided to the recipient must be made available in a way that allows him to store and reproduce them' (this requirement is compulsory in consumer cases and optional in non-consumer cases). Article 11.2 requires service providers to make available to the recipient 'appropriate, effective and accessible technical means allowing him to identify and correct input errors prior to the placing of the order' (again, this requirement is compulsory in consumer cases and optional in non-consumer cases, except for where the contract is concluded exclusively by exchange of email, etc. when it is completely exempted).

## 2.8 UK IMPLEMENTATION OF THE E-COMMERCE DIRECTIVE

The UK has implemented the E-Commerce Directive through the Electronic Commerce (EC Directive) Regulations 2002, SI 2002/2013 (as amended by SI 2003/115, SI 2003/2500 and SI 2004/1178). The regulations are virtually a complete reiteration of the Directive, but the following additional points are noteworthy:

- Regulation 13 renders it a breach of statutory duty for a service provider to breach the transparency provisions (para.6), including the rules concerning commercial communications (para.7) and unsolicited commercial communications (para.8), the rules concerning information about the technical steps for completing contracts (para.9(1)) and the rules about acknowledgement of orders (para.11(1)(a)). The court can award damages for breach of statutory duty.

- Regulation 14 enables the court to order compliance with the rules concerning the reproduction and storage of terms and conditions (para.9(3)).
- Regulation 15 gives the customer the right to rescind a contract where the rules concerning the technical means for identifying and correcting input errors have been breached (para.11(1)(b)).
- Regulation 20 gives the court the power to issue orders against ISPs to prevent infringement of rights irrespective of the exclusions of liabilities (paras.17 (mere conduit), 18 (caching) and 19 (hosting)).

Regulation 22 is also worth noting, as it contains rules for determining whether an ISP has notice of an infringement of rights. This says:

> **22. Notice for the purposes of actual knowledge**
>
> In determining whether a service provider has actual knowledge for the purposes of regulations 18(b)(v) and 19(a)(i), a court shall take into account all matters which appear to it in the particular circumstances to be relevant and, among other things, shall have regard to –
>
> (a) whether a service provider has received a notice through a means of contact made available in accordance with regulation 6(1)(c), and
> (b) the extent to which any notice includes –
>
> (i) the full name and address of the sender of the notice;
> (ii) details of the location of the information in question; and
> (iii) details of the unlawful nature of the activity or information in question.

## 2.9 KEY SIMILARITIES AND DIFFERENCES BETWEEN THE DISTANCE SELLING DIRECTIVES AND THE E-COMMERCE DIRECTIVE

Although there is a significant amount of overlap between the regimes in the Distance Selling Directives and the E-Commerce Directive, there are also very many differences. Most of these will be obvious from the above discussions, but the key distinctions are:

- The Distance Selling Directives cover a wider variety of distance contracts than the E-Commerce Directive. For example, while both are concerned with contracts made by email, the Distance Selling Directives cover distance contracts made over the telephone or via mail order for example, which can never fall within any recognised definition of e-commerce.
- The Distance Selling Directives are concerned only with contracting, whereas the E-Commerce Directive is concerned with a much wider

variety of issues, for example the legal recognition of electronic contracts, the lowering of barriers to market and the liability of ISPs.

- While the Distance Selling Directives are concerned only with consumer issues, the E-Commerce Directive is concerned with both consumer and non-consumer issues.

The key similarity for the purpose of this book is that all of the Directives are concerned with email to a greater or lesser extent. As such they are both highly pertinent within a consideration of email law. Another similarity is that they are all concerned with transparency issues, through their provisions on pre-contractual and contractual information. Another is that they are both concerned with unsolicited commercial communications.

## CHAPTER NOTES

1 For an interesting article about the dotcom bubble see the relevant Wikipedia entry at **http://en.wikipedia.org/wiki/Dot-com_bubble**. This article attributes the dotcom bubble to the period covering 1995 to 2001, with a climax in 2000.

2 The favourable treatment accorded to internet service providers still continues. For example, the Communications Data Retention Directive 2006/24/EC provides that Member States may delay the operation of the data retention provisions in the field of 'Internet access, Internet telephony and Internet e-mail' until March 2009.

3 Article 3(2). The exemption covers foodstuffs and beverages, including those supplied by regular roundsmen (such as milkmen), hotel accommodation, transport, catering and leisure (such as holidays, or sporting events). The exemption in Article 3(2) applies also to Articles 6 and 7(1).

4 The Directive does not define the meaning of durable medium, but its sister, the Financial Services Distance Selling Directive, does, at Article 2(f), which says that durable medium 'means any instrument which enables the consumer to store information addressed personally to him in a way accessible for future reference for a period of time adequate for the purposes of the information and which allows the unchanged reproduction of the information stored'.

5 See Note 12.

6 See Note 12 and Recital 18.

7 Examples given are foreign exchange, money market instruments, transferable securities, units in collective investment undertakings, financial-futures contracts, including equivalent cash-settled instruments, forward interest-rate agreements (FRAs), interest-rate, currency and equity swaps, options to acquire or dispose of any instruments referred to in this point including equivalent cash-settled instruments.

8 These are contracts for the sale or other disposition of an interest in land (except for a rental agreement), contracts for the construction of a building where the contract also provides for a sale or other disposition of an interest in land on which the building is constructed (except for a rental agreement), contracts relating to financial services, contracts concluded by means of an automated vending machine or automated commercial premises, contracts concluded with a telecommunications operator through the use of a public payphone and contracts concluded at an auction.

9 See Note 12.

10 Paragraph 9 says that this information does not have to be provided in a 'contract for the supply of services which are performed through the use of a means of distance communication, where those services are supplied on only one occasion and are invoiced by the operator of the means of distance communication'.
11 This covers most of the information required by reg.7 plus information about cancellation rights and procedures, the geographical address for the sending of complaints, information about any after-sales services and guarantees and the conditions for cancellation where the contract is of unspecified duration or of more than one year's duration.
12 The requirements within Annex II which certification-service-providers must meet to be able to issue qualified certificates are concerned with issues such as the reliability of the certification services, expertise and trustworthiness.
13 See Recital 17, which refers to the definition of information society service contained in Directive 98/34/EC of the European Parliament and of the Council laying down a procedure for the provision of information in the field of technical standards and regulations and of rules on Information Society Services. The definition in Directive 98/34/EC was inserted by Directive 98/48/EC of the European Parliament and of the Council of 20 July 1998 amending Directive 98/34/EC laying down a procedure for the provision of information in the field of technical standards and Directive 98/48/EC.

# CHAPTER 3

# Privacy and data protection

## 3.1 INTRODUCTION

Data protection laws within Europe developed in reaction to new technological developments, particularly computerisation, from which email has sprung. In the previous chapter it was submitted that data protection laws have helped to encourage the take-up and acceptance of use of email in two key ways. First, by guaranteeing a high level of protection for personal data undergoing processing they have encouraged user confidence in email and a successful, thriving economy in email services. Second, they have secured the free flow of personal information between countries, which is essential for email use. In this chapter, data protection laws are examined in more depth.

## 3.2 FROM THE BIRTH OF DATA PROTECTION TO THE DATA PROTECTION DIRECTIVE

The genus of harmonised data protection law in Europe was concern about the ambit and scope of Article 8 of the European Convention on Human Rights, which contains the right to privacy. Article 8 says:

1. Everyone has the right to respect for his private and family life, his home and his correspondence.
2. There shall be no interference by a public authority with the exercise of this right except such as is in accordance with the law and is necessary in a democratic society in the interests of national security, public safety or the economic well-being of the country, for the prevention of disorder or crime, for the protection of health or morals, or for the protection of the rights and freedoms of others.

The concern had two core components within it. First, it was doubted that Article 8 provided protection against interferences with privacy resulting from the use of new technologies. Second, it was doubted that Article 8 extended to provide protection against interferences with privacy in the private sector; this concern arose from the face of the wording of Article 8(2), which says that only public authorities fall within scope. These doubts have been addressed by data protection laws, which have extended and modified the right to privacy, although it is important to note that the latest iteration of data protection law focuses upon the protection of fundamental freedoms generally, albeit with specific and enhanced focus on privacy.

## 3.3 THE SCOPE OF THE RIGHT TO PRIVACY

The scope of the right to privacy is extensive and indeed it would be fair to say that the law has undergone a process of unprecedented evolution in recent years. For example, in *Peck* v. *United Kingdom* (2003) 36 EHRR 41, the European Court of Human Rights confirmed that Article 8 extended to the sharing of CCTV footage of an attempted suicide in a public place. In *Von Hannover* v. *Germany* (2006) 43 EHRR 7, the European Court of Human Rights also confirmed that Article 8 extends to the taking of photographs of a member of the Monaco Royal Family engaged in social pursuits in public and quasi-public places. In *Campbell* v. *Mirror Group Newspapers* [2004] UKHL 22, the House of Lords confirmed that the right to privacy extends to the taking of photographs of a person standing in the street outside a building used for meetings of Narcotics Anonymous. In *Douglas* v. *Hello Ltd* [2005] EWCA Civ 595, the Court of Appeal confirmed that the right to privacy, via the modified law of confidence, extends to the taking of photographs of a celebrity wedding reception, even though the claimants were contracted to a rival magazine for the publication of such photographs. In *McKennitt* v. *Ash* [2006] EWCA Civ 1714, the Court of Appeal confirmed that the right to privacy, via the modified law of confidence, extends to the publication of falsehoods in an unauthorised biography. In *Murray* v. *Express Newspapers plc* [2008] EWCA Civ 446, the Court of Appeal confirmed that the right to privacy extends to the taking of photographs of a famous writer's child in a public place. In *Mosley* v. *News Group Newspapers Ltd* [2008] EWHC 1777, the High Court confirmed that the right to privacy extends to the covert and unauthorised filming of unusual sex acts.

### 3.3.1 The right to privacy and the law of confidence – reasonable expectation of privacy

The UK has addressed its obligations under Article 8 through modification of the common law of confidence, to protect information where there is a reasonable expectation of privacy; the modification of the law of confidence is a judge-led process that was a necessary development due to the fact that s.6 of the Human Right Act 1998 requires the courts as public authorities to act compatibly with the European Convention on Human Rights, and s.2

requires the courts to take account of decisions of the European Court of Human Rights during the performance of their duties.

In the case of *A* v. *B plc* [2002] EWCA Civ 337, a decision of the Court of Appeal, Lord Woolf explained the development of the law of confidence to cover the right to privacy:

> A is a footballer with a premier division football club. B is a national newspaper. C is one of two women with whom A, who is a married man, had affairs. The injunction was granted to restrain B from publishing the stories which C and the other woman, D, had sold to B recounting their affairs with A. In using initials to describe the parties we are following the course adopted in the court below to protect the identity of A. D has taken no part in the proceedings.
>
> Since the coming into force of the Human Rights Act 1998 ('the 1998 Act') there has been an increase in the number of actions in which injunctions are being sought to protect the claimants from the publication of articles in newspapers on the grounds that the articles contain confidential information concerning the claimants, the publication of which, it is alleged, would infringe their privacy. Such actions can be against any part of the media.
>
> The applications for interim injunctions have now to be considered in the context of articles 8 and 10 of the European Convention of Human Rights ('ECHR'). These articles have provided new parameters within which the court will decide, in an action for breach of confidence, whether a person is entitled to have his privacy protected by the court or whether the restriction of freedom of expression which such protection involves cannot be justified. The court's approach to the issues which the applications raise has been modified because under section 6 of the 1998 Act, the court, as a public authority, is required not to act 'in a way which is incompatible with a Convention right'. The court is able to achieve this by absorbing the rights which articles 8 and 10 protect into the long-established action for breach of confidence. This involves giving a new strength and breadth to the action so that it accommodates the requirements of those articles.

In *Campbell* v. *Mirror Group Newspapers*, the House of Lords confirmed that the law of confidence will protect information where there is a reasonable expectation of privacy; Lord Nicholls said 'essentially the touchstone of private life is whether in respect of the disclosed facts the person in question had a reasonable expectation of privacy'.

### 3.3.2 The first stage of data protection – the Council of Europe's Resolutions

The first stage of data protection was the Council of Europe's Resolutions for protecting personal information stored in electronic data banks.

The first steps towards harmonised European legislation were taken by the Council of Europe in the late 1960s. In 1968, for example, the Council's Parliamentary Assembly issued a Recommendation that required its Committee of Experts on Human Rights to examine whether 'having regard to Article 8 of the Convention on Human Rights, the national legislation in the Member States adequately protects the right to privacy against violations which may be committed by the use of modern scientific and technical methods' and, if not, 'to make recommendations for the better protection of the right to privacy' (Recommendation 509 (1968) on human rights and modern scientific and technological developments, adopted 31 January 1968). The concerns of the Parliamentary Assembly identified by the Recommendation were that:

- there were 'serious dangers for the rights of the individual inherent in certain aspects of modern scientific and technological development';
- there was a belief that 'newly developed techniques such as phone-tapping, eavesdropping, surreptitious observation, the illegitimate use of official statistical and similar surveys to obtain private information, and subliminal advertising and propaganda are a threat to the rights and freedoms of individuals and, in particular, to the right to privacy'.

Although the Recommendation does not reveal any evidence to suggest that the Council's Parliamentary Assembly had foreseen the development of email or the internet, it does show that an important and powerful political and legislative body was concerned about technological developments. In effect the Parliamentary Assembly was laying down a clear marker that told Europe that it would seek to assert legal control over technology in a restricting manner in order to achieve its objectives, in this case the protection of the right to privacy. In other words, technology would not be allowed to develop outside of the control of human rights law.

The Committee of Experts soon concluded that Article 8 did not extend to cover the two core concerns identified earlier, which caused the Council of Europe to pass resolutions in 1973 and 1974[1] that effectively extended the right to privacy within Article 8 to private sector and public sector data banks. These extensions were intended to operate on a harmonised basis, in the sense that it was envisaged that Council of Europe Member States would implement equivalent national laws thereby creating an area of legal harmonisation within Europe. The harmonisation agenda has remained at the forefront of data protection law ever since.

The initial scope of data protection is best understood by reference to the 1973 Resolution whose principles applied to 'personal information stored in electronic data banks'. This phrase was defined in the following terms:

> For the purposes of this resolution, the term 'personal information' means information relating to individuals (physical persons), and the term 'electronic data bank' means any electronic data processing system which is used to handle personal information and to disseminate such information.

It is noteworthy that the explanatory notes to Resolution (74) 29 did express a favourable view about new technology saying 'the Preamble reaffirms that the use of computers for purposes of public administration should in general be regarded as a positive development. The purpose of the present resolution is not to oppose such use, but to reinforce it with certain guarantees.' However, despite the positive flavour of the Preamble, the Resolutions were firmly geared towards restrictions upon the use of technology, rather than overt encouragement. For example, the explanatory notes to Resolution (73) 22 almost read as an apologia for technology, saying:

> . . . a particular new source of possible intrusion into privacy has been created by the rapid growth and popularisation of computer technology. The purposes which computers are increasingly serving in the public and private sectors are by themselves not basically different from those served by more traditional forms of data storage and processing. What is setting computers apart from the traditional means of data storage and processing is the extraordinary ease with which they have overcome at a stroke a whole series of problems raised by the management of information: the great volume of data, the techniques for their storage and retrieval, their transmission over large distances, their correct interpretation and, finally, the speed with which all these operations can be performed. Thus, computers permit the building up in the form of 'data banks', of data collections or integrated networks of data collections. These 'data banks' are capable of providing instantly and over large distances massive information on individuals. While few would deny the great advantages offered by the application of electronic data processing techniques, there is a growing concern among the public about the possibility of improper use being made of sensitive personal information stored electronically.

The Resolutions' approach to data protection was based around key principles, most of which remain intact within current legislation. **Table 3.1** illustrates this by showing the principles within the Resolutions and their current manifestations within the Data Protection Act (DPA) 1998.

**Table 3.1** Comparison of data protection principles

| Resolution (73) 22 | Resolution (74) 29 | Data Protection Act 1998 |
|---|---|---|
| 1. The information stored should be accurate and should be kept up to date.<br><br>In general, information relating to the intimate private life of persons or information which might lead to unfair discrimination should not be recorded or, if recorded, should not be disseminated. | 1. As a general rule the public should be kept regularly informed about the establishment, operation and development of electronic data banks in the public sector. | 1. Personal data shall be processed fairly and lawfully and, in particular, shall not be processed unless –<br><br>(a) at least one of the conditions in Schedule 2 is met, and<br>(b) in the case of sensitive personal data, at least one of the conditions in Schedule 3 is also met. |

**Table 3.1** *Cont.*

| Resolution (73) 22 | Resolution (74) 29 | Data Protection Act 1998 |
|---|---|---|
| 2. The information should be appropriate and relevant with regard to the purpose for which it has been stored. | 2. The information stored should be:<br><br>a. obtained by lawful and fair means,<br>b. accurate and kept up to date,<br>c. appropriate and relevant to the purpose for which it has been stored.<br><br>Every care should be taken to correct inaccurate information and to erase inappropriate, irrelevant or obsolete information. | 2. Personal data shall be obtained only for one or more specified and lawful purposes, and shall not be further processed in any manner incompatible with that purpose or those purposes. |
| 3. The information should not be obtained by fraudulent or unfair means. | 3. Especially when electronic data banks process information relating to the intimate private life of individuals or when the processing of information might lead to unfair discrimination,<br><br>a. their existence must have been provided for by law, or by special regulation or have been made public in a statement or document, in accordance with the legal system of each member state;<br>b. such law, regulation, statement or document must clearly state the purpose of storage and use of such information, as well as the conditions under which it may be communicated either within the public administration or to private persons or bodies; | 3. Personal data shall be adequate, relevant and not excessive in relation to the purpose or purposes for which they are processed. |

**Table 3.1** *Cont.*

| Resolution (73) 22 | Resolution (74) 29 | Data Protection Act 1998 |
|---|---|---|
| | c. that data stored must be used for purposes other than those which have been defined unless exception is explicitly permitted by law, is granted by a competent authority or the rules for the use of the electronic data bank are amended. | |
| 4. Rules should be laid down to specify the periods beyond which certain categories of information should no longer be kept or used. | 4. Rules should be laid down to specify the time limits beyond which certain categories of information may not be kept or used. However, exceptions from this principle are acceptable if the use of the information for statistical, scientific or historical purposes requires its conservation for an indefinite duration. In that case, precautions should be taken to ensure that the privacy of the individuals concerned will not be prejudiced. | 4. Personal data shall be accurate and, where necessary, kept up to date. |
| 5. Without appropriate authorisation, information should not be used for purposes other than those for which it has been stored, nor communicated to third parties. | 5. Every individual should have the right to know the information stored about him. Any exception to this principle or limitation to the exercise of this right should be strictly regulated. | 5. Personal data processed for any purpose or purposes shall not be kept for longer than is necessary for that purpose or those purposes. |

**Table 3.1** *Cont.*

| Resolution (73) 22 | Resolution (74) 29 | Data Protection Act 1998 |
|---|---|---|
| 6. As a general rule, the person concerned should have the right to know the information stored about him, the purpose for which it has been recorded, and particulars of each release of this information. | 6. Precautions should be taken against any abuse or misuse of information. For this reason:<br>a. everyone concerned with the operation of electronic data processing should be bound by rules of conduct aimed at preventing the misuse of data and in particular by a duty to observe secrecy;<br>b. electronic data banks should be equipped with security systems which bar access to the data held by them to persons not entitled to obtain such information and which provide for the detection of misdirections of information, whether intentional or not. | 6. Personal data shall be processed in accordance with the rights of data subjects under this Act. |
| 7. Every care should be taken to correct inaccurate information and to erase, obsolete information or information obtained in an unlawful way. | 7. Access to information that may not be freely communicated to the public should be confined to the persons whose functions entitle them to take cognisance of it in order to carry out their duties. | 7. Appropriate technical and organisational measures shall be taken against unauthorised or unlawful processing of personal data and against accidental loss or destruction of, or damage to, personal data. |

**Table 3.1** *Cont.*

| Resolution (73) 22 | Resolution (74) 29 | Data Protection Act 1998 |
|---|---|---|
| 8. Precautions should be taken against any abuse or misuse of information.<br><br>Electronic data banks should be equipped with security systems which bar access to the data held by them to persons not entitled to obtain such information, and which provide for the detection of misdirection of information, whether intentional or not. | 8. When information is used for statistical purposes it should be released only in such a way that it is impossible to link information to a particular person. | 8. Personal data shall not be transferred to a country or territory outside the European Economic Area unless that country or territory ensures an adequate level of protection for the rights and freedoms of data subjects in relation to the processing of personal data. |
| 9. Access to the information stored should be confined to persons who have a valid reason to know it. The operating staff of electronic data banks should be bound by rules of conduct aimed at preventing the misuse of data and, in particular, by rules of professional secrecy. | | |
| 10. Statistical data should be released only in aggregate form and in such a way that it is impossible to link the information to a particular person. | | |

The bulk of the principles within the 1973 Resolution were concerned with the issues of fair and lawful obtaining of data, the purposes for which data are processed, data accuracy and relevancy, data security and transparency. These key elements are all covered by the principles within the DPA 1998. The only differences between the principles within these two regimes is that those within the DPA 1998 do not address the issue of statistical information and those within the 1973 Resolution do not deal with transfers to countries outside Europe, but remembering that the regimes are separated by a quarter century of thinking, it stands as a testament to the lucidity of the original thinking that the current regime is almost a complete and faithful reiteration of the original and, in any event, the issue of transfers to non-European countries was soon fully embedded within data protection thinking and was certainly a core component by the end of the 1970s.

### 3.3.3 The second stage of data protection – the Data Protection Convention

The second stage of data protection was extending its scope through the Data Protection Convention.

Naturally, over the course of the remainder of the 1970s thinking on data protection developed and by the turn of the decade a second consideration had emerged: in addition to protecting privacy rights, data protection laws should help to maintain free flows of personal information within the area of harmonisation. The Data Protection Convention aimed to put the regime on a more formal footing (Council of Europe Convention for the Protection of Individuals with regard to Automatic Processing of Personal Data, Treaty 108, Strasbourg, 28 January 1981; see **http://conventions.coe.int**). The Convention described its object and purpose at Article 1, in the following terms:

> The purpose of this convention is to secure in the territory of each Party for every individual, whatever his nationality or residence, respect for his rights and fundamental freedoms, and in particular his right to privacy, with regard to automatic processing of personal data relating to him ('data protection').

The core ambitions of the Convention are the same as those within the Resolutions and the principles express the same thinking. One of the main advances within the Convention lay in the fact that it contained the necessary constituent parts for a fully enforceable legal regime, as represented by its rules on sanctions and remedies (Article 10), designated authorities (Article 13) and the consultative committee (Article 18). However, for the purposes of encouraging the acceptance, take-up and use of email it was the introduction of rules on transborder data flows which have had the greatest impact, as they ameliorated many of the restricting qualities of data protection. Article 12 says:

> **Article 12 – Transborder flows of personal data and domestic law**
>
> 1. The following provisions shall apply to the transfer across national borders, by whatever medium, of personal data undergoing automatic processing or collected with a view to their being automatically processed.
> 2. A Party shall not, for the sole purpose of the protection of privacy, prohibit or subject to special authorisation transborder flows of personal data going to the territory of another Party.
> 3. Nevertheless, each Party shall be entitled to derogate from the provisions of paragraph 2:
>
>    a. insofar as its legislation includes specific regulations for certain categories of personal data or of automated personal data files, because of the nature of those data or those files, except where the regulations of the other Party provide an equivalent protection;

b. when the transfer is made from its territory to the territory of a non-contracting State through the intermediary of the territory of another Party, in order to avoid such transfers resulting in circumvention of the legislation of the Party referred to at the beginning of this paragraph.

The essence of the rule on transborder data flows is that any country that signs the Convention cannot restrict the flow of personal information from its territory to the territory of another contracting State merely on the grounds of privacy. As such, within the area of harmonisation personal data move freely. The consequences of this provision were profound, and while it is submitted that there was little reason for most people to foresee the arrival of the internet and email[2] back in 1981, the legal protection for free flows of information helped to create the kind of hospitable environment that the internet and email needed in order to develop and thrive. Indeed, it might be fair to say that had data protections laws developed differently, so as to be concerned only with the protection of privacy, they could have positively hindered the development of the internet and email.

Although the dual interests of privacy protection and free flows of personal data within Europe were first expressed in the Convention, it is worth noting that the year before, in 1980, the Organisation for Economic Cooperation and Development (OECD) expressed the same interest within its own data protection guidelines (OECD Guidelines on the Protection of Privacy and Transborder Flows of Personal Data, 23 September 1980), the preface to which says:

> The development of automatic data processing, which enables vast quantities of data to be transmitted within seconds across national frontiers, and indeed across continents, has made it necessary to consider privacy protection in relation to personal data. Privacy protection laws have been introduced, or will be introduced shortly, in approximately one half of OECD Member countries (Austria, Canada, Denmark, France, Germany, Luxembourg, Norway, Sweden and the United States have passed legislation. Belgium, Iceland, the Netherlands, Spain and Switzerland have prepared draft bills) to prevent what are considered to be violations of fundamental human rights, such as the unlawful storage of personal data, the storage of inaccurate personal data, or the abuse or unauthorised disclosure of such data.
>
> On the other hand, there is a danger that disparities in national legislations could hamper the free flow of personal data across frontiers; these flows have greatly increased in recent years and are bound to grow further with the widespread introduction of new computer and communications technology. Restrictions on these flows could cause serious disruption in important sectors of the economy, such as banking and insurance.
>
> For this reason OECD Member countries considered it necessary to develop Guidelines which would help to harmonise national privacy legislation and, while upholding such human rights, would at the same time prevent interruptions in international flows of data. They represent a consensus on basic principles which can be built into existing national legislation, or serve as a basis for legislation in those countries which do not yet have it.

### 3.3.4 The third stage of data protection – the work of the European Community

During the 1990s, European data protection laws made considerable advances through the auspices of the European Community (EC). Although the EC is a party to the Council of Europe Data Protection Convention and took proactive steps to encourage EC Member States to bring their national laws into harmonisation per the requirements of the Convention, the EC did reserve to itself the right to issue its own law (Commission Recommendation of 29 July 1981 relating to the Council of Europe Convention for the protection of individuals with regard to automatic processing of personal data (81/679/EEC)). By the end of the 1980s only a handful of EC Member States had ratified the Convention, which meant that there were still continuing obstacles to the free flow of personal data within Europe, which represented failure of the harmonisation agenda. This acted to motivate the European Commission to issue a proposal for a directive on data protection in 1990, under the internal market provisions of the Treaty of Rome. This culminated in the Data Protection Directive of 1995 (Directive 95/46/EC of the European Parliament and of the Council of 24 October 1995 on the protection of individuals with regard to the processing of personal data and on the free movement of such data) and the Telecommunications Data Protection Directive of 1997 (Directive 97/66/EC of the European Parliament and of the Council of 15 December 1997 concerning the processing of personal data and the protection of privacy in the telecommunications sector).

Without wishing to diminish the value of the work done by the Council of Europe, it might be fair to say that it was the EC's intervention that caused data protection laws to be fully embedded in Europe. In particular, it is significant that the Directive rendered the introduction of national data protections laws compulsory within the EC Member States, whereas the Convention rendered data protection an elective, or optional, issue.

### 3.3.5 The Data Protection Directive

The Data Protection Directive is considerably more detailed that the Data Protection Convention and the preceding Resolutions, consisting of some 72 recitals and 34 articles. Furthermore, in addition to regulating automated data processing it also regulates some kinds of manual documents, unlike the Convention and the Resolution which were concerned only with automated processing. However, these differences do not represent the key innovative step within the Directive, which was that it made the introduction of data protection laws compulsory within the European Community. The reason for this statement lies in the fact that Council of Europe Conventions are essentially voluntary measures, unlike EC directives, which oblige the Member States to implement transposing legislation. So, when viewed in this manner it is possible to see the Directive as a compulsory measure and for this reason the Directive represents a true advance over the Convention and a real enhancement of data protection.

### 3.3.6 The Telecommunications Data Protection Directive

The Telecommunications Data Protection Directive was the first piece of sectoral lawmaking for data protection, applying to the provision of publicly available telecommunications networks and services. It was repealed and replaced by the Privacy and Electronic Communications Directive 2002, which is discussed in **Chapter 4** along with the UK transposing instruments.

## 3.4 THE DATA PROTECTION ACT 1998

The privacy of emails containing personal data is guaranteed by the DPA 1998, which gives effect to the requirements of the Data Protection Convention and the Data Protection Directive. In summary, the DPA 1998 regulates the processing of personal data by data controllers. A 'data controller' is a person who determines both the purposes for which and the manner in which personal data are, or are to be, processed. A data controller can be a natural or legal person and when determining the purposes and manner of processing they can act either alone or jointly in common with others. A data controller is obliged to comply with the data protection principles (DPA 1998, s.4(1)).

There are two other actors within the regime: data subjects and data processors. A 'data subject' is the living individual who is the subject of personal data. A 'data processor' is a person or organisation that processes data on behalf of a data controller, but for these purposes employees of a data controller are considered to form part of the controller, not data processors.

### 3.4.1 The meaning of 'data'

According to DPA 1998, s.1(1) there are five categories of data, which are:

1. Information that is being processed by means of equipment operating automatically in response to instructions given for that purpose. This is a description of data held on computers and on computer controlled equipment.
2. Information that is recorded with the intention that is should be processed by means of equipment that operates automatically. This is a description of information that will be held on a computer or on

computer controlled equipment at a point in the future. Such information can be electronic in nature, as in the case of data that has been transferred from a computer to a CD or DVD, or it can be manual, as in the sense of a solicitor's handwritten attendance note that is in waiting to be typed up on a computer.

3. Information that is recorded as part of a relevant filing system or with the intention that it should form part of a relevant filing system. This is a description of manual data. A relevant filing system is a highly structured manual file, although the definition captures manual information that has yet to become incorporated into a structured file.
4. Information that does not fall into any of the preceding categories but forms part of an accessible record. Accessible records cover certain health, education and public records and they are always manual in nature (DPA 1998, s.68).
5. Recorded information held by a public authority that does not fall into any of the previous categories. Again, this is referring to purely manual data. Such data may be structured, but to a lesser degree of complexity than relevant filing systems, or it can be completely unstructured.

It is fair to say that an email can fall into any of these categories of data, depending upon whether it is held in electronic or manual form (in the sense of being a hard copy). Of course, an email will only gain the protections of the Act if it contains personal data (or, for the purposes of DPA 1998, s.55, amounts to either information contained in personal data or information extracted from personal data – see **Chapter 6** for discussion).

### 3.4.2 The meaning of 'personal data'

The DPA 1998 defines personal data in the following manner:

> 'personal data' means data which relate to a living individual who can be identified –
>
> (a) from those data, or
> (b) from those data and other information which is in the possession of, or is likely to come into the possession of, the data controller,
>
> and includes any expression of opinion about the individual and any indication of the intentions of the data controller or any other person in respect of the individual.

The corresponding definition within Article 2(a) of the Data Protection Directive is:

> 'Personal data' shall mean any information relating to an identified or identifiable natural person ('data subject'); an identifiable person is one who can be identified, directly or indirectly, in particular by reference to an identification number or to one or more factors specific to his physical, physiological, mental, economic, cultural or social identity.

### *Personal data and the* Durant *case*

Clearly, the definition of personal data has very wide scope, meaning that untruths are caught as well as facts, opinions and indications of intention. However, the leading domestic case on the meaning of personal data, *Durant* v. *Financial Services Authority* [2003] EWCA Civ 1746 (a decision of the Court of Appeal in 2003), has been widely criticised for narrowing the scope of the DPA 1998, due to the fact that it held that information processed by the Financial Services Authority (FSA) that identified the claimant did not 'relate' to him, for the purposes of the definition of personal data, but to his complaint about a bank. Up until that point, the general consensus of data protection practitioners was that any information that identified a person, 'related' to that person for the purposes of data protection.

The background of the case is as follows: Mr Durant was once a customer of Barclays Bank. He fell into dispute with Barclays and later commenced litigation, which was unsuccessful. He then made complaints to the FSA, which carried out an investigation. Again, Mr Durant failed to secure the outcome he felt that he deserved. Thus, he used his powers in DPA 1998, s.7 to gain access to the FSA's files. The FSA delivered information in response to the access request, but it withheld some information on the grounds that it was not personal data as it did not relate to Mr Durant, but to his complaint. This set the battlegrounds for the litigation.

In the light of the Court of Appeal's decision in *Durant*, the current state of the law in the UK is that mere references to a person are not enough to make data 'relate' to a person. Instead, something more tangible is required, which the Court of Appeal described as being an effect on an individual's privacy. In his leading judgment Lord Justice Auld said:

> It follows from what I have said that not all information retrieved from a computer search against an individual's name or unique identifier is personal data within the Act. Mere mention of the data subject in a document held by a data controller does not necessarily amount to his personal data. Whether it does so in any particular instance depends on where it falls in a continuum of relevance or proximity to the data subject as distinct, say, from transactions or matters in which he may have been involved to a greater or lesser degree. It seems to me that there are two notions that may be of assistance. The first is whether the information is biographical in a significant sense, that is, going beyond the recording of the putative data subject's involvement in a matter or an event that has no personal connotations, a life event in respect of which his privacy could not be said to be compromised. The second is one of focus. The information should have the putative data subject as its

> focus rather than some other person with whom he may have been involved or some transaction or event in which he may have figured or have had an interest, for example, as in this case, an investigation into some other person's or body's conduct that he may have instigated. In short, it is information that affects his privacy, whether in his personal or family life, business or professional capacity.

Unfortunately for those advising on data protection, the situation has become even more confused since the publication of an Opinion by the Article 29 Working Party. The Article 29 Working Party is an expert body established under Article 29 of the Data Protection Directive. It has various duties (see Article 30), which include the issuing of opinions on matters of interpretation. Its Opinion 'on the concept of personal data' is one such opinion (Opinion No.4/2007 on the concept of personal data, 20 June 2007, WP 136). This Opinion prefers a much wider approach to the meaning of personal data than the Court of Appeal, and there seems to be little room to doubt that had the Article 29 Working Party's formulation been applied in the *Durant* case the outcome would have been very different.

The Opinion focuses on the constituent parts of the definition of personal data contained in Article 2(a) of the Data Protection Directive and for the purposes of the words 'relating to', which were at the heart of the Court of Appeal's analysis in *Durant*, it gives the following assistance:

> In view of the cases mentioned above, and along the same lines, it could be pointed out that, in order to consider that the data 'relate' to an individual, a 'content' element OR a 'purpose' element OR a 'result' element should be present.
>
> The 'content' element is present in those cases where – corresponding to the most obvious and common understanding in a society of the word 'relate' – information is given about a particular person, regardless of any purpose on the side of the data controller or of a third party, or the impact of that information on the data subject. Information 'relates' to a person when it is 'about' that person, and this has to be assessed in the light of all circumstances surrounding the case. For example, the results of medical analysis clearly relate to the patient, or the information contained in a company's folder under the name of a certain client clearly relates to him. Or the information contained in a RFID [Radio Frequency Identification] tag or a bar code incorporated in an identity document of a certain individual relates to that person, as in future passports with a RFID chip.
>
> Also a 'purpose' element can be responsible for the fact that information 'relates' to a certain person. That 'purpose' element can be considered to exist when the data are used or are likely to be used, taking into account all the circumstances surrounding the precise case, with the purpose to evaluate, treat in a certain way or influence the status or behaviour of an individual.
>
> A third kind of 'relating' to specific persons arises when a 'result' element is present. Despite the absence of a 'content' or 'purpose' element, data can be considered to 'relate' to an individual because their use is likely to have an impact on a certain person's rights and interests, taking into account all the circumstances surrounding the precise case. It should be noted that it is not necessary that the potential result be a major impact. It is sufficient if the individual may be treated differently from other persons as a result of the processing of such data.

> These three elements (content, purpose, result) must be considered as alternative conditions, and not as cumulative ones. In particular, where the content element is present, there is no need for the other elements to be present to consider that the information relates to the individual. A corollary of this is that the same piece of information may relate to different individuals at the same time, depending on what element is present with regard to each one. The same information may relate to individual Titius because of the 'content' element (the data is clearly about Titius), AND to Gaius because of the 'purpose' element (it will be used in order to treat Gaius in a certain way) AND to Sempronius because of the 'result' element (it is likely to have an impact on the rights and interests of Sempronius). This means also that it is not necessary that the data 'focuses' on someone in order to consider that it relates to him. Resulting from the previous analysis, the question of whether data relate to a certain person is something that has to be answered for each specific data item on its own merits. In a similar way, the fact that information may relate to different persons should be kept in mind in the application of substantive provisions (e.g. on the scope of the right of access).

If the Article 29 Working Party's approach on the meaning of 'relating to' is applied to the facts in *Durant*, then the information processed by the FSA about Mr Durant's complaint against the bank would relate to him through the content element. It is also worth noting that in the final paragraph of the passage quoted above there is explicit rejection of the idea that data should focus on a person in order to relate to them, which seems to be a direct rejection of the Court of Appeal's approach in *Durant*. In making this final point, the author notes that the European Commission and the Article 29 Working Party have been highly critical of *Durant*, levying the charge that if *Durant* is correct on the face of the DPA 1998 then the UK has failed properly to transpose the Directive.

The Information Commissioner, who was represented on the Article 29 Working Party, has published his own guidance on the meaning of personal data that attempts to bridge the gap between *Durant* and the Opinion.[3] As regards Lord Justice Auld's notion of biographical significance, the Commissioner's guidance says:

> It is important to remember that it is not always necessary to consider 'biographical significance' to determine whether data is personal data. In many cases data may be personal data simply because its content is such that it is 'obviously about' an individual. Alternatively, data may be personal data because it is clearly 'linked to' an individual because it is about his activities and is processed with the purpose of determining or influencing the way in which that person is treated. You need to consider 'biographical significance' only where information is not 'obviously about' an individual or clearly 'linked to' him.

As regards Lord Justice Auld's notion of focus, the Commissioner's guidance says:

> Again, it is important to remember that it is not always necessary to consider 'focus' to determine whether data is personal data. In many cases data may be personal data because it is 'obviously about' an individual, or because it is clearly 'linked to' an individual because it is about the individual's activities. You need to consider the 'focus' of the data only where information is not 'obviously about' an individual or clearly 'linked to' them.

The Commissioner's guidance on biographical significance and focus is eminently sensible, but the fact remains that at the outer parameters of interpretation there still seems to be a massive gulf between the approach of the Court of Appeal and the approach of the Article 20 Working Party. The House of Lords recently had an opportunity to reconsider the *Durant* meaning of personal data in the case of *Child Support Agency* v. *The Scottish Information Commissioner* [2008] UKHL 47, a Freedom of Information Act (FOIA) 2000 case. This case concerned the interaction between the Freedom of Information (Scotland) Act 2002 and the DPA 1998. It was held that if personal data cannot be truly anonymised so as to render a person's identity undetectable by any third party, the public authority must not disclose that data to a third party unless that disclosure would be fully compliant with the data protection principles. The Information Commissioner and the Ministry of Justice intervened, to invite their Lordships' approval of the Commissioner's guidance on the meaning of personal data, but their Lordships declined the opportunity.

Another case which impacts upon the meaning of personal data is *Bavarian Lager Co Ltd (supported by European Data Protection Supervisor)* v. *Commission of the European Communities* [2008] 1 CMLR 35, a decision of the Court of First Instance of the European Communities. The case resulted from a UK law (Supply of Beer Order 1989) that effectively prevented German beers being sold as guest beers in tied public houses. The Commission considered this could be unlawful and commenced an investigation with a view to commencing proceedings against the UK. During the course of this investigation a meeting was held between representatives of the Commission, the UK government and various breweries from which Bavarian Lager was excluded. Bavarian Lager applied for access to the minutes of the meeting and these were supplied, absent the names of five attendees, which had been redacted. Bavarian Lager then pressed for the release of unredacted versions. The Commission refused, citing an exemption in the Community freedom of information legislation (Regulation (EC) No.1049/2001 of the European Parliament and of the Council of 30 May 2001 regarding public access to European Parliament, Council and Commission documents; see Article 4(1)(b)), which allows the Commission to refuse access to a document where disclosure would undermine the protection of privacy and the integrity of the individual, in particular in accordance with Community legislation regarding the protection of personal data. The Court of First Instance held that although the names of the attendees at the meeting constituted personal data disclosure would not undermine their privacy. It may therefore be argued that this approach to the meaning of personal data is irreconcilable with the Court of Appeal's approach in *Durant*; *Bavarian Lager* seems to be authority for the proposition that information does not need to affect a person's privacy to be personal data, which was the core holding of the Court of Appeal in *Durant*.

For the time being at least, *Durant* remains good law and the tension between the UK approach and the European approach is very unsatisfactory, making life unnecessarily difficult for data controllers. At some point the UK courts will have to bridge the gulf between domestic thinking on data protection and the consensus opinion at European level, but until then UK data controllers will have to take a judgment call on whether to follow the *Durant* approach or the approach of the Article 29 Working Party.

### *The meaning of 'sensitive personal data'*

A special form of personal data is 'sensitive personal data', of which there are eight types. Section 2 of the Act says:

> In this Act 'sensitive personal data' means personal data consisting of information as to –
>
> (a) the racial or ethnic origin of the data subject,
> (b) his political opinions,
> (c) his religious beliefs or other beliefs of a similar nature,
> (d) whether he is a member of a trade union within the meaning of the 1992 Trade Union and Labour Relations (Consolidation) Act 1992,
> (e) his physical or mental health or condition,
> (f) his sexual life,
> (g) the commission or alleged commission by him of any offence, or
> (h) any proceedings for any offence committed or alleged to have been committed by him, the disposal of such proceedings or the sentence of any court in such proceedings.

The European data protection framework has always recognised that sensitive personal data falls into a special category,[4] requiring greater protections than non-sensitive data.[5] Thus, for example, the DPA 1998 says that where a data controller wishes to rely upon the consent of the data subject to legitimise processing they need to obtain 'explicit' consent (see the first data protection principle and the first paragraphs to Scheds.2 and 3) wherever sensitive data are concerned, whereas with non-sensitive data there is no need for the consent to be explicit. The rationale behind the according of greater protections for sensitive data is, of course, that there is the potential for greater harm when sensitive data are unlawfully processed than with non-sensitive data.

### 3.4.3 The meaning of 'processing'

The Act defines 'processing' in the following terms:

> 'processing', in relation to information or data, means obtaining, recording or holding the information or data or carrying out any operation or set of operations on the information or data, including –
>
> (a) organisation, adaptation or alteration of the information or data,
> (b) retrieval, consultation or use of the information or data,
> (c) disclosure of the information or data by transmission, dissemination or otherwise making available, or
> (d) alignment, combination, blocking, erasure or destruction of the information or data [DPA 1998, s.1(1)];
>
> In this Act, unless the context otherwise requires –
>
> (a) 'obtaining' or 'recording', in relation to personal data, includes obtaining or recording the information to be contained in the data, and
> (b) 'using' or 'disclosing', in relation to personal data, includes using or disclosing the information contained in the data [DPA 1998, s.1(2)].

Clearly, processing has a very wide meaning and until a recent decision of the Court of Appeal, the consensus view of data protection practitioners was that it covered all operations relating to electronic data, including those operations conducted by human beings. However, the most recent case on the meaning of processing, the decision of the Court of Appeal in *Johnson* v. *Medical Defence Union* [2007] EWCA Civ 262, has injected considerable confusion into this area.

#### *The* Johnson *case*

*Johnson* concerned a decision by the MDU to withdraw professional indemnity insurance cover from the claimant, a medical practitioner with no adverse claims history. During the process that led to the withdrawal of cover, an employee of the defendant, Dr Roberts, was charged with the task of summarising the effect of a number of computer records relating to the claimant; these records contained the claimant's personal data. Dr Roberts read the computer records and then created a new computer record, referred to as a 'RAR', which contained the summary. In effect, computer data were subject to a process of human filtering which led to the creation of more computer data, an operation that is so mundane and routine that it seemed inconceivable that it would lead to a dispute on the meaning of processing. However, a dispute did arise.

The claimant complained that Dr Roberts's selection of information from the original records was unfair within the meaning of the first data protection principle, in that it created a false impression of the claimant thereby causing him to suffer loss and damage. Lord Justice Buxton rejected this argument, holding that the process of selection by Dr Roberts was a mental process performed by a human, not an act of processing within the meaning of the DPA 1998, with the result that the Act did not apply to that operation. He held:

> the difficulty for Mr Johnson remains that the selection, and thus the carrying out of operations, of which he complains was done by Dr Roberts, using her own judgement, and not by any computer or by any automatic means.

Lady Justice Arden did not share Lord Justice Buxton's conclusion on the meaning of processing, however, siding instead with the judge at first instance, Mr Justice Rimer:

> the expression 'personal data' in section 1(2)(a) [of the DPA 1998] includes putative personal data, that is information which will constitute 'personal data' when both the act of obtaining the information to be contained in the data and the act of inputting it onto a computer have been completed. On that basis, the selection by Dr Roberts of material and the placing of that material on to a computer constituted 'processing' for the purposes of section 1 of the 1998 Act. That conclusion is consistent with the directive, and the court is not precluded from coming to the conclusion that the selection of material is capable of being 'processing' by reason of the fact that the selection occurs before any information is put on to the computer.

However, Lord Justice Longmore sided with Lord Justice Buxton on the meaning of processing, holding that:

> To my mind when an individual decides what information to put into an automatic system, he or she is not automatically processing that information either partly or wholly. An exercise of judgment by an individual is not automatic at all. Indeed it is the antithesis of automaticity. It might be different if the information was being automatically inserted into a computer but, in this case, although the RAR form was created on computer by Dr Roberts it was not automatically processed at that stage. It was fed in by the exercise of human judgment.

Thus, on a majority decision the claimant lost on the meaning of processing and the appeal was dismissed, although when taking account of the judgment of the judge at first instance the decisions of all the judges involved in the case were equally split.

It is also troubling that Lord Justice Buxton sought to distinguish a decision of the Court of Appeal in *Campbell* v. *MGN Ltd* [2002] EWCA 1373, while Lady Justice Arden cited it in support of her judgment. (See also the decision of the House of Lords, [2004] UKHL 22, although there was no appeal on the meaning of processing for the purposes of the DPA 1998.)

In *Campbell* v. *MGN*, the supermodel Naomi Campbell complained that photographs showing her in the street outside a building used by Narcotics Anonymous published in *The Mirror* newspaper breached her privacy and the provisions of the DPA 1998, which led to an examination of the question whether such publication amounted to an act of processing. On this question the Court of Appeal was unanimous, with Lord Phillips, Master of the Rolls, holding:

> Accordingly we conclude that, where the data controller is responsible for the publication of hard copies that reproduce data that has previously been processed by means of equipment operating automatically, the publication forms part of the processing and falls within the scope of the Act.[6]

It is very difficult to reconcile the logic of Lord Justice Buxton's analysis with the intention of the Data Protection Directive and the decision of the Court of Appeal in *Campbell*, although in practical terms *Johnson* is unlikely to have much effect on data protection law at routine compliance level. However, it is the writer's opinion that the judgment of Lady Justice Arden should be preferred, not least because it is also compatible with the DPA 1998's interpretative provisions, which state that data also means information which is recorded with the intention that it should be processed by means of automated equipment (DPA 1998, s.1(1)(b)), although it is noticeable and somewhat surprising that the Court of Appeal in *Johnson* did not specifically address this point (see, for example, *CCN Credit Systems Ltd* v. *The Data Protection Registrar* (1991), **www.informationtribunal.gov.uk/Documents/decisions/ccn_systems.pdf**).

### 3.4.4 The meaning of 'relevant filing system'

Private sector manual data can fall within the scope of the DPA 1998 in a number of ways,[7] but the meaning of 'relevant filing system' causes problems for many data controllers. The DPA 1998 defines relevant filing system in the following terms:

> 'relevant filing system' means any set of information relating to individuals to the extent that, although the information is not processed by means of equipment operating automatically in response to instructions given for that purpose, the set is structured, either by reference to individuals or by reference to criteria relating to individuals, in such a way that specific information relating to a particular individual is readily accessible.

Central to the meaning of relevant filing system is the requirement that the structure of the file should make information 'readily accessible'. Unfortunately, the Act does not give any assistance with the meaning of this term and nor does the Data Protection Directive, which talks instead about personal data filing systems (see Article 2(c) which says '"personal data filing system" ("filing system") shall mean any structured set of personal data which are accessible according to specific criteria, whether centralized, decentralized or dispersed on a functional or geographical basis'). However, it is worth noting that Recital 27 to the Directive says that 'the content of a filing system must be structured according to specific criteria relating to individuals allowing easy access to the personal data'.

The leading domestic case on the meaning of relevant filing system is *Durant*. Lord Justice Auld held that:

> Parliament intended to apply the Act to manual records only if they are of sufficient sophistication to provide the same or similar ready accessibility as a computerised filing system. That requires a filing system so referenced or indexed that it enables the data controller's employee responsible to identify at the outset of his search with reasonable certainty and speed the file or files in which the specific data relating to the person requesting the information is located and to locate the relevant information about him within the file or files, without having to make a manual search of them. To leave it to the searcher to leaf through files, possibly at great length and cost, and fruitlessly, to see whether it or they contain information relating to the person requesting information and whether that information is data within the Act bears, as Mr. Sales said, no resemblance to a computerised search. It cannot have been intended by Parliament.

This passage shows that Lord Justice Auld was very much persuaded that relevant filing systems should enable a search of similar sophistication as that provided by computers. With respect to the judge, this does not reveal an appreciation of the true sophistication of computer searches, but the balance of his argument is certainly consistent with the intention of the Data Protection Directive and, indeed, his final conclusions are hard to fault:

> Accordingly, I conclude, as Mr. Sales submitted, that 'a relevant filing system' for the purpose of the Act, is limited to a system:
>
> 1) in which the files forming part of it are structured or referenced in such a way as clearly to indicate at the outset of the search whether specific information capable of amounting to personal data of an individual requesting it under section 7 is held within the system and, if so, in which file or files it is held; and
> 2) which has, as part of its own structure or referencing mechanism, a sufficiently sophisticated and detailed means of readily indicating whether and where in an individual file or files specific criteria or information about the applicant can be readily located.

The importance of relevant filing systems to this book is, of course, that hard copies of emails can be made; sometimes hard copies of emails will be stored in relevant filing systems, rendering them subject to the full scope of the DPA 1998.

## 3.5 COMPLIANCE OBLIGATIONS

### 3.5.1 Transparency

A central component of the legal framework for data protection, which has been present since the Council of Europe's first Resolution in 1973, is its requirement for transparency of data processing operations. The DPA 1998's transparency safeguards are various, with the main ones being:

- Data controllers are subject to regulatory and judicial scrutiny. The Information Commissioner is empowered to investigate controllers and to enforce the DPA 1998. He can bring criminal proceedings against seriously errant data controllers (i.e. those breaching the provisions that give rise to direct criminal liability and those breaching enforcement and information notices), while the data subject can take complaints to the Commissioner and can enforce their rights before the courts.
- The DPA 1998 promotes consensual processing; the first data protection principle refers to Scheds.2 and 3, which both refer to consensual processing. Although consent is not the only route to legitimate processing, for most processing operations it will be either the route of choice or necessity.
- The first and second data protection principles require controllers to be open about their reasons for processing, stating a purpose prior to the commencement of processing.
- The DPA 1998 obliges data controllers to register themselves and their processing operations with the Information Commissioner. If an obligation to notify exists, it is a crime to fail to do so or to fail to keep one's notification up to date.
- The data subject is empowered to serve 'access requests' on the data controller, which require the controller to provide core information about their processing operations.

### 3.5.2 Data protection principles

The DPA 1998's core compliance obligations are contained within the data protection principles. Section 4(4) of the Act says that 'it shall be the duty of a data controller to comply with the data protection principles in relation to all personal data with respect to which he is the data controller'. The principles are contained in Sched.1, Part I of the DPA 1998 and are accompanied by rules for their interpretation which are contained in Sched.1, Part II (see DPA 1998, Sched.1, Part II; s.4(2) says that the principles 'are to be interpreted in accordance with Part II of Schedule 1'). **Table 3.2** shows the principles side-by-side with their interpretation.

**Table 3.2** The data protection principles and their interpretation

| Sched.1, Part I – the principles | Sched.1, Part II – their interpretation |
|---|---|
| 1. Personal data shall be processed fairly and lawfully and, in particular, shall not be processed unless –<br><br>(a) at least one of the conditions in Schedule 2 is met, and<br>(b) in the case of sensitive personal data, at least one of the conditions in Schedule 3 is also met. | 1. (1) In determining for the purposes of the first principle whether personal data are processed fairly, regard is to be had to the method by which they are obtained, including in particular whether any person from whom they are obtained is deceived or misled as to the purpose or purposes for which they are to be processed.<br><br>(2) Subject to paragraph 2, for the purposes of the first principle data are to be treated as obtained fairly if they consist of information obtained from a person who –<br><br>(a) is authorised by or under any enactment to supply it, or<br>(b) is required to supply it by or under any enactment or by any convention or other instrument imposing an international obligation on the United Kingdom.<br><br>2. (1) Subject to paragraph 3, for the purposes of the first principle personal data are not to be treated as processed fairly unless –<br><br>(a) in the case of data obtained from the data subject, the data controller ensures so far as practicable that the data subject has, is provided with, or has made readily available to him, the information specified in sub-paragraph (3), and<br>(b) in any other case, the data controller ensures so far as practicable that, before the relevant time or as soon as practicable after that time, the data subject has, is provided with, or has made readily available to him, the information specified in sub-paragraph (3).<br><br>(2) In sub-paragraph (1)(b) 'the relevant time' means –<br><br>(a) the time when the data controller first processes the data, or<br>(b) in a case where at that time disclosure to a third party within a reasonable period is envisaged - |

**Table 3.2** *Cont.*

| Sched.1, Part I – the principles | Sched.1, Part II – their interpretation |
|---|---|
| | (i) if the data are in fact disclosed to such a person within that period, the time when the data are first disclosed,<br>(ii) if within that period the data controller becomes, or ought to become, aware that the data are unlikely to be disclosed to such a person within that period, the time when the data controller does become, or ought to become, so aware, or<br>(iii) in any other case, the end of that period.<br><br>(3) The information referred to in sub-paragraph (1) is as follows, namely –<br><br>(a) the identity of the data controller,<br>(b) if he has nominated a representative for the purposes of this Act, the identity of that representative,<br>(c) the purpose or purposes for which the data are intended to be processed, and<br>(d) any further information which is necessary, having regard to the specific circumstances in which the data are or are to be processed, to enable processing in respect of the data subject to be fair.<br><br>3. (1) Paragraph 2(1)(b) does not apply where either of the primary conditions in sub-paragraph (2), together with such further conditions as may be prescribed by the Secretary of State by order, are met.<br><br>(2) The primary conditions referred to in sub-paragraph (1) are –<br><br>(a) that the provision of that information would involve a disproportionate effort, or<br>(b) that the recording of the information to be contained in the data by, or the disclosure of the data by, the data controller is necessary for compliance with any legal obligation to which the data controller is subject, other than an obligation imposed by contract. |

**Table 3.2** *Cont.*

| Sched.1, Part I – the principles | Sched.1, Part II – their interpretation |
|---|---|
| | 4. (1) Personal data which contain a general identifier falling within a description prescribed by the Secretary of State by order are not to be treated as processed fairly and lawfully unless they are processed in compliance with any conditions so prescribed in relation to general identifiers of that description.<br><br>(2) In sub-paragraph (1) 'a general identifier' means any identifier (such as, for example, a number or code used for identification purposes) which –<br><br>(a) relates to an individual, and<br>(b) forms part of a set of similar identifiers which is of general application. |
| 2. Personal data shall be obtained only for one or more specified and lawful purposes, and shall not be further processed in any manner incompatible with that purpose or those purposes. | 5. The purpose or purposes for which personal data are obtained may in particular be specified –<br><br>(a) in a notice given for the purposes of paragraph 2 by the data controller to the data subject, or<br>(b) in a notification given to the Commissioner under Part III of this Act.<br><br>6. In determining whether any disclosure of personal data is compatible with the purpose or purposes for which the data were obtained, regard is to be had to the purpose or purposes for which the personal data are intended to be processed by any person to whom they are disclosed. |
| 3. Personal data shall be adequate, relevant and not excessive in relation to the purpose or purposes for which they are processed. | |
| 4. Personal data shall be accurate and, where necessary, kept up to date. | 7. The fourth principle is not to be regarded as being contravened by reason of any inaccuracy in personal data which accurately record information obtained by the data controller from the data subject or a third party in a case where – |

**Table 3.2** *Cont.*

| **Sched.1, Part I – the principles** | **Sched.1, Part II – their interpretation** |
|---|---|
| | (a) having regard to the purpose or purposes for which the data were obtained and further processed, the data controller has taken reasonable steps to ensure the accuracy of the data, and<br>(b) if the data subject has notified the data controller of the data subject's view that the data are inaccurate, the data indicate that fact. |
| 5. Personal data processed for any purpose or purposes shall not be kept for longer than is necessary for that purpose or those purposes. | |
| 6. Personal data shall be processed in accordance with the rights of data subjects under this Act. | 8. A person is to be regarded as contravening the sixth principle if, but only if –<br>(a) he contravenes section 7 by failing to supply information in accordance with that section,<br>(b) he contravenes section 10 by failing to comply with a notice given under subsection (1) of that section to the extent that the notice is justified or by failing to give a notice under subsection (3) of that section,<br>(c) he contravenes section 11 by failing to comply with a notice given under subsection (1) of that section, or<br>(d) he contravenes section 12 by failing to comply with a notice given under subsection (1) or (2)(b) of that section or by failing to give a notification under subsection (2)(a) of that section or a notice under subsection (3) of that section. |
| 7. Appropriate technical and organisational measures shall be taken against unauthorised or unlawful processing of personal data and against accidental loss or destruction of, or damage to, personal data. | 9. Having regard to the state of technological development and the cost of implementing any measures, the measures must ensure a level of security appropriate to – |

**Table 3.2** *Cont.*

| Sched.1, Part I – the principles | Sched.1, Part II – their interpretation |
|---|---|
| | (a) the harm that might result from such unauthorised or unlawful processing or accidental loss, destruction or damage as are mentioned in the seventh principle, and<br>(b) the nature of the data to be protected.<br><br>10 . The data controller must take reasonable steps to ensure the reliability of any employees of his who have access to the personal data.<br><br>11. Where processing of personal data is carried out by a data processor on behalf of a data controller, the data controller must in order to comply with the seventh principle –<br><br>(a) choose a data processor providing sufficient guarantees in respect of the technical and organisational security measures governing the processing to be carried out, and<br>(b) take reasonable steps to ensure compliance with those measures.<br><br>12. Where processing of personal data is carried out by a data processor on behalf of a data controller, the data controller is not to be regarded as complying with the seventh principle unless –<br><br>(a) the processing is carried out under a contract –<br>(i) which is made or evidenced in writing, and<br>(ii) under which the data processor is to act only on instructions from the data controller, and<br>(b) the contract requires the data processor to comply with obligations equivalent to those imposed on a data controller by the seventh principle. |

**Table 3.2** *Cont.*

| Sched.1, Part I – the principles | Sched.1, Part II – their interpretation |
|---|---|
| 8. Personal data shall not be transferred to a country or territory outside the European Economic Area unless that country or territory ensures an adequate level of protection for the rights and freedoms of data subjects in relation to the processing of personal data. | 13. An adequate level of protection is one which is adequate in all the circumstances of the case, having regard in particular to –<br><br>(a) the nature of the personal data,<br>(b) the country or territory of origin of the information contained in the data,<br>(c) the country or territory of final destination of that information,<br>(d) the purposes for which and period during which the data are intended to be processed,<br>(e) the law in force in the country or territory in question,<br>(f) the international obligations of that country or territory,<br>(g) any relevant codes of conduct or other rules which are enforceable in that country or territory (whether generally or by arrangement in particular cases), and<br>(h) any security measures taken in respect of the data in that country or territory.<br><br>14. The eighth principle does not apply to a transfer falling within any paragraph of Schedule 4, except in such circumstances and to such extent as the Secretary of State may by order provide.<br><br>15. (1) Where –<br><br>(a) in any proceedings under this Act any question arises as to whether the requirement of the eighth principle as to an adequate level of protection is met in relation to the transfer of any personal data to a country or territory outside the European Economic Area, and<br>(b) a Community finding has been made in relation to transfers of the kind in question,<br><br>that question is to be determined in accordance with that finding. |

**Table 3.2** *Cont.*

| Sched.1, Part I – the principles | Sched.1, Part II – their interpretation |
|---|---|
| | (2) In sub-paragraph (1) 'Community finding' means a finding of the European Commission, under the procedure provided for in Article 31(2) of the Data Protection Directive, that a country or territory outside the European Economic Area does, or does not, ensure an adequate level of protection within the meaning of Article 25(2) of the Directive. |

### *First data protection principle – fair and lawful processing*

The first data protection principle's focus on fair and lawful processing incorporates a wide range of issues and considerations. Fairness covers the fairness of the processing purpose, the fairness of the processing manner, the fairness of the processing operation and the fairness of the data controller's means of obtaining the personal data. The interpretation to the first principle shows that deception will result in the processing being automatically unfair, as will (in most cases) a failure to adhere to the transparency principles contained in para.2(3) of the interpretation, which require the controller to supply the data subject with core information about their identity and the processing purpose. Lawfulness covers not only lawfulness in the sense of DPA 1998 lawfulness, but general lawfulness. Thus, processing which is generally unlawful cannot be lawful for the purposes of data protection, even if the controller has obeyed all of the principles within the Act.

As can be seen, the first principle also refers to the conditions in Scheds.2 and 3, with the rule being that for the processing of personal data at least one of the conditions in Sched.2 should be satisfied, while for the processing of sensitive personal data it is also necessary for the data controller to satisfy at least one of the conditions in Sched.3. These conditions are sometimes referred to as the criteria for legitimate processing, echoing phraseology in the Data Protection Directive (Section II of the Directive is titled 'criteria for making data processing legitimate'). **Table 3.3** contains the full sets of conditions within Scheds.2 and 3.

**Table 3.3** Conditions referred to in the first data protection principle

| **Schedule 2 – personal data** | **Schedule 3 – sensitive personal data** |
|---|---|
| 1. The data subject has given his consent to the processing. | 1. The data subject has given his explicit consent to the processing of the personal data. |
| 2. The processing is necessary –<br>(a) for the performance of a contract to which the data subject is a party, or<br>(b) for the taking of steps at the request of the data subject with a view to entering into a contract. | 2. (1) The processing is necessary for the purposes of exercising or performing any right or obligation which is conferred or imposed by law on the data controller in connection with employment.<br>(2) The Secretary of State may by order –<br>(a) exclude the application of sub-paragraph (1) in such cases as may be specified, or<br>(b) provide that, in such cases as may be specified, the condition in sub-paragraph (1) is not to be regarded as satisfied unless such further conditions as may be specified in the order are also satisfied. |
| 3. The processing is necessary for compliance with any legal obligation to which the data controller is subject, other than an obligation imposed by contract. | 3. The processing is necessary –<br>(a) in order to protect the vital interests of the data subject or another person, in a case where –<br>(i) consent cannot be given by or on behalf of the data subject, or<br>(ii) the data controller cannot reasonably be expected to obtain the consent of the data subject, or<br>(b) in order to protect the vital interests of another person, in a case where consent by or on behalf of the data subject has been unreasonably withheld. |

**Table 3.3** *Cont.*

| **Schedule 2 – personal data** | **Schedule 3 – sensitive personal data** |
|---|---|
| 4. The processing is necessary in order to protect the vital interests of the data subject. | 4. The processing –<br><br>(a) is carried out in the course of its legitimate activities by any body or association which -<br>(i) is not established or conducted for profit, and<br>(ii) exists for political, philosophical, religious or trade-union purposes,<br>(b) is carried out with appropriate safeguards for the rights and freedoms of data subjects,<br>(c) relates only to individuals who either are members of the body or association or have regular contact with it in connection with its purposes, and<br>(d) does not involve disclosure of the personal data to a third party without the consent of the data subject. |
| 5. The processing is necessary –<br>(a) for the administration of justice,<br>(aa) for the exercise of any functions of either House of Parliament,<br>(b) for the exercise of any functions conferred on any person by or under any enactment,<br>(c) for the exercise of any functions of the Crown, a Minister of the Crown or a government department, or<br>(d) for the exercise of any other functions of a public nature exercised in the public interest by any person. | 5. The information contained in the personal data has been made public as a result of steps deliberately taken by the data subject. |
| 6. (1) The processing is necessary for the purposes of legitimate interests pursued by the data controller or by the third party or parties to whom the data are disclosed, except where the processing is unwarranted in any particular case by reason of prejudice to the rights and freedoms or legitimate interests of the data subject.<br><br>(2) The Secretary of State may by order specify particular circumstances in which this condition is, or is not, to be taken to be satisfied. | 6. The processing –<br><br>(a) is necessary for the purpose of, or in connection with, any legal proceedings (including prospective legal proceedings),<br>(b) is necessary for the purpose of obtaining legal advice, or<br>(c) is otherwise necessary for the purposes of establishing, exercising or defending legal rights.<br><br>7. (1) The processing is necessary – |

**Table 3.3** Conditions referred to in the first data protection principle

| **Schedule 2 – personal data** | **Schedule 3 – sensitive personal data** |
|---|---|
| | (a) for the administration of justice,<br>(aa) for the exercise of any functions of either House of Parliament,<br>(b) for the exercise of any functions conferred on any person by or under an enactment, or<br>(c) for the exercise of any functions of the Crown, a Minister of the Crown or a government department.<br><br>(2) The Secretary of State may by order –<br><br>(a) exclude the application of sub-paragraph (1) in such cases as may be specified, or<br>(b) provide that, in such cases as may be specified, the condition in sub-paragraph (1) is not to be regarded as satisfied unless such further conditions as may be specified in the order are also satisfied.<br><br>7A. (1) The processing –<br><br>(a) is either –<br>(i) the disclosure of sensitive personal data by a person as a member of an anti-fraud organisation or otherwise in accordance with any arrangements made by such an organisation; or<br>(ii) any other processing by that person or another person of sensitive personal data so disclosed; and<br>(b) is necessary for the purposes of preventing fraud or a particular kind of fraud.<br><br>(2) In this paragraph 'an anti-fraud organisation' means any unincorporated association, body corporate or other person which enables or facilitates any sharing of information to prevent fraud or a particular kind of fraud or which has any of these functions as its purpose or one of its purposes. [Inserted by Serious Crime Act 2007, s.7.] |

**Table 3.3** Conditions referred to in the first data protection principle

| Schedule 2 – personal data | Schedule 3 – sensitive personal data |
| --- | --- |
| | 8. (1) The processing is necessary for medical purposes and is undertaken by –<br><br>(a) a health professional, or<br>(b) a person who in the circumstances owes a duty of confidentiality which is equivalent to that which would arise if that person were a health professional.<br><br>(2) In this paragraph 'medical purposes' includes the purposes of preventative medicine, medical diagnosis, medical research, the provision of care and treatment and the management of healthcare services.<br><br>9. (1) The processing –<br><br>(a) is of sensitive personal data consisting of information as to racial or ethnic origin,<br>(b) is necessary for the purpose of identifying or keeping under review the existence or absence of equality of opportunity or treatment between persons of different racial or ethnic origins, with a view to enabling such equality to be promoted or maintained, and<br>(c) is carried out with appropriate safeguards for the rights and freedoms of data subjects.<br><br>(2) The Secretary of State may by order specify circumstances in which processing falling within sub-paragraph (1)(a) and (b) is, or is not, to be taken for the purposes of sub-paragraph (1)(c) to be carried out with appropriate safeguards for the rights and freedoms of data subjects. |
| 10. The personal data are processed in circumstances specified in an order made by the Secretary of State for the purposes of this paragraph.8 | |

### *Second data protection principle – processing to purpose*

The second data protection principle contains three important components: first, the processing must be for a purpose; second, the purpose itself must be specified and lawful; and third, any subsequent processing should not be incompatible with the original purpose.

It seems to be implicit with the second principle that the purpose behind the processing should be known prior to the commencement of the processing, which means prior to the collection of the data. As regards the communication of the purpose, the interpretation to the second principle shows that this can be given in two ways: either in the fair processing notice that is required by the first principle, or within the controller's notification of processing to the Information Commissioner under DPA 1998, s.18.

As regards the meaning of incompatibility, this has not yet been determined by a court, but in the recent case of *Secretary of State for the Home Office* v. *British Union for the Abolition of Vivisection, The Information Commissioner* [2008] EWHC 892 (QB), Mr Justice Eady reminded that 'one should try to give words contained in a statute their ordinary English meaning unless the context is such as to make clear that some specialist interpretation is required'. As such, incompatible is likely to mean contradictory.

A possible example of what amounts to compatible processing might be systems testing. Processing for systems testing purposes is a common and natural feature of computer-based processing and if it were somehow declared to be unlawful on the grounds of incompatibility it could lead, ultimately, either to stagnation in technological development (controllers would be unwilling to refresh their technology for fear of acting unlawfully) or to the failure of processing systems when an old piece of technology is replaced by a new, untried and untested one. When personal data are first obtained, the data controller will always have a core purpose in mind; this is the purpose referred to within the second data protection principle. In addition to the core purpose, one must remember that the platform of computerised processing will always result in processing operations that are ancillary to the core purpose. These ancillary operations are part and parcel of the provision of a good platform for the core processing operation. Examples would include data migration, data archiving and data backups, and many of these can rightly be mapped to elements within the data protection principles; for example, archiving can be legitimately expressed as a facet of the obligation of retention within the fifth principle or a facet of security within the seventh principle. These ancillary operations support the core purpose. As such they are compatible with the core purpose.

### *Third data protection principle – adequacy, relevancy and amount*

The third principle is one of the key 'data quality' principles. It provides that, in effect, the data must be sufficient for the purpose.

The issues expressed within the third principle have been the subject of consistent enforcement activity by the Information Commissioner (and predecessors). In the case of *Community Charge Registrar Officer of Rhondda Borough Council* v. *Data Protection Registrar* (1990)[9] it was held that requests for dates of birth were excessive. In the cases of *Community Charge Registration Officer of Runnymede Borough Council* v. *Data Protection Registrar*, *Community Charge Registration Officer of South Northamptonshire District Council* v. *Data Protection Registrar* and *Community Charge Registration Officer of Harrow Borough Council* v. *Data Protection Registrar* (1990)[10] it was held that the holding of property information on the Community Charges Register was excessive. However, in the case of *The Chief Constables of West Yorkshire, South Yorkshire and North West Wales* v. *The Information Commissioner* (2005)[11] it was held that the retention of old conviction data on the Police National Computer did not breach either the third data protection principle or the fifth principle, although the Tribunal reached the opposite decision in *Chief Constables of Humberside, Staffordshire, Northumbria, West Midlands and Greater Manchester* v. *Information Commissioner.*[12]

### *Fourth data protection principle – accuracy*

The obligations within the fourth principle are twofold. First, the data controller must ensure that data are accurate; this is a mandatory requirement. Second, the controller must keep the data up to date; this is mandatory to the extent that it is necessary to do so.

The interpretation provides the controller with some latitude where any inaccuracies result from the data subject or from third parties; the controller is required to take reasonable steps to ensure accuracy, rather than is required to ensure accuracy.

### *Fifth data protection principle – retention*

The fifth principle imposes both retention and deletion obligations on the controller; once the processing purpose has been fulfilled the data should be deleted or somehow rendered anonymous. On this point it is also worth mentioning Article 6(1) of the Directive on Privacy and Electronic Communications (2002/58/EC) (discussed at **Chapter 4**) which says that 'traffic data relating to subscribers and users processed and stored by the provider of a public communications network or publicly available electronic communications service must be erased or made anonymous when it is no longer needed for the purpose of the transmission of a communication'.

Indeed, on the point of anonymisation, Recital 26 of the Data Protection Directive says that 'the principles of protection shall not apply to data rendered anonymous in such a way that the data subject is no longer identifiable'. The Article 29 Working Party's opinion on the concept of personal data says the following about anonymisation:

> 'Anonymous data' in the sense of the Directive can be defined as any information relating to a natural person where the person cannot be identified, whether by the data controller or by any other person, taking account of all the means likely reasonably to be used either by the controller or by any other person to identify that individual. 'Anonymised data' would therefore be anonymous data that previously referred to an identifiable person, but where that identification is no longer possible. Recital 26 also refers to this concept when it reads that 'the principles of protection shall not apply to data rendered anonymous in such a way that the data subject is no longer identifiable'. Again, the assessment of whether the data allow identification of an individual, and whether the information can be considered as anonymous or not depends on the circumstances, and a case-by-case analysis should be carried out with particular reference to the extent that the means are likely reasonably to be used for identification as described in Recital 26. This is particularly relevant in the case of statistical information, where despite the fact that the information may be presented as aggregated data, the original sample is not sufficiently large and other pieces of information may enable the identification of individuals.

The Information Tribunal recently held that the retention of personal data on the Police National Computer breached the fifth principle (see *Chief Constables of Humberside, Staffordshire, Northumbria, West Midlands and Greater Manchester* v. *Information Commissioner*, EA/2007/0096,98,99,108, 127, 21 July 2008). In holding that the police had breached the fifth principle the Chairman of the Tribunal said:

> We consider the correct approach is that the police process data for what the Commissioner describes as their core purposes. In data protection terms this processing requires holding criminal intelligence on the PNC for so long as it is necessary for the police's core purposes. During the course of holding such data the police are under statutory obligations to allow access to or disclosure of such data to other bodies for their purposes. However we do not consider that Chief Constables are required under their statutory obligations to hold data they no longer require for core purposes. They are only required to provide data that they do hold at the time of the request for access. We heard evidence that Chief Constables have been weeding/deleting conviction data under the various codes of practice until the 2006 Guidelines, and even since then in exceptional cases. Therefore Chief Constables, in any case, are unable to provide all conviction data to these other bodies, only the data which is held on the PNC at the time of access or the request for access. If Chief Constables in accordance with good management practice and/or other statutory requirements, like their data protection obligations, as envisaged by the 2005 Code and the criteria used in MOPI, delete

conviction data or other intelligence from time to time, then in the Tribunal's view there is no counter or overriding obligation on them not to delete that data.

### *Sixth data protection principle – data subject rights*

The sixth data protection principle enhances the value of the data subject rights within DPA 1998, ss.7, 10, 11 and 12. The enhancement lies in the fact that a breach of the principles engages the Information Commissioner's right to take enforcement action.

### *Seventh data protection principle – data security*

While the data protection principles rank equally in importance, it is in the field of data security that we are witnessing the most rapid growth in regulatory action and legislative developments. There are many factors behind this activity, with the 'watershed' moment being the loss of two data disks by HM Revenue and Customs in November 2007, which achieved national and international press coverage; this has spurred on many proposals for legislative change, including the introduction of new criminal offences to cover the reckless mishandling of personal data. While it is true that data controllers face many different kinds of security risks, it remains the case that email presents one of the biggest risks to security.

The current climate in the field of data security is discussed at **Chapter 9**.

### *Eighth data protection principle – transborder data flows*

The eighth principle stands as a general prohibition against the sending of emails containing personal data from countries within the European Economic Area (EEA) to other countries that do not provide adequate protection for personal data as judged by EU standards. The interpretation of the eighth principle assists with determining whether a third country's protection is adequate.

The prohibition is not a complete one, however. There are a number of gateways permitting the lawful transfer of data to non-adequate countries, which include:

- with the consent of the data subject, where the transfer is necessary for contractual purposes, where the transfer is in the public interest and where the transfer is necessary for the protection of legal rights or the data subject's vital interests (DPA 1998, Sched.4);
- where the transfer is subject to approved contractual terms (DPA 1998, Sched.4 and Data Protection Directive, Article 26(4));
- where the transfer is in the context of a controller's Binding Corporate Rules (a scheme introduced by the European Commission under Data Protection Directive, Article 26(2));

- where the transfer is in the context of the US Safe Harbor scheme (approved by the European Commission under Data Protection Directive, Article 25(6)).

### *The principles as compliance challenges for email*

In combination the principles, their interpretation and the criteria for legitimacy provide a comprehensive code for the processing of personal data, but the character of email poses many compliance challenges for data controllers, as the examples within **Table 3.4** seek to demonstrate.

**Table 3.4** Email and the data protection principles: illustrative compliance challenges resulting from the nature and character of email

| | |
|---|---|
| First principle – fair, lawful and legitimate processing | One of the key aims of the first principle is that the collection of personal data should be fair, which requires, for example, the data controller to provide the data subject with an account of the purposes for which the data will be processed. Due to the large volumes of email, the wide usage within the organisation and email's tendency to act as a substitute for conversation, it is very hard for data controllers to be sure that data subjects are always provided with a full and proper account of the purposes. |
| Second principle – processing to purpose | If the organisation cannot be sure that the purposes were properly communicated to the data subject at the outset of processing, it may find it very difficult to demonstrate to the Information Commissioner or to the court that the processing operations remained consistent with the original purpose. |
| Third principle – sufficiency and amount | A common phenomenon of email use is a propensity to total retention and archiving. If every email is kept as a matter of policy (or practice), this creates a risk of excessive, irrelevant and unnecessary processing. |
| Fourth principle – accuracy | The definition of personal data includes opinions about the data subject. The conversational nature of email often embeds inaccurate opinions into the organisation's data banks. The long-term retention of email can also embed inaccuracy. |

**Table 3.4** *Cont.*

| | |
|---|---|
| Fifth principle – retention | Very often email users structure their inboxes in a manner that avoids their organisation's formal archiving systems, with the result that emails can be retained much longer than the period that is required to satisfy the processing purpose. Similarly, emails sent to home, for after-hours working, result in storage outside the formal system. |
| Sixth principle – data subject rights | Email proliferation, through wide copy circulation, blind copy circulation, teleworking and the number and variety of formal and informal storage systems can make it very difficult for organisations to comply with the data subject's right of access. |
| Seventh principle – security | Unencrypted emails are also a security risk. The fact that emails can be sent with attachments poses a security risk. |
| Eighth principle – international transfers | A defining feature of email is its ability to transcend normal, geographical controls. With one click of the mouse, personal data can be transferred to nearly every country outside Europe. |

### 3.5.3 Data subject rights

The DPA 1998 provides the data subject with a number of key rights. These are:

- A right of access to personal data, which includes a right to information about the data controller's processing operations (s.7).
- A right to prevent processing that is causing or is likely to cause substantial and unwarranted damage or distress (s.10). However, this right does not exist where the data subject has given their consent to the processing, or where the processing is necessary for the performance of a contract or where the processing is carried out in the data subject's vital interest.
- A right to request the cessation of processing for direct marketing purposes (s.11). Although the rules on the sending of direct marketing materials by email are contained in the Privacy and Electronic Communications (EC Directive) Regulations 2003, s.11 is still relevant within the context of the enforcement of the anti-spam rules (see **Chapter 4**).
- A right to prevent automatic processing of personal data that is done for the purposes of evaluating matters relating to the data subject, such as work performance, creditworthiness, reliability and conduct (s.12). It is

doubtful that it will be of much practical significance in the context of emails, rather it is aimed more at structured data within databases.

In all of these cases the data subject must direct their requests to the data controller. If the controller fails to comply, the data subject can commence legal action to enforce their rights. In addition to these rights, the data subject is entitled to commence court proceedings to seek the rectification, blocking, erasure or destruction of inaccurate data, although unlike the other rights the data subject is not required to make a prior request to the data controller as a condition precedent to litigation (DPA 1998, s.14).

*The right of access to personal data*

This is discussed at **Chapter 7**.

### 3.5.4 Enforcement by the data subject

In addition to data subjects' right to bring litigation to enforce their rights in respect of access to personal data, processing likely to cause substantial and unwarranted damage or distress, direct marketing, automated decisions and inaccuracies, they can also bring proceedings for compensation. DPA 1998, s.13 states:

> (1) An individual who suffers damage by reason of any contravention by a data controller of any of the requirements of this Act is entitled to compensation from the data controller for that damage.
> (2) An individual who suffers distress by reason of any contravention by a data controller of any of the requirements of this Act is entitled to compensation from the data controller for that distress if –
>
> (a) the individual also suffers damage by reason of the contravention, or
> (b) the contravention relates to the processing of personal data for the special purposes.
>
> (3) In proceedings brought against a person by virtue of this section it is a defence to prove that he had taken such care as in all the circumstances was reasonably required to comply with the requirement concerned.

In *Johnson* v. *Medical Defence Union* the Court of Appeal examined the meaning of damage for the purposes of s.13. By way of background (and in the words of Lord Justice Buxton) the claimant advanced his claim on the following basis:

> But he claims that his expulsion has caused him significant damage of a wider nature. He says he has had to disclose it to hospitals where he has, or has since sought, admitting rights or employment; and he asserts that it reflects that he was regarded by the MDU as a serious risk to its funds, which he says is likely to have had a chilling effect on hospitals who became aware of it. He claims it has

> damaged his professional reputation. He now asks to be compensated. His claim for compensation is brought under section 13 of the Data Protection Act 1998 ('the DPA') and is founded on the assertion that his expulsion was the consequence of the MDU's unfair processing of his personal data.

Lord Justice Buxton held that 'there is no compelling reason to think that "damage" in the Directive has to go beyond its root meaning of pecuniary loss'. Lady Justice Arden and Lord Justice Longmore agreed.

However, matters may not be so clear-cut. During his analysis of the meaning of s.13, Lord Justice Buxton said that 'if a party could establish that a breach of the requirements of the Directive had indeed led to a breach of his Article 8 [European Convention on Human Rights] rights, then he could no doubt recover for that breach under the Directive, without necessarily pursuing the more tortuous path of recovery for a breach of Article 8 as such', which brings into play the case of *Pfeifer* v. *Austria*, a judgment of the European Court of Human Rights (15 November 2007, Application No.12556/03). In this case the applicant alleged that the Austrian Courts had failed to protect his reputation against defamatory allegations made in a magazine. The European Court of Human Rights said that it:

> considers that a person's reputation, even if that person is criticised in the context of a public debate, forms part of his or her personal identity and psychological integrity and therefore also falls within the scope of his or her 'private life'. Article 8 therefore applies. This is not disputed by the parties.

Against this background it would seem that Lord Justice Buxton's words, albeit *obiter*, permit the bringing of a claim for compensation for reputational damage within proceedings based on the Data Protection Directive.

### 3.5.5 Enforcement by the Information Commissioner

The Information Commissioner's enforcement powers can be grouped into four categories:

- He can bring criminal proceedings against errant data controllers.
- He can take enforcement action under DPA 1998, s.40, if he considers that the data controller has contravened, or is contravening, any of the data protection principles.
- He can serve information notices on controllers under DPA 1998, ss.43 and 44, if he has either received a 'request for an assessment' under s.42, or if he reasonably requires information for the purposes of determining whether a controller has complied or is complying with the data protection principles.

- He can issue fines, if he considers that the data controller has breached the data protection principles.

*Fines*

The Criminal Justice and Immigration Act (CJIA) 2008, which received Royal Assent on 8 May 2008, has introduced a new power for the Information Commissioner to fine data controllers who are in serious contravention of the data protection principles. Section 144 of the CJIA 2008 inserts s.55A into the DPA 1998, which says:

**55A. Power of Commissioner to impose monetary penalty**

(1) The Commissioner may serve a data controller with a monetary penalty notice if the Commissioner is satisfied that –

(a) there has been a serious contravention of section 4(4) by the data controller,
(b) the contravention was of a kind likely to cause substantial damage or substantial distress, and
(c) subsection (2) or (3) applies.

(2) This subsection applies if the contravention was deliberate.
(3) This subsection applies if the data controller –

(a) knew or ought to have known –

(i) that there was a risk that the contravention would occur, and
(ii) that such a contravention would be of a kind likely to cause substantial damage or substantial distress, but

(b) failed to take reasonable steps to prevent the contravention.

(4) A monetary penalty notice is a notice requiring the data controller to pay to the Commissioner a monetary penalty of an amount determined by the Commissioner and specified in the notice.
(5) The amount determined by the Commissioner must not exceed the prescribed amount.
(6) The monetary penalty must be paid to the Commissioner within the period specified in the notice.
(7) The notice must contain such information as may be prescribed.
(8) Any sum received by the Commissioner by virtue of this section must be paid into the Consolidated Fund.
(9) In this section –

'data controller' does not include the Crown Estate Commissioners or a person who is a data controller by virtue of section 63(3);
'prescribed' means prescribed by regulations made by the Secretary of State.

The detail of the legal framework for fines has not yet been published, although in June 2008 the Information Commissioner anticipated that fines would be issued by the summer of 2009.

*Criminal proceedings*

The main criminal offences within the DPA 1998 are:

- Failure to notify processing operations and failure to keep notifications accurate and up to date (s.21). In summary, most data controllers are required to register with the Information Commissioner information about their processing operations.
- Failure to comply with an enforcement notice, information or special information notice (s.47).
- Unlawful obtaining of personal data, etc. (s.55). This is discussed in more depth at **Chapter 6**.
- Enforced subject access (s.56). The main situation where the crime of enforced subject access will be committed is during the recruitment of employees, when an employer requires a prospective employee to exercise their rights of access to personal data against another data controller as a condition of employment.
- Obstructing the execution of a warrant (s.56). The Information Commissioner can ask a Crown Court judge to grant a warrant allowing him to enter premises where he has reasonable grounds for suspecting that there has been a breach of the data protection principles or the commission of a crime and relevant evidence will be found on the premises.

The Commissioner may also bring criminal proceedings under s.77 of the FOIA 2000, where a person, in order to defeat a request for personal data made to a public authority under DPA 1998, s.7, 'alters, defaces, blocks, erases, destroys or conceals any record held by [a] public authority'.

Section 61 of the Act contains an important power that allows the Information Commissioner to prosecute company directors and similar officials for offences. Section 61 says:

> (1) Where an offence under this Act has been committed by a body corporate and is proved to have been committed with the consent or connivance of or to be attributable to any neglect on the part of any director, manager, secretary or similar officer of the body corporate or any person who was purporting to act in any such capacity, he as well as the body corporate shall be guilty of that offence and be liable to be proceeded against and punished accordingly.
>
> (2) Where the affairs of a body corporate are managed by its members subsection (1) shall apply in relation to the acts and defaults of a member in connection with his functions of management as if he were a director of the body corporate.

Bar the obstruction of warrant offence within Sched.9, which is a summary offence, all of the offences identified above are triable either way. Upon conviction in the Crown Court the defendant is liable to an unlimited fine, and upon conviction in the magistrates' court the fine is the statutory maximum, save for the obstruction of warrant offence, which is liable to a fine not exceeding level 5 on the standard scale.

However, the penalties regime for s.55 offences could be extended to cover custodial penalties, due to provisions within s.77 of the CJIA 2008. Section 77 gives the Secretary of State the power to introduce custodial penalties of up to 12 months' duration where the defendant is convicted in the magistrates' court and up to two years' duration where the defendant is convicted in the Crown Court.

### *Enforcement action*

The Information Commissioner's formal enforcement powers are contained in DPA 1998, ss.40, 43 and 44. Section 40 gives the Commissioner the power to serve an enforcement notice when he is satisfied that the data controller has contravened or is contravening any of the data protection principles. Section 43 gives the Commissioner the power to serve an information notice where he has either received a request for an assessment within the meaning of s.42 of the Act, or if he reasonably requires information for the purpose of determining whether there has been a breach of the principles. Section 44 gives the Commissioner the power to serve a special information notice, which is concerned with 'special purposes' processing, which is defined in s.3 of the Act as the purposes of journalism, artistic purposes and literary purposes.

An enforcement notice must require the data controller to either take or refrain from taking such steps as are specified in the notice, or it must require the controller to refrain from specified processing operations. These requirements are stated to be 'for complying with the principle or principles in question', which seems to indicate that the purpose of an enforcement is to achieve the data controller's compliance with the principles, rather than merely being declaratory of a breach, or a tool for punishment or example-setting.

The Commissioner's power to serve an enforcement notice is a discretionary one, however, and s.40(2) of the Act says that 'in deciding whether to serve an enforcement notice, the Commissioner shall consider whether the contravention has caused or is likely to cause any person damage or distress'.

Section 40 of the DPA 1998 says:

**40. Enforcement notices**

(1) If the Commissioner is satisfied that a data controller has contravened or is contravening any of the data protection principles, the Commissioners may serve him with a notice (in this Act referred to as 'an enforcement notice') requiring him, for complying with the principle or principles in question, to do either or both of the following –

(a) to take within such time as may be specified in the notice, or to refrain from taking after such time as may be so specified, such steps as are so specified, or
(b) to refrain from processing any personal data, or any personal data of a description specified in the notice, or to refrain from processing them for a purpose so specified or in a manner so specified, after such time as may be so specified.

(2) In deciding whether to serve an enforcement notice, the Commissioner shall consider whether the contravention has caused or is likely to cause any person damage or distress.
(3) An enforcement notice in respect of a contravention of the fourth data protection principle which requires the data controller to rectify, block, erase or destroy any inaccurate data may also require the data controller to rectify, block, erase or destroy any other data held by him and containing an expression of opinion which appears to the Commissioner to be based on the inaccurate data.
(4) An enforcement notice in respect of a contravention of the fourth data protection principle, in the case of data which accurately record information received or obtained by the data controller from the data subject or a third party, may require the data controller either –

(a) to rectify, block, erase or destroy any inaccurate data and any other data held by him and containing an expression of opinion as mentioned in subsection (3), or
(b) to take such steps as are specified in the notice for securing compliance with the requirements specified in paragraph 7 of Part II of Schedule 1 and, if the Commissioner thinks fit, for supplementing the data with such statement of the true facts relating to the matters dealt with by the data as the Commissioner may approve.

(5) Where –

(a) an enforcement notice requires the data controller to rectify, block, erase or destroy any personal data, or
(b) the Commissioner is satisfied that personal data which have been rectified, blocked, erased or destroyed had been processed in contravention of any of the data protection principles,

an enforcement notice may, if reasonably practicable, require the data controller to notify third parties to whom the data have been disclosed of the rectification, blocking, erasure or destruction; and in determining whether it is reasonably practicable to require such notification regard shall be had, in particular, to the number of persons who would have to be notified.
(6) An enforcement notice must contain –

(a) a statement of the data protection principle or principles which the Commissioner is satisfied have been or are being contravened and his reasons for reaching that conclusion, and
(b) particulars of the rights of appeal conferred by section 48.

(7) Subject to subsection (8), an enforcement notice must not require any of the provisions of the notice to be complied with before the end of the period within which an appeal can be brought against the notice and, if such

an appeal is brought, the notice need not be complied with pending the determination or withdrawal of the appeal.

(8) If by reason of special circumstances the Commissioner considers that an enforcement notice should be complied with as a matter of urgency he may include in the notice a statement to that effect and a statement of his reasons for reaching that conclusion; and in that event subsection (7) shall not apply but the notice must not require the provisions of the notice to be complied with before the end of the period of seven days beginning with the day on which the notice is served.

(9) Notification regulations (as defined by section 16(2)) may make provision as to the effect of the service of an enforcement notice on any entry in the register maintained under section 19 which relates to the person on whom the notice is served.

(10) This section has effect subject to section 46(1).

A data controller served with an enforcement notice has three choices. They can comply with the notice, or they can appeal against its service to the Information Tribunal under section 48 of the Act or they can apply to the Commissioner for its cancellation or variation. If the controller does nothing then the notice will have effect after the expiry of the time limit for appealing, which is 28 days [Information Tribunal (Enforcement Appeals) Rules 2005, SI 2005/14, r.5], and non-compliance will be an offence under section 47.

Section 41 gives the Information Commissioner the power to cancel or vary an enforcement notice. The Commissioner can act on his volition under s.41(1) to cancel or vary an enforcement notice 'if he considers that all or any of the provisions or an enforcement notice need not be complied with in order to ensure compliance with the data protection principle or principles to which it relates'. The Commissioner can also act to cancel or vary an enforcement notice upon receipt of an application from the data controller under s.41(2), if 'by reason of a change of circumstances, all or any part of the provisions of that notice need not be complied with in order to ensure compliance with the data protection principle or principles to which that notice relates'. However, a controller can only apply for cancellation or variation after expiry of the time limit for appealing. If the Commissioner refuses to vary or cancel following an application, the data controller can appeal the refusal.

Information notices and special information notices work in a similar manner to enforcement notices, save for two important differences. First, one of the grounds for service of an information notice is that the Commissioner has received a request for an assessment under s.42(1), which does not apply in the case of enforcement notices. Section 42(1) provides:

> A request may be made to the Commissioner by or on behalf of any person who is, or believes himself to be, directly affected by any processing of personal data for an assessment as to whether it is likely or unlikely that the processing has been or is being carried out in compliance with the provisions of this Act.

The second difference concerns variation and cancellation. Section 43(9) says that the Commissioner may cancel an information notice, but there is no corresponding power for him to vary an information notice. Furthermore, the Act does not contain a procedure that allows the data controller to apply for variation or cancellation. Data controllers receiving an information notice can appeal to the Information Tribunal under s.48 and, again, the appeal period is 28 days. See **Chapter 7** for a further discussion of information notices and the Commissioner's power to enter premises.

Section 49 identifies the grounds for an appeal. There are only two grounds: (1) the notice was not in accordance with the law; and (2) to the extent that the notice involved an exercise of discretion the Commissioner ought to have exercised his discretion differently. If the Tribunal is persuaded that the appeal should be allowed it will either cancel the notice or substitute its own decision. During the course of the appeal the Tribunal may review any determination of fact on which the notice was based.

## 3.6 EXEMPTIONS

The DPA 1998 comes equipped within many exemptions from its key obligations. These are contained in Part IV of the Act.

The opening section within Part IV, s.27, groups the exemptions into two categories, namely the 'subject information provisions' and the 'non-disclosure provisions'. Section 27 says:

**27. Preliminary**

(1) References in any of the data protection principles or any provision of Parts II and III to personal data or to the processing of personal data do not include references to data or processing which by virtue of this Part are exempt from that principle or other provision.

(2) In this Part 'the subject information provisions' means –

  (a) the first data protection principle to the extent to which it requires compliance with paragraph 2 of Part II of Schedule 1, and
  (b) section 7.

(3) In this Part 'the non-disclosure provisions' means the provisions specified in subsection (4) to the extent to which they are inconsistent with the disclosure in question.

(4) The provisions referred to in subsection (3) are –

  (a) the first data protection principle, except to the extent to which it requires compliance with the conditions in Schedules 2 and 3,
  (b) the second, third, fourth and fifth data protection principles, and
  (c) sections 10 and 14(1) to (3).

(5) Except as provided by this Part, the subject information provisions shall have effect notwithstanding any enactment or rule of law prohibiting or restricting the disclosure, or authorising the withholding, of information.

**Table 3.5** identifies the exemptions within Part IV and their scope.

**Table 3.5** The exemptions within Part IV of the DPA 1998

| Section | Category | Exemptions | Key points |
|---|---|---|---|
| 28 | National security | The principles; Parts II, III and V; ss.54A and 55. | The purpose of the exemption is safeguarding national security. It requires a certificate signed by a Minister of the Crown. Once the certificate is signed the data can be processed outside the reach of the Act. |
| 29 | Crime and taxation | 1. First principle (save for Scheds.2 and 3) and s.7. | 1. Applies to s.29(1); the purposes are the prevention or detection of crime, the apprehension of prosecution of offenders and the assessment or collection of taxes and duties. The exemptions apply if the application of those provisions would be 'likely to prejudice' the purposes. |
| | | 2. Subject information provisions. | 2. Applies to s.29(2); the discharging of statutory functions. Same 'likely to prejudice' test. |
| | | 3. Non-disclosure provisions. | 3. Applies to section 29(3); covers disclosure made for the purposes of section 29(1). Same 'likely to prejudice' test. |
| | | 4. Section 7. | 4. Applies to s.29(4); applies to risk assessment systems run by public authorities for purposes of assessment or collection of taxes, or dealing with crimes in respect payments from public funds. The exemption applies if required 'in the interests of the operation of the system'. |

**Table 3.5** *Cont.*

| Section | Category | Exemptions | Key points |
|---|---|---|---|
| 30 | Health, education and social work | Subject information provisions. | See SI 2000/413, SI 2000/414, SI 2000/415. |
| 31 | Regulatory activity | Subject information provisions. | The purpose of the exemption is to ensure the effective discharge of regulatory functions where the application of the provisions would be likely to prejudice the proper discharge of those functions. |
| 32 | Journalist, literature and art | Sections 7, 10, 12 and 14(1)–(3). | The purpose is to protect freedom of expression where publication of journalistic, literary or artistic material is in the public interest. The exemption applies if the controller reasonably believes that compliance with the provisions would be incompatible with the purposes. |
| 33 | Research, history and statistics | Second and fifth principle and section 7. | The purpose is to allow the continued processing of personal data for statistical purposes without undue hindrance from the provisions in question. However, the processing cannot be used to support measures or decisions with respect to individual data subjects and it must be conducted so as not to cause substantial damage or distress. |
| 33A | Manual data held by public authorities | 1. First, second, third, fifth, sixth (save for ss.7 and 14) seventh, eighth principles; ss.10–12; s.13 (save for s.7 and fourth principle); Part III and s.55. | 1. Applies to s.33A(1). The purpose is to remove hindrances to the holding of unstructured manual data within the public sector. |

**Table 3.5** *Cont.*

| Section | Category | Exemptions | Key points |
|---|---|---|---|
| | | 2. All of the above, the remaining principles and the remaining provisions of Part II. | 2. Applies to s.33A(2) and covers personnel matters in the public sector, such as appointments, removals, pay, discipline and pensions. |
| 34 | Information available to public under an enactment | Subject information provisions; fourth principle; s.14(1)–(3); non-disclosure provisions. | The purpose is to limit the operation of the Act where there is other legislation governing the disclosure of information to the public, other than the FOIA 2000. |
| 35 | Disclosures required by law or made in connection with legal proceedings | Non-disclosure provisions. | This covers disclosures ordered by the court and disclosures connected with legal proceedings, in order to remove any DPA 1998 bars to disclosure. |
| 35A | Parliamentary privilege | First principle (save for Scheds.2 and 3); second, third, fourth and fifth principles; s.7; ss.10 and 14(1)–(3). | The exemptions apply for the purpose of avoiding an infringement of the privileges of the Houses of Parliament. |
| 36 | Domestic purposes | Principles and Parts II and III. | This takes processing for personal, family, household and recreational purposes outside the scope of the Act. |
| 37 | Miscellaneous | See Sched.7. | |
| 38 | Powers to make further exemptions by order | See SI 2000/419. | |

The meaning of the non-disclosure provisions was discussed recently by the Information Tribunal, in an appeal against enforcement notices issued by the Information Commissioner against various police forces that ordered them to delete personal data retained on the Police National Computer (*Chief Constables of Humberside, Staffordshire, Northumbria, West Midlands and Greater Manchester* v. *Information Commissioner*, EA/2007/0096, 98,99, 108,127, 21 July 2008). The police argued that the construction of

DPA 1998, s.29, which contains exemptions from the non-disclosure provisions where the processing is for crime and taxation purposes, meant that the enforcement notice was wrong in law, because it ordered deletion of the data on the basis that its retention breached the third and fifth data protection principle, whereas the non-disclosure provisions exempt the controller from the requirement to comply with the third and fifth principles. The Tribunal rejected this argument, holding that the non-disclosure provisions extended only to disclosures in breach of the first data protection principle. The Chairman of the Tribunal said:

> The Enforcement Notices focus on the retention of information, and on breaches of DPP3 and DPP5 (except in the case of SP). The intention, we believe behind the provision, is that personal data can be disclosed for the limited purposes set out in section 29(1) even if otherwise in breach of DPP1. It does not apply to DPP3 and DPP5.

The holding attracts criticism. It is clear from the definition of 'non-disclosure provisions' in s.27(4) that they extend to the third and fifth principles; to say that the exemption within s.29(1) does not apply to these principles cannot be correct. Furthermore, a disclosure of data cannot be possible if they are not retained, a point which the Information Tribunal appreciated within a passage that seemingly undermines the previous one:

> It is unrealistic to consider DPPs 3 and 5 in complete isolation to the other DPPs when considering the data controller's purposes which will usually involve all aspects of processing. Retention is the fundamental requirement because without data no processing can take place whatever the purpose.

## CHAPTER NOTES

1 The first fruits of the study conducted by the Committee of Experts were two Resolutions, Resolution (73) 22 on the protection of the privacy of individuals vis-à-vis electronic data banks in the private sector and Resolution (74) 29 on the protection of the privacy of individuals vis-à-vis electronic data banks in the public sector. These Resolutions continued the restricting agenda expressed in Recommendation 509. However, it is worth noting that the explanatory notes to Resolution (74) 29 did express a favourable view about new technology saying 'the Preamble reaffirms that the use of computers for purposes of public administration should in general be regarded as a positive development. The purpose of the present resolution is not to oppose such use, but to reinforce it with certain guarantees'.

2 Resolution (74) 29 supports this point. Within the explanatory notes it was said that 'the public is not sufficiently informed about the new information technology'.

3 'Data Protection Technical Guidance – Determining what is personal data', v1.0, 21 August 2007: **www.ico.gov.uk/upload/documents/library/data_protection/detailed_specialist_guides/personal_data_flowchart_v1_with_preface001.pdf**.

4 The Data Protection Directive refers to 'special categories of data'; see Article 8, which says 'Member States shall prohibit the processing of personal data revealing racial or ethnic origin, political opinions, religious or philosophical beliefs, trade-union membership, and the processing of data concerning health or sex life'.

5 It will be recalled that the first principle of the Council of Europe's 1973 Resolution operated to prohibit the storage and dissemination of information 'which might lead to unfair discrimination'.

6 See para.107 of Lord Phillips's judgment. See also para.104 where he said 'The Directive and the Act define processing as "any operation or set of operations". At one end of the process "obtaining the information" is included, and at the other end "using the information". While neither activity in itself may sensibly amount to processing, if that activity is carried on by, or at the instigation of, a "data controller", as defined, and is linked to automated processing of the data, we can see no reason why the entire set of operations should not fall within the scope of the legislation. On the contrary, we consider that there are good reasons why it should.'

7 In addition to relevant filing systems, private sector manual data can fall within the scope of the DPA 1998 it if is recorded with the intention that it should be processed by equipment operating automatically, if it is recorded with the intention that it should form part of a relevant filing system, if it forms part of an accessible record and if it is extracted from data held on a computer and the computer form still exists. In the public sector, because of the concept of record information held by a public authority, a much greater amount of data will fall within the scope of the Act. Furthermore, accessible records are much more extensive in the public sector than in the private sector.

8 See the Data Protection (Processing of Sensitive Personal Data) Order 2000, SI 2000/417; Data Protection (Processing of Sensitive Personal Data) (Elected Representatives) Order 2002, SI 2002/2905; and Data Protection (Processing of Sensitive Personal Data) Order 2006.

9 See **www.informationtribunal.gov.uk/Documents/decisions/community_charge.pdf**.

10 See **www.informationtribunal.gov.uk/Documents/decisions/community_charge_last.pdf**.

11 See **www.informationtribunal.gov.uk/Documents/decisions/north_wales_police.pdf**.

12 EA/2007/0096,98,99,108,127, 21 July 2008; **www.informationtribunal.gov.uk/Documents/decisions/ChiefConstables_v_ICfinal_Decision_20Jul08.pdf**.

CHAPTER 4

# Communications privacy

## 4.1 INTRODUCTION

The point has already been made that Article 8 of the European Convention on Human Rights protects the privacy of communications, and in the previous chapter we saw how the European data protection regime has built upon Article 8 to extend the right to privacy to processing operations involving personal data. The Privacy and Electronic Communications Directive 2002 (PECD), as amended by the Communications Data Retention Directive 2006 (CDRD), contains the EU legal framework for the protection of privacy in the context of the provision of publicly available electronic communications services in public communications networks. Article 3 of PECD identifies the services that are subject to regulation, saying (at Article 3(1)):

> This Directive shall apply to the processing of personal data in connection with the provision of publicly available electronic communications services in public communications networks in the Community.

However, it should not be forgotten that despite the application of PECD, the Data Protection Directive will apply to the processing of personal data via email in any event; PECD does not oust the Data Protection Directive, but builds upon its protections. Indeed, Article 1(2) says that PECD's provisions 'particularise and complement' the Data Protection Directive.

PECD differs from the Data Protection Directive in two material ways. First, whereas the Data Protection Directive focuses upon data controllers and data subjects, PECD focuses on the providers of publicly available communications services and networks and subscribers to and users of such services. Second, PECD extends the scope of protection to 'the legitimate interests of subscribers who are legal persons' (Article 1(2)).

As the vast bulk of email is conveyed over public communications networks, it follows that the protections within PECD extend to email. Likewise, the obligations placed upon the providers of publicly available communications services extend to control their use of email, both expressly and impliedly.

The Directive contains a number of provisions that do not have any connection with the use of email (particularly the provisions concerning the presentation and restriction of calling and connected line identification (Article 8) and the provisions concerning automatic call forwarding (see Article 11), which are both concerned with voice telephony) and a number of provisions that may have a substantial effect on email in the future, but do not do so now (particularly the provisions concerning itemised billing (Article 7) and the provisions concerning directories of subscribers (Article 12)). These provisions are not discussed here. Instead, this chapter focuses on the provisions concerning security, confidentiality of communications, traffic and location data,[1] and unsolicited communications. In summary, these provisions provide that:

- providers of publicly available communications services must safeguard the security of their services, working in cooperation with the network provider;
- interception and surveillance of electronic communications such as email is prohibited, save for in cases of compelling public interest;
- communications data are subject to mandatory retention periods, which Member States can set at between six months and two years; and
- 'spam' emails are subject to 'opt-in' and 'opt-out' rules.

In the UK the key provisions are contained in the Regulation of Investigatory Powers Act 2000, the Telecommunications (Lawful Business Practice) (Interception of Communications) Regulations 2000, SI 2000/2699, the Privacy and Electronic Communications (EC Directive) Regulations 2003, SI 2003/2426 and the Data Retention (EC Directive) Regulations 2007, SI 2007/2199. These instruments are supported by a plethora of statutory instruments, many codes of practice and countless pieces of regulatory guidance. There is also a healthy body of case law, most of which emanates from the European Court of Human Rights.

## 4.2 SECURITY OF COMMUNICATIONS SERVICES

The European data protection regime has always required data controllers to keep personal data safe and secure (see Article 17 of the Data Protection Directive) and PECD is no different. Article 4 states:

> 1. The provider of a publicly available electronic communications service must take appropriate technical and organisational measures to safeguard security of its services, if necessary in conjunction with the provider of the public communications network with respect to network security. Having regard to

the state of the art and the cost of their implementation, these measures shall ensure a level of security appropriate to the risk presented.

2. In case of a particular risk of a breach of the security of the network, the provider of a publicly available electronic communications service must inform the subscribers concerning such risk and, where the risk lies outside the scope of the measures to be taken by the service provider, of any possible remedies, including an indication of the likely costs involved.

As with Article 17 of the Data Protection Directive, Article 4 of PECD requires communications service providers to take appropriate technical and organisational security measures. Again, there is a state of the art requirement within the obligation, a requirement to take account of cost and a requirement to take account of the nature of the prevailing security risks. Where Article 4 of PECD differs from Article 17 of the Data Protection Directive is in its focus on the security of the services rather than the security of the personal data itself, in its requirement for cooperation between the service provider and the network provider and in its requirement for notification of network security risks and remedial measures.

The Privacy and Electronic Communications (EC Directive) Regulations 2003 provide an almost verbatim transposition of the security requirement into domestic law (see reg.5). However, there is a divergence between the Regulations and the Directive on the issue of communication of information about risk: whereas the Directive requires the communication of information about a 'particular risk', the Regulations only require such communication where the risk is 'significant'. At the date of publication of this book, this distinction has not been litigated, but the law on data security is undergoing a process of change and it remains entirely possible that there will be judicial consideration of this point in due course.

In the light of the growing appreciation of the extent of data security breaches and the harm they can cause, an area where the law may develop concerns the reporting of occurrences of security breaches. Indeed, in 2007 the European Commission stated its desire for the introduction of a reporting of security breach obligation into the legal framework for electronic communications.[2] Article 13a.3 of the proposed amending Directive says:

> Member States shall ensure that undertakings providing public communications networks or publicly available electronic communications services notify the national regulatory authority of any breach of security or integrity that had a significant impact on the operation of networks or services.
>
> Where appropriate, the national regulatory authority concerned shall inform the national regulatory authorities in other Member States and the Authority. Where disclosure of the breach is in the public interest, the national regulatory authority may inform the public.
>
> Every three months, the national regulatory authority shall submit a summary report to the Commission on the notifications received and the action taken in accordance with this paragraph.

## 4.3 CONFIDENTIALITY OF COMMUNICATIONS (INCLUDING SURVEILLANCE AND INTERCEPTION)

Article 5 of PECD is titled 'Confidentiality of the communications' and it says:

> 1. Member States shall ensure the confidentiality of communications and the related traffic data by means of a public communications network and publicly available electronic communications services, through national legislation. In particular, they shall prohibit listening, tapping, storage or other kinds of interception or surveillance of communications and the related traffic data by persons other than users, without the consent of the users concerned, except when legally authorised to do so in accordance with Article 15(1). This paragraph shall not prevent technical storage which is necessary for the conveyance of a communication without prejudice to the principle of confidentiality.
> 2. Paragraph 1 shall not affect any legally authorised recording of communications and the related traffic data when carried out in the course of lawful business practice for the purpose of providing evidence of a commercial transaction or of any other business communication.
> 3. Member States shall ensure that the use of electronic communications networks to store information or to gain access to information stored in the terminal equipment of a subscriber or user is only allowed on condition that the subscriber or user concerned is provided with clear and comprehensive information in accordance with Directive 95/46/EC, inter alia about the purposes of the processing, and is offered the right to refuse such processing by the data controller. This shall not prevent any technical storage or access for the sole purpose of carrying out or facilitating the transmission of a communication over an electronic communications network, or as strictly necessary in order to provide an information society service explicitly requested by the subscriber or user.

When viewed from the perspective of Article 5, the confidentiality of communications concerns two activities: the interception of communications and the surveillance of communications. Clearly, these activities are central to all concepts of privacy, hence why they are subject to tight legal controls.

It will be noticed that Article 5(1) refers to Article 15(1), which permits the EU Member States to adopt legislative measures to restrict the protections within Article 5 'when such restriction constitutes a necessary, appropriate and proportionate measure within a democratic society to safeguard national security (i.e. State security), defence, public security, and the prevention, investigation, detection and prosecution of criminal offences or of unauthorised use of the electronic communication system'. These carve-outs mirror closely the carve-outs from the right to privacy contained in Article 8(2) of the European Convention on Human Rights. Thus, Member States may legislate to allow for the interception of communications, as has happened in the UK, with the Regulation of Investigatory Powers Act 2000, for example.

Article 5(3) of PECD is designed to provide users of communications with protection from covert collection of their information and it works in two ways. First, it prevents network and service providers from warehousing communications sent over communications networks. Second, it prevents the collection of data from the user's terminal equipment, which in the case of email means the user's PC, mobile telephone and other handheld devices.[3] The only exceptions to these provisions are for informed prior consent and technically essential collection and access. The provisions of Article 5(3) are transposed faithfully by the Privacy and Electronic Communications (EC Directive) Regulations 2003 (see reg.6).

The legal framework for interceptions is contained in the Regulation of Investigatory Powers Act 2000 (for Scotland see Regulation of Investigatory Powers (Scotland) Act 2000), while the provisions of Article 5(2) are transposed into domestic law by the Telecommunications (Lawful Business Practice) (Interception of Communications) Regulations 2000.

## 4.4 RETENTION OF TRAFFIC DATA (INCLUDING LOCATION DATA)

The retention of traffic data is addressed by Articles 5, 6 and 15 of PECD. Traffic data is described as 'any data processed for the purpose of the conveyance of a communication on an electronic communications network or for the billing thereof'. Location data is a subset of traffic data and is described as 'any data processed in an electronic communications network, indicating the geographic position of the terminal equipment of a user of a publicly available electronic communications service'.

Traffic data and location data are distinct from the content of a communication; they are information *about* a communication. Whether alone, or in conjunction with the content, they can provide a great deal of information about the communication and the participants in the communication. As such, the processing of traffic and location data carries with it a significant potential for infringement of privacy rights and expectations of confidentiality. Emails generally result in the processing of traffic and location data by the communications service and network providers and, of course, this data is highly attractive to a great many people, from precision marketing companies, through to law enforcement agencies.

As we have already seen, Article 5(1) contains a general prohibition against the storage of traffic data without legal authorisation in accordance with Article 15(1), although this does not apply to technical storage 'which is necessary for the conveyance of a communication'. These rules are expanded upon by Article 6. First, Article 6(1) sets out the general rule that traffic data must either be deleted or made anonymous, saying 'traffic data relating to subscribers and users processed and stored by the provider of a public communications network or publicly available electronic communications service must be erased or made anonymous when it is no longer needed for the purpose of the transmission of a communication', but it then goes on to say that this is 'without prejudice to paragraphs 2, 3 and 5 of this Article and Article 15(1)'. The effects of Article 6(2) and (3) are as follows:[4]

- Article 6(2) allows traffic data to be processed for 'the purposes of subscriber billing and interconnection payments'. In order words, traffic data need not be erased or made anonymous while it is still needed for invoicing purposes, which, of course, is entirely logical. However, this right of retention is limited by the words 'to the end of the period during which the bill may lawfully be challenged or payment pursued' (in practice the effect of this limitation can be downplayed; for example, payments can be pursued for the duration of the limitation period for contractual debts).
- Article 6(3) allows traffic data to be processed for marketing purposes and for the purposes of providing value added services, again without being erased or being made anonymous. This right of retention can potentially endure for years, but as it is consent-based it cannot endure for longer than the consent.

Thus, when Articles 5 and 6 are read together it can be concluded that they provide only very limited grounds for the retention of traffic data, but when they are read in conjunction with Article 15(1) it can be seen that the EU framework permits significantly greater data retention rights and obligations. Furthermore, in addition to the legislative measures mentioned earlier, Article 15(1) allows Member States to adopt measures to 'provide for the retention of data for a limited period'.

Collectively these provisions provide an extremely confusing set of rules for the retention of traffic data. On the one hand PECD seeks to limit the holding of traffic and location data, thereby upholding the right to privacy within Article 8(1) of the European Convention on Human Rights; but on the other hand it allows Member States to set their own additional retention rules by way of carve-out from the right to privacy along the lines envisaged by Article 8(2) of the Convention. As such, PECD created a situation in which the rules on retention of traffic and location data could differ from State to State. It is this problem which is addressed by the Communications Data Retention Directive.

### 4.4.1 The anonymisation of location data

The confusion increases when the rules governing the anonymisation of location data are considered. The starting point within Article 9 of PECD is that location data can only be processed if they are made anonymous, unless the processing is done for the purposes of a value added service[5] and then only with the subscriber's or user's consent. However, as in the case of traffic data,

Article 15(1) allows Member States to pass their own derogating legislation, with the potential for differing results. Again, the Communication Data Retention Directive addresses this problem.

### 4.4.2 The Communications Data Retention Directive

PECD, like the Data Protection Directive, was adopted as an internal market measure, under Article 95 of the Treaty Establishing the European Community (the Treaty of Rome). These measures are designed to further the proper establishment and functioning of the internal market through processes of legal harmonisation across the Member States. Harmonisation is not intended to achieve exactness in the laws of the Member States, however, but, conversely, it will be appreciated that considerable divergences will undermine the harmonisation process and, in theory at least, cause damage to the internal market. Unfortunately, as far as the European Commission was concerned, PECD gave Member States an unacceptable margin of manoeuvre, which is why it proposed the adoption of the Communications Data Retention Directive.

The driving force behind the Communications Data Retention Directive is concern that different national rules on the retention of traffic and location data act to impede the effective discharge of law enforcement functions. Indeed, a perusal of the recitals makes it plain that the Directive is serving law enforcement ambitions. However, to be lawful it was necessary to present the Directive as an internal market measure, hence the recitals say (at Recital 6):

> The legal and technical differences between national provisions concerning the retention of data for the purpose of prevention, investigation, detection and prosecution of criminal offences present obstacles to the internal market for electronic communications, since service providers are faced with different requirements regarding the types of traffic and location data to be retained and the conditions and periods of retention.

This Directive amends PECD, requiring Member States to adopt measures to ensure the retention of 'data'. It also contains provisions about access to retained data and the storage of it.

The first noticeable feature of the Directive is that it introduces the concept of 'data', which did not appear in PECD; PECD was only concerned with location data and traffic data. Article 2(2)(a) defines data as 'traffic data and location data and the related data necessary to identify the subscriber or user'. This third component, 'data necessary to identify the subscriber or user', serves a very specific purpose: it operates to prevent the anonymisation of traffic and location data, which was one of the central aims of Articles 6 and 9 of PECD (it will be recalled that these articles allowed anonymisation as an alternative to deletion); obviously, anonymised data is of little use to law enforcement agencies that wish to identify parties to communications. The Directive does not contain any new rules about the retention of the content of a communication, so the rules in PECD are preserved; see Article 1(2) (and see also Recital 13, which says that the Directive 'relates only to data generated or processed as a consequence of a communication or a communication service and does not relate to data that are the content of the information communicated').

Of course, the central aim of the Directive is data retention and the 'obligation to retain' is contained in Article 3. This says:

> 1. By way of derogation from Articles 5, 6 and 9 of Directive 2002/58/EC, Member States shall adopt measures to ensure that the data specified in Article 5 of this Directive are retained in accordance with the provisions thereof, to the extent that those data are generated or processed by providers of publicly available electronic communications services or of a public communications network within their jurisdiction in the process of supplying the communications services concerned.
> 2. The obligation to retain data provided for in paragraph 1 shall include the retention of the data specified in Article 5 relating to unsuccessful call attempts where those data are generated or processed, and stored (as regards telephony data) or logged (as regards Internet data), by providers of publicly available electronic communications services or of a public communications network within the jurisdiction of the Member State concerned in the process of supplying the communication services concerned. This Directive shall not require data relating to unconnected calls to be retained.

It is very interesting that Article 3 describes the obligation to retain as derogation from Articles 5, 6 and 9 of PECD, because this acts to distinguish the obligation from the Member States' discretionary powers within Article 15(1) of PECD. Indeed, this point is borne out by Article 11 of the Directive, which inserts a new paragraph 1a into Article 15 that says:

> 1a. Paragraph 1 shall not apply to data specifically required by Directive 2006/24/EC of the European Parliament and of the Council of 15 March 2006 on the retention of data generated or processed in connection with the provision of publicly available electronic communications services or of public communications networks to be retained for the purposes referred to in Article 1(1) of that Directive.

Article 5 identifies six categories of data to be retained. These are:

- data necessary to trace and identify the source of a communication;
- data necessary to identify the destination of a communication;
- data necessary to identify the date, time and duration of a communication;
- data necessary to identify the type of a communication;

- data necessary to identify users' communication equipment or what purports to be their equipment; and
- data necessary to identify the location of mobile communication equipment.

When viewed in combination, it is patently clear that the retention obligation significantly impacts upon the privacy of communications, but as the recitals say 'data relating to the use of electronic communications are particularly important and therefore a valuable tool in the prevention, investigation, detection and prosecution of criminal offences, in particular organised crime' (Recital 7) and so the interference is justified on the grounds of necessity.[6]

Article 6 contains the rules on the retention period, stating that Member States are to ensure the retention of the data identified in Article 5 'for periods of not less than six months and not more than two years from the date of the communication'. In the light of the Directive's stated concern about the prejudice caused to the internal market and to law enforcement resulting from the 'different requirements regarding the types of traffic and location data to be retained and the conditions and periods of retention' (Recital 6), the wide margin of manoeuvre seems a little strange. The two-year long-stop retention period is not immovable however, as Article 12 says that 'a Member State facing particular circumstances that warrant an extension for a limited period of the maximum retention period referred to in Article 6 may take the necessary measures'.

Article 15, which is titled 'Transposition', required Member States to bring their implementing laws into force by 15 September 2007, but this is subject to an important exception contained in Article 15(3), which says:

> Until 15 March 2009, each Member State may postpone application of this Directive to the retention of communications data relating to Internet Access, Internet telephony and Internet e-mail. Any Member State that intends to make use of this paragraph shall, upon adoption of this Directive, notify the Council and the Commission to that effect by way of a declaration. The declaration shall be published in the Official Journal of the European Union.

The UK, like many other Member States, has taken advantage of Article 15(3) to postpone the application of the Directive to the retention of communications data relating to internet access, internet telephony and internet email, but when the period of grace expires for internet service providers (ISPs) it will become necessary to focus again on the recitals, which say that 'as regards the retention of data relating to Internet e-mail and Internet telephony, the obligation to retain data may apply only in respect of data from the providers' or the network providers' own services' (Recital 13).

The UK's transposition of the Directive is found in the Data Retention (EC Directive) Regulations 2007, SI 2007/2199 (these regulations were made on 26 July 2007 and came into force on 1 October 2007). Regulation 5 identifies the data to be retained, but as the UK has taken advantage of the power in Article 15(3) to postpone the retention obligation in the case of ISPs it refers only to fixed and mobile telephony data. This means that new Regulations will be required to meet the March 2009 deadline for ISPs. While the retention period for telephony data is set at 12 months from the date of the communication (reg.4(2)), it remains to be seen if a different period will be set for ISPs and email.

*Access to retained data*

Articles 4 and 8 address access issues. Article 4 says that network and service providers are only to provide retained data to 'competent authorities', while Article 8 says that data are to be retained in that they and other necessary related information 'can be transmitted upon request to the competent authorities without undue delay'. This topic is examined at **Chapter 7**.

### 4.4.3 Unsolicited communications

One of the biggest irritants within the world of email is spam. PECD treats spam and other unsolicited communications as a privacy issue, with Recital 40 stating:

> Safeguards should be provided for subscribers against intrusion of their privacy by unsolicited communications for direct marketing purposes in particular by means of automated calling machines, telefaxes, and e-mails, including SMS messages. These forms of unsolicited commercial communications may on the one hand be relatively easy and cheap to send and on the other may impose a burden and/or cost on the recipient. Moreover, in some cases their volume may also cause difficulties for electronic communications networks and terminal equipment. For such forms of unsolicited communications for direct marketing, it is justified to require that prior explicit consent of the recipients is obtained before such communications are addressed to them. The single market requires a harmonised approach to ensure simple, Community-wide rules for businesses and users.

The rules on spam are contained in Article 13, and they differ depending upon whether the recipient of the email is a natural or legal person, whether there is a prior commercial relationship between the sender and the subscriber and whether the sender's identity is concealed. In brief, the rules are as follows:

- Direct marketing emails may only be sent to subscribers who are natural persons with their prior consent (Article 13(1)), unless there is a pre-existing commercial relationship (Article 13(2)).
- Subject to there being a pre-existing commercial relationship between the sender of the email and the subscriber (Article 13(2)), Member States

must afford sufficient protection to the legitimate interests of subscribers who are legal persons (Article 13(5)).

- If there is a pre-existing commercial relationship between the sender of the email and the subscriber, direct marketing emails may be sent, provided that the subscriber was given a chance to refuse them when their email address was first collected (Article 13(2)). This rule applies whether the subscriber is a natural or legal person.
- Direct marketing emails where the sender's identity is concealed or disguised are banned, as are direct marketing emails without a valid return address for receipt of requests for cessation (Article 13(4)).

A form of language has developed in the data protection legal fraternity which describes these rules as 'opt-ins', 'opt-outs' and 'soft opt-ins'. The rule that direct marketing emails may only be sent to subscribers who are natural persons with their prior consent is known as opt-in. The rule that says they may be sent to subscribers where there is a pre-existing commercial relationship is known as soft opt-in. The rule that Member States must afford sufficient protection to the legitimate interests of subscribers who are legal persons is said to give them the option of using either an opt-in or an opt-out, with the idea behind opt-out being that direct marketing emails may be lawfully sent until such time as the subscribers act for cessation.

The UK's transposition of these rules is contained in regs.22 and 23 of the 2003 Regulations. Regulation 22 provides as follows:

> (1) This regulation applies to the transmission of unsolicited communications by means of electronic mail to individual subscribers. [Regulation 2(1) defines an individual as 'a living individual and includes an unincorporated body of such individuals'.]
>
> (2) Except in the circumstances referred to in paragraph (3), a person shall neither transmit, nor instigate the transmission of, unsolicited communications for the purposes of direct marketing by means of electronic mail unless the recipient of the electronic mail has previously notified the sender that he consents for the time being to such communications being sent by, or at the instigation of, the sender.
>
> (3) A person may send or instigate the sending of electronic mail for the purposes of direct marketing where –
>
> (a) that person has obtained the contact details of the recipient of that electronic mail in the course of the sale or negotiations for the sale of a product or service to that recipient;
>
> (b) the direct marketing is in respect of that person's similar products and services only; and
>
> (c) the recipient has been given a simple means of refusing (free of charge except for the costs of the transmission of the refusal) the use of his contact details for the purposes of such direct marketing, at the time that the details were initially collected, and, where he did not initially refuse the use of the details, at the time of each subsequent communication.

(4) A subscriber shall not permit his line to be used in contravention of paragraph (2).

As reg.22 applies only to subscribers who are natural persons and as reg.23 deals only with the ban on the sending of direct marketing emails where the sender's identity or address is concealed, it follows that direct marketing emails to corporate subscribers can be sent until such time as the corporate subscriber asks for them to stop.

### *Enforcing the anti-spam rules*

Regulation 31 of the 2003 Regulations extends the enforcement provisions within the Data Protection Act (DPA) 1998 (see **Chapter 3**) to cover the Regulations. However, the Regulations are also subject to the enforcement regime within the Enterprise Act 2002.

#### ENFORCEMENT UNDER THE ENTERPRISE ACT 2002

The Information Commissioner has been designated (under the Enterprise Act 2002 (Part 8 Designated Enforcers: Criteria for Designation, Designation of Public Bodies as Designated Enforcers and Transitional Provisions) Order 2003, SI 2003/1399) as an enforcer for the purposes of Part 8 of the Enterprise Act 2002; and PECD has been designated as a listed Directive for the purposes of s.210 (Enterprise Act 2002 (Part 8 Community Infringements Specified UK Laws) (Amendment) Order 2005, SI 2005/2418). The net effect of these designations is that the Information Commissioner is entitled to use the enforcement mechanisms in the Enterprise Act to enforce regs.19–24 of the 2003 Regulations.

The Enterprise Act 2002 opened up two additional enforcement mechanisms for the Commissioner, namely undertakings (s.219) and enforcement orders (s.215). In both cases the Commissioner is empowered to make a person cease activities that breach the PEC Regulations. If undertakings are obtained, the Commissioner can go on to seek an enforcement order if they are subsequently breached.

Enforcement orders are made by the High Court (s.217), upon an application by the Commissioner. Prior to making an application the Commissioner must engage in a process known as consultation (s.214), unless the case is one of urgency (applications for interim enforcement orders can be made in cases of urgency: s.218). Consultation, which lasts for 14 days (seven days in the case of applications for interim enforcement orders), is the means by which the offender is given an opportunity to desist or make representations. If the offender fails to comply with the Commissioner's requests, or fails to put up credible representations, court action can be commenced after the expiry of the consultation period.

If the court makes an enforcement order, or if the offender agrees to give undertakings, part of the process can include a requirement for the offender to publish a corrective statement, which can extend to informing the data subject of the remedial steps that will be taken to prevent further abuse of their privacy rights under the PEC Regulations. Breach of an enforcement order is a contempt of court, punishable by fine or imprisonment.

When the enforcement powers in the Enterprise Act 2002 are compared with those in the DPA 1998, the following similarities and differences are identified.

The enforcement provisions within the DPA 1998 extend to all aspects of data protection: DPA 1998, s.40(1) allows the Commissioner to serve an enforcement notice if is he is satisfied that the data controller has contravened or is contravening the data protection principles. This means that the DPA 1998 provisions have much wider scope than the powers under the Enterprise Act 2002. Another important distinction is that the enforcement provisions within the DPA 1998 extend to positive action, rather than just cessation of action (DPA 1998, s.40(1)(a)).

Furthermore, enforcement under the DPA 1998 does not contain a consultation provision. However, in the light of the Commissioner's current approach to enforcement, which has been guided by the Information Tribunal, the Commissioner will generally serve a preliminary enforcement notice setting out in draft the action required, upon which the offender's representations are offered. The preliminary enforcement notice procedure is not a statutory procedure, but its effect is comparable with the consultation procedure in the Enterprise Act 2002.

The route by which the Commissioner may take a case to court under the enforcement provisions in the DPA 1998 is different to the route set out in the Enterprise Act 2002. Under DPA 1998, s.48 the data controller can appeal an enforcement notice to the Information Tribunal and if an appeal is made the case cannot proceed to court until after (a) the appeal has been concluded in the Commissioner's favour and (b) the data controller has breached the enforcement notice. Of course, if the data controller fails to appeal the enforcement notice the notice will be effective and the Commissioner will be able to proceed directly to court if the controller subsequently breaches its terms.

The court forums are also different under the DPA 1998 and the Enterprise Act 2002. If the Commissioner wishes to take court action following a breach of an enforcement notice he will commence proceedings in the criminal courts. All Enterprise Act proceedings are brought in the civil courts (the High Court, as mentioned earlier), including proceedings for contempt.

In conclusion, there are important material differences between the enforcement provisions in the Enterprise Act 2002 and the DPA 1998, albeit the same outcomes can be achieved, namely fines and imprisonment in both cases. If the Enterprise Act 2002 is to be viewed as providing stronger powers than the DPA 1998, the distinction lies in the fact that the Commissioner has a more direct route to court under the Enterprise Act 2002 in disputed cases.

### ENFORCEMENT BY SUBSCRIBERS AND USERS

Subscribers and users who are individuals can use their powers within DPA 1998, s.11 to request the cessation of direct marketing emails. If the sender fails to comply with a request for cessation, the subscriber or user can then bring court proceedings under s.11(2), for an order requiring the sender to stop. Presumably they can also use DPA 1998, s.10 to provide the foundations for court action, on the basis that direct marketing emails cause substantial and unwarranted damage or distress.

Regulation 30 of the 2003 Regulations gives 'any person who suffers damage by reason of any contravention of any of the requirements' of the Regulations the right to bring proceedings for compensation. This right extends to legal persons as well as natural persons. However, the meaning of damage as set out in *Johnson* v. *Medical Defence Union* acts to curtail the effectiveness of this remedy.

Finally, reg.32 gives an aggrieved person the right to request the Information Commissioner to exercise his extended enforcement powers under DPA 1998, Part V.

### ENFORCEMENT BY NETWORK OPERATORS AND SERVICE PROVIDERS

In the case of *Microsoft Corporation* v. *McDonald (t/a Bizads)* [2006] EWHC 3410 (Ch) the court was required to consider whether a communications service provider, Microsoft, had locus to bring injunctive proceedings under reg.22 of the 2003 Regulations; the defendant was a notorious 'spammer', who sent spam via Microsoft's Hotmail system. Mr Justice Lewison held that Microsoft did have locus and he granted the injunction:

> The threshold question, as it seems to me, is whether Microsoft Corporation has a cause of action under these Regulations at all. That is to be determined according to the normal principles applicable to deciding whether a private person (whether a natural person or a corporation) has a cause of action for breach of a statutory requirement. The court must first be satisfied that the person who claims the cause of action was within the class of persons for whose protection the relevant statutory requirement was imposed. Second, the court must be satisfied that the terms in which the statutory requirement was imposed enables a claim for relief to be brought.
>
> As I have said the domestic regulations were made in order to conform with the provisions of the Directive and part of the policy of the Directive was, in my judgment, to protect the providers of electronic communications' systems Consequently, I am satisfied that Microsoft is within the class of persons for whose benefit the statutory requirement was imposed.

## 4.5 DOMESTIC RULES ON INTERCEPTION

UK domestic rules on interception of communications are contained in the Regulation of Investigatory Powers Act (RIPA) 2000 (for Scotland see the Regulation of Investigatory Powers (Scotland) Act 2000). RIPA 2000 also deals with the acquisition and disclosure of communications data, surveillance and the use of covert intelligence sources, the investigation of electronic data that are protected by encryption, the role of the Interception of Communications Commissioner, the scrutiny of investigatory powers and the functions of the intelligence services and various miscellany.

RIPA 2000 is the successor to the Interception of Communications Act 1985. Its enactment was triggered by the adoption of the Telecommunications Data Protection Directive 1997 and the decision of the European Court of Human Rights in the *Halford* v. *UK* case (1997). It is a very complex piece of legislation and as far as emails are concerned, it is the Act's chapters on interception, the acquisition and disclosure of communications data, and the investigation of electronic data protected by encryption that are most relevant.

### 4.5.1 Interception

Section 1 of RIPA 2000 criminalises unlawful interceptions of communications. There are three offences within s.1, namely:

- interception of a communication in the course of its transmission by means of a public postal service (s.1(1)(a));
- interception of a communication in the course of its transmission by means of a public telecommunications system (s.1(1)(b)); and
- interception of a communication in the course of its transmission by means of a private telecommunications system (s.1(2)).

In each of these cases a crime will only be committed where the interception takes place in the United Kingdom and is intentional. In the third case, interception within private telecommunications systems, there are circumstances where criminal liability is excluded (s.1(2), (6)), but even in such cases there will still be residual civil liability if the interception is without lawful authority (s.1(3)).

The concept of interception is very complex. Key questions are:

- What is a communication?
- What is an interception?
- What is meant by the phrase 'in the course of transmission'?
- What is the difference between a public telecommunications system and a private telecommunications system?
- What constitutes lawful authority?

### *What is a communication?*

We have already learned that an email consists of (a) content and (b) traffic and location data. Bearing this in mind, will there be an interception for the purposes of RIPA 2000 where only the content is intercepted, or can an interception for these purposes only take place in respect of traffic and location data, or does it not matter what part of the communication is intercepted?

The answer to this question is contained in s.2(2), which defines the meaning of interception. This section talks about the making of 'some or all of the contents of the communication available'. So, on the face of s.2(2), interception for the purposes of RIPA 2000 is referring to the interception of the *content* of the communication, not interception of its traffic and location data.

Section 2(5)(a) reinforces this view, saying that interception does not include references to 'any conduct that take place in relation only to so much of the communication as consists in any traffic data' and s.2(5)(b) says that interception does not cover the situation where the interceptor gains 'only so much access to a communication as is necessary for the purpose of identifying traffic data'.

It should be noted that RIPA 2000 also concerns itself with 'communications data'. For example, in the context of interceptions carried out pursuant to warrants, s.21(4) says that the conduct authorised by an interception warrant shall be taken to include 'conduct for obtaining related communications data' (see s.5(6)(b)). This means that we have been introduced to four concepts of non-content data, namely traffic data, location data, data and communications data. **Table 4.1** shows how these terms have been defined within PECD, the Data Retention Directive and RIPA 2000.

**Table 4.1** Types of data

| Types of data | PECD 2002 | CDRD 2006 | RIPA 2000 |
|---|---|---|---|
| Traffic data | Article 2(b):<br><br>'traffic data' means any data processed for the purpose of the conveyance of a communication on an electronic communications network or for the billing thereof | | Sections 2(9) and 21(6):<br><br>In this section 'traffic data', in relation to any communication, means –<br><br>(a) any data network or for the identifying, or billing thereof purporting to identify, any person, apparatus or location to or from which the communication is or may be transmitted,<br>(b) any data identifying or selecting, or purporting to identify or select, apparatus through which, or by means of which, the communication is or may be transmitted,<br>(c) any data comprising signals for the actuation of apparatus used for the purposes of a telecommunication system for effecting (in whole or in part) the transmission of any communication, and<br>(d) any data identifying the data or other data as data comprised in or attached to a particular communication, |

**Table 4.1** *Cont.*

| Types of data | PECD 2002 | CDRD 2006 | RIPA 2000 |
|---|---|---|---|
| | | | but that expression includes data identifying a computer file or computer program access to which is obtained, or which is run, by means of the communication to the extent only that the file or program is identified by reference to the apparatus in which it is stored. |
| Location data | Article 2(c):<br><br>'location data' means any data processed in an electronic communications network, indicating the geographic position of the terminal equipment of a user of a publicly available electronic communications service | | |
| Data | | Article 2(a):<br><br>'data' means traffic data and location data and the related data necessary to identify the subscriber or user | |
| Communications Data | | | Section 21(4):<br><br>'In this Chapter "communications data" means any of the following – |

**Table 4.1** *Cont.*

| Types of data | PECD 2002 | CDRD 2006 | RIPA 2000 |
|---|---|---|---|
| | | | (a) any traffic data comprised in or attached to a communication (whether by the sender or otherwise) for the purposes of any postal service or telecommunication system by means of which it is being or may be transmitted;<br>(b) any information which includes none of the contents of a communication (apart from any information falling within paragraph (a)) and is about the use made by any person –<br>(i) of any postal service or telecommunications service; or<br>(ii) in connection with the provision to or use by any person of any telecommunications service, of any part of a telecommunication system;<br>(c) any information not falling within paragraph (a) or (b) that is held or obtained, in relation to persons to whom he provides the service, by a person providing a postal service or telecommunications service. |

### *What constitutes an interception?*

At this juncture it is worth looking at s.2(2) in full. This says:

> For the purposes of this Act, but subject to the following provisions of this section, a person intercepts a communication in the course of its transmission by means of a telecommunication system if, and only if, he –
>
> (a) so modifies or interferes with the system, or its operation,
> (b) so monitors transmissions made by means of the system, or
> (c) so monitors transmissions made by wireless telegraphy to or from apparatus comprised in the system,
>
> as to make some or all of the contents of the communication available, while being transmitted, to a person other than the sender or intended recipient of the communication.

The new points that we draw from this section are that:

- interception can take many forms of activity;
- an interception must involve someone other than the parties to the communication gaining access to the content of the communication;
- an interception can only take place while the communication is being transmitted – it is impossible to intercept a communication after it has been transmitted.

### *'In the course of transmission'*

With telephone conversations it is relatively easy to determine when the communication is being transmitted: the transmission commences when the sound waves generated by the speaker's voice hit the microphone in the speaker's handset and it ends at the point when the sound waves leave the speaker in the recipient's handset. For an interception to occur the activity must take place somewhere between these two points, but this does not require the interceptor to be listening in 'real time', as s.2(8) of RIPA 2000 makes clear:

> For the purposes of this section the cases in which any contents of a communication are to be taken to be made available to a person while being transmitted shall include any case in which any of the contents of the communication, while being transmitted, are diverted or recorded so as to be available to a person subsequently.

In the light of this section a third party can 'bug' a telephone conversion during the transmission, record it to some form of storage, listen to it many days later and still commit an interception.

Of course many communications over telecommunications systems – nowadays probably the majority – do not take place in real time. For example, a telephone caller might reach an answering machine service and with email a delay between its sending and receipt is the norm while the email languishes on a server somewhere waiting to be downloaded to the recipient's inbox. So, how does RIPA 2000 deal with these eventualities?

Section 2(7) contains the answers, saying:

> For the purposes of this section the times while a communication is being transmitted by means of a telecommunication system shall be taken to include any time when the system by means of which the communication is being, or has been, transmitted is used for storing it in a manner that enables the intended recipient to collect it or otherwise to have access to it.

This section shows that an interception can take place while the communication is in storage. In the case of email, s.2(7) will cover the situation where they are waiting on a server to be downloaded by the intended recipient. However, once the email reaches the intended recipient's inbox an interception cannot occur, even if the intended recipient does not then open it or read it. This is because of the inclusion of the phrase 'collect it or otherwise to have access to it'; when a person successfully downloads an email to their inbox they can be said to have collected it.

### *Lawful authority*

#### INTERCEPTION WITHOUT A WARRANT; CONDUCT AUTHORISED UNDER RIPA 2000, s.3

RIPA 2000, s.3 is concerned with interception without a warrant and it describes four situations that will amount to lawful authority.

The first situation is the most straightforward, applying where the interceptor has the consent of the parties to the communication, or where the interceptor has 'reasonable grounds for believing' that they have this consent (s.3(1)).

The second situation is where the interceptor has the consent of one of the parties to the communication and 'surveillance by means of that interception has been authorised under Part II' of RIPA 2000 (s.3(2)). Part II of RIPA 2000 is concerned with two types of surveillance, intrusive surveillance and directed surveillance, but it is only directed surveillance that is relevant to this form of lawful authority.[7] (Part II is also concerned with the use of covert human intelligence sources, but these have no role within the form of lawful authority contained in s.3(2).)

To understand what directed surveillance is, it is first necessary to understand what intrusive surveillance is. 'Intrusive surveillance' is defined in s.26(2) as covert surveillance that is carried out in relation to anything taking place on residential premises or within a private vehicle that involves the presence of an individual in the premises or vehicle. Section 26(2) defines 'directed surveillance' as surveillance that is not intrusive, is undertaken for the purposes of a specific investigation or operation, is likely to result in the obtaining of private information about a person and is carried out in circumstances where it would be reasonably practicable to seek an authorisation. Authorisations for directed surveillance are required for surveillance performed in the interests of national security, for the purpose of preventing or detecting crime or preventing disorder, in the interests of the economic wellbeing of the United Kingdom, in the interests of public safety, for the purpose of protecting public health and for the purpose of assessing or collecting tax (s.28(3); the Secretary of State may specify other purposes). The public authorities that are entitled to grant authorisations for directed surveillance are identified in RIPA 2000, Sched.1.[8] Each authority has a designated person for the purpose of these authorisations (SI 2003/3171 and SI 2005/1084 identify the persons designated for these purposes).

The third situation is where the interceptor is the provider or a telecommunications service, or is acting on the provider's behalf, and it takes place for purposes connected with the provision or operation of the service or for purposes connected with the enforcement of any enactment relating to the use of the service (s.3(3)). This would cover, for example, interception by a public telecommunications service provider for the purposes of establishing whether a person was guilty of improper use of the network (see Communications Act 2003, s.127, discussed at **Chapter 6**).

The fourth situation concerns wireless telegraphy and would cover emails sent from a mobile telephone or other portable device (s.3(4)). To apply, the interception must be authorised by a person designated by Wireless Telegraphy Act 2006, s.48 for the purposes of the grant of wireless licences, or the prevention or detection of anything that constitutes interference with wireless telegraphy, or for the purpose of enforcing certain provisions of the Wireless Telegraphy Act 2006.

## INTERCEPTION OF BUSINESS COMMUNICATIONS AUTHORISED UNDER RIPA 2000, s.4

RIPA 2000, s.4 is concerned with various forms of lawful interception, including interception in prisons (s.4(4)) and high security hospitals (s.4(5)) and the interception of communications of persons situated outside the United Kingdom (s.4(1)), but the type which has the greatest everyday consequences concerns the interception of business communications. Section 4(2) says:

> Subject to subsection (3), the Secretary of State may by regulations authorise any such conduct described in the regulations as appears to him to constitute a legitimate practice reasonably required for the purpose, in connection with the carrying on of any business, of monitoring or keeping a record of –

(a) communications by means of which transactions are entered into in the course of that business; or
(b) other communications relating to that business or taking place in the course of its being carried on.

Section 4(3) says:

> Nothing in any regulations under subsection (2) shall authorise the interception of any communication except in the course of its transmission using apparatus or services provided by or to the person carrying on the business for use wholly or partly in connection with that business.

The Telecommunications (Lawful Business Practice) (Interception of Communications) Regulations 2000, SI 2000/2699 were made pursuant to the power in s.4(2). These are discussed at **Chapter 7**.

INTERCEPTION PURSUANT TO A WARRANT UNDER RIPA 2000, s.4

This is discussed at **Chapter 7**.

*Criminal offences*

This is discussed at **Chapter 6**.

## 4.6 SELECTED CASE LAW ON COMMUNICATIONS PRIVACY

The European Court of Human Rights has given judgment in a series of landmark cases on communications privacy, which analyse the right to privacy within Article 8 of the European Convention on Human Rights. The main cases are considered below, together with two recent domestic decisions. However, by way of reminder Article 8 of the Convention provides as follows:

> 1. Everyone has the right to respect for his private and family life, his home and his correspondence.
> 2. There shall be no interference by a public authority with the exercise of this right except such as is in accordance with the law and is necessary in a democratic society in the interests of national security, public safety or the economic well-being of the country, for the prevention of disorder or crime, for the protection of health or morals, or for the protection of the rights and freedoms of others.

### 4.6.1 *Klass* v. *Germany* (1978)

In *Klass v. Germany* (European Court of Human Rights, Application No.5029/71, 6 September 1978), the applicants alleged that a German law that permitted surveillance of postal and telecommunications, including interception, breached their right to privacy for two reasons. First, it did not require those undertaking surveillance to notify those affected. Second, it did not allow those affected to challenge a decision to undertake surveillance before the courts.

The court held that while there was no evidence that the applicants had been affected by surveillance they were entitled to bring proceedings because they lived under the 'menace' of surveillance. Furthermore, the court held that surveillance of communications constituted an interference with the right to privacy. Therefore, the question was whether the interference was justified.

The court dismissed the applicants' allegation of a breach of Article 8. Prominent within the court's reasoning were the following matters.

- The law under review defined precisely the purposes of surveillance, namely the safeguarding of national security and the prevention of disorder and crime. In defining these purposes, the law limited the scope of surveillance.
- The law contained adequate safeguards against abuse. For example, it required a factual basis for surveillance, it limited surveillance to a measure of last resort, it covered surveillance only of specific suspects and their contacts and it required the authorisation of a senior government official.
- Although the law excluded the possibility of judicial supervision within the courts it did make detailed provision for administrative supervision.
- The law limited the duration of surveillance to three months and it prevented the use of information obtained during surveillance for other purposes.

*Klass* is also interesting in that it reveals judicial concerns about espionage and terrorism. These concerns remain ever present:

> As the Delegates observed, the Court, in its appreciation of the scope of the protection offered by Article 8 (art. 8), cannot but take judicial notice of two important facts. The first consists of the technical advances made in the means of espionage and, correspondingly, of surveillance; the second is the development of terrorism in Europe in recent years. Democratic societies nowadays find themselves threatened by highly sophisticated forms of espionage and by terrorism, with the result that the State must be able, in order effectively to counter such threats, to undertake the secret surveillance of subversive elements operating within its jurisdiction. The Court has therefore to accept that the existence of some legislation granting powers of secret surveillance over the mail, post and telecommunications

is, under exceptional conditions, necessary in a democratic society in the interests of national security and/or for the prevention of disorder or crime.

### 4.6.2 *Malone* v. *United Kingdom* (1984)

In *Malone* v. *United Kingdom* (European Court of Human Rights, Application No.8691/79, 2 August 1984), the Applicant complained of unlawful interception of his telephone calls by the police as well as the 'metering' of his calls. By way of background, Malone was prosecuted for handling stolen goods and during the course of his trial it came to light that he had been the subject of interception by the police. The extent of the interception was unknown, however, as the UK government declined to provide details.

The judgment provides a very interesting account of the legal history of interception of postal communications and telecommunications through to 1981. At that time interception was subject to administrative controls, not statutory controls. The key elements of the administrative provisions were as follows:

- Telephone calls could be intercepted only pursuant to a warrant issued by the Home Secretary.
- A warrant would only be granted in respect of 'really serious' offences, where normal methods of investigation had been tried and failed or would be unlikely to succeed and only if there was good reason to think that the interception would be likely to lead to an arrest and conviction.
- Applications for warrants had to be made in writing, containing a statement of the purpose that the interception served and a summary of the facts and circumstances supporting the request.
- Applications could only be made by a senior official at the Metropolitan Police Service, or by a Chief Constable at another force.
- The warrant had to specify the telephone number to be intercepted and the name of the subscriber.
- Warrants were time limited to two months' duration, although they could be renewed if the original reasons for grant remained valid.
- The Home Secretary could delegate powers to make changes to the terms of warrants to a senior civil servant.
- Warrants had to be discontinued if they were no longer necessary.
- Individuals were not informed of the interception of their calls.
- The system was subject to independent scrutiny by a senior judge.
- Information obtained through a warrant could not be tendered in evidence.
- Records of communications had to be destroyed when no longer required.

Following *Klass* the court held that the interception of Malone's telephone calls by the police amounted to an interference with his right to privacy as guaranteed by Article 8 of the Convention, which left the question whether the interference was in accordance with law and necessary in a democratic society.

On the question of whether the interference was in accordance with the law, the court observed that this meant that the law must be adequately accessible by the citizen and formulated with sufficient precision so as to enable the citizen to be able to regulate their conduct. The court said:

> the law must be sufficiently clear in its terms to give citizens an adequate indication as to the circumstances in which and the conditions on which public authorities are empowered to resort to this secret and potentially dangerous interference with the right to respect for private life and correspondence.

It was common ground between the parties that the Home Secretary's power to order interception was lawful, in the sense that the power derived from legislation. The issue for determination, as the court explained, was whether the law was sufficiently precise so as to enable a person to be sure of the circumstances in which the discretionary power to order interception would be exercised. The court posited the question:

> whether, under domestic law, the essential elements of the power to intercept communications were laid down with reasonable precision in accessible legal rules that sufficiently indicated the scope and manner of exercise of the discretion conferred on the relevant authorities.

On the question of discretions the court gave detailed guidance on the required quality of discretionary laws, reinforcing the point that where the exercise of discretion is not open to scrutiny the laws have to be clear on the scope of discretions in order to prevent abuse:

> Since the implementation in practice of measures of secret surveillance of communications is not open to scrutiny by the individuals concerned or the public at large, it would be contrary to the rule of law for the legal discretion granted to the executive to be expressed in terms of an unfettered power. Consequently, the law must indicate the scope of any such discretion conferred on the competent authorities and the manner of its exercise with sufficient clarity, having regard to the legitimate aim of the measure in question, to give the individual adequate protection against arbitrary interference.

When measured against these requirements, the court found that the laws of England and Wales were sadly lacking in clarity. The court concluded that:

> Nonetheless, on the evidence before the Court, it cannot be said with any reasonable certainty what elements of the powers to intercept are incorporated in legal rules and what elements remain within the discretion of the executive. In view of the attendant obscurity and uncertainty as to the state of the law in this essential respect, the Court cannot but reach a similar conclusion to that of the Commission. In the opinion of the Court, the law of England and Wales does not

> indicate with reasonable clarity the scope and manner of exercise of the relevant discretion conferred on the public authorities. To that extent, the minimum degree of legal protection to which citizens are entitled under the rule of law in a democratic society is lacking.

Having concluded that the laws were not of sufficient quality, the court felt that it did not have to examine whether they were necessary in a democratic society. However, the court did provide useful guidance on the subject matter that would be considered during an analysis of this issue:

> Undoubtedly, the existence of some law granting powers of interception of communications to aid the police in their function of investigating and detecting crime may be 'necessary in a democratic society . . . for the prevention of disorder or crime', within the meaning of paragraph 2 of Article 8. The Court accepts, for example, the assertion in the [UK] Government's White Paper that in Great Britain 'the increase of crime, and particularly the growth of organised crime, the increasing sophistication of criminals and the ease and speed with which they can move about have made telephone interception an indispensable tool in the investigation and prevention of serious crime'. However, the exercise of such powers, because of its inherent secrecy, carries with it a danger of abuse of a kind that is potentially easy in individual cases and could have harmful consequences for democratic society as a whole. This being so, the resultant interference can only be regarded as 'necessary in a democratic society' if the particular system of secret surveillance adopted contains adequate guarantees against.

The second issue concerned the metering of Mr Malone's telephone calls. The process of metering, as the court described, 'involves the use of a device (a meter check printer) which registers the numbers dialled on a particular telephone and the time and duration of each call'. The use of the meter check printer did not involve interception: rather it captured what we would now call traffic data, which as the court found, 'a supplier of a telephone service may in principle legitimately obtain, notably in order to ensure that the subscriber is correctly charged or to investigate complaints or possible abuses of the service'.

The evidence before the court was that British Telecommunications would make this data available to the police without the consent of the subscriber, but the court found that 'there would appear to be no legal rules concerning the scope and manner of exercise of the discretion enjoyed by the public authorities'. As such, although the release of the data was lawful in the sense that there were domestic laws that enabled the police to issue subpoenas for it, the practice was not in accordance with law within the meaning of Article 8(2) of the Convention, with the result that Article 8 was infringed.

In direct response to this decision Parliament passed the Interception of Communications Act 1985, but that Act was successfully challenged in *Halford* v. *United Kingdom*, which triggered its replacement, the Regulation of Investigatory Powers Act 2000. However, it is very interesting to note that despite the failings in the law identified by *Malone*, the current statutory framework for interceptions mirrors very closely the administrative provisions identified by the court.

### 4.6.3 *Huvig* v. *France* (1990)

In *Huvig* v. *France* (European Court of Human Rights, Application No.11105/84, 24 April 1990), the applicants complained that there had been a violation of Article 8 as a result of the interception of their business and private telephone calls that took place in the mid-1970s. The interception took place pursuant to a warrant issued by an investigating judge, who was examining allegations of tax evasion and fraud. The applicants were prosecuted and convicted of these offences and served custodial sentences despite trying to have the prosecutions declared nullities on the grounds that their privacy, which was legally protected, had been infringed.

The court analysed the French laws that were applicable at the time. Although the court found that an investigating judge had the legal right to 'take all the investigative measures he deems useful for establishing the truth' and that post and telecommunications authorities were legally obliged to comply with requests for monitoring of telephone calls made by an investigating judge or by a senior police officer acting under a judicial warrant, there was no express statutory power that permitted an investigating judge to order interception.

There was also a significant amount of law on the issuing of warrants, including much settled case law. For example, investigating judges could only issue a warrant where there was a presumption that a specific offence had been committed and that offence gave rise to the investigation; interception could not be accompanied by 'any subterfuge or ruse' and interception could only be carried out 'in such a way that the exercise of the rights of the defence cannot be jeopardised'.

Relying upon the decisions in *Klass* and *Malone* the court once again confirmed that interception amounted 'without any doubt' to an interference with the applicants' rights under Article 8 and would be a violation unless carried out in accordance with the law, in pursuit of a legitimate aim and necessary in a democratic society.

Regarding whether the interception was in accordance with law, the court summarised the issue in the following manner:

> The expression 'in accordance with the law', within the meaning of Article 8 § 2 (art. 8–2), requires firstly that the impugned measure should have some basis in domestic law; it also refers to the quality of the law in question, requiring that it should be accessible to the person concerned, who must moreover be able to foresee its consequences for him, and compatible with the rule of law.

The court had no hesitation in finding that interception had a basis in French law; the fact that there was a substantial body of case law on the subject was very influential in the court's thinking. It also found that there was no issue with regard to the requirement regarding the quality of the law; it was 'accessible'.

The court was much more troubled about the question of foreseeability, however, and it reminded that:

> Tapping and other forms of interception of telephone conversations represent a serious interference with private life and correspondence and must accordingly be based on a 'law' that is particularly precise. It is essential to have clear, detailed rules on the subject, especially as the technology available for use is continually becoming more sophisticated.

The court referred to the various safeguards that the French government had identified, such as the rule against subterfuge, but it noted that only some of them were part of the Code of Criminal Procedure, while others had not even been the subject of case law. The court therefore concluded that 'the system does not for the time being afford adequate safeguards against various possible abuses'. In illustration it said:

> For example, the categories of people liable to have their telephones tapped by judicial order and the nature of the offences which may give rise to such an order are nowhere defined. Nothing obliges a judge to set a limit on the duration of telephone tapping. Similarly unspecified are the procedure for drawing up the summary reports containing intercepted conversations; the precautions to be taken in order to communicate the recordings intact and in their entirety for possible inspection by the judge (who can hardly verify the number and length of the original tapes on the spot) and by the defence; and the circumstances in which recordings may or must be erased or the tapes be destroyed, in particular where an accused has been discharged by an investigating judge or acquitted by a court. The information provided by the Government on these various points shows at best the existence of a practice, but a practice lacking the necessary regulatory control in the absence of legislation or case-law.

In the light of these findings the court held that 'French law, written and unwritten, does not indicate with reasonable clarity the scope and manner of exercise of the relevant discretion conferred on the public authorities', concluding that there had been a breach of Article 8. As a result of this finding it was not necessary for the court to form any conclusions on the other issues.

### 4.6.4 ***Niemietz* v. *Germany* (1992)**

In the case of *Niemietz* v. *Germany* (1992) 16 EHRR 97, a government authority conducted a search of the office of a lawyer for papers involving one of the lawyer's clients. The court rejected an argument run by the government that Article 8 did not protect the lawyer against the search but stated that there was no reason of principle why 'the notion of "private life" should be taken to exclude activities of a business nature.' (para.29). In addition, the court noted that it is not always possible to distinguish which of an individual's activities form part of his or her business life and which do not.

### 4.6.5 ***Halford* v. *United Kingdom* (1997)**

In *Halford* v. *United Kingdom* (1997) 24 EHRR 523, the court examined the compatibility of the Interception of Communications Act 1985, which had been introduced in response to *Malone*, with Article 8. In brief, the 1985 Act applied to interception of communications over public, not private, telecommunications systems. The Act did not provide the subjects of interception with any legal remedies; the only recourse open to interception subjects was the making of complaints to the Interception of Communications Tribunal, but the Tribunal did not have the power to confirm that interception had actually taken place.

By way of background, Alison Halford was appointed to the post of Assistant Chief Constable of Merseyside Police in 1983. Over the following seven years she made eight unsuccessful applications for promotion to the position of Deputy Chief Constable. She believed that she was blocked by the Chief Constable, who opposed her support for equal treatment for women. In 1990 Ms Halford commenced proceedings against the Chief Constable and the Home Office in the Industrial Tribunal, alleging sex discrimination. These proceedings led to a campaign being waged against her, which included the interception of her telephone calls and, eventually, a disciplinary proceeding that resulted in her suspension.

Within the course of the Industrial Tribunal proceedings, Ms Halford tried to make an issue of the interception, but she was prevented from doing so by the 1985 Act. Therefore, she brought a complaint before the Interception of Communication Tribunal, but this was dismissed without confirmation that interception had actually taken place.

Ms Halford believed that calls from her office telephones and her home telephone had been intercepted. The office telephones formed part of a private telecommunications system however, not part of the public system. As such, the 1985 Act did not apply to these acts of interception. The home phone was connected to the public system, meaning that the 1985 Act applied, but because of the constraints placed upon the Interception of Communications Tribunal Ms Halford had no way of knowing if interception had actually taken place. However, during the course of the proceedings before the European Court, the UK government admitted that there was a reasonable likelihood that calls from Ms Halford's office telephones had been intercepted. It made no such admissions in respect of calls from her home telephone.

The court held that the UK had infringed Article 8.

### 4.6.6 *Copland* v. *UK* (2007)

In *Copland* v. *UK* (62617/00 [2007] ECJ 253), the European Court of Human Rights considered the monitoring of an employee's telephone, email and internet use by her employer. The court found that the employer's monitoring breached the employee's right to respect for private life. In this instance, since the employee had been given no warning that her calls would be monitored, the court found that she had a reasonable expectation that calls made from her work telephone and communications from her email and her internet use would remain private. It held that the collection and storage without her knowledge of personal information relating to her telephone, email and internet use amounted to an interference with her Article 8 rights.

The *Copland* case clearly illustrates the dangers of employers operating without an appropriate policy when monitoring employees' electronic communications. Crucially, in this case the employer had no policy extant which might have enabled it to argue that the employee's expectation of privacy was reduced when using her employer's email, telephone and internet systems. (At the time of the monitoring that was in issue, the DPA 1998 and RIPA 2000 were not in force, so there was no domestic law in the UK regulating monitoring.) The case also emphasises the need for employers who monitor employees to ensure that those employees are aware that their communications could be monitored and that there is a good reason for such monitoring in every case.

### 4.6.7 *McGowan* v. *Scottish Water* (2004)

In the case of *McGowan* v. *Scottish Water* [2005] IRLR 167, the Scottish Employment Appeal Tribunal (EAT) considered the case of an employee being monitored by Scottish Water on the basis of a suspicion that the employee was falsifying timesheets relating to call-outs and periods when it was necessary for the employee to attend his place of work, which was a water treatment plant. Scottish Water appointed private investigators to film the activities of the employee and the video footage was subsequently referred to in disciplinary hearings. The employee was dismissed following the disciplinary hearings, as a result of which he brought proceedings for unfair dismissal. The EAT found that the surveillance was proportionate in the circumstances, although the surveillance of an employee by his employer is capable of infringing the employee's right to a private life. In this case the issue was, given the conduct of which the employee was suspected, whether the employer's actions were proportionate in the circumstances. On the facts, the EAT found that the actions of Scottish Water in conducting the monitoring was justified.

This case demonstrates that, where employees are monitored, this is likely to be an infringement of their right to a private life. An employer would have to justify the monitoring on the basis that the infringement is proportionate and, therefore, need to consider whether the business need justifies the intrusion into the employee's privacy, examine how the monitoring is undertaken and consider alternatives. In the context of the McGowan case, it is material that the employee was suspected of having committed a criminal offence, Scottish Water had considered other less intrusive methods of monitoring (the installation of cameras at the water treatment plant) but this was not regarded as effective as the appointment of private investigators.

### 4.6.8 *Fosh* v. *Cardiff University* (2008)

In *Fosh* v *Cardiff University* (EAT, 23/01/2008) the appellant was a former employee of the university. Whilst employed by the university, the employee had helped a student bring a claim of race discrimination against the university which, in the opinion of the university, amounted to a serious conflict of interest. The employee refused to cease acting for the student when asked to do so and was suspended, during which time a search of her email account was authorised. The employee was subsequently dismissed. The grounds for dismissal included acting in conflict of interest by representing the student, being inappropriately involved in a student's application for a fellowship and criticising her head of department in abusive terms.

The employment tribunal dismissed the claims of unfair dismissal and victimisation under the emanation of the state and had acted in breach of Article 8, thereby making her dismissal unfair. The tribunal dismissed the claim and the case was appealed to the EAT which dismissed the employee's appeal. In relation to the search of the employee's email account, the EAT held that the university had not breached Article 8. In reaching this decision, it made an assumption, without deciding the point, that the university was an emanation of the state. The EAT was satisfied that the search of the employee's emails was authorised in accordance with the internal rules of the university and that the university was also entitled to rely on the provisions of RIPA 2000. The EAT was satisfied that the tribunal was entitled to conclude on that basis that there had been no violation of Article 8.

## CHAPTER NOTES

1 PECD refers to traffic and location data, CDRD refers to data and RIPA 2000 refers to communications data and traffic data. For current purposes it might be easier to view communications data and data as generic terms for traffic data and location data.

2 See the Commission Proposal for a Directive of the European Parliament and of the Council amending Directives 2002/21/EC on a common regulatory framework for electronic communications networks and services, 2002/19/EC on access to, and interconnection of, electronic communications networks and services, and 2002/20/EC on the authorisation of electronic communications networks and services, COM(2007) 697 final, 13 November 2007. See **http://ec.europa.eu/information_society/policy/ecomm**.

3 Recital 24 gives examples of how the rule against the gathering of data from the user's terminal equipment can be breached. It says that 'so-called spyware, web bugs, hidden identifiers and other similar devices can enter the user's terminal equipment without their knowledge in order to gain access to information, to store information or to trace the activities of the user and may seriously intrude upon the privacy of these users'. However, Recital 25 legitimises the use of cookies saying these can be 'a legitimate and useful tool, for example, in analysing the effectiveness of website design and advertising, and in verifying the identity of users engaged in on-line transactions'.

4 Article 6(5) is concerned with the identity of persons who are entitled to process traffic data, saying 'processing of traffic data, in accordance with paras.1, 2, 3 and 4, must be restricted to persons acting under the authority of providers of the public communications networks and publicly available electronic communications services handling billing or traffic management, customer enquiries, fraud detection, marketing electronic communications services or providing a value added service, and must be restricted to what is necessary for the purposes of such activities'.

5 A value added service is described as 'any service which requires the processing of traffic data or location data other than traffic data beyond what is necessary for the transmission of a communication or the billing thereof'. Recital 18 gives a number of examples of value added services saying they may consist of advice on least expensive tariff packages, route guidance, traffic information, weather forecasts and tourist information.

6 See Recital 9, which says that 'because retention of data has proved to be such a necessary and effective investigative tool for law enforcement in several Member States, and in particular concerning serious matters such as organised crime and terrorism, it is necessary to ensure that retained data are made available to law enforcement authorities for a certain period, subject to the conditions provided for in this Directive. The adoption of an instrument on data retention that complies with the requirements of Article 8 of the ECHR is therefore a necessary measure'.

7 See the definition of intrusive surveillance within RIPA 2000, s.26. Section 26(4)(a) excludes from the definition of intrusive surveillance and 'surveillance consisting in any such interception of a communication as falls within section 48(4)'. Section 48(4) refers to interception over a telecommunications system where one party to the communication has consented to interception and there is no interception warrant authorising the interception: in other words, s.48(4) is repeating the key elements of the form of lawful authority set out in s.3(2).

8 See also the Regulation of Investigatory Powers (Directed Surveillance and Covert Human Intelligence Sources) Order 2003, SI 2003/3171; and the Regulation of Investigatory Powers (Directed Surveillance and Covert Human Intelligence Sources) (Amendment) Order 2005, SI 2005/1084.

# CHAPTER 5

# Substantive law issues – civil

## 5.1 INTRODUCTION

Although email is a new form of communication, its use and operation is subject to the usual laws of the jurisdiction. In this chapter, important provisions of substantive law are discussed as they apply to email. Of course, this chapter cannot cover all of the detail and nuances of the substantive laws that are identified; rather it is intended to provide the reader with a basic overview of the provisions that are most likely to be engaged through the use of email. With this purpose in mind, the approach taken in this chapter is to identify and state the key elements of relevant legislation supported by useful extracts of case law.

## 5.2 CONFIDENTIALITY

An area of the law that is ripe for engagement by the misuse of email is the law of confidence (see, for example, *Pennwell Publishing (UK) Ltd* v. *Ornstien* [2007] EWHC 1570). If information has the necessary quality of confidence and it is imparted or communicated in circumstances giving rise to a duty of confidence it will amount to a breach of that duty to disclose the information without the consent of the person to whom the duty is owed, unless there is an overriding public interest in non-disclosure. (Confidentiality does not attach to trivial or useless information; see, for example, the comments of Lord Goff in the *Spycatcher* case. See also *Moorgate Tobacco Co Ltd* v. *Philip Morris Ltd (No.2)* (1984) 156 CLR 414. The public interest defence to a claim of unlawful disclosure of confidential information was originally known as the iniquity rules; see *Gartside* v. *Outram* (1857) 26 LJ Ch.) Furthermore, the person to whom the duty of confidence is owed can also take legal action to restrain anticipated disclosures.

Information does not have to be completely secret to be confidential, although information that is freely circulating in the public domain will lose its quality of confidence, as was confirmed in the *Spycatcher* case, *Attorney-General* v. *Guardian Newspapers Ltd (No.2)* [1990] 1 AC 109. Instead, the law looks for relative secrecy; for example, in *HRH Prince of Wales* v. *Associated Newspapers Ltd* [2007] EWHC 1685 the claimant was successful in restraining the publication of extracts from his private diaries despite the fact that he had circulated parts of them amongst his friends and advisers. See also, for example, *Schering Chemicals Ltd* v. *Falkman Ltd* [1982] 1 QB 1; *Creation Records Ltd* v. *News Group Newspapers Ltd* [1997] EMLR 44; and *Franchi* v. *Franchi* [1967] RPC 149.

### 5.2.1 *Coco* v. *Clark* – the classic statement of the law

The classic statement of the law can be found in *Coco* v. *A.N. Clark (Engineers) Ltd* [1969] RPC 41, a decision of Mr Justice Megarry:

> In my judgment, three elements are normally required if, apart from contract, a case of breach of confidence is to succeed. First, the information itself, in the words of Lord Greene, M.R. in the *Saltman* case on page 215, must 'have the necessary quality of confidence about it'. Secondly, that information must have been imparted in circumstances importing an obligation of confidence. Thirdly, there must be an unauthorised use of that information to the detriment of the party communicating it. I must briefly examine each of these requirements in turn.
>
> First, the information must be of a confidential nature. As Lord Greene said in the *Saltman* case at page 215 'something which is public property and public knowledge' cannot per se provide any foundation for proceedings for breach of confidence. However confidential the circumstances of communication, there can be no breach of confidence in revealing to others something which is already common knowledge. But this must not be taken too far. Something that has been constructed solely from materials in the public domain may possess the necessary quality of confidentiality: for something new and confidential may have been brought into being by the application of the skill and ingenuity of the human brain. Novelty depends on the thing itself, and not upon the quality of its constituent parts. Indeed, often the more striking the novelty, the more commonplace its components, Mr. Mowbray demurs to the concept that some degree of originality is requisite. But whether it is described as originality or novelty or ingenuity or otherwise, I think there must be some product of the human brain which suffices to confer a confidential nature upon the information: and, expressed in those terms, I think that Mr. Mowbray accepts the concept.
>
> The difficulty comes, as Lord Denning, M.R. pointed out in the *Seager* case on page 931, when the information used is partly public and partly private; for then the recipient must somehow segregate the two and, although free to use the former, must take no advantage of the communication of the latter. To this subject I must in due course return. I must also return to a further point, namely, that where confidential information is communicated in circumstances of confidence the obligation thus created endures, perhaps in a modified form, even after all the information has been published or is ascertainable by the public; for the recipient must not use the communication as a spring-board (see the *Seager* case, page 931 and 933). I should add that, as shown by *Cranleigh Precision Engineering Ltd.* v. *Bryant* [1965] 1 W.L.R. 1293, [1966] R.P.C. 81; the mere simplicity of an idea does not prevent it being confidential (see pages 1309 and 1310). Indeed, the simpler an idea, the more likely it is to need protection.

The second requirement is that the information must have been communicated in circumstances importing an obligation of confidence. However secret and confidential the information, there can be no binding obligation of confidence if that information is blurted out in public or is communicated in other circumstances which negative any duty of holding it confidential. From the authorities cited to me, I have not been able to derive any very precise idea of what test is to be applied in determining whether the circumstances import an obligation of confidence. In the *Argyll* case at page 330, Ungoed-Thomas, J. concluded his discussion of the circumstances in which the publication of marital communications should be restrained as being confidential by saying 'If this was a well-developed jurisdiction doubtless there would be guides and tests to aid in exercising it'. In the absence of such guides or tests he then in effect concluded that part of the communications there in question would on any reasonable test emerge as confidential. It may be that that hard-worked creature, the reasonable man, may be pressed into service once more; for I do not see why he should not labour in equity as well as at law. It seems to me that if the circumstances are such that any reasonable man standing in the shoes of the recipient of the information would have realised that upon reasonable grounds the information was being given to him in confidence, then this should suffice to impose upon him the equitable obligation of confidence. In particular, where information of commercial or industrial value is given on a business-like basis and with some avowed common object in mind, such as a joint venture or the manufacture of articles by one party for the other, I would regard the recipient as carrying a heavy burden if he seeks to repel a contention that he was bound by an obligation of confidence: see the *Saltman* case at page 216. On that footing, for reasons that will appear, I do not think I need explore this head further. I merely add that I doubt whether equity would intervene unless the circumstances are of sufficient gravity; equity ought not to be invoked merely to protect trivial tittle-tattle, however confidential.

Thirdly, there must be an unauthorised use of the information to the detriment of the person communicating it. Some of the statements of principle in the cases omit any mention of detriment; others include it. At first sight, it seems that detriment ought to be present if equity is to be induced to intervene; but I can conceive of cases where a plaintiff might have substantial motives for seeking the aid of equity and yet suffer nothing which could fairly be called detriment to him, as when the confidential information shows him in a favourable light but gravely injures some relation or friend of his whom he wishes to protect. The point does not arise for decision in this case, for detriment to the plaintiff plainly exists. I need therefore say no more than that although for the purposes of this case I have stated the proposition in the stricter form, I wish to keep open the possibility of the true proposition being that in the wider form.

In the *Spycatcher* case, Lord Goff summarised the effect of the law as to how a duty of confidence arises, being where confidential information comes to a person's knowledge in circumstances where they have notice that the information is confidential:

My Lords, it is tempting in this case to embark upon an exegesis of the law relating to breach of confidence. That temptation must however, in my opinion, be resisted – if only because, as I see the case, subject to one important and difficult point (which, to my mind unfortunately, does not seem to have been the subject of argument in the courts below), the applicable principles of law appear to me to be

> relatively straightforward and non-controversial. This may well be because I have derived so much assistance from the judgments in the courts below; though that provides yet another reason why I should not attempt to do more than state the applicable principles of law in broad terms.
>
> I start with the broad general principle (which I do not intend in any way to be definitive) that a duty of confidence arises when confidential information comes to the knowledge of a person (the confidant) in circumstances where he has notice, or is held to have agreed, that the information is confidential, with the effect that it would be just in all the circumstances that he should be precluded from disclosing the information to others. I have used the word 'notice' advisedly, in order to avoid the (here unnecessary) question of the extent to which actual knowledge is necessary; though I of course understand knowledge to include circumstances where the confidant has deliberately closed his eyes to the obvious. The existence of this broad general principle reflects the fact that there is such a public interest in the maintenance of confidences, that the law will provide remedies for their protection.

As such, it is the nature or quality of the information and the nature of the relationships which determine whether information is subject to a duty of confidence. It is not necessary for the duty to be expressly stated by the parties; it can arise impliedly (see, for example, *Argyll* v. *Argyll* [1967] Ch 302). Indeed, in many cases, particularly those involving photo-journalism, the duty of confidence arises because the defendant acted without the claimant's knowledge or consent, either through trickery or some form of deceit or due to the invasive abilities of the long lens (see, for example, *Lord Ashburton* v. *Pape* [1913] 2 Ch 469 and *Prince Albert* v. *Strange* (1849) 1 De G & Sm 652).

### 5.2.2 In what circumstances will the recipient of an email be bound by a duty of confidence?

A recipient of an email receiving confidential information will be bound by a duty of confidence if they have notice of the fact that the information is confidential, which can arise from an express 'confidentiality notice', or because it would be obvious to a reasonable person that the information is confidential. A third party who turns a blind eye will be caught by the duty of confidence (see, for example, *Thomas* v. *Pearce* [2000] FSR 718).

### 5.2.3 Types of confidential information

The situations in which the courts have held that there was a duty of confidence are wide and varied. In *Argyll* v. *Argyll* the court was concerned with marital relations, and as *Mosley* v. *News Group Newspapers Ltd* [2008] EWCA Civ 337 confirms, this has been extended to extra-marital sexual relationships with prostitutes. (See the discussion at **Chapter 3** for the relationship between the right to privacy within Article 8 of the European Convention on Human Rights and the law of confidence.) In the *Spycatcher* case the confidential information was governmental secrets (see also

*Attorney-General* v. *Blake* [2001] 1 AC 268). In *Saltman Engineering Co Ltd* v. *Campbell Engineering Co Ltd* (1948) 65 RPC 203 the confidential information was commercial information, as in trade secrets (see also *Seager* v. *Copydex Ltd* [1967] 1 WLR 923 and *Fraser* v. *Evans* [1969] 1 QB 349). In *Douglas* v. *Hello Ltd* [2005] EWCA Civ 595 the confidential information was essentially private information that had been sold for commercial value.

### 5.2.4 Defences

If there is a public interest in disclosure, that will defeat a claim for breach of confidence. The public interest defence started out as the iniquity rule, but it has since developed to cover many different interests. For example, in *Tournier* v. *National Provincial and Union Bank of England* [1924] 1 KB 46 the Court of Appeal identified four qualifications to the duty of confidence in a customer-banking relationship, namely where:

- disclosure of confidential information is required by law;
- there is a duty to disclose the information to the public;
- the interests of the bank require disclosure; or
- the customer has either expressly or impliedly agreed to the disclosure.

The public interest defence has legitimised disclosures where serious harm could be caused to the public, which covers cases were serious harm has already been caused; see *Stone* v. *South East Coast Strategic Health Authority* [2006] EWHC 1668 (Admin). This was held in *Beloff* v. *Pressdram Ltd* [1973] 1 All ER 241 and *Lion Laboratories Ltd* v. *Evans* [1985] QB 526, but there is a considerable distinction to be drawn between matters of public interest and matters that interest the public.

The existence of the public interest defence to non-consensual disclosures of confidential information is expressly recognised by the Data Protection Act 1998, s.7(4) which permits the disclosure of information about third parties in response to a data subject's access request (s.7(6)(a) requires the data controller to have regard to any duty of confidence owed to the third party), while the exemption provisions in Part IV provide a number of gateways to the non-consensual disclosure of personal data (see **Chapter 3** for a list of exemptions).

### 5.2.5 Remedies

A person whose confidence has been breached can sue for an injunction to prevent further breaches, damages, accounts of profits and delivery up and destruction of materials. Injunctions can be sought to prevent anticipated breaches.

## 5.3 COPYRIGHT

The law of copyright interacts with the world of email in a variety of ways, but the ones under analysis in this section are, first, the way email can be used to create a literary work; and second, the way email can be used to commit a copyright infringement, through the distribution of copyright protected works as attachments to emails. In addition, the main defences to claims of copyright infringement are identified, as are the remedies and sanctions for breach. Finally, the issue of vicarious liability is discussed.

The distribution of copyright protected work via email is a serious problem on many levels. First, a situation has arisen through the development of technologies, such as Apple's iTunes, where it is now regarded as being culturally acceptable for people to make electronic copies of their CD and DVD collections for playing on their portable devices, despite the fact that this is generally unlawful under domestic copyright laws. These copies are usually held on computers with internet access and email software and so it is only natural for people to think that if it is acceptable for them to make copies for use on their portable devices it is also acceptable for them to email copies to their contacts. Indeed, as the penetration of technologies such as iTunes into younger parts of the community increases, so does the chance of further copyright infringement through the distribution of infringing copies by email.

Second, there is the ease by which copies of electronic data can be made and the ease by which the copies can be distributed. In the same way that it is easy for a person to make and email copies of their CD and DVD collections, it is easy for a person to copy electronic files that are accessible through the internet. Text files, sound and music files and video and image files can be copied and distributed with just a few clicks of a mouse; no special skills or software are generally required.

Third, there is a real problem within the workplace with monitoring and regulating computer use. Most employers still allow their staff to use work systems for personal use, and there are significant privacy law and employment law obstacles to successful workplace monitoring of systems use. This means that the workplace can become a hive of infringing activities, with serious problems for vicarious liability.

This discussion is merely illustrative of the nature of the problem posed by email use and, of course, it is worth remembering that the vast majority of copyright infringements through the use of email will go undetected and unpunished. However, despite the relatively illusive nature of most incidences of copyright infringement, cases concerning breach by email are likely to go to court with increasing frequency.

See, for example, *Cembrit Blunn Ltd* v. *Apex Roofing Services LLP* [2007] EWHC 111, which concerned a dispute about the quality of roofing tiles supplied by a company to one of their customers. Senior employees at the supplier exchanged emails about the quality of their tiles after the customer refused to pay. The customer acquired a copy of one of the emails, which it then circulated to third parties. The judge, Kitchin J, held that this breached the supplier's copyright in the email. See, also, *Chan Nai Ming* v. *HKSAR* [2007] 3 HKC 255, which concerned the distribution of electronic versions of pirate movies over a peer-to-peer network. The defendant argued that he had not infringed the Hong Kong Copyright Ordinance because, he argued, the word 'copy' required distribution in a tangible form. In other words, he argued that infringement could not occur through the distribution of an electronic form, but only through a physical copy. The court rejected this argument and in doing so drew an analogy with infringing material being distributed as attachments to emails, holding that the internet, as a network of connected computers, was effectively a tangible means of distribution.

### 5.3.1 The use of email to create a literary work

Many people may think of copyright as an intellectual property right for works of artistic merit or quality, and while many copyright works will display such features, these are not essential qualities for subsistence of the right. Copyright can subsist in emails via the protections for literary works, a category of protected work that does not require any 'highbrow' components. Provided that the email is original and is the product of sufficient skill, judgment or labour, copyright will be created when the email is typed or, as the law prefers, 'recorded'. Indeed, copyright has been held to subsist in a wide variety of literary works which display none of the features of great, or even average, literature. Examples include football fixture lists (*Football League* v. *Littlewoods* [1959] Ch 637) and televisions listings (*Independent Television Publications* v. *Time Out* [1984] FSR 64). Indeed, in the well known case of *University of London Press* v. *University Tutorial Press* [1916] 2 Ch 601 Peterson J observed that a literary work is one 'which is expressed in print or writing, irrespective of the question whether the quality or style is high'.

The starting point in a consideration of copyright in emails as literary works is Copyright, Designs and Patents Act (CDPA) 1988, s.1, which says:

**1. Copyright and copyright works**

(1) Copyright is a property right which subsists in accordance with this Part in the following descriptions of work –

  (a) original literary, dramatic, musical or artistic works,
  (b) sound recordings, films or broadcasts and
  (c) the typographical arrangement of published editions.

(2) In this Part 'copyright work' means a work of any of those descriptions in which copyright subsists.

(3) Copyright does not subsist in a work unless the requirements of this Part with respect to qualification for copyright protection are met (see section 153 and the provisions referred to there).

Section 3(1) of the CDPA 1988 then goes on to say that a literary work 'means any work, other than a dramatic or musical work, which is written, spoken or sung'. However, copyright will only come into being when the literary work is 'recorded, in writing or otherwise' (s.3(2)). The requirement that the work should be recorded is a cornerstone upon which copyright law is built; many lawyers talk about copyright protecting the 'expression' of an idea, rather than the idea itself, a defining feature of copyright which is subsumed within the concept of recording (see *Baigent v Random House Group Ltd* [2007] EWCA Civ 247 for a detailed discussion on the difference between ideas and expression of ideas). As regards the distinction between ideas and the expression of them, sometimes the demarcation between the two is difficult to identify. The complexity within the law here is illustrated excellently by the words of Lord Hoffmann in *Designers Guild Ltd* v. *Russell Williams (Textiles) Ltd (Trading as Washington DC)* [2000] 1 WLR 2416, where he said the following:

> My Lords, if one examines the cases in which the distinction between ideas and the expression of ideas has been given effect, I think it will be found that they support two quite distinct propositions. The first is that a copyright work may express certain ideas which are not protected because they have no connection with the literary, dramatic, musical or artistic nature of the work. It is on this ground that, for example, a literary work which describes a system or invention does not entitle the author to claim protection for his system or invention as such. The same is true of an inventive concept expressed in an artistic work. However striking or original it may be, others are (in the absence of patent protection) free to express it in works of their own: see *Kleeneze Ltd.* v. *D.R.G. (U.K.) Ltd* [1984] F.S.R. 399. The other proposition is that certain ideas expressed by a copyright work may not be protected because, although they are ideas of a literary, dramatic or artistic nature, they are not original, or so commonplace as not to form a substantial part of the work.

From the perspective of email, the recording component will always be satisfied due to the manual and technological steps that are required to create them, although it is generally assumed that the recording requires a degree of permanence. Of course, from an evidential perspective, permanence is required if a case for copyright infringement is to stand anything near reasonable prospects of success.

So, for email as a literary work, the essential questions within a consideration of copyright are:

1. Is the email original?
2. Is the email the product of sufficient skill, judgment or labour?

As already stated, the originality of the work lies in its expression, not in the idea giving rise to the expression. Thus, an author who writes a new book about old ideas can expect to acquire copyright in the work, which will explain how copyright can subsist in history books; after all, as Lord Bingham said in *Designers Guild*, 'there is no new thing under the sun'. Similarly, an original review of a previous work can acquire copyright. Again, referring to *University of London Press* v. *University Tutorial Press*, the words of Peterson J shed considerable light on the meaning of originality:

> The word 'original' does not in this connection mean that the work must be the expression of original or inventive thought. Copyright Acts are not concerned with the originality of ideas, but with the expression of thought, and, in the case of 'literary work', with the expression of thought in print or writing. The originality which is required relates to the expression of the thought. But the Act does not require that the expression must be in an original or novel form, but that the work must not be copied from another work – that it should originate from the author.

The requirement that the email should be the product of sufficient skill, judgment or labour can be regarded as a facet of originality, but it also stands to illustrate that there is a *de minimis* principle within copyright protection for literary works, in the sense that there is a minimum degree of effort that needs to be invested in the expression of the idea (see, for example, *Cramp* v. *Smythson* [1944] AC 329), although this does not mean that a work has to be particularly long or complicated to satisfy the requirement of sufficient skill, judgment or labour (see, for example, *Express Newspapers* v. *Liverpool Daily Post* [1985] FSR 306).

Of course, because of the character of email (particularly its ability to add attachments) it is possible to breach copyright in many different kinds of work: sound files, video files and image files are commonly circulated by email, as are spreadsheets, which might contain databases, and copies of broadcasts. Email users and advisers may, therefore, gain assistance from understanding how the CDPA 1988 treats non-literary works. **Table 5.1** identifies other protected materials, in which copyright is regularly infringed through the attachment of files to emails.

**Table 5.1** Non-literary works in which copyright may subsist

| | |
|---|---|
| Databases | **3A. Databases**<br>(1) In this Part 'database' means a collection of independent works, data or other materials which –<br>(a) are arranged in a systematic or methodical way, and<br>(b) are individually accessible by electronic or other means.<br>(2) For the purposes of this Part a literary work consisting of a database is original if, and only if, by reason of the selection or arrangement of the contents of the database the database constitutes the author's own intellectual creation. |
| Artistic works | **4. Artistic works**<br>(1) In this Part 'artistic work' means –<br>(a) a graphic work, photograph, sculpture or collage, irrespective of artistic quality,<br>(b) a work of architecture being a building or a model for a building, or<br>(c) a work of artistic craftsmanship. |
| Sound recordings | **5A. Sound recordings**<br>(1) In this Part 'sound recording' means –<br>(a) a recording of sounds, from which the sounds may be reproduced, or<br>(b) a recording of the whole or any part of a literary, dramatic or musical work, from which sounds reproducing the work or part may be produced,<br>regardless of the medium on which the recording is made or the method by which the sounds are reproduced or produced. |
| Films | **5B. Films**<br>(1) In this Part 'film' means a recording on any medium from which a moving image may by any means be produced.<br>(2) The sound track accompanying a film shall be treated as part of the film for the purposes of this Part.<br>(3) Without prejudice to the generality of subsection (2), where that subsection applies –<br>(a) references in this Part to showing a film include playing the film sound track to accompany the film,<br>(b) references in this Part to playing a sound recording, or to communicating a sound recording to the public, do not include playing or communicating the film sound track to accompany the film, |

**Table 5.1** *Cont.*

| | |
|---|---|
| | (c) references in this Part to copying a work, so far as they apply to a sound recording, do not include copying the film sound track to accompany the film, and<br>(d) references in this Part to the issuing, rental or lending of copies of a work, so far as they apply to a sound recording, do not include the issuing, rental or lending of copies of the sound track to accompany the film. |
| Broadcasts | **6. Broadcasts**<br>(1) In this Part a 'broadcast' means an electronic transmission of visual images, sounds or other information which –<br>(a) is transmitted for simultaneous reception by members of the public and is capable of being lawfully received by them, or<br>(b) is transmitted at a time determined solely by the person making the transmission for presentation to members of the public,<br>and which is not excepted by subsection (1A); and references to broadcasting shall be construed accordingly.<br>(1A) Excepted from the definition of 'broadcast' is any internet transmission unless it is –<br>(a) a transmission taking place simultaneously on the internet and by other means,<br>(b) a concurrent transmission of a live event, or<br>(c) a transmission of recorded moving images or sounds forming part of a programme service offered by the person responsible for making the transmission, being a service in which programmes are transmitted at scheduled times determined by that person. |

### 5.3.2 Preliminary issues, including who owns copyright?

CDPA 1988, Part I, Ch.II deals with infringement of copyright, of which there are two kinds, namely primary infringement and secondary infringement. A key difference between the two kinds of infringement is that in cases of primary infringement there is no requirement upon the right-holder to show that the defendant knew or intended to infringe, unlike for secondary infringement where there is a mental component within breach. However, the fundamental basis of both forms of infringement is that the infringing person assumes the rights of the copyright owner. The essential right of the copyright owner is the exclusive right to make copies of the work (see also CDPA 1988, Part I, Ch.IV for the moral rights, such as the right to be identified as the author), for the duration of the right (for the rules on duration of copyright see CDPA 1988, ss.12–15 the duration of copyright for literary, dramatic, musical and artistic works is 70 years from the end of the calendar year in which the author dies). In the *Designers Guild* case[1] Lord Bingham said:

> The law of copyright rests on a very clear principle: that anyone who by his or her own skill and labour creates an original work of whatever character shall, for a limited period, enjoy an exclusive right to copy that work. No one else may for a season reap what the copyright owner has sown.

Of course, in any dispute over copyright one of the initial questions is, who is the owner of copyright? This is dealt with by CDPA 1988, s.11, which says that the first owner of copyright is the author of the work:

> **11. First ownership of copyright**
>
> (1) The author of a work is the first owner of any copyright in it, subject to the following provisions.
> (2) Where a literary, dramatic, musical or artistic work, or a film, is made by an employee in the course of his employment, his employer is the first owner of any copyright in the work subject to any agreement to the contrary.

The meaning of author is dealt with in s.9:

> **9. Authorship of work**
>
> (1) In this Part 'author', in relation to a work, means the person who creates it.
> (2) That person shall be taken to be –
>
> (aa) in the case of a sound recording, the producer;
> (ab) in the case of a film, the producer and the principal director;
> (b) in the case of a broadcast, the person making the broadcast (see section 6(3)) or, in the case of a broadcast which relays another broadcast by reception and immediate re-transmission, the person making that other broadcast;
> (d) in the case of the typographical arrangement of a published edition, the publisher.

Section 11(2) records the fact that copyright in works created by employees belongs to their employers. This means that special care should be taken when the person creating the work is self-employed, perhaps as a subcontractor or a consultant. In such cases the self-employed person will be treated as the author, even where they receive a fee for creating the work. In order for copyright to be transferred from the author to another person, a written assignment is required (see CDPA 1988, s.90(3)).

### 5.3.3 Primary infringement

For primary infringement, the initial consideration is CDPA 1988, s.16, which sets out the exclusive rights of the owner. Section 16 provides:

**16. The acts restricted by copyright in a work**

(1) The owner of the copyright in a work has, in accordance with the following provisions of this Chapter, the exclusive right to do the following acts in the United Kingdom –

(a) to copy the work (see section 17);
(b) to issue copies of the work to the public (see section 18);
(ba) to rent or lend the work to the public (see section 18A);
(c) to perform, show or play the work in public (see section 19);
(d) to communicate the work to the public (see section 20);
(e) to make an adaptation of the work or do any of the above in relation to an adaptation (see section 21);

and those acts are referred to in this Part as the 'acts restricted by the copyright'.

(2) Copyright in a work is infringed by a person who without the licence of the copyright owner does, or authorises another to do, any of the acts restricted by the copyright.

(3) References in this Part to the doing of an act restricted by the copyright in a work are to the doing of it –

(a) in relation to the work as a whole or any substantial part of it, and
(b) either directly or indirectly;

and it is immaterial whether any intervening acts themselves infringe copyright.

(4) This Chapter has effect subject to –

(a) the provisions of Chapter III (acts permitted in relation to copyright works), and
(b) the provisions of Chapter VII (provisions with respect to copyright licensing).

From s.16 we can gather the following:

- An infringement will occur if the defendant does any of the restricted acts without the permission of the owner, or authorises another to do any of the restricted acts.

- The infringing act does not need to take place in respect of the entire work, but a substantial part.
- Infringement can be direct or indirect.
- Copyright is not an absolute right, but qualified.

CDPA 1988, s.27 defines an 'infringing copy' in the following terms:

**27. Meaning of 'infringing copy'**

(1) In this Part 'infringing copy', in relation to a copyright work, shall be construed in accordance with this section.
(2) An article is an infringing copy if its making constituted an infringement of the copyright in the work in question.

Much of the litigation in the field of electronic copyright infringement has involved respect of 'peer-to-peer' (P2P) file sharing, with the first and most famous case involving Napster. The P2P file sharing world has encompassed many varieties of activities, usually as a result of the organisations at the centre of the networks trying to keep one step ahead of the copyright owners by making distinguishing changes to their operations in light of prior cases, but when stripped down to their bare essentials they all operate in the same way and for the same purpose, namely to introduce members of the P2P network to one another so that they can share copies of the files stored on their personal computers. As such, most of the interest in the field concerns the copying and distribution of perfect digital copies of files, which, when viewed from the perspective of the owner's case against the file sharers themselves, seems to involve relatively straightforward issues of law. The complexity within P2P litigation generally arises from the perspective of the owner's case against the organisation at the heart of the network; the basic accusation against the organisation is that they are facilitating copyright infringement by the members of the network, which is met with the response that while infringement does occur through the use of their systems, this is an unfortunate by-product of file sharing which, after all, also serves many legitimate purposes. In other words, P2P file sharing is not unlawful per se. Of course, copyright owners have woken up to the fact that their cases against the file sharers are legally more straightforward and there is plenty of evidence to show that copyright owners are now very willing to go after the file sharers directly.

Therefore, in respect of infringement of copyright by the distribution of infringing copies of works as attachments to email, the copyright owner's case against the sender of the email is likely to be relatively straightforward; the nature of attachments is such that, provided that the owner can prove that copyright subsists, they should be able to show both direct and substantial primary infringement.

When assessing whether primary infringement has occurred, the most obvious starting point is CDPA 1988, s.17, which addresses infringement through the making of copies. Section 17 says:

**17. Infringement of copyright by copying**

(1) The copying of the work is an act restricted by the copyright in every description of copyright work; and references in this Part to copying and copies shall be construed as follows.
(2) Copying in relation to a literary, dramatic, musical or artistic work means reproducing the work in any material form.
This includes storing the work in any medium by electronic means.
(3) In relation to an artistic work copying includes the making of a copy in three dimensions of a two-dimensional work and the making of a copy in two dimensions of a three-dimensional work.
(4) Copying in relation to a film or broadcast includes making a photograph of the whole or any substantial part of any image forming part of the film or broadcast.
(5) Copying in relation to the typographical arrangement of a published edition means making a facsimile copy of the arrangement.
(6) Copying in relation to any description of work includes the making of copies which are transient or are incidental to some other use of the work.

Let's start with the example of a computer user copying a CD music disk to their computer hard drive, a procedure often called 'format shifting'. Absent specific permission from the copyright holder, which could be contained within the terms and conditions relating to the purchase of the CD in the first place, the copying will be a primary infringement under CDPA 1988, s.17, regardless of the fact that there is a 'fair dealing' defence in s.29 (however, see CDPA 1988, s.56, which deals with transfer of copies of works in electronic form). Thus, the act of copying that is preparatory to the sending of a music file by email is likely to be an infringement in many cases.

Of course, the whole point of sending attachments by email is the making of a communication, and in cases of copyright infringement through this medium it will be CDPA 1988, s.18 that will be the first port of call for rights owners. Section 18 says:

**18. Infringement by issue of copies to the public**

(1) The issue to the public of copies of the work is an act restricted by the copyright in every description of copyright work.
(2) References in this Part to the issue to the public of copies of a work are to –
   (a) the act of putting into circulation in the EEA copies not previously put into circulation in the EEA by or with the consent of the copyright owner, or
   (b) the act of putting into circulation outside the EEA copies not previously put into circulation in the EEA or elsewhere.

(3) Reference in this Part to the issue to the public of copies of a work do not include –

(a) any subsequent distribution, sale, hiring or loan of copies previously put into circulation (but see section 18A: infringement by rental or lending), or

(b) any subsequent importation of such copies into the United Kingdom or another EEA state,

except so far as paragraph (a) of subsection (2) applies to putting into circulation in the EEA copies previously put into circulation outside the EEA.

When s.18 is read in the light of s.17, it is easy to conclude that where a person makes a copy of a work that is itself an infringing copy, it will then amount to a breach of s.18 to email that copy to another person. However, s.18 extends much further than this, as it is also a standalone provision, meaning that s.18 can be breached even where the making of the copy itself was authorised. Thus, a person might purchase a CD subject to terms and conditions that entitle them to make an electronic copy, but this will not authorise the distribution of the electronic version to third parties by email.

### *Substantial copying and indirect infringement*

As s.16 makes clear, the CDPA 1988 does not require that the infringing act should take place in respect of the entire work; it is sufficient for a case of primary infringement to be made out if the infringing act takes place in respect of a substantial part of the work, but, of course, if the entire work is taken the case will be much easier to prove.

Copying of a substantial part can be determined on a quantitative basis, but very often a qualitative assessment is required because some parts of a work can be more important, or substantial, than other parts.[2] In *Designers Guild* Lord Hoffmann expressed this in the following terms:

> Although the term 'substantial part' might suggest a quantitative test, or at least the ability to identify some discrete part which, on quantitative or qualitative grounds, can be regarded as substantial, it is clear upon the authorities that neither is the correct test. *Ladbroke (Football) Ltd.* v. *William Hill (Football) Ltd.* [1964] 1 W.L.R. 273 establishes that substantiality depends upon quality rather than quantity.

There is also a middle ground between these points, where the assessment needs to be both qualitative and quantitative. Lord Hoffmann continued in *Designers Guild*:

> Generally speaking, in cases of artistic copyright, the more abstract and simple the copied idea, the less likely it is to constitute a substantial part. Originality, in the

> sense of the contribution of the author's skill and labour, tends to lie in the detail with which the basic idea is presented.

Another important variable is whether there has been unadulterated copying or some alteration to the work by the defendant, because a point can be reached whereby the defendant's alterations are so great that nothing of the original work survives, whereas unadulterated copying can support a case of infringement where only a small part of the work is copied, although only very minor copying may not be substantial.

Indirect infringement occurs where the defendant imitates the protected work, as would happen where they take a photograph of a protected painting or sculpture.

### 5.3.4 Secondary infringement

Secondary infringement of copyright is dealt with in CDPA 1988, ss.22–6, which cover secondary infringement by importing an infringing copy (s.22), by possessing or dealing with an infringing copy (s.23), by providing the means for making an infringing copy (s.24), by permitting the use of premises for an infringing performance (s.25) and by provision of apparatus for an infringing performance (s.26). The most likely case of secondary infringement which will be engaged through the use of email is dealing. Section 23 says:

> **23. Secondary infringement: possessing or dealing with infringing copy**
>
> The copyright in a work is infringed by a person who, without the licence of the copyright owner –
>
> (a) possesses in the course of a business,
> (b) sells or lets for hire, or offers or exposes for sale or hire,
> (c) in the course of a business exhibits in public or distributes, or
> (d) distributes otherwise than in the course of a business to such an extent as to affect prejudicially the owner of the copyright,
>
> an article which is, and which he knows or has reason to believe is, an infringing copy of the work.

Infringement by dealing requires a commercial purpose and either actual or constructive knowledge. It is not inconceivable that the email will be used to deal with infringing copies in the manner contemplated by s.23.

### 5.3.5 Defences

Aside from arguments about whether the work under analysis is protected by copyright or whether the copying is substantial, the main defence to a case of copyright infringement involving emails will be 'fair dealing', which requires the court to consider the overall fairness of the defendant's actions in the light of the circumstances as a whole. However, the scope of the defence is very limited.

The first fair dealing defence is contained in CDPA 1988, s.29 and it concerns both non-commercial research and private study and it can be maintained in cases of infringement concerning literary, dramatic, musical and artistic work and in respect of published editions. However, it does not extend to sound recordings or films, meaning that the copying of CD and DVD libraries will never fall within the defence. Implicit within fair dealing here is acknowledgement of the copyright, unless that would be impossible. Section 29 says:

**29. Research and private study**

(1) Fair dealing with a literary, dramatic, musical or artistic work for the purposes of research for a non-commercial purpose does not infringe any copyright in the work provided that it is accompanied by a sufficient acknowledgement.
(1B) No acknowledgement is required in connection with fair dealing for the purposes mentioned in subsection (1) where this would be impossible for reasons of practicality or otherwise.
(1C) Fair dealing with a literary, dramatic, musical or artistic work for the purposes of private study does not infringe any copyright in the work.

The scope of this fair dealing defence does not extend beyond the educational and academic purpose. Provided that the copier can bring themselves within the scope of s.29 they would be permitted, for example, to include copyright work in an email to their tutor.

The second fair dealing defence is contained in s.30. This covers criticism, reviews and news reporting. Although its scope is limited, it is still a very powerful and valuable defence, particularly as it legitimises many otherwise infringing acts by press and media organisations in the context of the reporting of current affairs. Again, the copyright must be acknowledged, save for news reporting in broadcasts, films and by sound due to impossibility. Section 30 says:

**30. Criticism, review and news reporting**

(1) Fair dealing with a work for the purpose of criticism or review, of that or another work or of a performance of a work, does not infringe any copyright in the work provided that it is accompanied by a sufficient acknowledgement and provided that the work has been made available to the public.

(1A) For the purposes of subsection (1) a work has been made available to the public if it has been made available by any means, including –

(a) the issue of copies to the public;
(b) making the work available by means of an electronic retrieval system;
(c) the rental or lending of copies of the work to the public;
(d) the performance, exhibition, playing or showing of the work in public;
(e) the communication to the public of the work,

but in determining generally for the purposes of that subsection whether a work has been made available to the public no account shall be taken of any unauthorised act.

(2) Fair dealing with a work (other than a photograph) for the purpose of reporting current events does not infringe any copyright in the work provided that (subject to subsection (3)) it is accompanied by a sufficient acknowledgement.

(3) No acknowledgement is required in connection with the reporting of current events by means of a sound recording, film or broadcast where this would be impossible for reasons of practicality or otherwise.

### 5.3.6 Remedies

Copyright infringement is actionable at the suit of the owner. CDPA 1998, s.96 makes it clear that the owner's range of remedies are very wide:

**96. Infringement actionable by copyright owner**

(1) An infringement of copyright is actionable by the copyright owner.

(2) In an action for infringement of copyright all such relief by way of damages, injunctions, accounts or otherwise is available to the plaintiff as is available in respect of the infringement of any other property right.

The owner's right to damages is limited, however, to cases where the defendant had actual or constructive knowledge of the subsistence of copyright. If this defence is overcome the court can award 'additional damages' if it is just to do so, having regard to all the circumstances of the case including the flagrancy of the infringement and the extent to which the defendant benefited from the infringement, which to all intents and purposes extends beyond the usual compensatory approach to damages to an almost 'punitive' basis of assessment. Section 97 says:

**97. Provisions as to damages in infringement action**

(1) Where in an action for infringement of copyright it is shown that at the time of the infringement the defendant did not know, and had no reason to believe, that copyright subsisted in the work to which the action relates, the plaintiff is not entitled to damages against him, but without prejudice to any other remedy.

> (2) The court may in an action for infringement of copyright having regard to all the circumstances, and in particular to –
>
> (a) the flagrancy of the infringement, and
> (b) any benefit accruing to the defendant by reason of the infringement,
>
> award such additional damages as the justice of the case may require.

Of course, in litigation for infringement the owner will have to prove that the defendant has infringed the owner's copyright. In other words, the claimant must prove the connection between the two works. This is a matter of evidence and it will not be assumed by the court. If the defendant arrived at his work independently of the claimant's then the case will fail, despite the similarities. Balancing this point, where there are striking similarities between the works the defendant will be expected to provide an explanation of his working processes. This point is well illustrated by *Harman Pictures* v. *Osborne and others*. In this case, the plaintiff owned the film rights in a book about the Charge of the Light Brigade. At one point the plaintiff entered into discussions with the defendants, who were film producers and distributors, about a possible sale of the rights to them or a joint film venture. Subsequently the plaintiff learned that the defendants were planning to make their own film about the Charge. In proceedings for an injunction the defendants denied infringement, saying that their screenplay was the result of independent work, but the author of their screenplay did not present any evidence about how long he had been working on the screenplay. In granting the injunction the judge, Goff J (as he then was) said:

> For this purpose, and at this stage, in my judgment the lack of explanation by John Osborne how or when he worked and how long it took him, is of fundamental importance. All I have is a bare assertion that he did not base the script upon the book. That being sworn to must, of course, be regarded seriously, but I find it impossible to think that he can have produced this large script ready for 'shooting' (at any rate as he claims independently) without some kind of sketch plan and probably extensive notes or trial drafts of the whole or parts of it. All these will emerge on discovery, and may well serve either to corroborate or discredit his evidence. It is also, I think, remarkable that instead of John Osborne (who knows) saying even in outline what sources he consulted and how he arrived at his selection, or even taking one or two examples of common situations and giving his own explanation, he has left it to his solicitor, who does not know what happened, to compile a list of sources, and he then says they have truly identified many but not all of the sources of which he availed himself in each particular.

### 5.3.7 Vicarious liability

An organisation can be held vicariously liable for the infringements of its employees.

### 5.3.8 Crime

CDPA 1988, s.107 makes it a criminal offence to deal in infringing articles. Section 107(1) says:

**107. Criminal liability for making or dealing with infringing articles etc**

(1) A person commits an offence who, without the licence of the copyright owner –

- (a) makes for sale or hire, or
- (b) imports into the United Kingdom otherwise than for his private and domestic use, or
- (c) possesses in the course of a business with a view to committing any act infringing the copyright, or
- (d) in the course of a business –
  - (i) sells or lets for hire, or
  - (ii) offers or exposes for sale or hire, or
  - (iii) exhibits in public, or
  - (iv) distributes, or
- (e) distributes otherwise than in the course of a business to such an extent as to affect prejudicially the owner of the copyright, an article which is, and which he knows or has reason to believe is, an infringing copy of a copyright work.

The maximum penalty for a criminal offence under the CDPA 1988 is 10 years' imprisonment (s.107(4)).

## 5.4 DEFAMATION

As a medium for communication, email lends itself perfectly to the publication of defamatory materials. Indeed, cases about defamation by email are now starting to appear before the courts with increasing frequency. For example, in the recent case of *Gentoo Group Ltd (formerly Sunderland Housing Co Ltd)* v. *Hanratty* [2008] EWHC 627 (QB) the claimant, who was a social landlord, sued on the basis of an email campaign against it. In *Akinleye* v. *East Sussex Hospitals NHS Trust* [2008] EWHC 68 (QB), a hospital trust investigating the performance of the claimant, a departing employee, made an enquiry of one of the claimant's former employers, another trust, about his performance as an echo-cardiographer, which was answered by an email that the claimant alleged was defamatory. *Claire McBride* v. *The Body Shop International plc* [2007] EWHC 1658 concerned allegedly defamatory emails in the context of an employment disciplinary matter.

### 5.4.1 Forms of defamation

A defamatory statement can take one or two forms: it can either be a slander or a libel. The distinction between slander and libel lies in the permanence of the statement. A spoken defamatory statement or one in temporary form will be a slander, whereas a written defamatory statement or one in permanent form will be a libel. If a claim is to be founded on slander, the claimant will be expected to prove financial loss ('special damage') in most cases,[3] a criterion that is not present within libel claims. In reference to libel Lord Bingham said the following in *Jameel* v. *Wall Street Journal Europe SPRL (No.3)* [2006] UKHL 44:

> The tort of libel has long been recognised as actionable per se. Thus where a personal plaintiff proves publication of a false statement damaging to his reputation without lawful justification, he need not plead or prove special damage in order to succeed. Proof of injury to his reputation is enough.

### 5.4.2 Publication

One of the key questions at the heart of a claim in defamation is whether the defendant has published to a third person a defamatory statement about the claimant, or is responsible for such publication. For these purposes publication means the communication of information from the publisher to publishee, and publication will take place when the communication is heard or read by the publishee, not when the communication is spoken or written. Every new defamatory communication is a standalone, independent tort, actionable in its own right, as was established long ago in the case of *Duke of Brunswick* v. *Harmer* (1849) 14 QB 185. In the recent case of *Loutchansky* v. *Times Newspapers Ltd and others* [2001] EWCA Civ 1805, Lord Phillips MR said the following about *Duke of Brunswick*:

> It is a well established principle of the English law of defamation that each individual publication of a libel gives rise to a separate cause of action, subject to its own limitation period. *Duke of Brunswick* v *Harmer* 14 QB 185 provides a striking illustration of this principle. On 19 September 1830 an article was published in the 'Weekly Dispatch'. The limitation period for libel was then six years. The article defamed the Duke of Brunswick. Seventeen years after its publication an agent of the Duke purchased a back number containing the article from the 'Weekly Dispatch''s office. Another copy was obtained from the British Museum. The Duke sued on those two publications. The defendant contended that the cause of action was time-barred, relying on the original publication date. The Court of Queen's Bench held that the delivery of a copy of the newspaper to the plaintiff's agent constituted a separate publication in respect of which suit could be brought.

Thus, if X publishes a defamatory statement about the claimant to Y, and Y then communicates it to Z, both X and Y will be liable to the claimant for their respective publications, provided of course that they are unable to satisfy one of the defences. If Z then communicates the defamatory statement to another person, Z will be liable too.

Applying this to email, it will be appreciated that it is very easy for a person receiving an email to republish it, by use of the forward function and in no time at all an email can be circulating all around the globe. This 'viral' nature of email poses significant challenges for a person who is defamed, but in terms of defamation law the principles are straightforward: each person who forwards an email will be liable to the claimant.

### 5.4.3 Identification of the claimant

A claimant in a defamation claim will not be able to succeed if they are unable to show that the defamatory statement referred to them. In most cases this will not be an issue as the statement will identify the claimant by name, but this is not always the case. There are many instances of people being named by innuendo, due to a wide range of 'pointers', with well known cases including *Lloyd* v. *David Syme & Co* [1986] AC 350 (an allegation that a cricket match involving the West Indies team had been rigged, which the team captain alleged had defamed him), *Hayward* v. *Thompson* [1982] QB 47 (a newspaper article that alleged that a wealthy donor to the Liberal Party had been connected to a criminal investigation relating to the Jeremy Thorpe affair was said to have identified the claimant due to the paucity of wealthy donors to the Liberals) and *Youssoupoff* v. *MGN Pictures* (1934) 50 TLR 581 (a film about the murder of Rasputin which portrayed his killer's wife having sex with the monk, which enabled his real life killer's wife to sue for libel). The key issue in 'identification by innuendo' cases is whether a reasonable reader will understand the statement to be referring to the claimant, although where the pointers require special knowledge the question will be whether a reasonable reader with that special knowledge will understand the statement to be referring to the claimant. On these issues the claimant may adduce evidence from witnesses as to what they understood the statement to be saying, although this evidence does not bind the court; the question of identification is an objective issue. In cases like these the court adopts a two-stage approach. The first question is whether the statement is capable of identifying the claimant. This is a question of law for the judge. The second question is whether the statement did identify the claimant, which is a question of fact for the jury.

Similar considerations apply in respect of class libel. A statement may identify a class of people, and if the class is sufficiently small it will be possible for all members of the class to maintain that they have been identified.

### 5.4.4 Is the statement defamatory?

Assuming that a statement has been published, the first question will be, is the statement defamatory? This requires identification of the words complained of and identification of the meaning conveyed by the statement to the ordinary or reasonable person. The starting point is that the statement should be given its natural or ordinary meaning, although this is subject to acceptance of the fact that the ordinary or reasonable person will be capable of reading between the lines. However, the statement complained of should be considered in its full context, which is sometimes referred to as the 'bane and antidote' rule, and the publisher's intention in making the statement is irrelevant. However, if the statement consists of materials that would require special knowledge to understand, in the sense that the ordinary reader would not be able to discern the true meaning, the statement will contain an innuendo and it will be the innuendo which is the meaning. For example, slang, dialect and code may convey special meaning to people with special skills. Likewise, if a statement which on its face appears neutral or insignificant conveys another meaning to a person with special skill or knowledge, perhaps revealing hypocrisy within the person who is the subject of the statement, that innuendo will be the meaning.

Once the meaning of the statement has been identified, the next question is whether it is capable of being defamatory. This is a question of law for the judge. If the statement is capable of being defamatory, the next question is whether it is *actually* defamatory, which is a question of fact for the jury. Mere falsity on its own will not be enough to make a statement defamatory. Instead it must be one that tends to cause a reasonable person, a right-thinking member of society, to think worse of the claimant. In other words, the statement must have a negative effect on the reputation of the claimant, one that could cause a reasonable person to shun or avoid the claimant. There are many ways in which a statement can harm a person's reputation, for example, accusing a person of being a criminal, avoiding their financial obligations, or of having loose morals or being incompetent in their trade or profession.

However, before a court can conclude that a statement is defamatory it will also need to consider the range of defences that are open to the publisher. The starting point is that there is a presumption that the statement is false, with the burden being on the defendant to prove that it is true. If the defendant can prove that the statement is true, or substantially true, that will be the end of the matter. If not, the defendant will have to resort to the defences of fair comment and privilege. However, the fair comment and privilege defence cannot succeed where the statement is made maliciously.

### 5.4.5 Justification defence

The defence of justification applies where the defamatory statement is true or substantially true and it does not matter if the defendant is actuated by malice. In *Reynolds* v. *Times Newspapers Ltd* [1999] 3 WLR 1010 Lord Nicholls said:

> The defence of qualified privilege must be seen in its overall setting in the law of defamation. Historically the common law has set much store by protection of reputation. Publication of a statement adversely affecting a person's reputation is actionable. The plaintiff is not required to prove that the words are false. Nor, in the case of publication in a written or permanent form, is he required to prove he has been damaged. But, as Littledale J. said in *McPherson* v. *Daniels* (1829) 10 B. & C. 263, 272, 'the law will not permit a man to recover damages in respect of an injury to a character which he does not or ought not to possess'. Truth is a complete defence. If the defendant proves the substantial truth of the words complained of, he thereby establishes the defence of justification. With the minor exception of proceedings to which the Rehabilitation of Offenders Act 1974 applies, this defence is of universal application in civil proceedings. It avails a defendant even if he was acting spitefully.

There is a presumption of falsity in defamation law and the defendant carries the burden of proving justification, on the balance of probabilities. There is an important exception to the presumption of falsity and that concerns cases where the claimant complains that they have been defamed by an allegation of commission of a criminal offence. The rule is that a conviction is conclusive proof of the commission of the offence.

A statement can be substantially true if it addresses the 'sting' of the defamatory meaning contended for by the claimant. Thus, the presence of minor errors within an otherwise true statement will not defeat the defence of justification. On the other hand, if the statement is true it cannot have a defamatory meaning and the defendant will not need to plead justification.

The truth which the defendant has to prove in a justification defence is the truth of the meaning of the statement. If the defendant can prove the truth of certain matters within the statement, the defence of justification will fail if the truth is less serious that the true meaning of the statement complained of. However, the rule against repetition prevents a defendant from succeeding in a defence of justification to a claim arising from their reporting of another's defamatory statement by merely proving that the allegation was made. Instead, where a defendant reports another's defamatory statement they will have to prove the allegation is true to succeed on a justification defence.

Very often the defendant will make a range of separate and distinct allegations against the claimant, some of which will be true and some of which will be false. In these situations s.5 of the Defamation Act 1952 applies, which says:

**5. Justification**

> In an action for libel or slander in respect of words containing two or more distinct charges against the plaintiff, a defence of justification shall not fail by reason only that the truth of every charge is not proved if the words not proved to be true do not materially injure the plaintiff's reputation having regard to the truth of the remaining charges.

Section 5 makes it clear that the defence of justification will not be defeated by some falsities within the statement. However, a comparison of the gravity of the true allegations and the gravity of the false allegations needs to be carried out. If the false allegation is significantly more serious that the true one, the defence of justification will be defeated.

Furthermore, s.5 does not prevent the claimant from suing on one specific allegation within a range of separate and distinct allegations. If the claimant chooses to do so and the defendant fails to prove that the allegation complained of is true, the defendant will not be able to avail themselves of s.5 to prove the truth of the allegation that the claimant did not sue on. In the recent case of *Rath* v. *Guardian News and Media Limited, Ben Goldacre* [2008] EWHC 398 this point was identified and agreed by the parties. In the words of Mr Justice Tugendhat:

> It is common ground that a claimant is entitled to isolate in the words complained of a 'separate and distinct' defamatory statement, if there is one, and that the Defendants are not then entitled to assert the truth of other defamatory statements by way of justification.

However, if the separate and distinct allegations contain a common sting, the defendant could rely on s.5 even if the claimant chooses to sue on only one allegation. The common sting approach to separate and distinct allegations was at the heart of *Polly Peck (Holdings) plc and others* v. *Trelford and others* [1986] QB 1000 Lord Justice O'Conner said:

> Whether a defamatory statement is separate and distinct from other defamatory statements contained in the publication is a question of fact and degree in each case. The several defamatory allegations in their context may have a common sting, in which event they are not to be regarded as separate and distinct allegations. The defendant is entitled to justify the sting, and once again it is fortuitous that what is in fact similar fact evidence is found in the publication.

### 5.4.6 Fair comment defence

The fair comment defence can be taken in respect of defamatory statements of opinion. This distinguishes it from the justification defence, which, to recap, can only apply to defamatory statements that are true. However, it is important to appreciate that for the defence to apply the comment has to be based on facts that are true, or substantially true; in other words, the comment has to have a sufficient factual basis. This rule is modified for cases where the comment is based on defamatory statements that are protected by privilege. In these situations the defamatory 'facts' can be false but the fair comment defence will still apply. All of this is subject to the defendant showing that they honestly held their opinion and the publication of it being in the public interest. If the defendant's comment is made maliciously, the defence will fail, but for these purposes malice means the opinion not being honestly held; the defendant's motive for making the comment is irrelevant provided that their opinion is honestly held.

There will be situations in which the comment is based on a range of facts, only some of which will be false. The question is whether the presence of falsity can deprive the defendant from relying upon the fair comment defence, bearing in mind the condition that the factual basis behind the opinion must be true. The answer to this question is found in s.6 of the Defamation Act 1952, which says:

> **6. Fair comment**
>
> In an action for libel or slander in respect of words consisting partly of allegations of fact and partly of expression of opinion, a defence of fair comment shall not fail by reason only that the truth of every allegation of fact is not proved if the expression of opinion is fair comment having regard to such of the facts alleged or referred to in the words complained of as are proved.

Section 6 will save the defendant where some of the 'facts' are false, provided that the opinion can be supported by reference to the facts that are proved to be true.

The requirement to prove that the subject matter of the comment must be in the public interest causes difficulties. In *Jameel* v. *Wall Street Journal Europe SPRL (No.3)* [2006] UKHL 44 Lord Bingham reminded that it 'has been repeatedly and rightly said that what engages the interest of the public may not be material which engages the public interest'. In the same case Lord Hoffmann said:

> The question of whether the material concerned a matter of public interest is decided by the judge. As has often been said, the public tends to be interested in many things which are not of the slightest public interest and the newspapers are not often the best judges of where the line should be drawn. It is for the judge to apply the test of public interest.

As regards whether the comment must be fair, it seems that this component is no longer a feature of the fair comment defence. The issue is one of honestly held opinions. In *Reynolds* v. *Times Newspapers Ltd* [1999] 3 WLR 1010 Lord Nicholls said:

> Traditionally one of the ingredients of this defence is that the comment must be fair, fairness being judged by the objective standard of whether any fair-minded person could honestly express the opinion in question. Judges have emphasised the latitude to be applied in interpreting this standard. So much so, that the time has come to recognise that in this context the epithet 'fair' is now meaningless and misleading. Comment must be relevant to the facts to which it is addressed. It cannot be used as a cloak for mere invective. But the basis of our public life is that the crank, the enthusiast, may say what he honestly thinks as much as the reasonable person who sits on a jury. The true test is whether the opinion, however exaggerated, obstinate or prejudiced, was honestly held by the person expressing it: see Diplock J. in *Silkin* v. *Beaverbrook Newspapers Ltd.* [1958] 1 W.L.R. 743, 747.

### 5.4.7 Privilege defence

Where a statement is protected by privilege, a claim in defamation will fail even if the statement is false. For these purposes there are two kinds of privilege, namely absolute privilege and qualified privilege. As the name implies, absolute privilege acts as a complete bar to the bringing of proceedings. Qualified privilege is only a partial bar; it can be defeated if the statement is malicious, which will be the case where the defendant published their statement knowing it to be wrong, or if they were reckless as to its truth.

#### *Absolute privilege*

Absolute privilege, while very powerful, applies in only a small number of circumstances. The main ones are statements made in judicial or quasi-judicial proceedings, statements made in Parliament and in Parliamentary proceedings and statements contained in reports of court proceedings, providing they are fair, accurate and contemporaneously reported. The rules on reporting of court proceedings are contained in s.14 of the Defamation Act 1996, which says:

> **14. Reports of court proceedings absolutely privileged**
>
> (1) A fair and accurate report of proceedings in public before a court to which this section applies, if published contemporaneously with the proceedings, is absolutely privileged.
> (2) A report of proceedings which by an order of the court, or as a consequence of any statutory provision, is required to be postponed shall be treated as published contemporaneously if it is published as soon as practicable after publication is permitted.
> (3) This section applies to –
>
> (a) any court in the United Kingdom,
> (b) the European Court of Justice or any court attached to that court,
> (c) the European Court of Human Rights, and

(d) any international criminal tribunal established by the Security Council of the United Nations or by an international agreement to which the United Kingdom is a party.

In paragraph (a) 'court' includes any tribunal or body exercising the judicial power of the State.

## *Qualified privilege*

As regards qualified privilege there are three broad categories to be considered, namely 'duty and interest', media publications in the public interest (sometimes called *Reynolds* privilege or the defence of responsible journalism) and fair and accurate reporting. The second category, media publications in the public interest, is really a specialised subset of the first. Due to the frequency with which press and media companies are making use of email for the delivery and distribution of journalism, *Reynolds* privilege is an issue of substantial importance within a consideration of the interaction between email and the law of defamation.

### MALICE

As mentioned earlier, the defence of qualified privilege will be defeated by malice. In the recent case of *Rackham* v. *Sandy* [2005] EWHC 482 (QB) Mr Justice Gray said the following on malice:

> Were the Defendants – or, more accurately, was any of the Defendants – abusing the occasion in the sense that he was actuated by malice? The burden of proving malice rests on the Claimant, who has to establish his case by evidence of a cogency commensurate with the seriousness of charge. In the context of a defence of qualified privilege, malice may take the form of either a dominant improper motive or an absence of honest belief in the truth of what was published or both.

One of the leading judgments on the meaning of malice within the context of qualified privilege is Lord Diplock's in *Horrocks* v. *Lowe* [1975] AC 135, which is worth considering at some length:

> . . . in all cases of qualified privilege there is some special reason of public policy why the law accords immunity from suit – the existence of some public or private duty, whether legal or moral, on the part of the maker of the defamatory statement which justifies his communicating it or of some interest of his own which is entitled to protect by doing so. If he uses the occasion for some other reason he loses the protection of the privilege.
>
> So, the motive with which the defendant on a privileged occasion made a statement defamatory of the plaintiff becomes crucial. The protection might, however, be illusory if the onus lay on him to prove that he was actuated solely by a sense of the relevant duty or a desire to protect the relevant interest. So he is entitled to be protected by the privilege unless some other dominant and improper motive on his part is proved. 'Express malice' is the term of art descriptive of such a motive.

Broadly speaking, it means malice in the popular sense of a desire to injure the person who is defamed and this is generally the motive which the plaintiff sets out to prove. But to destroy the privilege the desire to injure must be the dominant motive for the defamatory publication; knowledge that it will have that effect is not enough if the defendant is nevertheless acting in accordance with a sense of duty or in bona fide protection of his own legitimate interests.

The motive with which a person published defamatory matter can only be inferred from what he did or said or knew. If it be proved that he did not believe that what he published was true this is generally conclusive evidence of express malice, for no sense of duty or desire to protect his own legitimate interests can justify a man in telling deliberate and injurious falsehoods about another, save in the exceptional case where a person may be under a duty to pass on, without endorsing, defamatory reports made by some other person.

Apart from those exceptional cases, what is required on the part of the defamer to entitle him to the protection of the privilege is positive belief in the truth of what he published or, as it is generally though tortologously termed, 'honest belief'. If he publishes untrue defamatory matter recklessly, without considering or caring whether it be true or not, he is in this, as in other branches of the law, treated as if he knew it to be false. But indifference to the truth of what he publishes is not to be equated with carelessness, impulsiveness or irrationality in arriving at a positive belief that it is true. The freedom of speech protected by the law of qualified privilege may be availed of by all sorts and conditions of men. In affording to them immunity from suit if they have acted in good faith in compliance with a legal or moral duty or in protection of a legitimate interest the law must take them as it finds them. In ordinary life it is rare indeed for people to form their beliefs by a process of logical deduction from facts ascertained by a rigorous search for all available evidence and a judicious assessment of its probative value. In greater or in less degree according to their temperaments, their training, their intelligence, they are swayed by prejudice, rely on intuition instead of reasoning, leap to conclusions on inadequate evidence and fail to recognise the cogency of material which might case doubt on the validity of the conclusions they reach. But despite the imperfection of the mental process by which the belief is arrive at it may still be 'honest', that is, a positive belief that the conclusions they have reached are true. The law demands no more.

Even a positive belief in the truth of what is published on a privileged occasion-which is presumed unless the contrary is proved-may not be sufficient to negative express malice if it can be proved that the defendant misused the occasion for some purpose other than that for which the privilege is accorded by the law. The commonest case is where the dominant motive which actuates the defendant is not a desire to perform the relevant duty or to protect the relevant interest, but to give vent to his personal spite or ill will towards the person he defames. If this be proved, then even positive belief in the truth of what is published will not enable the defamer to avail himself of the protection of the privilege to which he would otherwise have been entitled. There may be instances of improper motives which destroy the privilege apart from personal spite. A defendant's dominant motive may have been to obtain some private advantage unconnected with the duty or the interest which constitutes the reason for the privilege. If so, he loses the benefit of the privilege despite his positive belief that what he said or wrote was true.

Judges and juries should, however, be very slow to draw the inference that a defendant was so far actuated by improper motives as to deprive him of the protection of the privilege unless they are satisfied that he did not believe that what he said or wrote was true or that he was indifferent to its truth or falsity. The motives

> with which human beings act are mixed. They find it difficult to hate the sin but love the sinner. Qualified privilege would be illusory, and the public interest that it is meant to serve defeated, if the protection which it affords were lost merely because a person, although acting in compliance with a duty or in protection of a legitimate interest, disliked the person whom he defamed or was indignant at what he believed to be that person's conduct and welcomed the opportunity of exposing it. It is only where his desire to comply with the relevant duty or to protect the relevant interest plays no significant part in his motives for publishing what he believes to be true that 'express malice' can properly be found.

## DUTY AND INTEREST

The duty and interest category is non-statutory and it arises where both parties to the communication have either a duty or interest in the communication. What amounts to sufficient duty or interest is a fact sensitive issue, which is determined objectively, but for duty there are legal, social and moral duties to consider and for interest this generally arises in commercial and financial situations. If there is no reciprocity in the relationship between the maker of the statement and the recipient of it the defence of qualified privilege will fail. In the recent case of *Rackham* v. *Sandy*[4] [2005] EWHC 482 (QB), Mr Justice Gray summarised the principles within the defence of qualified privilege in the following terms:

> It will be convenient if, at this stage of the judgment and before coming to the facts in more detail, I summarised the principles of law applicable in this case. The classic definition of the circumstances under which a publication will be protected by qualified privilege at common law is to be found in *Adam* v *Ward* [1917] AC 309, per Lord Atkinson at 334: 'A privileged occasion . . . is an occasion where the person who makes communication has an interest or duty, legal, social or moral to make it to the person to whom it is made, and the person to whom it is made has a corresponding interest or duty to receive it. This reciprocity is essential'.

Situations where either a duty or interest will arise in the communication of a defamatory statement so as to engage the defence of qualified privilege include where the maker of the statement is responding to an inquiry, perhaps a police investigation or in the context of an internal workplace investigation into misconduct and where the maker of the statement is seeking redress of a grievance. Another situation that will be of interest to lawyers is where the communication is circulated within a membership body or association, as happened in *Kearns* v. *General Council of the Bar* [2003] 1 WLR 1357. In *Kearns* the Bar Council issued a circular to all heads of chambers which reached over 10,000 barristers. The circular wrongly informed barristers not to accept instructions from the claimant on the grounds that they were not solicitors. In the subsequent libel proceedings the Bar Council successfully claimed qualified privilege. Lord Justice Simon Brown, who gave the leading judgment in the case, gave the following summary of the facts and the issue:

> The present appeal concerns neither media publications nor an assertion of malice. The question arises here in the context of a communication between the Bar Council and its 10,132 members. The offending publication was a letter written by Mr Mark Stobbs, the head of the Bar Council's Professional Standards and Legal Services Department to all heads of chambers and senior clerks/practice managers. The letter concerned the Bar's Code of Conduct. It was written in the mistaken belief that the appellants are not solicitors. Undoubtedly it was libellous. Undoubtedly it was untrue. For the purposes of this appeal we must assume it was unverified. Was it nevertheless a publication made on an occasion protected by qualified privilege?

Simon Brown LJ was clearly very sympathetic to the claimant's plight, but he was clearly bound to find for the Bar Council. These concluding parts of his judgment illustrate the extent of the benefit within the qualified privilege defence for professional associations that publish defamatory statements:

> I would not wish to part from this appeal without expressing some considerable sympathy for these appellants. Were this to have been a media publication and Reynolds therefore to apply, there could be no question of qualified privilege attaching. And the Reynolds approach, one reflects, attaches on occasion to publications circulating no more widely and hardly more generally than in the present case - consider, for example, the Saudi Arabian newspaper with a circulation of some 1,500 readers in *Al-Fagih* -v- *HH Saudi Research Marketing (UK) Limited* [2001] EWCA Civ 1634. The law with regard to non-media publications, however, is different. Here, as Lord Diplock observed in *Horrocks* -v- *Lowe*, a man's right to 'vindicate his reputation against calumny' gives way to 'the competing public interest in permitting men to communicate frankly and freely with one another . . . if they have acted in good faith in compliance with a legal or moral duty or in protection of a legitimate interest' and in these cases 'the law demands no more' than that the defendant shall have honestly believed what he said. With regard to these duty or interest cases the law has decided that 'the common convenience and welfare of society' (*Toogood* -v- *Spyring*) is better served by allowing full and frank communication than by requiring the communicator to act responsibly. The media publisher, by contrast, has above all to act responsibly. There are, of course, a number of policy considerations in play here, some in conflict. They include considerations of legal certainty and the right to freedom of expression (a right enjoyed no less by those outside than those inside the media). Where in any particular type of case the balance should be struck raises deep and difficult questions. These are not, however, presently before us. No-one suggests on this appeal that we could or should be modifying the law. On the conventional approach to common law qualified privilege I am clear that in the circumstances of the present case the appellants must suffer and the respondent succeed.

## *REYNOLDS* PRIVILEGE – MEDIA PUBLICATIONS IN THE PUBLIC INTEREST AND RESPONSIBLE JOURNALISM

The next area of qualified privilege concerns media publications on matters of public interest, which is a variant of the duty-interest form in the sense that the press carries a duty to report matters which are in the public interest.

This form of qualified privilege provides a public interest defence to defamation claims for responsible journalism and it was first expressed in *Reynolds* v. *Times Newspapers Ltd* [1999] 3 WLR 1010. Before turning to the analysis, it is important to note that email is now an important vehicle for distribution of journalism. For example, a visit to the BBC website will reveal that every article is accompanied by a function that allows the reader to email the article 'to a friend'. As such this form of qualified privilege is likely to be of increasing important in the field of defamation.

The background to the *Reynolds* case was described by Lord Nicholls:

> The events giving rise to these proceedings took place during a political crisis in Dublin in November 1994. The crisis culminated in the resignation of Mr. Reynolds as Taoiseach (prime minister) of Ireland and leader of the Fianna Fáil party. The reasons for Mr. Reynolds' resignation were of public significance and interest in the United Kingdom because of his personal identification with the Northern Ireland peace process. Mr. Reynolds was one of the chief architects of that process. He announced his resignation in the Dáil (the House of Representatives) of the Irish Parliament on Thursday, 17 November 1994. On the following Sunday, 20 November, the 'Sunday Times' published in its British mainland edition an article entitled 'Goodbye gombeen man.' The article was the lead item in its world news section and occupied most of one page. The article was sub-headed 'Why a fib too far proved fatal for the political career of Ireland's peacemaker and Mr. Fixit'. On the same day the Irish edition of the 'Sunday Times' contained a three page article headed 'House of Cards' concerning the fall of the Government. This article differed in a number of respects from the British mainland edition.

The House of Lords held that the duty and interest form of qualified privilege could cover journalistic activities, if the public had a right to know the information that was being published. This construction satisfies the reciprocity element within the duty-interest. The considerations within this 'public interest defence' as identified by Lord Nicholls are:

1. The seriousness of the allegation. The more serious the charge, the more the public is misinformed and the individual harmed, if the allegation is not true.
2. The nature of the information, and the extent to which the subject-matter is a matter of public concern.
3. The source of the information. Some informants have no direct knowledge of the events. Some have their own axes to grind, or are being paid for their stories.
4. The steps taken to verify the information.
5. The status of the information. The allegation may have already been the subject of an investigation which commands respect.
6. The urgency of the matter. News is often a perishable commodity.
7. Whether comment was sought from the defendant. He may have information others do not possess or have not disclosed. An approach to the defendant will not always be necessary.
8. Whether the article contained the gist of the plaintiff's side of the story.

9. The tone of the article. A newspaper can raise queries or call for an investigation. It need not adopt allegations as statements of fact.
10. The circumstances of the publication, including the timing.

However, Lord Nicholls did not consider that *The Sunday Times* had established the public interest defence. The article was one-sided and it presented allegation as fact. Lord Nicholls said:

> Was the information in the 'Sunday Times' article information the public was entitled to know? The subject matter was undoubtedly of public concern in this country. However, these serious allegations by the newspaper, presented as statements of fact but shorn of all mention of Mr. Reynolds' considered explanation, were not information the public had a right to know. I agree with the Court of Appeal this was not a publication which should in the public interest be protected by privilege in the absence of proof of malice.

Lord Nicholls anticipated that 'over time, a valuable corpus of case law will be built up' in the area of qualified privilege, which has happened (see, for example, *Bonnick* v. *Morris* [2003] 1 AC 300).

Perhaps the most important case since *Reynolds* is *Jameel* v. *Wall Street Journal Europe SPRL (No.3)* [2006] UKHL 44, a decision of the House of Lords. The facts of the case as summarised by Lord Bingham are:

> On 6 February 2002 the newspaper published the article which gave rise to these proceedings. It was headed 'Saudi Officials Monitor Certain Bank Accounts' with a smaller sub-heading 'Focus Is on Those With Potential Terrorist Ties'. It bore the by-line of James M Dorsey, an Arabic-speaking reporter with specialist knowledge of Saudi Arabia, and acknowledged the contribution of Glenn Simpson, a staff writer in Washington. The gist of the article, succinctly stated in the first paragraph, was that the Saudi Arabian Monetary Authority, the Kingdom's central bank, was, at the request of US law enforcement agencies, monitoring bank accounts associated with some of the country's most prominent businessmen in a bid to prevent them from being used, wittingly or unwittingly, for the funnelling of funds to terrorist organisations. This information was attributed to 'U.S. officials and Saudis familiar with the issue'. In the second paragraph a number of companies and individuals were named, among them 'the Abdullatif Jamil Group of companies' who, it was stated later in the article, 'couldn't be reached for comment'.

The main issue on the appeal was the extent to which the defendant could rely upon qualified privilege as arising in *Reynolds*. In other words, was the publication of the report in the public interest? Repeating the opinion of Lord Nicholls in *Reynolds*, Lord Hoffmann described the test facing the defendant as being one of 'responsible journalism' and he saw three issues to be key, namely 'the steps taken to verify the story, the opportunity given to the Jameel group to comment and the propriety of publication in the light of US diplomatic policy at the time'. On a majority decision the House of Lords held that the defence had been made out; publication of the story was in the public interest, sufficient steps had been taken to verify the story and the claimant had been given an opportunity to comment. Baroness Hale said:

> If ever there was a story which met the test, it must be this one. In the immediate aftermath of 9/11, it was in the interests of the whole world that the sources of funds for such atrocities be identified and if possible stopped. There was and should have been a lively public debate about this. Given the nationalities of the hi-jackers, this focussed particularly upon the efforts of the Saudi Arabian authorities. Anti-Saudi feeling was running high in some places. Information that the Saudis were actively co-operating, not only with the United Nations, but also with the United States was of great importance to that debate. This was, in effect, a pro-Saudi story, but one which, for internal reasons, the Saudi authorities were bound to deny. Without names, its impact would be much reduced.
>
> Secondly, the publisher must have taken the care that a responsible publisher would take to verify the information published. The actual steps taken will vary with the nature and sources of the information. But one would normally expect that the source or sources were ones which the publisher had good reason to think reliable, that the publisher himself believed the information to be true, and that he had done what he could to check it. We are frequently told that 'fact checking' has gone out of fashion with the media. But a publisher who is to avoid the risk of liability if the information cannot later be proved to be true would be well-advised to do it. Part of this is, of course, taking reasonable steps to contact the people named for their comments. The requirements in 'reportage' cases, where the publisher is simply reporting what others have said, may be rather different, but if the publisher does not himself believe the information to be true, he would be well-advised to make this clear. In any case, the tone in which the information is conveyed will be relevant to whether or not the publisher has behaved responsibly in passing it on.
>
> Once again, as my noble and learned friend Lord Hoffmann has demonstrated, the publication of this story passed this test. We have to judge the steps which are known to have been taken against the background of the style and tone of the publication in general and the article in particular. This is not a newspaper with an interest in publishing any sensational information however inaccurate (or even in some cases invented). It is, as the journalist quoted by my noble and learned friend said, 'gravely serious' (indeed some might find it seriously dull). We need more such serious journalism in this country and our defamation law should encourage rather than discourage it.
>
> In short, My Lords, if the public interest defence does not succeed on the known facts of this case, it is hard to see it ever succeeding.

### *Fair and accurate reporting*

Section 15 of the Defamation Act 1996 is the sibling of s.14 and it sets out the circumstances in which certain reports and statements will be covered by qualified privilege. Section 15 says:

**15. Reports, etc. protected by qualified privilege**

(1) The publication of any report or other statement mentioned in Schedule 1 to this Act is privileged unless the publication is shown to be made with malice, subject as follows.

(2) In defamation proceedings in respect of the publication of a report or other statement mentioned in Part II of that Schedule, there is no defence under this section if the plaintiff shows that the defendant –

(a) was requested by him to publish in a suitable manner a reasonable letter or statement by way of explanation or contradiction, and

(b) refused or neglected to do so.

For this purpose 'in a suitable manner' means in the same manner as the publication complained of or in a manner that is adequate and reasonable in the circumstances.

(3) This section does not apply to the publication to the public, or a section of the public, of matter which is not of public concern and the publication of which is not for the public benefit.

(4) Nothing in this section shall be construed –

(a) as protecting the publication of matter the publication of which is prohibited by law, or

(b) as limiting or abridging any privilege subsisting apart from this section.

As can be seen, there are two kinds of reports and statements falling within the scope of s.15. As far as reports are concerned in both cases they have to be 'fair and accurate'. The first kind of report and statement is one falling within Sched.1, Part I being ones 'having qualified privilege without explanation or contradiction'. In summary, these reports and statements will be protected by qualified privilege provided that they are of public concern and made for the public benefit, are not malicious and are not prohibited by law. The second kind is one falling within Sched.1, Part I being one that is 'privileged subject to explanation or contradiction'. The same conditions apply as with the first kind, but if the defendant fails to comply with the claimant's request for publications of the claimant's reasonable letter or statement of explanation or correction the defence will be lost. The defendant bears the burden of proof on the issues of public concern and public benefit. Regarding fairness and accuracy, again the burden is on the defendant to prove these matters. Total accuracy is not required, only substantial accuracy, but if the report or statement contains a substantial inaccuracy the defence will be defeated, particularly in the context of omission of material matters, a failing that can render the report or statement unfair. **Table 5.2** identifies the reports that fall within Sched.1.

**Table 5.2** Reports protected by qualified privilege under the Defamation Act 1996

| Schedule 1, Part I | Schedule 1, Part II |
|---|---|
| Statements having qualified privilege without explanation or contradiction | Statements privileged subject to explanation or contradiction |
| A fair and accurate report of proceedings in public of a legislature anywhere in the world. | (1) A fair and accurate copy of or extract from a notice or other matter issued for the information of the public by or on behalf of –<br>(a) a legislature in any member State or the European Parliament;<br>(b) the government of any member State, or any authority performing governmental functions in any member State or part of a member State, or the European Commission;<br>(c) an international organisation or international conference.<br>(2) In this paragraph 'governmental functions' includes police functions. |
| A fair and accurate report of proceedings in public before a court anywhere in the world. | A fair and accurate copy of or extract from a document made available by a court in any member State or the European Court of Justice (or any court attached to that court), or by a judge or officer of any such court. |
| A fair and accurate report of proceedings in public of a person appointed to hold a public inquiry by a government or legislature anywhere in the world. | (1) A fair and accurate report of proceedings at any public meeting or sitting in the United Kingdom of –<br>(a) a local authority, local authority committee or in the case of a local authority which are operating executive arrangements the executive of that authority or a committee of that executive;<br>(b) a justice or justices of the peace acting otherwise than as a court exercising judicial authority;<br>(c) a commission, tribunal, committee or person appointed for the purposes of any inquiry by any statutory provision, by Her Majesty or by a Minister of the Crown, a member of the Scottish Executive, the Welsh Ministers or the Counsel General to the Welsh Assembly Government or a Northern Ireland Department; |

**Table 5.2** *Cont.*

| Schedule 1, Part I | Schedule 1, Part II |
|---|---|
| | (d) a person appointed by a local authority to hold a local inquiry in pursuance of any statutory provision;<br>(e) any other tribunal, board, committee or body constituted by or under, and exercising functions under, any statutory provision.<br><br>(1A) In the case of a local authority which are operating executive arrangements, a fair and accurate record of any decision made by any member of the executive where that record is required to be made and available for public inspection by virtue of section 22 of the Local Government Act 2000 or of any provision in regulations made under that section. |
| A fair and accurate report of proceedings in public anywhere in the world of an international organisation or an international conference | (1) A fair and accurate report of proceedings at any public meeting held in a member State.<br>(2) In this paragraph a 'public meeting' organisation or an international conference. means a meeting bona fide and lawfully held for a lawful purpose and for the furtherance or discussion of a matter of public concern, whether admission to the meeting is general or restricted. |
| A fair and accurate copy of or extract from any register or other document required by law to be open to public inspection. | (1) A fair and accurate report of proceedings at a general meeting of a UK public company.<br>(2) A fair and accurate copy of or extract from any document circulated to members of a UK public company –<br><br>(a) by or with the authority of the board of directors of the company,<br>(b) by the auditors of the company, or<br>(c) by any member of the company in pursuance of a right conferred by any statutory provision.<br><br>(3) A fair and accurate copy of or extract from any document circulated to members of a UK public company which relates to the appointment, resignation, retirement or dismissal of directors of the company. |

**Table 5.2** *Cont.*

| **Schedule 1, Part I** | **Schedule 1, Part II** |
| --- | --- |
| A notice or advertisement published by or on the authority of a court, or of a judge or officer of a court, anywhere in the world. | A fair and accurate report of any finding or decision of any of the following descriptions of association, formed in the United Kingdom or another member State, or of any committee or governing body of such an association – <br><br>(a) an association formed for the purpose of promoting or encouraging the exercise of or interest in any art, science, religion or learning, and empowered by its constitution to exercise control over or adjudicate on matters of interest or concern to the association, or the actions or conduct of any person subject to such control or adjudication;<br>(b) an association formed for the purpose of promoting or safeguarding the interests of any trade, business, industry or profession, or of the persons carrying on or engaged in any trade, business, industry or profession, and empowered by its constitution to exercise control over or adjudicate upon matters connected with that trade, business, industry or profession, or the actions or conduct of those persons;<br>(c) an association formed for the purpose of promoting or safeguarding the interests of a game, sport or pastime to the playing or exercise of which members of the public are invited or admitted, and empowered by its constitution to exercise control over or adjudicate upon persons connected with or taking part in the game, sport or pastime;<br>(d) an association formed for the purpose of promoting charitable objects or other objects beneficial to the community and empowered by its constitution to exercise control over or to adjudicate on matters of interest or concern to the association, or the actions or conduct of any person subject to such control or adjudication. |

**Table 5.2** *Cont.*

| Schedule 1, Part I | Schedule 1, Part II |
|---|---|
| A fair and accurate copy of or extract from matter published by or on the authority of a government or legislature anywhere in the world. | (1) A fair and accurate report of, or copy of or extract from, any adjudication, report, statement or notice issued by a body, officer or other person designated for the purposes of this paragraph –<br>(a) for England and Wales or Northern Ireland, by order of the Lord Chancellor, and<br>(b) for Scotland, by order of the Secretary of State. |
| A fair and accurate copy of or extract from matter published anywhere in the world by an international organisation or an international conference. | |

## 5.5 DISCRIMINATION

Unfortunately, email also lends itself perfectly to the dissemination of discriminatory materials. The reason for this probably lies in the fact that people use email in an informal manner, often as a substitute for conversation rather than as a substitute for written correspondence, without giving much, if any, thought to the fact that emails have a degree of permanence and are disclosable in litigation. Thus, the primary focus of this part is how discrimination can occur through the use of email or how email can be evidence of discrimination. There are a number of ways in which an email can be discriminatory or act as evidence of discrimination, for example:

- People can send emails to groups of people. The selection of the members of the group may reflect underlying discriminatory behaviour, whether intentional or innocent or somewhere in between. For example, an email might invite only the male members of a workplace to a regular social engagement, or only heterosexual members, or only white members, or only young members, or only able-bodied members.
- The physical components within the use of email might be discriminatory to disabled persons. For example, a blind person might be able to sustain a claim for disability discrimination because their employer failed to make sufficient adaptations, such as the provision of text reader applications.

- The words used in the email might be discriminatory in themselves. Sadly, racist, sexist, ageist and homophobic emails are still very regular occurrences.

The scope of prohibited acts is vast. Legislation currently exists to prohibit discrimination on the grounds of age, disability, marital and civil partnership status, race, religion, sexual orientation and sex. A work of this nature can only scratch at the surface of the complex worlds of discrimination law, but it is hoped that the following discussion will bring home the message that emails can cause people and organisations significant problems from the perspective of discrimination law.

This part focuses only on discrimination in the workplace.

### 5.5.1 Age discrimination

The main legislation in the field of age discrimination is the Employment Equality (Age) Regulations (EE(A)R) 2006, SI 2006/1031, which came into force on 1 October 2006. The regulations apply to age discrimination in the field of employment and vocational training. In addition to the employer-employee relationship, the regulations cover contract workers (reg.9), pension schemes (reg.11), office holders (reg.12), the police (reg.13), barristers (reg.15), advocates (reg.16) and partnerships (reg.17).

The regulations apply to those in employment at establishments in Great Britain and to applicants for employment. Regulation 7 says:

**7. Applicants and employees**

(1) It is unlawful for an employer, in relation to employment by him at an establishment in Great Britain, to discriminate against a person –

(a) in the arrangements he makes for the purpose of determining to whom he should offer employment;
(b) in the terms on which he offers that person employment; or
(c) by refusing to offer, or deliberately not offering, him employment.

(2) It is unlawful for an employer, in relation to a person whom he employs at an establishment in Great Britain, to discriminate against that person –

(a) in the terms of employment which he affords him;
(b) in the opportunities which he affords him for promotion, a transfer, training, or receiving any other benefit;
(c) by refusing to afford him, or deliberately not affording him, any such opportunity; or
(d) by dismissing him, or subjecting him to any other detriment.

(3) It is unlawful for an employer, in relation to employment by him at an establishment in Great Britain, to subject to harassment a person whom he employs or who has applied to him for employment.

(4) Subject to paragraph (5), paragraph (1)(a) and (c) does not apply in relation to a person –

(a) whose age is greater than the employer's normal retirement age or, if the employer does not have a normal retirement age, the age of 65; or

(b) who would, within a period of six months from the date of his application to the employer, reach the employer's normal retirement age or, if the employer does not have a normal retirement age, the age of 65.

(5) Paragraph (4) only applies to a person to whom, if he was recruited by the employer, regulation 30 (exception for retirement) could apply.

(6) Paragraph (2) does not apply to benefits of any description if the employer is concerned with the provision (for payment or not) of benefits of that description to the public, or to a section of the public which includes the employee in question, unless –

(a) that provision differs in a material respect from the provision of the benefits by the employer to his employees; or

(b) the provision of the benefits to the employee in question is regulated by his contract of employment; or

(c) the benefits relate to training.

(7) In paragraph (2)(d) reference to the dismissal of a person from employment includes reference –

(a) to the termination of that person's employment by the expiration of any period (including a period expiring by reference to an event or circumstance), not being a termination immediately after which the employment is renewed on the same terms; and

(b) to the termination of that person's employment by any act of his (including the giving of notice) in circumstances such that he is entitled to terminate it without notice by reason of the conduct of the employer.

(8) In paragraph (4) 'normal retirement age' is an age of 65 or more which meets the requirements of section 98ZH of the 1996 Act.

The regulations also apply to members and prospective members of occupational pension schemes and, in limited circumstances, to persons after employment has ended (reg.24).

The regulations identify four kinds of discrimination, namely:

- discrimination on the grounds of age (reg.3);
- discrimination by way of victimisation (reg.4);
- instructions to discriminate (reg.5);
- harassment (reg.5).

### *Discrimination on the grounds of age*

Discrimination on the grounds of age falls into two categories, namely direct discrimination and indirect discrimination. Unlike cases of direct disability discrimination, direct age discrimination can be justified. Indirect age discrimination, like indirect disability discrimination, can be justified also. Regulation 3 says:

**3. Discrimination on grounds of age**

(1) For the purposes of these Regulations, a person ('A') discriminates against another person ('B') if –

(a) on grounds of B's age, A treats B less favourably than he treats or would treat other persons, or
(b) A applies to B a provision, criterion or practice which he applies or would apply equally to persons not of the same age group as B, but –

(i) which puts or would put persons of the same age group as B at a particular disadvantage when compared with other persons, and
(ii) which puts B at that disadvantage,

and A cannot show the treatment or, as the case may be, provision, criterion or practice to be a proportionate means of achieving a legitimate aim.

(2) A comparison of B's case with that of another person under paragraph (1) must be such that the relevant circumstances in the one case are the same, or not materially different, in the other.
(3) In this regulation –

(a) 'age group' means a group of persons defined by reference to age, whether by reference to a particular age or a range of ages; and
(b) the reference in paragraph (1)(a) to B's age includes B's apparent age.

Direct discrimination is addressed in reg.3(1)(a) and occurs if the employer treats the complainant less favourably on the grounds of age when compared to other persons. However, the treatment will be justified if it is a proportionate means of achieving a legitimate aim. Regarding the burden of proof the complainant need only prove facts that would allow the Employment Tribunal to conclude in the absence of a sufficient explanation from the employer that the reason for the unfavourable treatment was age. As regards justification, to succeed with the defence the employer needs to go further than proving that there was a legitimate aim behind the less favourable treatment; the employer also has to show that the treatment was proportionate, in other words, was appropriate and reasonably necessary for achieving the legitimate aim.

Indirect discrimination is addressed in reg.3(1)(b). The essence of indirect discrimination is:

- the employer applies against the complainant a provision, criterion or practice; and
- the provision, criterion or practice is applied against persons of a different age group to the complainant; and
- the provision, criterion or practice would be likely to put a persons of the complainant's age group at a particular disadvantage; and

- the provision, criterion or practice actually puts the complainant at a disadvantage; and
- the provision, criterion or practice is not justified.

### *Discrimination by way of victimisation*

The essence of victimisation is that the complainant is treated less favourably than other persons due to having taken advantage of their protections under the regulations, whether through Employment Tribunal proceedings or by making a complaint, or has given evidence in such proceedings or assisted others in their bringing of complaints or proceedings under the regulations. Victimisation cannot be justified. Regulation 4 says:

> **4. Discrimination by way of victimisation**
>
> (1) For the purposes of these Regulations, a person ('A') discriminates against another person ('B') if he treats B less favourably than he treats or would treat other persons in the same circumstances, and does so by reason that B has –
>
> (a) brought proceedings against A or any other person under or by virtue of these Regulations;
>
> (b) given evidence or information in connection with proceedings brought by any person against A or any other person under or by virtue of these Regulations;
>
> (c) otherwise done anything under or by reference to these Regulations in relation to A or any other person; or
>
> (d) alleged that A or any other person has committed an act which (whether or not the allegation so states) would amount to a contravention of these Regulations,
>
> or by reason that A knows that B intends to do any of those things, or suspects that B has done or intends to do any of them.
>
> (2) Paragraph (1) does not apply to treatment of B by reason of any allegation made by him, or evidence or information given by him, if the allegation, evidence or information was false and not made (or, as the case may be, given) in good faith.

Victimisation under reg.4 follows the same pattern as under disability discrimination legislations.

### *Instructions to discriminate*

Discriminating against a person because they refuse to comply with an instruction that they should discriminate, or because they complain after being issued with an instruction to discriminate, is also unlawful and cannot be justified. Regulation 5 says:

**5. Instructions to discriminate**

For the purposes of these Regulations, a person ('A') discriminates against another person ('B') if he treats B less favourably than he treats or would treat other persons in the same circumstances, and does so by reason that –

(a) B has not carried out (in whole or in part) an instruction to do an act which is unlawful by virtue of these Regulations, or
(b) B, having been given an instruction to do such an act, complains to A or to any other person about that instruction.

## *Harassment*

The way in which harassment is formulated in reg.6 of the EE(A)R 2006 means that emails are very likely to be vehicles for harassment. Harassment occurs where a person's dignity is violated or where an intimidating, hostile, degrading, humiliating or offensive environment is created for the person of a specific age group. Although the test of harassment is an objective one, the feelings of the harassed person are relevant considerations.

As regards the requirement that the conduct should be unwarranted, the EE(A)R 2006 do not impose an obligation on the employee to communicate a message to the employer that it is unwarranted. Rather, the question of whether conduct is unwarranted is a question of fact for the Employment Tribunal to decide.

Regulation 6 says:

**6. Harassment on grounds of age**

(1) For the purposes of these Regulations, a person ('A') subjects another person ('B') to harassment where, on grounds of age, A engages in unwanted conduct which has the purpose or effect of –
 (a) violating B's dignity; or
 (b) creating an intimidating, hostile, degrading, humiliating or offensive environment for B.
(2) Conduct shall be regarded as having the effect specified in paragraph (1)(a) or (b) only if, having regard to all the circumstances, including in particular the perception of B, it should reasonably be considered as having that effect.

## *Vicarious liability*

An employer will be liable for any unlawful acts committed by its employees during the course of their employment, irrespective of whether such acts were done with the employer's knowledge or approval. The employer has a defence of taking all reasonable steps to prevent the discrimination. Regulation 25 says:

**25. Liability of employers and principals**

(1) Anything done by a person in the course of his employment shall be treated for the purposes of these Regulations as done by his employer as well as by him, whether or not it was done with the employer's knowledge or approval.
(2) Anything done by a person as agent for another person with the authority (whether express or implied, and whether precedent or subsequent) of that other person shall be treated for the purposes of these Regulations as done by that other person as well as by him.
(3) In proceedings brought under these Regulations against any person in respect of an act alleged to have been done by an employee of his it shall be a defence for that person to prove that he took such steps as were reasonably practicable to prevent the employee from doing that act, or from doing in the course of his employment acts of that description.

### 5.5.2 Disability discrimination

The main legislation in the field of disability discrimination is the Disability Discrimination Act (DDA) 1995, as amended by the Disability Discrimination Act 1995 (Amendment) Regulations 2003, SI 2003/1673, and the Disability Discrimination Act 2005. References to DDA 1995 in this section are to the 1995 Act as amended by the 2003 Regulations and 2005 Act.

The DDA 1995 covers a number of different fields. Part II of the Act concerns the employment field; Part III concerns the provision of goods, facilities and services, the functions of public authorities, the activities of private clubs and the disposition of premises; Part IV concerns the provision of education; and Part V concerns public transport.

The meaning of disability and disabled is contained in DDA 1995, s.1:

**1. Meaning of 'disability' and 'disabled person'**

(1) Subject to the provisions of Schedule 1, a person has a disability for the purposes of this Act if he has a physical or mental impairment which has a substantial and long-term adverse effect on his ability to carry out normal day-to-day activities.
(2) In this Act 'disabled person' means a person who has a disability.

For these purposes, 'substantial' means more than minor or trivial and 'long-term' means that the effect has lasted or is likely to last at least 12 months, or it is likely to last for the rest of the person's life, or if it is likely to recur if in remission (DDA 1995, Sched.1, para.2(1), (2)). The kinds of impairments which are regarded as affecting a person's ability to carry out their normal day-to-day activities are those which affect the person's mobility, manual dexterity, physical coordination, continence, ability to lift, carry or otherwise move everyday objects, speech, hearing or eyesight, memory or ability to concentrate, learn or understand or their perception of the risk of danger

(Sched.1, para.4(1)). It is question of fact whether a condition is or is not substantial.

The Disability Discrimination (Meaning of Disability) Regulations 1996, SI 1996/1455 provide interpretation on the meaning of impairment. Conditions that are not regarded as being impairments for the purpose of the DDA 1995 are alcohol, nicotine and substance addictions (SI 1996/1455, reg.3), unless they result from being medically prescribed or from medical treatment, tendencies to start fires, theft, physical or sexual abuse, exhibitionism and voyeurism (reg.4), hay fever, unless it aggravates another condition (reg.4), tattoos and non-medical body piercings (reg.5). Severe disfigurement can amount to an impairment however (DDA 1995, Sched.1, para.3), as can controlled or corrected impairments, if the absence of control or correction would have a substantial adverse effect on the person concerned (DDA 1995, Sched.1, para.6). A person with cancer, HIV or multiple sclerosis is deemed to have a disability (DDA 1995, Sched.1, para.6A).

In the case of *Goodwin* v. *The Patent Office* [1999] IRLR 4 the Employment Appeal Tribunal provided detailed guidance on the approach to be adopted by the Employment Tribunal when determining whether or not a person is disabled. In particular, the Employment Tribunal must have regard to the 'pleadings' in the case (the originating application and the response), it must adopt a purposive approach to construction of the legislation and it must have regard to the Code of Practice on Disability Discrimination issued by the Secretary of State under DDA 1995, s.3.

### *Disability discrimination in the employment field*

The employment field is exceptionally wide, covering the traditional employer-employee relationship (DDA 1995, ss.4, 4A) as well as contract workers (s.4B), office holders (ss.4C–4F), partnerships (ss.6A–6C), occupational pension schemes (ss.4G–4K) and barristers and advocates (ss.7A–7D). In this section the traditional employer-employee relationship is discussed, but the principles outlined below are of general application.

The DDA 1995 makes it unlawful for an employer to discriminate against a disabled person and to subject a disabled person to harassment. The Act covers the steps leading to the creation of the employer-employee relationship as well as events occurring thereafter. DDA 1995, s.4 says:

**4. Employers: discrimination and harassment**

(1) It is unlawful for an employer to discriminate against a disabled person –

(a) in the arrangements which he makes for the purpose of determining to whom he should offer employment;

(b) in the terms on which he offers that person employment; or
(c) by refusing to offer, or deliberately not offering, him employment.

(2) It is unlawful for an employer to discriminate against a disabled person whom he employs –

(a) in the terms of employment which he affords him;
(b) in the opportunities which he affords him for promotion, a transfer, training or receiving any other benefit;
(c) by refusing to afford him, or deliberately not affording him, any such opportunity; or
(d) by dismissing him, or subjecting him to any other detriment.

(3) It is also unlawful for an employer, in relation to employment by him, to subject to harassment –

(a) a disabled person whom he employs; or
(b) a disabled person who has applied to him for employment.

(4) Subsection (2) does not apply to benefits of any description if the employer is concerned with the provision (whether or not for payment) of benefits of that description to the public, or to a section of the public which includes the employee in question, unless –

(a) that provision differs in a material respect from the provision of the benefits by the employer to his employees;
(b) the provision of the benefits to the employee in question is regulated by his contract of employment; or
(c) the benefits relate to training.

(5) The reference in subsection (2)(d) to the dismissal of a person includes a reference –

(a) to the termination of that person's employment by the expiration of any period (including a period expiring by reference to an event or circumstance), not being a termination immediately after which the employment is renewed on the same terms; and
(b) to the termination of that person's employment by any act of his (including the giving of notice) in circumstances such that he is entitled to terminate it without notice by reason of the conduct of the employer.

(6) This section applies only in relation to employment at an establishment in Great Britain.

'Discrimination' and 'harassment' are defined in ss.3A and 3B in the following terms:

**3A. Meaning of 'discrimination'**

(1) For the purposes of this Part, a person discriminates against a disabled person if –

(a) for a reason which relates to the disabled person's disability, he treats him less favourably than he treats or would treat others to whom that reason does not or would not apply, and
(b) he cannot show that the treatment in question is justified.

(2) For the purposes of this Part, a person also discriminates against a disabled person if he fails to comply with a duty to make reasonable adjustments imposed on him in relation to the disabled person.

(3) Treatment is justified for the purposes of subsection (1)(b) if, but only if, the reason for it is both material to the circumstances of the particular case and substantial.

(4) But treatment of a disabled person cannot be justified under subsection (3) if it amounts to direct discrimination falling within subsection (5).

(5) A person directly discriminates against a disabled person if, on the ground of the disabled person's disability, he treats the disabled person less favourably than he treats or would treat a person not having that particular disability whose relevant circumstances, including his abilities, are the same as, or not materially different from, those of the disabled person.

(6) If, in a case falling within subsection (1), a person is under a duty to make reasonable adjustments in relation to a disabled person but fails to comply with that duty, his treatment of that person cannot be justified under subsection (3) unless it would have been justified even if he had complied with that duty.

**3B. Meaning of 'harassment'**

(1) For the purposes of this Part, a person subjects a disabled person to harassment where, for a reason which relates to the disabled person's disability, he engages in unwanted conduct which has the purpose or effect of –

  (a) violating the disabled person's dignity, or
  (b) creating an intimidating, hostile, degrading, humiliating or offensive environment for him.

(2) Conduct shall be regarded as having the effect referred to in paragraph (a) or (b) of subsection (1) only if, having regard to all the circumstances, including in particular the perception of the disabled person, it should reasonably be considered as having that effect.

### *Types of disability discrimination and harassment in the employment field*

Reading DDA 1995, ss.3A and 3B in conjunction with s.55 (which deals with victimisation), there are five broad categories of claim that a disabled person can bring under the DDA 1995. These are:

- direct discrimination, which happens when on the grounds of their disability a person is treated less favourably than a person without that disability (DDA 1995, s.3A(5));
- disability-related discrimination, which happens when for a reason relating to their disability a person is treated less favourably than others to whom that reason does not apply, but if the treatment can be objectively justified it will not amount to discrimination (s.3A(1));
- failure to make reasonable adjustments (s.3A(6));

- harassment (s.3B);
- victimisation (s.55).

A complaint about disability discrimination is brought before the Employment Tribunal (s.17A(1)).

### *Direct discrimination*

Cases of direct discrimination can never be justified, and in order to determine whether direct discrimination has occurred the treatment of the disabled person must be compared with the treatment of a person having the same abilities as the disabled person, but not the disability. If the comparator is treated more favourably, that will amount to direct discrimination, unless the employer can show that the reason for different treatment was not the disability.

### *Disability-related discrimination*

In disability-related discrimination cases the disabled person only has to show that the reason for their treatment was related to their disability and that they were treated differently than a person to whom the reason for treatment did not apply. Once this has been established, the employer will have to justify the treatment, failing which a claim of disability discrimination will be made out.

An example of disability-related discrimination would be a failure to include a disabled person in an email invitation to a work social occasion, perhaps a lunch at a local restaurant. In this situation the failure to issue an invitation would be 'treatment' for the purposes of DDA 1995, s.3A(1). If the reason for not inviting the disabled person is because their impaired mobility would slow down the journey to and from the restaurant and thereby reduce the time available for the meal, the treatment would be disability-related and the disabled person would succeed in a discrimination claim, unless the employer could justify it.

### *Failure to make adjustments*

Discrimination on the grounds of failing to make adjustments builds upon the employer's duty in DDA 1995, s.4A. This says:

> **4A. Employers: duty to make adjustments**
>
> (1) Where –
>
> (a) a provision, criterion or practice applied by or on behalf of an employer, or
> (b) any physical feature of premises occupied by the employer,

places the disabled person concerned at a substantial disadvantage in comparison with persons who are not disabled, it is the duty of the employer to take such steps as it is reasonable, in all the circumstances of the case, for him to have to take in order to prevent the provision, criterion or practice, or feature, having that effect.

(2) In subsection (1), 'the disabled person concerned' means –

  (a) in the case of a provision, criterion or practice for determining to whom employment should be offered, any disabled person who is, or has notified the employer that he may be, an applicant for that employment;
  (b) in any other case, a disabled person who is –
    (i) an applicant for the employment concerned, or
    (ii) an employee of the employer concerned.

(3) Nothing in this section imposes any duty on an employer in relation to a disabled person if the employer does not know, and could not reasonably be expected to know –

  (a) in the case of an applicant or potential applicant, that the disabled person concerned is, or may be, an applicant for the employment; or
  (b) in any case, that that person has a disability and is likely to be affected in the way mentioned in subsection (1).

The scope of the phrase 'provision, criterion or practice' is very wide and it would incorporate text reading software for blind and partially sighted users of email and modified input devices, such as voice recognition software, for those with impaired mobility. Guidance on the issues that employers should consider when addressing the question of reasonable adjustments is contained in DDA 1995, Sched.18B and includes the extent to which the adjustment would prevent the disabled person being substantially disadvantaged, the financial cost of the adjustment, the extent of the disruption caused by the adjustment, the administrative costs of the adjustment, the financial resources of the employer and the size of the employer's undertaking. Examples of the kinds of steps that employers may need to take are also included in Sched.18B and they include the modification of equipment and the provision of readers and interpreters, which can easily be construed to mean that email facilities should be appropriately adapted for disabled users.

### *Harassment*

Harassment within the meaning of DDA 1995, s.3B has the same effect as harassment under the EE(A)R 2006 (see **5.5.1** above).

### *Victimisation*

The prohibition on victimisation is contained in DDA 1995, s.55. Victimisation occurs where the employer ('A') treats a person ('B') less favourably than other persons whose circumstances are the same as B and does so for one or more of the following reasons:

- B has brought proceedings against A or any other person under this Act; or
- B has given evidence or information in connection with such proceedings brought by any person; or
- B has otherwise done anything under, or by reference to, the Act in relation to A or any other person; or
- B alleges that A or any other person has (whether or not the allegation so states) contravened this Act; or
- A believes or suspects that B has done or intends to do any of those things.

*Vicarious liability*

The principles of vicarious liability are the same as those within the EE(A)R 2006 (see **5.5.1** above). DDA 1995, s.58 says:

**58. Liability of employers and principals**

(1) Anything done by a person in the course of his employment shall be treated for the purposes of this Act as also done by his employer, whether or not it was done with the employer's knowledge or approval.
(2) Anything done by a person as agent for another person with the authority of that other person shall be treated for the purposes of this Act as also done by that other person.
(3) Subsection (2) applies whether the authority was –

(a) express or implied; or
(b) given before or after the act in question was done.

(4) Subsections (1) and (2) do not apply in relation to an offence under section 57(4).
(5) In proceedings under this Act against any person in respect of an act alleged to have been done by an employee of his, it shall be a defence for that person to prove that he took such steps as were reasonably practicable to prevent the employee from –

(a) doing that act; or
(b) doing, in the course of his employment, acts of that description.

### 5.5.3 Race and sex discrimination

Race and sex discrimination laws have a relatively long pedigree within the jurisdiction. These topics are considered together, because the legislative framework in these areas is very similar. The legislative framework is contained in the Race Relations Act (RRA) 1976 and the Sex Discrimination Act (SDA) 1975, although both Acts have been heavily amended over the years, in particular to take account of various harmonising laws of the EU. Key amending laws include the Race Relations Act 1976 (Amendment) Regulations 2003, SI 2003/1626; the Sex Discrimination Act 1975 (Amendment) Regulations 2003, SI 2003/1657 (see also the Sex Discrimination Act 1975 (Amendment) Regulations 2008, SI 2008/656); and the Civil Partnership Act 2004 (which amended SDA 1975, s.3 to make it unlawful to discriminate in the employment field against persons who are civil partners).

Both Acts cover much more than the employment field (for example, the supply of goods and services), but it is only the employment field that is considered below. The respective provisions of the Acts prohibiting discrimination in the field of employment are RRA 1976, s.4 and SDA 1975, s.6.

RRA 1976, s.4 says:

**4. Applicants and employees**

(1) It is unlawful for a person, in relation to employment by him at an establishment in Great Britain, to discriminate against another –

- (a) in the arrangements he makes for the purpose of determining who should be offered that employment; or
- (b) in the terms on which he offers him that employment; or
- (c) by refusing or deliberately omitting to offer him that employment.

(2) It is unlawful for a person, in the case of a person employed by him at an establishment in Great Britain, to discriminate against that employee –

- (a) in the terms of employment which he affords him; or
- (b) in the way he affords him access to opportunities for promotion, transfer or training, or to any other benefits, facilities or services, or by refusing or deliberately omitting to afford him access to them; or
- (c) by dismissing him, or subjecting him to any other detriment.

(2A) It is unlawful for an employer, in relation to employment by him at an establishment in Great Britain, to subject to harassment a person whom he employs or who has applied to him for employment.

(3) Except in relation to discrimination falling within section 2 or discrimination on grounds of race or ethnic or national origins, subsections (1) and (2) do not apply to employment for the purposes of a private household.

(4) Subsection (2) does not apply to benefits, facilities or services of any description if the employer is concerned with the provision (for payment or not) of benefits, facilities or services of that description to the public, or to a section of the public comprising the employee in question, unless –

- (a) that provision differs in a material respect from the provision of the benefits, facilities or services by the employer to his employees; or
- (b) the provision of the benefits, facilities or services to the employee in question is regulated by his contract of employment; or
- (c) the benefits, facilities or services relate to training.

(4A) In subsection (2)(c) reference to the dismissal of a person from employment includes, where the discrimination is on grounds of race or ethnic or national origins, reference –

(a) to the termination of that person's employment by the expiration of any period (including a period expiring by reference to an event or circumstance), not being a termination immediately after which the employment is renewed on the same terms; and
(b) to the termination of that person's employment by any act of his (including the giving of notice) in circumstances such that he is entitled to terminate it without notice by reason of the conduct of the employer.

SDA 1975, s.6 says:

**6. Applicants and employees**

(1) It is unlawful for a person, in relation to employment by him at an establishment in Great Britain, to discriminate against a woman –

(a) in the arrangements he makes for the purpose of determining who should be offered that employment, or
(b) in the terms on which he offers her that employment, or
(c) by refusing or deliberately omitting to offer her that employment.

(2) It is unlawful for a person, in the case of a woman employed by him at an establishment in Great Britain, to discriminate against her –

(a) in the way he affords her access to opportunities for promotion, transfer or training, or to any other benefits, facilities or services, or by refusing or deliberately omitting to afford her access to them, or
(b) by dismissing her, or subjecting her to any other detriment.

(2A) It is unlawful for an employer, in relation to employment by him at an establishment in Great Britain, to subject to harassment –

(a) a woman whom he employs, or
(b) a woman who has applied to him for employment.

(2B) For the purposes of subsection (2A), the circumstances in which an employer is to be treated as subjecting a woman to harassment shall include those where –

(a) a third party subjects the woman to harassment in the course of her employment, and
(b) the employer has failed to take such steps as would have been reasonably practicable to prevent the third party from doing so.

(2C) Subsection (2B) does not apply unless the employer knows that the woman has been subject to harassment in the course of her employment on at least two other occasions by a third party.

(2D) In subsections (2B) and (2C), 'third party' means a person other than –

(a) the employer, or
(b) a person whom the employer employs,

and for the purposes of those subsections it is immaterial whether the third party is the same or a different person on each occasion.

[Subsections (4)–(6) are omitted.]

Although SDA 1975, s.6 refers to women, it is important to note that the SDA 1975 is also concerned with discrimination against men (and by reason of s.2A the SDA 1975 also provides protection to transsexuals). SDA 1975, s.2 says:

**2. Sex discrimination against men**

(1) Section 1, and the provisions of Parts II and III relating to sex discrimination against women, are to be read as applying equally to the treatment of men, and for that purpose shall have effect with such modifications as are requisite.
(2) In the application of subsection (1) no account shall be taken of special treatment afforded to women in connection with pregnancy or childbirth.

There are four main kinds of discrimination in the field, namely:

- direct discrimination;
- indirect discrimination;
- victimisation;
- harassment.

### *Direct and indirect discrimination*

The meaning of direct and indirect discrimination is dealt with in s.1 of both Acts. RRA 1976, s.1 says:

**1. Racial discrimination**

(1) A person discriminates against another in any circumstances relevant for the purposes of any provision of this Act if –
  (a) on racial grounds he treats that other less favourably than he treats or would treat other persons; or
  (b) he applies to that other a requirement or condition which he applies or would apply equally to persons not of the same racial group as that other but –
    (i) which is such that the proportion of persons of the same racial group as that other who can comply with it is considerably smaller than the proportion of persons not of that racial group who can comply with it; and
    (ii) which he cannot show to be justifiable irrespective of the colour, race, nationality or ethnic or national origins of the person to whom it is applied; and
    (iii) which is to the detriment of that other because he cannot comply with it.

(1A) A person also discriminates against another if, in any circumstances relevant for the purposes of any provision referred to in subsection (1B), he applies to that other a provision, criterion or practice which he applies or would apply equally to persons not of the same race or ethnic or national origins as that other, but –

(a) which puts or would put persons of the same race or ethnic or national origins as that other at a particular disadvantage when compared with other persons,
(b) which puts that other at that disadvantage, and
(c) which he cannot show to be a proportionate means of achieving a legitimate aim.

SDA 1975, s.1 says:

**1. Direct and indirect discrimination against women**

(1) In any circumstances relevant for the purposes of any provision of this Act, other than a provision to which subsection (2) applies, a person discriminates against a woman if –

(a) on the ground of her sex he treats her less favourably than he treats or would treat a man, or
(b) he applies to her a requirement or condition which he applies or would apply equally to a man but –

(i) which is such that the proportion of women who can comply with it is considerably smaller than the proportion of men who can comply with it, and
(ii) which he cannot show to be justifiable irrespective of the sex of the person to whom it is applied, and
(iii) which is to her detriment because she cannot comply with it.

(2) In any circumstances relevant for the purposes of a provision to which this subsection applies, a person discriminates against a woman if –

(a) on the ground of her sex, he treats her less favourably than he treats or would treat a man, or
(b) he applies to her a provision, criterion or practice which he applies or would apply equally to a man, but –

(i) which puts or would put women at a particular disadvantage when compared with men,
(ii) which puts her at that disadvantage, and
(iii) which he cannot show to be a proportionate means of achieving a legitimate aim.

There are two elements within direct discrimination. First, the employee must be subject to less favourable treatment when compared with another person, meaning that the legislation takes a comparative approach. Second, the less favourable treatment must be on the grounds of race or sex. Direct discrimination cannot be justified, unlike in cases of direct age discrimination. The concept of less favourable treatment is assessed objectively (see, for example,

*Burrett* v. *West Birmingham Health Authority* [1994] IRLR 7), but it is not the same as unfavourable treatment; merely unfavourable treatment will not found a claim in race or sex discrimination if persons of the opposite sex or different racial groups are subjected to the same unfavourable treatment (see, for example, *Bahl* v. *The Law Society* [2004] EWCA 1070).

Those bringing discrimination cases before the Employment Tribunal have the burden of proving[5] that they have been treated less favourably, which will require them to identify a comparator, of the opposite sex or from a different racial group.[6] The comparator can be a real person or a hypothetical person if a real comparator cannot be found. The comparator's characteristics must be the same as the complainant's or not materially different.[7] If the complainant is able to prove that they have been treated less favourably, the next issue is whether the less favourable treatment is on the grounds of racial group[8] or sex.[9] At this stage the burden is on the employer to show that the less favourable treatment was not on a prohibited ground. The less favourable treatment complained of has to be causally connected to a prohibited ground and the Employment Tribunal adopts the 'but for' test when determining this issue.

The legislative formulation for indirect discrimination is very similar to that for indirect disability discrimination. The essence of indirect discrimination is that the employer treats all of its employees the same but there is a disparity in effect that is due to either sex or racial grounds. In cases of indirect sex discrimination, which fall within SDA 1975, s.1(2)(b), the employer applies a provision, criterion or practice to the complainant which although it applies equally to persons of the opposite sex it puts the complainant's sex at particular disadvantage and puts the complainant at an actual disadvantage. However, indirect sexual discrimination can be justified, on the basis that is proportionate and pursues a legitimate aim.

The position is slightly more complex in cases of indirect racial discrimination, due to the fact that there are two tests contained within RRA 1976, s.1. Section 1(1)(b) applies to cases of indirect discrimination on the grounds of nationality and colour, while s.1(1A) applies in cases of indirect discrimination on the grounds of race and ethnic or national origin. Section 1(1A) has applied to these areas since 9 July 2003 and it will cover the bulk of indirect discrimination cases. The formulation is identical to indirect sex discrimination.

The justification defence is found in RRA 1976, s.1(1A)(c) and in SDA 1975, s.1(2) and is a 'proportionate means of achieving a legitimate aim'.[10] The burden of proof rests on the employer and the test is an objective one. The Employment Tribunal is required when assessing a justification defence to balance the discriminatory effect of the provision, criterion or practice against the reasonable needs of the employer.

### *Harassment*

The protections from harassment are contained in RRA 1976, s.3A and SDA 1975, s.4A. Again, the formulation of harassment follows the formulation for harassment in age and disability discrimination cases. RRA 1976, s.3A says:

> **3A. Harassment**
>
> (1) A person subjects another to harassment in any circumstances relevant for the purposes of any provision referred to in section 1(1B) where, on grounds of race or ethnic or national origins, he engages in unwanted conduct which has the purpose or effect of –
>
> (a) violating that other person's dignity, or
> (b) creating an intimidating, hostile, degrading, humiliating or offensive environment for him.
>
> (2) Conduct shall be regarded as having the effect specified in paragraph (a) or (b) of subsection (1) only if, having regard to all the circumstances, including in particular the perception of that other person, it should reasonably be considered as having that effect.

SDA 1975, s.4A says:

> **4A. Harassment, including sexual harassment**
>
> (1) For the purposes of this Act, a person subjects a woman to harassment if –
>
> (a) he engages in unwanted conduct that is related to her sex or that of another person and has the purpose or effect –
>
> (i) of violating her dignity, or
> (ii) of creating an intimidating, hostile, degrading, humiliating or offensive environment for her,
>
> (b) he engages in any form of unwanted verbal, non-verbal or physical conduct of a sexual nature that has the purpose or effect –
>
> (i) of violating her dignity, or
> (ii) of creating an intimidating, hostile, degrading, humiliating or offensive environment for her, or
>
> (c) on the ground of her rejection of or submission to unwanted conduct of a kind mentioned in paragraph (a) or (b), he treats her less favourably than he would treat her had she not rejected, or submitted to, the conduct.
>
> (2) Conduct shall be regarded as having the effect mentioned in sub-paragraph (i) or (ii) of subsection (1)(a) or (b) only if, having regard to all the circumstances, including in particular the perception of the woman, it should reasonably be considered as having that effect.
> (3) For the purposes of this Act, a person ('A') subjects another person ('B') to harassment if –

(a) A, on the ground that B intends to undergo, is undergoing or has undergone gender reassignment, engages in unwanted conduct that has the purpose or effect –

(i) of violating B's dignity, or
(ii) of creating an intimidating, hostile, degrading, humiliating or offensive environment for B, or

(b) A, on the ground of B's rejection of or submission to unwanted conduct of a kind mentioned in paragraph (a), treats B less favourably than A would treat B had B not rejected, or submitted to, the conduct.

(4) Conduct shall be regarded as having the effect mentioned in sub-paragraph (i) or (ii) of subsection (3)(a) only if, having regard to all the circumstances, including in particular the perception of B, it should reasonably be considered as having that effect.
(5) Subsection (1) is to be read as applying equally to the harassment of men, and for that purpose shall have effect with such modifications as are requisite.
(6) For the purposes of subsections (1) and (3), a provision of Part 2 or 3 framed with reference to harassment of women shall be treated as applying equally to the harassment of men, and for that purpose will have effect with such modifications as are requisite.

It is worth noting, however, that there is no specific protection from harassment on the grounds of nationality, colour, marital status, pregnancy, maternity leave or civil partnership status.

SDA 1975, s.4A(1)(b) deals specifically with sexual harassment, which is unwanted verbal, non-verbal or physical conduct of a sexual nature. Sexual harassment covers physical behaviour such as touching, patting, pinching and brushing-up. Verbal conduct falling within the scope of this section would include propositions and asking for dates. The most serious cases of harassment are crimes under the Criminal Justice and Public Order Act 1994 and the Protection from Harassment Act 1997.

### *Victimisation*

The prohibitions against victimisation are contained in RRA 1976, s.2 and SDA 1975, s.4. RRA 1976, s.2 says:

**2. Discrimination by way of victimisation**

(1) A person ('the discriminator') discriminates against another person ('the person victimised') in any circumstances relevant for the purposes of any provision of this Act if he treats the person victimised less favourably than in those circumstances he treats or would treat other persons, and does so by reason that the person victimised has –

(a) brought proceedings against the discriminator or any other person under this Act; or

(b) given evidence or information in connection with proceedings brought by any person against the discriminator or any other person under this Act; or
(c) otherwise done anything under or by reference to this Act in relation to the discriminator or any other person; or
(d) alleged that the discriminator or any other person has committed an act which (whether or not the allegation so states) would amount to a contravention of this Act,

or by reason that the discriminator knows that the person victimised intends to do any of those things, or suspects that the person victimised has done, or intends to do, any of them.

(2) Subsection (1) does not apply to treatment of a person by reason of any allegation made by him if the allegation was false and not made in good faith.

SDA 1975, s.4 says:

**4. Discrimination by way of victimisation**

(1) A person ('the discriminator') discriminates against another person ('the person victimised') in any circumstances relevant for the purposes of any provision of this Act if he treats the person victimised less favourably than in those circumstances he treats or would treat other persons, and do so by reason that the person victimised has –

(a) brought proceedings against the discriminator or any other person under this Act or the Equal Pay Act 1970 or sections 62 to 65 of the Pensions Act 1995, or
(b) given evidence or information in connection with proceedings brought by any person against the discriminator or any other person under this Act or the Equal Pay Act 1970 or sections 62 to 65 of the Pensions Act 1995, or
(c) otherwise done anything under or by reference to this Act or the Equal Pay Act 1970 or sections 62 to 65 of the Pensions Act 1995 in relation to the discriminator or any other person, or
(d) alleged that the discriminator or any other person has committed an act which (whether or not the allegation so states) would amount to a contravention of this Act or give rise to a claim under the Equal Pay Act 1970 or under sections 62 to 65 of the Pensions Act 1995

or by reason that the discriminator knows the person victimised intends to do any of those things, or suspects the person victimised has done, or intends to do, any of them.

(2) Subsection (1) does not apply to treatment of a person by reason of any allegation made by him if the allegation was false and not made in good faith.

(3) For the purposes of subsection (1), a provision of Part II or III framed with reference to discrimination against women shall be treated as applying equally to the treatment of men and for that purpose shall have effect with such modifications as are requisite.

These sections approach victimisation in the same way as age and disability discrimination. They protect people who have brought proceedings, those who have given evidence in proceedings, those who have done anything under or by reference to the RRA 1976 or SDA 1975 and those who have alleged a contravention of the RRA or SDA. These things are often called 'protected acts'. People who are protected from victimisation are protected from less favourable treatment, as in the sense of direct discrimination.

### *Vicarious liability*

The vicarious liability provisions in the RRA 1976 and SDA 1975 are found in s.32 and s.41 respectively. RRA 1976, s.32 says:

> **32. Liability of employers and principals**
>
> (1) Anything done by a person in the course of his employment shall be treated for the purposes of this Act (except as regards offences thereunder) as done by his employer as well as by him, whether or not it was done with the employer's knowledge or approval.
> (2) Anything done by a person as agent for another person with the authority (whether express or implied, and whether precedent or subsequent) of that other person shall be treated for the purposes of this Act (except as regards offences thereunder) as done by that other person as well as by him.
> (3) In proceedings brought under this Act against any person in respect of an act alleged to have been done by an employee of his it shall be a defence for that person to prove that he took such steps as were reasonably practicable to prevent the employee from doing that act, or from doing in the course of his employment acts of that description.

SDA 1975, s.41 says:

> **41. Liability of employers and principals**
>
> (1) Anything done by a person in the course of his employment shall be treated for the purposes of this Act as done by his employer as well as by him, whether or not it was done with the employer's knowledge or approval.
> (2) Anything done by a person as agent for another person with the authority (whether express or implied, and whether precedent or subsequent) of that other person shall be treated for the purposes of this Act as done by that other person as well as by him.
> (3) In proceedings brought under this Act against any person in respect of an act alleged to have been done by an employee of his it shall be a defence for that person to prove that he took such steps as were reasonably practicable to prevent the employee from doing that act, or from doing in the course of his employment acts of that description.

*Remedies*

The victim of discrimination can bring enforcement proceedings before the Employment Tribunal. In such proceedings the Tribunal has three broad powers:

- It can make a declaration of rights, under RRA 1976, s.56 and under SDA 1975, s.65.
- It can award compensation, under the same sections.
- It can make recommendations for remedial action to be taken by the employer, again under the same sections.

There is no cap on the amount of compensation that the Tribunal can award[11] and in vicarious liability cases it can also order individuals engaged in discrimination to pay compensation to the victim, in addition to an order against the employer. The purpose of compensation is to restore the victim to the position they would have been in had they not been discriminated against. This can cover loss of earnings and compensation for injury to feelings if the victim has suffered anger, upset or humiliation. If the victim's distress amounts to a psychiatric condition, damages can be awarded for personal injury also. The Tribunal may also award aggravated and exemplary damages where the discrimination is the result of exceptional or contumelious conduct or motive.

If the case is one of indirect sex discrimination, the Tribunal may award compensation even if the discrimination was unintentional, although there is no equivalent power for unintentional indirect discrimination in race cases.

RRA 1976, s.56 says:

**56. Remedies on complaint under s. 54**

(1) Where an employment tribunal finds that a complaint presented to it under section 54 is well-founded, the tribunal shall make such of the following as it considers just and equitable –

(a) an order declaring the rights of the complainant and the respondent in relation to the act to which the complaint relates;

(b) an order requiring the respondent to pay to the complainant compensation of an amount corresponding to any damages he could have been ordered by a county court or by a sheriff court to pay to the complainant if the complaint had fallen to be dealt with under section 57;

(c) a recommendation that the respondent take within a specified period action appearing to the tribunal to be practicable for the purpose of obviating or reducing the adverse effect on the complainant of any act of discrimination to which the complaint relates.

(4) If without reasonable justification the respondent to a complaint fails to comply with a recommendation made by an employment tribunal under subsection (1)(c), then, if it thinks it just and equitable to do so –

(a) the tribunal may increase the amount of compensation required to be paid to the complainant in respect of the complaint by an order made under subsection (1)(b); or

(b) if an order under subsection (1)(b) could have been made but was not, the tribunal may make such an order.

SDA 1975, s.65 says:

**65. Remedies on complaint under section 63**

(1) Where an employment tribunal finds that a complaint presented to it under section 63 is well-founded the tribunal shall make such of the following as it considers just and equitable –

(a) an order declaring the rights of the complainant and the respondent in relation to the act to which the complaint relates;

(b) an order requiring the respondent to pay to the complainant compensation of an amount corresponding to any damages he could have been ordered by a county court or by a sheriff court to pay to the complainant if the complaint had fallen to be dealt with under section 66;

(c) a recommendation that the respondent take within a specified period action appearing to the tribunal to be practicable for the purpose of obviating or reducing the adverse effect on the complainant of any act of discrimination to which the complaint relates.

(1A) In applying section 66 for the purposes of subsection (1)(b), no account shall be taken of subsection (3) of that section.

(1B) As respects an unlawful act of discrimination falling within section 1(2)(b) or section 3(1)(b), if the respondent proves that the provision, criterion or practice in question was not applied with the intention of treating the complainant unfavourably on the ground of his sex or (as the case may be) fulfilment of the condition in section 3(2), an order may be made under subsection (1)(b) only if the employment tribunal –

(a) makes such order under subsection (1)(a) and such recommendation under subsection (1)(c) (if any) as it would have made if it had no power to make an order under subsection (1)(b); and

(b) (where it makes an order under subsection (1)(a) or a recommendation under subsection (1)(c) or both) considers that it is just and equitable to make an order under subsection (1)(b) as well.

(3) If without reasonable justification the respondent to a complaint fails to comply with a recommendation made by an employment tribunal under subsection (1)(c), then, if they think it just and equitable to do so –

(a) the tribunal may increase the amount of compensation required to be paid to the complainant in respect of the complaint by an order made under subsection (1)(b), or

(b) if an order under subsection (1)(b) was not made, the tribunal may make such an order.

The Tribunal's powers in age, disability, religion or belief and sexual orientation discrimination cases are similar.

### 5.5.4 Religion or belief and sexual orientation discrimination

Discrimination on the grounds of sexual orientation and on the grounds of religion or belief is also unlawful. The relevant provisions are contained in the Employment Equality (Sexual Orientation) Regulations 2003, SI 2003/1661 (which were amended in 2003 and 2004) and the Employment Equality (Religion or Belief) Regulations 2003, SI 2003/1660 (which were amended in 2003). These regulations came into force on 1 December 2003 and 2 December 2003 respectively, and they follow closely the pattern of the SDA 1975 and the RRA 1976.

### 5.5.5 Harassment

The Protection from Harassment Act (PHA) 1997 prohibits harassment. In the light of how the prohibition is constructed it will be very easy for a person to commit harassment through the use of email.[12] The prohibition against harassment is contained in PHA 1997, s.1 and says:

> **1. Prohibition of harassment**
>
> (1) A person must not pursue a course of conduct –
>
> (a) which amounts to harassment of another, and
> (b) which he knows or ought to know amounts to harassment of the other.
>
> (1A) A person must not pursue a course of conduct –
>
> (a) which involves harassment of two or more persons, and
> (b) which he knows or ought to know involves harassment of those persons, and
> (c) by which he intends to persuade any person (whether or not one of those mentioned above) –
>
> (i) not to do something that he is entitled or required to do, or
> (ii) to do something that he is not under any obligation to do;
>
> (2) For the purposes of this section, the person whose course of conduct is in question ought to know that it amounts to or involves harassment of another if a reasonable person in possession of the same information would think the course of conduct amounted to or involved harassment of the other.
> (3) Subsection (1) or (1A) does not apply to a course of conduct if the person who pursued it shows –
>
> (a) that it was pursued for the purpose of preventing or detecting crime,
> (b) that it was pursued under any enactment or rule of law or to comply with any condition or requirement imposed by any person under any enactment, or
> (c) that in the particular circumstances the pursuit of the course of conduct was reasonable.

The essential ingredients of harassment are therefore:

- the pursuit of a course of conduct;
- that amounts to harassment of another; and
- that the harasser knows or ought to know amounts to harassment.

PHA 1997, s.7(2) says that harassment includes 'alarming the person or causing the person distress'. Section 7(3) says that a course of conduct in respect of an individual is conduct on at least two occasions, and in the case of conduct in respect of two or more persons conduct on at least one occasion in relation to each. While the PHA 1997 recognises that conduct includes speech, it can also cover harassment by email. The question whether the alleged harasser knew or ought to have known that their conduct amounted to harassment is an objective one and will be judged against the standards of a reasonable person.

Harassment is a criminal offence as well as a civil wrong. The maximum penalty on conviction is six months' imprisonment and a £5,000 fine. In civil proceedings the court can award damages and can issue a restraining order. PHA 1997, ss.2 and 3 say:

**2. Offence of harassment**

(1) A person who pursues a course of conduct in breach of section 1(1) or (1A) is guilty of an offence.
(2) A person guilty of an offence under this section is liable on summary conviction to imprisonment for a term not exceeding six months, or a fine not exceeding level 5 on the standard scale, or both.

**3. Civil remedy**

(1) An actual or apprehended breach of section 1(1) may be the subject of a claim in civil proceedings by the person who is or may be the victim of the course of conduct in question.
(2) On such a claim, damages may be awarded for (among other things) any anxiety caused by the harassment and any financial loss resulting from the harassment.
(3) Where –

(a) in such proceedings the High Court or a county court grants an injunction for the purpose of restraining the defendant from pursuing any conduct which amounts to harassment, and
(b) the plaintiff considers that the defendant has done anything which he is prohibited from doing by the injunction,

the plaintiff may apply for the issue of a warrant for the arrest of the defendant.

Section 1 of the PHA 1997 contains three narrow defences for a person who has pursued a course of conduct that amounts to harassment. The first defence is that the course of conduct was pursued for the purposes of preventing or detecting crime, and will obviously be of assistance to law enforcement agencies. The second defence is that the course of conduct was authorised under an enactment. The third defence is that the course of conduct was reasonable in the particular circumstances.

The PHA 1997 also criminalises behaviour that puts a person in fear of violence. Section 4 says:

**4. Putting people in fear of violence**

(1) A person whose course of conduct causes another to fear, on at least two occasions, that violence will be used against him is guilty of an offence if he knows or ought to know that his course of conduct will cause the other so to fear on each of those occasions.

(2) For the purposes of this section, the person whose course of conduct is in question ought to know that it will cause another to fear that violence will be used against him on any occasion if a reasonable person in possession of the same information would think the course of conduct would cause the other so to fear on that occasion.

(3) It is a defence for a person charged with an offence under this section to show that –

(a) his course of conduct was pursued for the purpose of preventing or detecting crime,

(b) his course of conduct was pursued under any enactment or rule of law or to comply with any condition or requirement imposed by any person under any enactment, or

(c) the pursuit of his course of conduct was reasonable for the protection of himself or another or for the protection of his or another's property.

(4) A person guilty of an offence under this section is liable –

(a) on conviction on indictment, to imprisonment for a term not exceeding five years, or a fine, or both, or

(b) on summary conviction, to imprisonment for a term not exceeding six months, or a fine not exceeding the statutory maximum, or both.

(5) If on the trial on indictment of a person charged with an offence under this section the jury find him not guilty of the offence charged, they may find him guilty of an offence under section 2.

(6) The Crown Court has the same powers and duties in relation to a person who is by virtue of subsection (5) convicted before it of an offence under section 2 as a magistrates' court would have on convicting him of the offence.

### *Vicarious liability*

An employer can be held vicariously liable for harassment committed by an employee. The question of vicarious liability as it applies to the PHA 1997 was central to the decision of the House of Lords in *Majrowski* v. *Guy's, St. Thomas' NHS Trust* [2006] UKHL 34. Lord Nichols gave the following opinion:

Against that legislative background I turn to the Trust's case. The principal thrust of the Trust's submissions is that the 1997 Act was primarily a legislative response to the public order problem of stalking. The Act was not aimed at the workplace. It is a public order provision designed to punish perpetrators for the anxiety and upset they cause to victims, not blameless employers who happen to be solvent and available as a target for litigation. Vicarious liability would have consequences for employers which Parliament cannot have intended. Vicarious liability would mean that a blameless employer would be liable in damages in respect of a cause of action wherein damages are recoverable for anxiety short of personal injury, foreseeability of damage is not an essential ingredient, and the limitation period is six years and not the usual period applicable to personal injury claims. The deterrent effect of ordering the perpetrator to pay compensation would be undermined by drawing litigation away from the very person guilty of the offence. Vicarious liability would increase very considerably the volume of claims based on stress, anxiety or other emotional problems at work. The courts would be unable to strike out unmeritorious claims. The burden on employers, insurers and the administration of justice would be wholly unjustified.

I am not persuaded by these arguments. Neither the terms nor the practical effect of this legislation indicate that Parliament intended to exclude the ordinary principle of vicarious liability.

As to the terms of the legislation, by section 3 Parliament created a new cause of action, a new civil wrong. Damages are one of the remedies for this wrong, although they are not the primary remedy. Parliament has spelled out some particular features of this new wrong: anxiety is a head of damage, the limitation period is six years, and so on. These features do not in themselves indicate an intention to exclude vicarious liability. Vicarious liability arises only if the new wrong is committed by an employee in the course of his employment, as already described. The acts of the employee must meet the 'close connection' test. If an employee's acts of harassment meet this test, I am at a loss to see why these particular features of this newly created wrong should be thought to place this wrong in a special category in which an employer is exempt from vicarious liability. It is true that this new wrong usually comprises conduct of an intensely personal character between two individuals. But this feature may also be present with other wrongs which attract vicarious liability, such as assault.

Nor does imposition of criminal liability only on the perpetrator of the wrong, and on a person who aids, abets, counsels or procures the harassing conduct, point to a different conclusion. Conversion, assault and battery may attract criminal liability as well as civil liability, but this does not exclude vicarious liability.

I turn to the practical effect of the legislation. Vicarious liability for an employee's harassment of another person, whether a fellow employee or not, will to some extent increase employers' burdens. That is clear. But, here again, this does not suffice to show Parliament intended to exclude the ordinary common law principle of vicarious liability. Parliament added harassment to the list of civil wrongs. Parliament did so because it considered the existing law provided insufficient protection for victims of harassment. The inevitable consequence of Parliament creating this new wrong of universal application is that at times an employee will commit this wrong in the course of his employment. This prompts the question: why should an employer have a special dispensation in respect of the newly-created wrong and not be liable if an employee commits this wrong in the course of his employment? The contemporary rationale of employers' vicarious liability is as applicable to this new wrong as it is to common law torts.

Take a case where an employee, in the course of his employment, harasses a non-employee, such as a customer of the employer. In such a case the employer would be liable if his employee had assaulted the customer. Why should this not equally be so in respect of harassment? In principle, harassment arising from a dispute between two employees stands on the same footing. If, acting in the course of his employment, one employee assaults another, the employer is liable. Why should harassment be treated differently?

## CHAPTER NOTES

1 *Designers Guild Ltd* v. *Russell Williams (Textiles) Ltd (trading as Washington DC)* (2000) House of Lords WL 1720247. This complex case provides an excellent review of some of the key principles within the law of copyright infringement and, perhaps, a number of important lessons on how best to challenge on appeal the decision of a court of first instance. As regards the facts Lord Miller provides an excellent summary: 'Both parties design and sell fabrics and wallpapers. The plaintiffs brought proceedings against the defendants for infringement of the copyright in one of their designs. The trial judge (Mr. Lawrence Collins QC) found that the defendants had prior access to the copyright work and that their design reproduced many of its features. He rejected the defendants' evidence of independent origin, and found that their design was copied from and reproduced a substantial part of the copyright work. He accordingly gave judgment for the plaintiffs. The defendants appealed to the Court of Appeal, but they did so on a very narrow ground. They abandoned most of the grounds in their notice of appeal, and did not challenge the Judge's findings of fact, in particular that the defendants' design was copied from and reproduced features of the copyright work. They contented themselves with challenging his conclusion that what they had taken was a substantial part of the copyright work.'

2 For a discussion on the quantitative and qualitative issues within substantial copying see, for example, *Ladbroke* v. *William Hill* [1964] 1 WLR 273. For a more recent case on the meaning of 'substantial copying' see *JHP Ltd* v. *BBC Worldwide Ltd, Trustees of the Estate of Terry Nation* [2008] EWHC [757], a case involving Daleks. See also See *Baigent* v. *Random House Group Ltd* [2007] EWCA Civ 247.

3 Special damage does not need to be shown in slanders involving an allegation of unchastity on the part of a woman, an allegation of the commission of a crime punishable by imprisonment, an allegation that the claimant is suffering from leprosy or venereal disease and an allegation likely to damage the claimant's reputation in relation to his office, profession, trade or business.

4 See also the opinion of Lord Bingham in *Jameel* v. *Wall Street Journal Europe SPRL (No.3)* [2006] UKHL 44, where he said 'underlying the development of qualified privilege was the requirement of a reciprocal duty and interest between the publisher and the recipient of the statement in question'.

5 SDA 1975, s.63A reverses the burden of proof once the complainant has proved facts from which the Employment Tribunal could conclude that the employer has committed an act of sex discrimination or harassment.

6 But see SDA 1975, s.3A for discrimination on the grounds of pregnancy or maternity leave; there is no longer a requirement to compare a pregnant person or one on maternity leave with a person of the opposite sex. See also RRA 1976, s.1(2), which is concerned with racial segregation; this says: 'It is hereby declared that, for the purposes of this Act, segregating a person from other persons on racial

grounds is treating him less favourably than they are treated'. As such there is no requirement for a comparator in racial segregation cases, as segregation by its very nature is less favourable treatment.

7 For example, RRA 1976, s.3(4) says 'a comparison of the case of a person of a particular racial group with that of a person not of that group under section 1(1) or (1A) must be such that the relevant circumstances in the one case are the same, or not materially different, in the other'. Similar provisions are found in SDA 1975, s.5(3).

8 'Racial group' is defined in RRA 1976, s.3(1) and covers colour, race, nationality, ethnic or national origins.

9 For these purposes sex discrimination also covers discrimination on the grounds of gender reassignment, discrimination on the grounds of pregnancy or maternity leave and discrimination on the grounds of marital or civil partnership status.

10 The justification defence in cases of indirect racial discrimination on the grounds of colour is different and is contained in RRA 1976, s.1(1)(b)(ii).

11 See the Employment Tribunals (Interest on Awards in Discrimination Cases) Regulations 1996, SI 1996/2803 for sex discrimination cases and the Race Relations (Remedies) Act 1994 for race discrimination cases.

12 See *R.* v. *Marchese* [2008] EWCA Crim 389 for a case involving harassment by SMS (text message). See *Attorney-General's Reference (No.113 of 2007)* [2008] EWCA Crim 22 for a case involving harassment by letter. See *R.* v. *Merrick* [2007] EWCA Crim 1159 for a case involving harassment by email.

# CHAPTER 6

# Substantive law issues – criminal

## 6.1 INTRODUCTION

The criminal law touches upon email in many different ways. For example, email might be used in the commission of a crime, such as where email is used to distribute indecent materials, or it can be used to plan crimes or it can be the target of crime. Therefore, law enforcement agencies routinely seek access to emails, as part of their investigations and, naturally, emails are receivable in evidence at court.

This chapter examines four important areas of substantive criminal law which regularly impact on email: 'data theft' offences under the Data Protection Act (DPA) 1998; the offence of unlawful interception under the Regulation of Investigatory Powers Act (RIPA) 2000; offences under the Computer Misuse Act (CMA) 1990; and 'hate mail'.

## 6.2 'DATA THEFT' OFFENCES WITHIN DATA PROTECTION ACT 1998, S.55

As discussed in **Chapters 3** and **4**, the processing of personal data is highly regulated by data protection laws. Of course, effective regulation requires appropriate sanctions for serious breaches of the law, which is why Article 24 of the Data Protection Directive says:

> The Member States shall adopt suitable measures to ensure the full implementation of the provisions of this Directive and shall in particular lay down the sanctions to be imposed in case of infringement of the provisions adopted pursuant to this Directive.

The DPA 1998 has, so far, taken a narrow position on the question of criminality, rendering only a few categories of breaches directly subject to the criminal law. Within this limited category of criminal offences[1] the most prominent is 'data theft', a colloquial term for the series of offences contained within s.55 of the Act.[2] In 'data theft' offences the target of the crime is personal data; as such, s.55 will be concerned with emails where emails contain personal data.

### 6.2.1 The Information Commissioner and the Criminal Justice and Immigration Act 2008

The Information Commissioner has successfully elevated DPA 1998, s.55 to a position of almost unparalleled prominence within the data protection regime, due to strong advocacy of the need to introduce custodial penalties for those convicted of the most serious cases of 'data theft'.

To explain, in May 2006 the Information Commissioner used a previously unused power within DPA 1998, s.52(2) to lay before Parliament a special report on s.55 offences. This report was called *What price privacy? The unlawful trade in confidential personal information* (HC 1056). The thrust of the Commissioner's case is that there is a 'pervasive and widespread "industry" devoted to the illegal buying and selling of [personal] information', which is an offence under s.55, and custodial penalties are required to stamp out the industry. Therefore, he made the following proposal:

> The crime at present carries no custodial sentence. When cases involving the unlawful procurement or sale of confidential personal information come before the courts, convictions often bring no more than a derisory fine or a conditional discharge. Low penalties devalue the data protection offence in the public mind and mask the true seriousness of the crime, even within the judicial system. They likewise do little to deter those who seek to buy or supply confidential information that should rightly remain private. The remedy I am proposing is to introduce a custodial sentence of up to two years for persons convicted on indictment, and up to six months for summary convictions. The aim is not to send more people to prison but to discourage all who might be tempted to engage in this unlawful trade, whether as buyers or suppliers.

The Commissioner benefited from government support; in July 2006 the Department for Constitutional Affairs published a consultation on the proposal for the introduction of custodial penalties (*Increasing penalties for deliberate and wilful misuse of personal data*, CP 9/06). In February 2007 the government formally declared its intention to introduce custodial penalties and this resulted in draft legislation being introduced in the Criminal Justice and Immigration Bill 2007. In May 2008 the Criminal Justice and Immigration Act (CJIA) 2008 received Royal Assent. Section 77 says:

> **77. Power to alter penalty for unlawfully obtaining etc. personal data**
>
> (1) The Secretary of State may by order provide for a person who is guilty of an offence under section 55 of the Data Protection Act 1998 (c. 29) (unlawful obtaining etc. of personal data) to be liable –
>
> (a) on summary conviction, to imprisonment for a term not exceeding the specified period or to a fine not exceeding the statutory maximum or to both,
>
> (b) on conviction on indictment, to imprisonment for a term not exceeding the specified period or to a fine or to both.

(2) In subsection (1)(a) and (b) 'specified period' means a period provided for by the order but the period must not exceed –

(a) in the case of summary conviction, 12 months (or, in Northern Ireland, 6 months), and
(b) in the case of conviction on indictment, two years.

(3) The Secretary of State must ensure that any specified period for England and Wales which, in the case of summary conviction, exceeds 6 months is to be read as a reference to 6 months so far as it relates to an offence committed before the commencement of section 282(1) of the Criminal Justice Act 2003 (c. 44) (increase in sentencing powers of magistrates' courts from 6 to 12 months for certain offences triable either way).
(4) Before making an order under this section, the Secretary of State must consult –

(a) the Information Commissioner,
(b) such media organisations as the Secretary of State considers appropriate, and
(c) such other persons as the Secretary of State considers appropriate.

(5) An order under this section may, in particular, amend the Data Protection Act 1998.

Thus, the stage is set for the introduction of custodial penalties in the future.[3]

DPA 1998, s.55, which has been amended by CJIA 2008, s.78 to introduce a specific public interest defence for journalists, now reads:

**55. Unlawful obtaining etc. of personal data**

(1) A person must not knowingly or recklessly, without the consent of the data controller –

(a) obtain or disclose personal data or the information contained in personal data, or
(b) procure the disclosure to another person of the information contained in personal data.

(2) Subsection (1) does not apply to a person who shows –

(a) that the obtaining, disclosing or procuring –

(i) was necessary for the purpose of preventing or detecting crime, or
(ii) was required or authorised by or under any enactment, by any rule of law or by the order of a court,

(b) that he acted in the reasonable belief that he had in law the right to obtain or disclose the data or information or, as the case may be, to procure the disclosure of the information to the other person,
(c) that he acted in the reasonable belief that he would have had the consent of the data controller if the data controller had known of the obtaining, disclosing or procuring and the circumstances of it,
(ca) that he acted –

(i) for the special purposes,
(ii) with a view to the publication by any person of any journalistic, literary or artistic material, and
(iii) in the reasonable belief that in the particular circumstances the obtaining, disclosing or procuring was justified as being in the public interest, or

(d) that in the particular circumstances the obtaining, disclosing or procuring was justified as being in the public interest.

(3) A person who contravenes subsection (1) is guilty of an offence.
(4) A person who sells personal data is guilty of an offence if he has obtained the data in contravention of subsection (1).
(5) A person who offers to sell personal data is guilty of an offence if –

(a) he has obtained the data in contravention of subsection (1), or
(b) he subsequently obtains the data in contravention of that subsection.

(6) For the purposes of subsection (5), an advertisement indicating that personal data are or may be for sale is an offer to sell the data.
(7) Section 1(2) does not apply for the purposes of this section; and for the purposes of subsections (4) to (6), 'personal data' includes information extracted from personal data.
(8) References in this section to personal data do not include references to personal data which by virtue of section 28 or 33A are exempt from this section.

There are five key offences within DPA 1998, s.55, namely:

- obtaining personal data, or the information contained in personal data;
- disclosing personal data, or the information contained in personal data;
- procuring the disclosure of information contained in personal data;
- selling personal data; and
- offering to sell personal data.

For all of these offences the *mens rea* is knowledge, or recklessness, as to the absence of the data controller's consent. Knowledge for these purposes means actual knowledge, while the test of recklessness is the one identified by the House of Lords in *R.* v. *G* [2004] 1 AC 1034.

### 6.2.2 The meaning of obtaining, etc.

The first issue within DPA 1998, s.55 is the *actus reus* of obtaining, disclosing, procuring, selling and offering to sell personal data, etc. As regards the meaning of 'obtaining' and 'disclosing', it is worth noting that s.55(7) ousts s.1(2) of the Act; s.1(2) contained indicative definitions of obtaining and disclosing. Thus, the intention of the Act is to apply the ordinary dictionary definitions. As regards 'procuring', this also requires an ordinary dictionary definition, but the word does appear in many pieces of legislation and has been subject to much judicial consideration. In *Attorney-General's Reference (No.1 of 1975)* [1975] QB 773 it was said that 'to procure means to produce by endeavour'.

### 6.2.3 Personal data, information contained in personal data and information extracted from personal data

The next issue is whether that which has been obtained (etc.) is personal data, or 'information contained in personal data', or 'information extracted from personal data'. The meaning of personal data is discussed at **Chapter 3**, but what is the meaning of 'information contained in personal data' and 'information extracted from personal data'?

Clearly, the use of three different phrases means that s.55 is concerned with three scenarios. In the first kind the defendant obtains (etc.) personal data from the data controller. As s.55 necessarily envisages the movement of information from the controller to the defendant, it would seem that where personal data are obtained there cannot be any change to the nature or form of the information during its movement. So, for example, if a person steals a physical item, such as a computer or a relevant filing system, in order to obtain the information within, the information within will remain as personal data in the defendant's hands, as they have the same nature and form as they had while they were in the controller's hands.

Of course, there are many more ways of obtaining information. For example, in *What price privacy?* the Information Commissioner was concerned mainly with 'blagging' offences, which are offences of pretext, where criminals falsely hold themselves out as being persons with legitimate entitlements to the data being sought. In blagging cases the target of the crime is specifically the information, rather than the item containing the information, with the preferred modus operandi of the blagger being a fraudulent telephone call to a call centre. So, in cases of blagging the defendant obtains the information within personal data, not the personal data. The nature of blagging, as opposed to the theft of physical items containing personal data, is that information is learned, which is a purely mental process, learned information cannot be personal data, as it is not processed by a computer, or held within a relevant filing system. (For a discussion on the distinction between processing and mental activities performed by humans, see *Johnson* v. *Medical Defence Union*, discussed at **Chapter 3**.)

The phrase 'information extracted from personal data' applies only to the sale offences, but it would seem to serve a similar function to the phrase 'information contained in personal data' in s.55(1), to cover situations where the information sold was not personal data in the hands of the criminal, either because when in the criminal's hands it was not processed, or it was not held in a relevant filing system (or equivalent), or it did not relate to an identifiable living individual. The phrase 'extracted from' may also mean extrapolation, although perhaps only in special and limited circumstances, such as where the extrapolation is logically derived from the personal data; for example, if personal data says that a person's birthday is 14 February, a logical extrapolation might be to say that the person's star sign is Aquarius; or a scientist might be able to extrapolate from a piece of DNA that a person has a particular genetic disorder.

In other words, s.55 requires consideration of both the nature and form of the data when in the possession or control of the data controller and its nature and form when in the possession or control of the defendant.

The leading case on s.55 is *R.* v. *Rooney* [2006] EWCA Crim 1841. In this case the defendant, a human resources administrator with Staffordshire Police, was convicted of unlawfully obtaining and unlawfully disclosing information contained in personal data. After accessing the human resources database she informed her sister that her ex-partner, a police officer, was living in a place called Tunstall, with his new partner. On appeal, the defendant argued that merely saying that people lived in Tunstall was not personal data, with the result that her conviction was unsound. Mr Justice Bean gave the leading judgment of the Court of Appeal:

> He [defence counsel] submits that to say that the couple lived in Tunstall does not sufficiently identify them and accordingly cannot amount to personal data.
>
> Mr Wood for the Crown says that it is sufficient that the reference to Tunstall should have been 'information contained in personal data'. In our view that is correct. The total sum of the information (at least as to identity and place of residence) contained on the database about P.C. Syred and/or Miss Booth was personal data. The information that they lived in Tunstall was part of 'the information contained in personal data'. Mr Hegarty does not submit that, and it would be absurd if, an offence was only committed if the whole of the information contained in personal data was improperly obtained or improperly disclosed. The town or village (whichever it was) in which they lived was quite clearly 'information contained in personal data' capable of constituting the offence. The information itself does not have to include the identity of the individual, particularly since in the present case the recipient of the information knew very well who was being talked about. Accordingly, there is, in our judgment, no basis for saying that the conviction on count 11 was in any way flawed in law or unsafe or unsatisfactory.

### 6.2.4 Defences

DPA 1998, s.55(2) sets out the defences, of which there are five. The new defence at s.55(2)(ca), introduced by CJIA 2008, s.78, was designed to assuage the concerns of press and media organisations that the introduction of custodial sentences could threaten the profession of investigative journalism.

## 6.3 OFFENCE OF UNLAWFUL INTERCEPTION UNDER RIPA 2000

In summary, there are two situations where interception of an email can be a crime: when an email is intercepted over a public telecommunications system without lawful authority; and when an email is intercepted over a private system without lawful authority.

### 6.3.1 Intercepting a communication over a public telecommunications system

RIPA 2000, s.1(1) sets out the offence of unlawful interception of a communication during the course of its transmission over a public telecommunications system. It says:

> It shall be an offence for a person intentionally and without lawful authority to intercept, at any place in the United Kingdom, any communication in the course of its transmission by means of –
>
> (a) a public postal service; or
> (b) a public telecommunication system.

Within this section are four key components:

- What is meant by interception?
- What is a public telecommunication system?
- What is meant by intentionally?
- What amounts to lawful authority?

*Meaning of interception*

The meaning of interception is discussed at **Chapter 4**, in the context of communications privacy. To recap, RIPA 2000, s.2 defines interception as making the contents of a communication available to a person other than the sender or intended recipient while in the course of transmission.

*What is a public telecommunication system?*

RIPA 2000, s.2(1) says:

> 'public telecommunications service' means any telecommunications service which is offered or provided to, or to a substantial section of, the public in any one or more parts of the United Kingdom;
>
> 'public telecommunication system' means any such parts of a telecommunication system by means of which any public telecommunications service is provided as are located in the United Kingdom;

> 'telecommunications service' means any service that consists in the provision of access to, and of facilities for making use of, any telecommunication system (whether or not one provided by the person providing the service); and
> 'telecommunication system' means any system (including the apparatus comprised in it) which exists (whether wholly or partly in the United Kingdom or elsewhere) for the purpose of facilitating the transmission of communications by any means involving the use of electrical or electro-magnetic energy.

This arduous approach to definitions certainly does not make RIPA 2000 any easier to understand, but it does tell us that the public telecommunication system extends as far as private residences and business premises, due to the fact that the meaning of telecommunication system incorporates 'apparatus', which covers the user's terminal equipment; terminal equipment includes telephones and PCs, which are found in private premises.

### *What is meant by intentionally?*

Intent is part of the *mens rea* of interception offences. The leading authority on the meaning of intent for the purposes of murder is *R.* v. *Woollin* [1999] 1 AC 82, HL. See also Criminal Justice Act 1967, s.8.

### *What amounts to lawful authority?*

RIPA 2000, s.1(5) says:

> Conduct has lawful authority for the purposes of this section if, and only if –
>
> (a) it is authorised by or under section 3 or 4;
> (b) it takes place in accordance with a warrant under section 5 ('an interception warrant'); or
> (c) it is in exercise, in relation to any stored communication, of any statutory power that is exercised (apart from this section) for the purpose of obtaining information or of taking possession of any document or other property;

Section 3 says:

> **3. Lawful interception without an interception warrant**
>
> (1) Conduct by any person consisting in the interception of a communication is authorised by this section if the communication is one which, or which that person has reasonable grounds for believing, is both –
>
> (a) a communication sent by a person who has consented to the interception; and
> (b) a communication the intended recipient of which has so consented.
>
> (2) Conduct by any person consisting in the interception of a communication is authorised by this section if –

(a) the communication is one sent by, or intended for, a person who has consented to the interception; and
(b) surveillance by means of that interception has been authorised under Part II.

(3) Conduct consisting in the interception of a communication is authorised by this section if –

(a) it is conduct by or on behalf of a person who provides a postal service or a telecommunications service; and
(b) it takes place for purposes connected with the provision or operation of that service or with the enforcement, in relation to that service, of any enactment relating to the use of postal services or telecommunications services.

(4) Conduct by any person consisting in the interception of a communication in the course of its transmission by means of wireless telegraphy is authorised by this section if it takes place –

(a) with the authority of a designated person under section 48 of the Wireless Telegraphy Act 2006 (interception and disclosure of wireless telegraphy messages); and
(b) for purposes connected with anything falling within subsection (5).

(5) Each of the following falls within this subsection –

(a) the grant of wireless telegraphy licences under the Wireless Telegraphy Act 2006;
(b) the prevention or detection of anything which constitutes interference with wireless telegraphy; and
(c) the enforcement of –

(i) any provision of Part 2 (other than Chapter 2 and sections 27 to 31) or Part 3 of that Act, or
(ii) any enactment not falling within subparagraph (i);

that relates to such interference.

Section 3 is concerned with four situations, all of which amount to lawful authority for the purposes of interception.

- The interceptor has reasonable grounds for believing that the sender and intended recipient both consented to the interception.
- Either the sender or intended recipient consents to the interception and the interception is authorised as a form of surveillance under RIPA 2000, Part II.
- The interception is by, or on behalf of, the provider of a telecommunications system and is carried out for purposes connected with the provision of the service.
- The interception is of wireless communications (in other words, mobile communications) and is authorised in accordance with the Wireless Telegraphy Act 2006.

See **Chapter 7** for a discussion of interception warrants under s.5 and the interception of business communications authorised under s.4.

### 6.3.2 Intercepting a communication over a private telecommunication system

The criminal offence of interception over a private telecommunications system is contained in RIPA 2000, s.1(2), which says:

> It shall be an offence for a person –
>
> (a) intentionally and without lawful authority, and
> (b) otherwise than in circumstances in which his conduct is excluded by subsection (6) from criminal liability under this subsection,
>
> to intercept, at any place in the United Kingdom, any communication in the course of its transmission by means of a private telecommunication system.

#### *What is a private telecommunication system?*

Dealing first with the meaning of private telecommunication system, RIPA 2000, s.2(1) says:

> 'private telecommunication system' means any telecommunication system which, without itself being a public telecommunication system, is a system in relation to which the following conditions are satisfied –
>
> (a) it is attached, directly or indirectly and whether or not for the purposes of the communication in question, to a public telecommunication system; and
> (b) there is apparatus comprised in the system which is both located in the United Kingdom and used (with or without other apparatus) for making the attachment to the public telecommunication system.

In the previous section the point was made that the public telecommunication system extends as far as private premises, which begs the question, in what circumstances will a system be a private one? Clearly, the answer does not lie in the fact that private residences and business premises are not open to the public.

Perhaps the best way of conceptualising the difference between a public and private system is to consider the situation in the workplace. If the workplace has a dedicated, private exchange for internal telephone calls, or an intranet for internal emails, these will be private systems for the purpose of RIPA 2000, provided that they are physically connected to a public system; the system will be private in the sense that internal phone calls and internal emails will be transmitted over the private system without touching a public system, but a connection between an internal system and a public system will exist if it is possible to make external telephone calls or send emails externally. If it is impossible to reach the outside world from the internal systems, the systems will not be private ones within the meaning of RIPA 2000, despite the fact that they are private in every other sense of the word.

### *Exclusion of criminal liability*

If the internal system is a private telecommunications system in the sense described, the situations in which criminal liability are excluded are very narrow. These situations are contained in RIPA 2000, s.1(6) and to fall within the exclusions the interceptor has to be 'the person with a right to control the operation or the use of the system' or be acting with 'the express or implied consent' of the system controller. The person with the right to control the use of a private system may differ from organisation to organisation, but in all cases it is a person with executive powers. That person will be able to give interception rights to others, including to law enforcement agencies.

Even if criminal liability is excluded by operation of s.1(6), those persons whose communications are intercepted will be able to bring civil proceedings if the interception is without lawful authority. RIPA 2000, s.1(3) says:

> Any interception of a communication which is carried out at any place in the United Kingdom by, or with the express or implied consent of, a person having the right to control the operation or the use of a private telecommunication system shall be actionable at the suit or instance of the sender or recipient, or intended recipient, of the communication if it is without lawful authority and is either –
>
> (a) an interception of that communication in the course of its transmission by means of that private system; or
>
> (b) an interception of that communication in the course of its transmission, by means of a public telecommunication system, to or from apparatus comprised in that private telecommunication system.

Section 1(3) is an expansive provision that covers not only interception of communications over private systems, but interception of communications between public systems and private ones. For example, if a person was to send an email from their home computer to a person at a business with a private system, they would be able to bring civil proceedings under s.1(3) if the communication was intercepted without lawful authority and it would not matter if the interception actually took place within the public system or within the private system.

## 6.4 COMPUTER MISUSE ACT 1990

The CMA 1990 creates a series of criminal offences that legislate against unauthorised access to computer material, unauthorised acts that impact upon the operation of computers, and the use of computers to commit other crimes. All of these crimes can impact on email.

However, it is interesting to note that the Act does not actually define the word 'computer', thereby leaving it to the courts to apply the ordinary dictionary definition. This means, of course, that the Act will extend much further than the desktop or laptop PC.

### 6.4.1 Unauthorised access to computer material

The offence of unauthorised access to computer material is contained in s.1, which reads as follows:

> (1) A person is guilty of an offence if –
>
> (a) he causes a computer to perform any function with intent to secure access to any program or data held in any computer, or to enable any such access to be secured;
> (b) the access he intends to secure, or to enable to be secured, is unauthorised; and
> (c) he knows at the time when he causes the computer to perform the function that that is the case.
>
> (2) The intent a person has to have to commit an offence under this section need not be directed at –
>
> (a) any particular program or data;
> (b) a program or data of any particular kind; or
> (c) a program or data held in any particular computer.

The offence in s.1 is now an 'either way' offence, meaning that it can be tried either in the Crown Court or in the magistrates' court (this is a change brought about by the Police and Justice Act 2006, prior to which the offence could only be tried in the magistrates' court).

#### *The first component – causing a computer to perform any function with intent, etc.*

The first component of the offence (set out in s.1(1)(a)), shows that the offence is protecting the information *within* computers, rather than the computer itself. (However, the purpose of s.1 has been described as protecting the integrity of computers, see e.g. *R.* v. *Bow Street Metropolitan Stipendiary Magistrate, ex p. United States (No.2)* [2000] 2 AC 216.) This component is itself compromised of two elements. The first element is part of the *actus reus* of the offence, in that the defendant must cause the computer to perform a function. The meaning of 'causes a computer to perform any function' is so broadly drawn that it would cover merely turning the computer on, a conclusion which arises from the wording at s.17(2)(c) when read in combination with the wording at s.17(3). The second element forms part of the *mens rea*, i.e. the function must be performed with intent to secure access, or with intent to enable access to be secured. (See, for example, *Ellis* v. *DPP (No.1)* [2001] EWHC Admin 362, which concerned the unauthorised use of a university computer by an alumni, who was browsing the internet.)

A critical part of the first component of the offence is the meaning of 'secure access to any program or data'. This is defined in s.17(2)–(4):

> (2) A person secures access to any program or data held in a computer if by causing a computer to perform any function he –
>
> (a) alters or erases the program or data;
> (b) copies or moves it to any storage medium other than that in which it is held or to a different location in the storage medium in which it is held;
> (c) uses it; or
> (d) has it output from the computer in which it is held (whether by having it displayed or in any other manner);
>
> and references to access to a program or data (and to an intent to secure such access or to enable such access to be secured) shall be read accordingly.
>
> (3) For the purposes of subsection (2)(c) above a person uses a program if the function he causes the computer to perform –
>
> (a) causes the program to be executed; or
> (b) is itself a function of the program.
>
> (4) For the purposes of subsection (2)(d) above –
>
> (a) a program is output if the instructions of which it consists are output; and
> (b) the form in which any such instructions or any other data is output (and in particular whether or not it represents a form in which, in the case of instructions, they are capable of being executed or, in the case of data, it is capable of being processed by a computer) is immaterial.

These definitions act to illustrate further the breadth of the offence and, indeed, it is difficult to see how a person can cause a computer to perform a function and then fail to secure access within the meaning of the Act. Perhaps the best way of understanding this point is to consider the meaning of 'use of a program'. Section 17(3) shows that 'use' includes causing a program to be executed. This would cover the mere turning on of a computer, because turning on a computer causes programs to be executed. However, there is still a substantial difference between use of a program in this sense and actual access to computer data. Indeed, a person could be convicted of an offence under s.1 without gaining actual access to anything meaningful. (In *R.* v. *Bow Street Metropolitan Stipendiary Magistrate, ex p. United States*

*(No.2)*, Lord Hobhouse said 's.1(1) creates an offence which can be committed as a result of having an intent to secure unauthorised access without in fact actually succeeding in accessing any data'.)

The meaning of s.1(1)(a) was examined in *Attorney-General's Reference (No.1 of 1991)* [1993] QB 94, following the acquittal of a defendant who gained access to a computer to obtain a large discount for himself from the price of goods that he was buying; at trial he successfully argued that s.1(1)(a) requires the use of two computers, the first being the one that the defendant causes to function and the second being the one that the defendant intended to secure access to. The Court of Appeal rejected this construction. Lord Taylor said:

> [The defendant's counsel] argued successfully before the judge, and sought to argue before this court, that that final phrase [in section 1(1)(a)], 'held in any computer,' should really be read as 'held in any other computer,' or alternatively should be read as 'held in any computer except the computer which has performed the function.'
>
> To read those words in that way, in our judgment, would be to give them a meaning quite different from their plain and natural meaning. It is a trite observation, when considering the construction of statutes, that one does not imply or introduce words which are not there when the plain and natural meaning is clear. In our judgment there are no grounds whatsoever for implying, or importing the word 'other' between 'any' and 'computer,' or excepting the computer which is actually used by the offender from the phrase 'any computer' at the end of the subsection (1)(a) .

### *The second component – access that is unauthorised*

The second component of the offence, which is contained in s.1(1)(b), is that the access must be unauthorised. This component forms part of the *actus reus* of the offence. The meaning of authorisation is given in s.17(5), which says:

> (5) Access of any kind by any person to any program or data held in a computer is unauthorised if –
>
> (a) he is not himself entitled to control access of the kind in question to the program or data; and
>
> (b) he does not have consent to access by him of the kind in question to the program or data from any person who is so entitled.

The leading case on s.17(5) is *R.* v. *Bow Street Metropolitan Stipendiary Magistrate, ex p. United States (No.2)*,[4] a decision of the House of Lords. The facts of the case are relatively straightforward: an American Express employee passed confidential account information to one Mr Allison; she did not have authority to access the information in question, let alone to disclose it to Allison. Allison was charged with being in conspiracy with the American Express employee to secure unauthorised access to an American Express computer with intent to commit further offences of forgery of charge cards and theft of money. Lord Hobhouse said:

> Section 17 is an interpretation section. Subsection (2) defines what is meant by access and securing access to any program or data. It lists four ways in which this may occur or be achieved. Its purpose is clearly to give a specific meaning to the phrase 'to secure access.' Subsection (5) is to be read with subsection (2). It deals with the relationship between the widened definition of securing access and the scope of the authority which the relevant person may hold. That is why the subsection refers to 'access of any kind' and 'access of the kind in question.' Authority to view data may not extend to authority to copy or alter that data. The refinement of the concept of access requires a refinement of the concept of authorisation. The authorisation must be authority to secure access of the kind in question. As part of this refinement, the subsection lays down two cumulative requirements of lack of authority. The first is the requirement that the relevant person be not the person entitled to control the relevant kind of access. The word 'control' in this context clearly means authorise and forbid. If the relevant person is so entitled, then it would be unrealistic to treat his access as being unauthorised. The second is that the relevant person does not have the consent to secure the relevant kind of access from a person entitled to control, i.e. authorise, that access.
>
> Subsection (5) therefore has a plain meaning subsidiary to the other provisions of the Act. It simply identifies the two ways in which authority may be acquired-by being oneself the person entitled to authorise and by being a person who has been authorised by a person entitled to authorise. It also makes clear that the authority must relate not simply to the data or program but also to the actual kind of access secured. Similarly, it is plain that it is not using the word 'control' in a physical sense of the ability to operate or manipulate the computer and that it is not derogating from the requirement that for access to be authorised it must be authorised to the relevant data or relevant programme or part of a programme. It does not introduce any concept that authority to access one piece of data should be treated as authority to access other pieces of data 'of the same kind' notwithstanding that the relevant person did not in fact have authority to access that piece of data. Section 1 refers to the intent to secure unauthorised access to any programme or data. These plain words leave no room for any suggestion that the relevant person may say: 'Yes, I know that I was not authorised to access that data but I was authorised to access other data of the same kind.'

### *The third component – knowledge that the access is unauthorised*

The third component of the offence, which is contained in s.1(1)(c), is that the defendant must know that their access is unauthorised. Again, this forms part of the *mens rea*. It is important to note that s.1(1)(c) is concerned with actual knowledge, not constructive knowledge or recklessness.

### *Intent need not be directed to particular programs, data or computers*

Section 1(2) reinforces the message that the offence is very broad, in that the intent to secure unauthorised access need not be directed at any particular program or data. Again, using the example of unauthorised access through mere turning on of a computer it is easy to see how that offence would not be directed at a particular program or data.

### 6.4.2 Unauthorised access with intent to commit other crimes

CMA 1990, s.2 builds upon the access offence in s.1, where the defendant intends to commit or facilitate the commission of further offences for which the sentence is fixed by law (such as murder) or where a sentence of imprisonment of five or more years could be imposed.

> **2. Unauthorised access with intent to commit or facilitate commission of further offences**
>
> (1) A person is guilty of an offence under this section if he commits an offence under section 1 above ('the unauthorised access offence') with intent –
>
> (a) to commit an offence to which this section applies; or
> (b) to facilitate the commission of such an offence (whether by himself or by any other person);
>
> and the offence he intends to commit or facilitate is referred to below in this section as the further offence.
>
> (2) This section applies to offences –
>
> (a) for which the sentence is fixed by law; or
> (b) for which a person of twenty-one years of age or over (not previously convicted) may be sentenced to imprisonment for a term of five years (or, in England and Wales, might be so sentenced but for the restrictions imposed by section 33 of the Magistrates' Courts Act 1980).
>
> (3) It is immaterial for the purposes of this section whether the further offence is to be committed on the same occasion as the unauthorised access offence or on any future occasion.
>
> (4) A person may be guilty of an offence under this section even though the facts are such that the commission of the further offence is impossible.
>
> (5) A person guilty of an offence under this section shall be liable –
>
> (a) on summary conviction, to imprisonment for a term not exceeding six months or to a fine not exceeding the statutory maximum or to both; and
> (b) on conviction on indictment, to imprisonment for a term not exceeding five years or to a fine or to both.

Section 2 is really a facilitative offence, therefore prosecutors may decide to prefer charges for the substantive offence, rather than for the s.2 offence, as happened in the case of *Holmes* v. *The Governor of Brixton Prison* [2004] EWHC 2020 (Admin), where the defendant was charged with obtaining money by deception, after allegedly misusing computer systems at a bank where he was a temporary employee. During proceedings for habeus corpus Mr Justice Burnton observed:

> *Davies* v *Flackett* is not binding authority for the proposition that deception of a machine or computer is not deception for the purposes of the Theft Act. Ackner J so stated in terms in his judgment in that case. We nonetheless accept that 'The prevailing opinion is that it is not possible in law to deceive a machine' . . . In the modern world, where internet banking involves the transfer of funds by the use of passwords and PIN numbers, and within banks and other organisations funds can be transferred by the misuse of passwords (as in the present case), it is regrettable that obtaining by means of PIN numbers, passwords and the like operating on computers by a person who knows that he has no right to do so is not a substantive offence of theft or a cognate offence . . . So far as the alleged deception of the bank's computer in the present case is concerned, we say no more about it, other than to draw attention to the provisions of section 2 of the Computer Misuse Act 1990, which might have been used to frame a charge in the present case: c.f. *Attorney General's Reference (No. 1 of 1991)*1 [1993] QB 94.

### 6.4.3 Unauthorised acts intending to impair the operation of computers

From 1 October 2008, CMA 1990, s.3 will be replaced by a new section, which is currently found in Police and Justice Act 2006, s.36. The new s.3, which is the focus of this part, reads as follows:

> **3. Unauthorised acts with intent to impair, or with recklessness as to impairing, operation of computer, etc.**
>
> (1) A person is guilty of an offence if –
>
> (a) he does any unauthorised act in relation to a computer;
> (b) at the time when he does the act he knows that it is unauthorised; and
> (c) either subsection (2) or subsection (3) below applies.
>
> (2) This subsection applies if the person intends by doing the act –
>
> (a) to impair the operation of any computer;
> (b) to prevent or hinder access to any program or data held in any computer;
> (c) to impair the operation of any such program or the reliability of any such data; or
> (d) to enable any of the things mentioned in paragraphs (a) to (c) above to be done.
>
> (3) This subsection applies if the person is reckless as to whether the act will do any of the things mentioned in paragraphs (a) to (d) of subsection (2) above.
> (4) The intention referred to in subsection (2) above, or the recklessness referred to in subsection (3) above, need not relate to –
>
> (a) any particular computer;
> (b) any particular program or data; or
> (c) a program or data of any particular kind.
>
> (5) In this section –
>
> (a) a reference to doing an act includes a reference to causing an act to be done;
> (b) 'act' includes a series of acts;

(c) a reference to impairing, preventing or hindering something includes a reference to doing so temporarily.

(6) A person guilty of an offence under this section shall be liable –

(a) on summary conviction in England and Wales, to imprisonment for a term not exceeding 12 months or to a fine not exceeding the statutory maximum or to both;

(b) on summary conviction in Scotland, to imprisonment for a term not exceeding six months or to a fine not exceeding the statutory maximum or to both;

(c) on conviction on indictment, to imprisonment for a term not exceeding ten years or to a fine or to both.

In summary, a person will be guilty of an offence under the new s.3 if they do or cause to be done any unauthorised act, or series of acts, in relation to a computer with knowledge that the act is unauthorised and with intent to impair the operation of any computer (etc.), or if they are reckless as to the impairment (etc.). The intention, or recklessness, need not relate to any particular computer, program or data, or to any program or data of any particular kind, which echoes the approach within s.1, and the impairment (etc.) can be temporary.

The situations where s.3 has been engaged include where a person sent out a series of emails containing viruses which were detected internationally (see *R.* v. *Vallor* [2003] EWCA Crim 288: the defendant pleaded guilty to three offences committed over a six-week period, but he appealed his sentence of two years' imprisonment for each offence); where an ex-employee tampered with three company websites belonging to his former employer (*R.* v. *Lindesay* [2001] EWCA Crim. 1720); and where hackers broke into a computer system belonging to Bloomberg (*Zezev* v. *Governor of Brixton Prison* [2002] EWHC 589). In the final case, the court considered the meaning of impairing reliability, and the Lord Chief Justice, Lord Woolf, said:

> The question of the meaning of the words 'reliability of such data' has in the first place to be considered against the language used by the draftsman in the section itself. If a computer is caused to record information which shows that it came from one person, when it in fact came from someone else, that manifestly affects its reliability.

### *Meaning of 'unauthorised'*

The meaning of unauthorised is contained in CMA 1990, s.17(8), which says:

(8) An act done in relation to a computer is unauthorised if the person doing the act (or causing it to be done) –

(a) is not himself a person who has responsibility for the computer and is entitled to determine whether the act may be done; and
(b) does not have consent to the act from any such person.

In this subsection 'act' includes a series of acts.

The meaning of authorisation was analysed in *DPP* v. *Lennon* [2006] EWHC 1201 (Admin), an appeal by way of case stated from a decision of the District Judge holding that the defendant had no case to answer despite 'mail-bombing' his former employer's email server, which received over 500,000 spam emails ('spam' in the sense that the sender's identity was disguised). The defendant argued that the emails were not unauthorised as the defendant's email server had been installed for the specific purpose of receiving emails. In rejecting this argument Mr Justice Jack said:

> I agree, and it is not in dispute, that the owner of a computer which is able to receive emails is ordinarily to be taken as consenting to the sending of emails to the computer. His consent is to be implied from his conduct in relation to the computer. Some analogy can be drawn with consent by a householder to members of the public to walk up the path to his door when they have a legitimate reason for doing so, and also with the use of a private letter box. But that implied consent given by a computer owner is not without limit. The point can be illustrated by the same analogies. The householder does not consent to a burglar coming up his path. Nor does he consent to having his letter box choked with rubbish. That second example seems to me to be very much to the point here. I do not think that it is necessary for the decision in this case to try to define the limits of the consent which a computer owner impliedly gives to the sending of emails. It is enough to say that it plainly does not cover emails which are not sent for the purpose of communication with the owner, but are sent for the purpose of interrupting the proper operation and use of his system. That was the plain intent of Mr Lennon in using the Avalanche program. The difference can be demonstrated in this way. If Mr Lennon had telephoned Ms Rhodes and requested consent to send her an email raising a point about the termination of his employment, she would have been puzzled as to why he bothered to ask and said that of course he might. If he had asked if he might send the half million emails he did send, he would have got a quite different answer. In short the purpose of Mr Lennon in sending the half million emails was an unauthorised purpose and the use made of D&G's email facility was an unauthorised use.

### *Unauthorised acts in relation to removable storage media*

CMA 1990 reveals an interesting situation concerning data in removable storage media. Where those data are in removable storage media they will only gain the protection of s.3 when the removable media is actually held in the computer; once the media are removed from the computer CMA 1990 will not apply. CMA 1990, s.17(6) says:

(6) References to any program or data held in a computer include references to any program or data held in any removable storage medium which is for the

time being in the computer; and a computer is to be regarded as containing any program or data held in any such medium.

Of course, the construction of s.17(6) does not mean that data held in removable storage media are not protected while out of the computer. If those data are personal data they will be protected by section 55 of the Data Protection Act. Likewise, if those data are altered or erased so as to affect the physical condition of the removable media, the Criminal Damage Act 1971 will be engaged.[5]

## 6.5 'HATE MAIL'

It is a sad fact of life that emails are often used to send nasty, threatening and obscene communications. Not surprisingly, the sending of such communications can often be an offence.

### 6.5.1 Malicious Communications Act 1988

The Malicious Communications Act 1988 criminalises the sending of hate mail, which includes email. It covers the sending of indecent, grossly offensive, threatening and false communications where the purpose is to cause distress or anxiety. However, there is a defence for reasonable threats that support a demand. Section 1 says:

**1. Offence of sending letters etc. with intent to cause distress or anxiety**

(1) Any person who sends to another person –

(a) a letter, electronic communication or article of any description which conveys –

(i) a message which is indecent or grossly offensive;
(ii) a threat; or
(iii) information which is false and known or believed to be false by the sender; or

(b) any article or electronic communication which is, in whole or part, of an indecent or grossly offensive nature,

is guilty of an offence if his purpose, or one of his purposes, in sending it is that it should, so far as falling within paragraph (a) or (b) above, cause distress or anxiety to the recipient or to any other person to whom he intends that it or its contents or nature should be communicated.

(2) A person is not guilty of an offence by virtue of subsection (1)(a)(ii) above if he shows –

(a) that the threat was used to reinforce a demand made by him on reasonable grounds; and

(b) that he believed, and had reasonable grounds for believing, that the use of the threat was a proper means of reinforcing the demand.

(2A) In this section 'electronic communication' includes –

(a) any oral or other communication by means of an electronic communications network; and
(b) any communication (however sent) that is in electronic form.

(3) In this section references to sending include references to delivering or transmitting and to causing to be sent, delivered or transmitted and 'sender' shall be construed accordingly.
(4) A person guilty of an offence under this section shall be liable on summary conviction to imprisonment for a term not exceeding six months or to a fine not exceeding level 5 on the standard scale, or to both.

### 6.5.2 Communications Act 2003

The Communications Act 2003 also contains a series of offences against hate mail. These include sending, or causing to be sent, grossly offensive, indecent, obscene or menacing communications over the public network, which covers emails. It is also an offence to send false messages for the purpose of causing annoyance, inconvenience or needless anxiety and an offence to persistently use the network for these purposes. Section 127 states:

**127 Improper use of public electronic communications network**

(1) A person is guilty of an offence if he –

(a) sends by means of a public electronic communications network a message or other matter that is grossly offensive or of an indecent, obscene or menacing character; or
(b) causes any such message or matter to be so sent.

(2) A person is guilty of an offence if, for the purpose of causing annoyance, inconvenience or needless anxiety to another, he –

(a) sends by means of a public electronic communications network, a message that he knows to be false,
(b) causes such a message to be sent; or
(c) persistently makes use of a public electronic communications network.

(3) A person guilty of an offence under this section shall be liable, on summary conviction, to imprisonment for a term not exceeding six months or to a fine not exceeding level 5 on the standard scale, or to both.
(4) Subsections (1) and (2) do not apply to anything done in the course of providing a programme service (within the meaning of the Broadcasting Act 1990 (c. 42)).

The leading case on s.127 is *DPP* v. *Collins* [2006] UKHL 40. Collins was charged with making grossly offensive telephone calls to his MP and leaving racially offensive messages. The House of Lords held that the purpose of s.127(1)(a) of the Communications Act 2003 is to prohibit the use of the public communications system for the transmission of communications that contravene the basic standards of society. Lord Bingham said:

> First, the object of section 127(1)(a) and its predecessor sections is not to protect people against receipt of unsolicited messages which they may find seriously objectionable. That object is addressed in section 1 of the Malicious Communications Act 1988 , which does not require that messages shall, to be proscribed, have been sent by post, or telephone, or public electronic communications network. The purpose of the legislation which culminates in section 127(1)(a) was to prohibit the use of a service provided and funded by the public for the benefit of the public for the transmission of communications which contravene the basic standards of our society. A letter dropped through the letterbox may be grossly offensive, obscene, indecent or menacing, and may well be covered by section 1 of the 1988 Act, but it does not fall within the legislation now under consideration.
>
> Secondly, it is plain from the terms of section 127(1)(a) , as of its predecessor sections, that the proscribed act, the actus reus of the offence, is the sending of a message of the proscribed character by the defined means. The offence is complete when the message is sent. Thus it can make no difference that the message is never received, for example because a recorded message is erased before anyone listens to it. Nor, with respect, can the criminality of a defendant's conduct depend on whether a message is received by A, who for any reason is deeply offended, or B, who is not. On such an approach criminal liability would turn on an unforeseeable contingency. The respondent did not seek to support this approach.

### 6.5.3 Protection from Harassment Act 1997

The Protection from Harassment Act 1997 is discussed in **Chapter 5**. To recap, s.2 of this Act makes it an offence for a person to pursue a course of conduct that amounts to harassment of another, which they know or ought to know amounts to harassment of the other person.

### 6.5.4 Miscellaneous offences

Offences may also be committed where emails are used to intimidate persons connected with animal research organisations (Serious Organised Crime and Police Act 2005, s.146); where they are used to distribute visual images or sounds that are intended to stir up racial hatred (Public Order Act 1986, s.21); where they are possessed with the intention of stirring up racial hatred (Public Order Act 1986, s.23); and where they are used to cause racial or religious harassment (Crime and Disorder Act 1998, s.31).

## CHAPTER NOTES

1 Breaches of the data protection principles can lead indirectly to criminality after the Information Commissioner has commenced enforcement action under DPA

1998, ss.40, 43 and 44. Failure to comply with enforcement and information notices is a crime; see s.47.

2 Section 55 is not concerned with theft; intangible information cannot amount to property for the purposes of the Theft Act 1968 and therefore cannot be stolen; see *Oxford* v. *Moss* (1979) 68 Cr App R 183.

3 See *Attorney-General's Reference (No.140 of 2004)* [2004] EWCA, where an administrator at the DVLA was jailed for misconduct in public office following conviction of offences under s.55.

4 See also *DPP* v. *Bignell* [1998] 1 CrAppR, which concerned personal use of the Police National Computer by two police officers, through the medium of an innocent police computer operator; the defendants were cleared of charges under s.1, because their access was not unauthorised, despite the fact that they were using the computer for personal, not policing, reasons. The correctness of the acquittal was accepted by the House of Lords in the *Allison* case.

5 See Criminal Damage Act 1971, s.10(5), inserted by the Police and Justice Act 2006, Sched.14, para.2, from a day to be appointed. This reads 'for the purposes of this Act a modification of the contents of a computer shall not be regarded as damaging any computer or computer storage medium unless its effect on that computer or computer storage medium impairs its physical condition'.

# CHAPTER 7

# Access regimes and email as evidence

## 7.1 INTRODUCTION

There are many routes by which access to emails can be compelled. For example, the compulsory disclosure of information is an important facet of many regulatory regimes. This chapter examines some of the main routes to access that are encountered in ordinary, day-to-day legal practice and the extent to which emails are admissible in evidence. Litigation disclosure is examined in **Chapter 8**.

## 7.2 ACCESS UNDER THE 'INFORMATION ACTS'

The Data Protection Act (DPA) 1998 and the Freedom of Information Act (FOIA) 2000 both contain very important access mechanisms which can affect email; indeed, the FOIA 2000 was enacted for the specific purpose of opening a gateway to public sector information. The main access regime within the DPA 1998 is commonly known as 'subject access', as it is one that benefits the data subject, the living individual to whom personal data relate. However, there are additional access regimes within the Act, namely the right given to the Information Commissioner to serve information notices and special information notices, as part of his enforcement powers under Part V of the DPA 1998, and the right given to the Commissioner to apply for search warrants under Sched.9 to the Act. The access regime within the FOIA 2000 is commonly known as the 'general right of access', which is taken from the title of s.1 of the Act.

### 7.2.1 Subject access under the DPA 1998

The right of access to personal data is governed by DPA 1998, ss.7–9A and Sched.1 and a series of orders.[1]

As the DPA 1998 is notorious for the complexity and obscurity of its drafting, it is worth repeating ss.7, 8 and 9A in full (s.9 contains some modifying provisions for cases where the data controller is a credit reference agency):

**7. Right of access to personal data**

(1) Subject to the following provisions of this section and to sections 8, 9 and 9A, an individual is entitled –

(a) to be informed by any data controller whether personal data of which that individual is the data subject are being processed by or on behalf of that data controller,

(b) if that is the case, to be given by the data controller a description of –

(i) the personal data of which that individual is the data subject,

(ii) the purposes for which they are being or are to be processed, and

(iii) the recipients or classes of recipients to whom they are or may be disclosed,

(c) to have communicated to him in an intelligible form –

(i) the information constituting any personal data of which that individual is the data subject, and

(ii) any information available to the data controller as to the source of those data, and

(d) where the processing by automatic means of personal data of which that individual is the data subject for the purpose of evaluating matters relating to him such as, for example, his performance at work, his credit worthiness, his reliability or his conduct, has constituted or is likely to constitute the sole basis for any decision significantly affecting him, to be informed by the data controller of the logic involved in that decision-taking.

(2) A data controller is not obliged to supply any information under subsection (1) unless he has received –

(a) a request in writing, and

(b) except in prescribed cases, such fee (not exceeding the prescribed maximum) as he may require.

(3) Where a data controller –

(a) reasonably requires further information in order to satisfy himself as to the identity of the person making a request under this section and to locate the information which that person seeks, and

(b) has informed him of that requirement,

the data controller is not obliged to comply with the request unless he is supplied with that further information.

(4) Where a data controller cannot comply with the request without disclosing information relating to another individual who can be identified from that information, he is not obliged to comply with the request unless –

(a) the other individual has consented to the disclosure of the information to the person making the request, or

(b) it is reasonable in all the circumstances to comply with the request without the consent of the other individual.

(5) In subsection (4) the reference to information relating to another individual includes a reference to information identifying that individual as the source of the information sought by the request; and that subsection is not to be construed as excusing a data controller from communicating so much of the information sought by the request as can be communicated without disclosing the identity of the other individual concerned, whether by the omission of names or other identifying particulars or otherwise.

(6) In determining for the purposes of subsection (4)(b) whether it is reasonable in all the circumstances to comply with the request without the consent of the other individual concerned, regard shall be had, in particular, to –

(a) any duty of confidentiality owed to the other individual,
(b) any steps taken by the data controller with a view to seeking the consent of the other individual,
(c) whether the other individual is capable of giving consent, and
(d) any express refusal of consent by the other individual.

(7) An individual making a request under this section may, in such cases as may be prescribed, specify that his request is limited to personal data of any prescribed description.

(8) Subject to subsection (4), a data controller shall comply with a request under this section promptly and in any event before the end of the prescribed period beginning with the relevant day.

(9) If a court is satisfied on the application of any person who has made a request under the foregoing provisions of this section that the data controller in question has failed to comply with the request in contravention of those provisions, the court may order him to comply with the request.

(10) In this section –

'prescribed' means prescribed by the Secretary of State by regulations:
'the prescribed maximum' means such amount as may be prescribed:
'the prescribed period' means forty days or such other period as may be prescribed:
'the relevant day', in relation to a request under this section, means the day on which the data controller receives the request or, if later, the first day on which the data controller has both the required fee and the information referred to in subsection (3).

(11) Different amounts or periods may be prescribed under this section in relation to different cases.

**8. Provisions supplementary to section 7**

(1) The Secretary of State may by regulations provide that, in such cases as may be prescribed, a request for information under any provision of subsection (1) of section 7 is to be treated as extending also to information under other provisions of that subsection.

(2) The obligation imposed by section 7(1)(c)(i) must be complied with by supplying the data subject with a copy of the information in permanent form unless –

(a) the supply of such a copy is not possible or would involve disproportionate effort, or
(b) the data subject agrees otherwise;

and where any of the information referred to in section 7(1)(c)(i) is expressed in terms which are not intelligible without explanation the copy must be accompanied by an explanation of those terms.

(3) Where a data controller has previously complied with a request made under section 7 by an individual, the data controller is not obliged to comply with a subsequent identical or similar request under that section by that individual unless a reasonable interval has elapsed between compliance with the previous request and the making of the current request.

(4) In determining for the purposes of subsection (3) whether requests under section 7 are made at reasonable intervals, regard shall be had to the nature of the data, the purposes for which the data are processed and the frequency with which the data are altered.

(5) Section 7(1)(d) is not to be regarded as requiring the provision of information as to the logic involved in any decision-taking if, and to the extent that, the information constitutes a trade secret.

(6) The information to be supplied pursuant to a request under section 7 must be supplied by reference to the data in question at the time when the request is received, except that it may take account of any amendment or deletion made between that time and the time when the information is supplied, being an amendment or deletion that would have been made regardless of the receipt of the request.

(7) For the purposes of section 7(4) and (5) another individual can be identified from the information being disclosed if he can be identified from that information, or from that and any other information which, in the reasonable belief of the data controller, is likely to be in, or to come into, the possession of the data subject making the request.

. . .

**9A. Unstructured personal data held by public authorities**

(1) In this section 'unstructured personal data' means any personal data falling within paragraph (e) of the definition of 'data' in section 1(1), other than information which is recorded as part of, or with the intention that it should form part of, any set of information relating to individuals to the extent that the set is structured by reference to individuals or by reference to criteria relating to individuals.

(2) A public authority is not obliged to comply with subsection (1) of section 7 in relation to any unstructured personal data unless the request under that section contains a description of the data.

(3) Even if the data are described by the data subject in his request, a public authority is not obliged to comply with subsection (1) of section 7 in relation to unstructured personal data if the authority estimates that the cost of complying with the request so far as relating to those data would exceed the appropriate limit.

(4) Subsection (3) does not exempt the public authority from its obligation to comply with paragraph (a) of section 7(1) in relation to the unstructured

personal data unless the estimated cost of complying with that paragraph alone in relation to those data would exceed the appropriate limit.

(5) In subsections (3) and (4) 'the appropriate limit' means such amount as may be prescribed by the Secretary of State by regulations, and different amounts may be prescribed in relation to different cases.

(6) Any estimate for the purposes of this section must be made in accordance with regulations under section 12(5) of the Freedom of Information Act 2000.

### *The extent of the entitlements*

The right of access actually consists of a series of distinct entitlements. These are:

- The data subject is entitled to be told whether the data controller is processing their personal data, which includes circumstances where the controller has engaged a data processor (DPA 1998, s.7(1)(a)).
- The data subject is entitled to a description of that personal data (s.7(1)(b)(i)).
- The data subject is entitled to a description of the purposes for which their data are being processed (s.7(1)(b)(ii)).
- The data subject is entitled to a description of the recipients or classes of recipients to whom their data are or may be disclosed (s.7(1)(b)(iii)).
- The data subject is entitled to have their information 'communicated' to them, in an intelligible form (s.7(1)(c)(i)). This obligation is complied with through the supply of a copy of the information in a permanent form, unless that would require a disproportionate effort or unless the data subject otherwise agrees (s.8(2)).
- The data subject is entitled to have communicated to them, in an intelligible form, any information that the data controller has about the source of the personal data (s.7(c)(ii)).

### *Exercising the right of access and the time for compliance*

The right of access is exercisable in writing (DPA 1998, s.7(2)(a)) and in most cases the data controller can charge a £10 fee before replying (s.7(2)(b)). The data controller may also seek information to verify the data subject's identity and to locate the data sought (s.7(3)). Once the fee has been paid the data controller has 40 days to supply the information (s.7(8)).

### *The information to be provided, including third party data*

The information that is to be provided is that in existence at the date of receipt of the request (DPA 1998, s.8(6)); see *Smith* v. *Lloyd's Bank plc* [2005] EWHC 246). However, the data controller may be able to avoid complying with a request for personal data if to comply would require the disclosure of information relating to another identifiable person (s.7(4)), although the controller must disclose as much of the information as is possible without identifying the other person (s.7(5)), which in appropriate cases brings with it an obligation to consider redaction and other anonymisation processes (s.7(4)(a)). If the other person consents to the disclosure no problem arises (s.7(4)(a)), but the data controller can still release the other person's information without their consent if it is reasonable to do so in all the circumstances (s.7(4)(b)). On the question of reasonableness, in the event of a dispute the court and the Information Commissioner are to have regard to any duty of confidentiality, any steps taken by the data controller to obtain consent, whether the other person is capable of giving consent and any express refusal of consent (s.7(6)).

In *Durant* v. *Financial Services Authority* Auld LJ said (see paras.64–7 inclusive):

> It is important for data controllers to keep in mind the two stage thought process that section 7(4) contemplates and for which section 7(4)–(6) provides.
>
> The first is to consider whether information about any other individual is necessarily part of the personal data that the data subject has requested. I stress the word 'necessarily' for the same reason that I stress the word 'cannot' in the opening words of section 7(4) , 'Where a data controller cannot comply with the request without disclosing information about another individual who can be identified from the information'. If such information about another is not necessarily part of personal data sought, no question of section 7(4) balancing arises at all. The data controller, whose primary obligation is to provide information, not documents, can, if he chooses to provide that information in the form of a copy document, simply redact such third party information because it is not a necessary part of the data subject's personal data.
>
> The second stage, that of the section 7(4) balance, only arises where the data controller considers that the third party information necessarily forms part of the personal data sought. In that event, it is tempting to adopt Mr. Sales's submission that, where the status of an individual is obvious and his or her identity is immaterial or of little legitimate value to the data subject, it would normally be reasonable to withhold information identifying that person in the absence of his consent. However, it is difficult to think in the abstract of information identifying another person and any other information about him which would be so bound up with the data subject as to qualify as his personal data, yet be immaterial or of little legitimate value to him. Much will depend, on the one hand, on the criticality of the third party information forming part of the data subject's personal data to the legitimate protection of his privacy, and, on the other, to the existence or otherwise of any obligation of confidence to the third party or any other sensitivity of the third party disclosure sought. Where the third party is a recipient or one of a class of recipients who might act on the data to the data subject's disadvantage (section 7(1)(b)(iii)), his right to protect his privacy may weigh heavily and obligations of confidence to the third party(ies) may be non-existent or of less weight. Equally, where the third party is the source of the information, the data subject may have a strong case for his identification if he needs to take action to correct some damaging inaccuracy, though here countervailing considerations of an

obligation of confidentiality to the source or some other sensitivity may have to be weighed in the balance. It should be remembered that the task of the court in this context is likely to be much the same as that under section 7(9) in the exercise of its general discretion whether to order a data controller to comply with the data subject's request (see para. 74 below). In short, it all depends on the circumstances whether it would be reasonable to disclose to a data subject the name of another person figuring in his personal data, whether that person is a source, or a recipient or likely recipient of that information, or has a part in the matter the subject of the personal data. Beyond the basic presumption or starting point to which I referred in paragraph 55 above, I believe that the courts should be wary of attempting to devise any principles of general application one way or the other.

However, as I have indicated, on the facts of the case, the redaction issue is barely worth all the attention given to it in the arguments. It is clear from the Judge's examination of the documents and the evidence to this Court of Mr. Davies that all the redactions, save arguably two, do not constitute 'personal data' for the reasons I have given, and the Act does not, therefore, entitle Mr. Durant to that information. As to those two redactions, they were of the name of an FSA employee which, in itself, can have been of little or no legitimate value to Mr. Durant and who had understandably withheld his or her consent because Mr. Durant had abused him or her over the telephone.

### *Failure to comply with the right of access*

The data subject's right of access to personal data is one that can pose significant difficulties for data controllers, particularly when the use of email is not subject to tight controls within the organisation. However, data controllers are not obliged to go to inordinate lengths to locate personal data that may fall within the scope of a subject access request and it is worth noting a first instance decision of the High Court, *Ezsias* v. *The Welsh Ministers* [2007] All ER(D) 65, which held that organisations are required to perform a reasonable and proportionate search to locate personal data; depending upon the facts of the case such a search can fall far short of a total search of the data within the organisation. Additionally, the provisions of s.8(2) should be noted, which effectively exempt the data controller from complying with s.7(1)(c), if that was otherwise to amount to disproportionate effort.

Aside from arguments about reasonableness and the application of any exemptions, if a data controller fails to comply with a subject access it faces two serious consequences. First, the data subject can bring proceedings before the court, under s.7(9), for an order that the controller shall comply with the access request. If the data subject does commence litigation under s.7(9), the court can inspect any disputed materials for the purpose of determining whether any information therein are required to be disclosed (s.15(2)). Second, the controller faces enforcement action by the Information Commissioner, as a failure to comply with an access request constitutes a breach of the sixth data protection principle. The Information Commissioner may commence enforcement action under s.40 if he is satisfied that the controller has contravened or is contravening any of the principles.

*Exemptions*

DPA 1998, Part IV is titled 'Exemptions'. It contains a wide series of exemptions from many of the provisions of the Act, including from subject access. Schedule 7 contains further miscellaneous exemptions. The right of access is further modified by a series of orders made under s.30.

### 7.2.2 Information notices under the DPA 1998

**Chapter 3** introduced the concepts of enforcement notices and information notices, which form part of the Information Commissioner's suite of enforcement powers under DPA 1998, Part V. Information notices and special information notices can both be used by the Commissioner to gain access to emails.

Under DPA 1998, s.43 the Commissioner can serve a data controller with an information notice if he has received a 'request for an assessment' of the controller's processing from a person under DPA 1998, s.42 (s.42(1) provides that a person may request the Commissioner to assess 'whether it is likely or unlikely that the processing has been or is being carried out in compliance with the provisions of [the Data Protection Act]' if they believe that they have been directly affected by the processing), or if he reasonably requires information for the purpose of determining whether or not the controller's processing is in compliance with the data protection principles. Section 43 says:

**43. Information notices**

(1) If the Commissioner –

(a) has received a request under section 42 in respect of any processing of personal data, or

(b) reasonably requires any information for the purpose of determining whether the data controller has complied or is complying with the data protection principles,

he may serve the data controller with a notice (in this Act referred to as 'an information notice') requiring the data controller, within such time as is specified in the notice, to furnish the Commissioner, in such form as may be so specified, with such information relating to the request or to compliance with the principles as is so specified.

(2) An information notice must contain –

(a) in a case falling within subsection (1)(a), a statement that the Commissioner has received a request under section 42 in relation to the specified processing, or

(b) in a case falling within subsection (1)(b), a statement that the Commissioner regards the specified information as relevant for the purpose of determining whether the data controller has complied, or is complying, with the data protection principles and his reasons for regarding it as relevant for that purpose.

(3) An information notice must also contain particulars of the rights of appeal conferred by section 48.

(4) Subject to subsection (5), the time specified in an information notice shall not expire before the end of the period within which an appeal can be brought against the notice and, if such an appeal is brought, the information need not be furnished pending the determination or withdrawal of the appeal.

(5) If by reason of special circumstances the Commissioner considers that the information is required as a matter of urgency, he may include in the notice a statement to that effect and a statement of his reasons for reaching that conclusion; and in that event subsection (4) shall not apply, but the notice shall not require the information to be furnished before the end of the period of seven days beginning with the day on which the notice is served.

(6) A person shall not be required by virtue of this section to furnish the Commissioner with any information in respect of –

(a) any communication between a professional legal adviser and his client in connection with the giving of legal advice to the client with respect to his obligations, liabilities or rights under this Act, or

(b) any communication between a professional legal adviser and his client, or between such an adviser or his client and any other person, made in connection with or in contemplation of proceedings under or arising out of this Act (including proceedings before the Tribunal) and for the purposes of such proceedings.

(7) In subsection (6) references to the client of a professional legal adviser include references to any person representing such a client.

(8) A person shall not be required by virtue of this section to furnish the Commissioner with any information if the furnishing of that information would, by revealing evidence of the commission of any offence other than an offence under this Act, expose him to proceedings for that offence.

(9) The Commissioner may cancel an information notice by written notice to the person on whom it was served.

(10) This section has effect subject to section 46(3).

The Commissioner's power to serve a special information notice is contained in DPA 1998, s.44. This applies where he has received a request for an assessment under s.42 or where court proceedings brought by a data subject against a controller have been stayed under s.32 to enable the Commissioner to determine whether the processing is for the 'special purposes' with a 'view to publication' (s.32(4)(b)). To explain, the special purposes are defined in DPA 1998, s.3 as being processing for the purposes of journalism, artistic purposes and literary purposes. Due to the provisions of s.32, special purposes processing is exempt from most aspects of the DPA 1998, including most of the data subject rights. Thus, if litigation is commenced by a data subject and it is claimed by the controller that the processing is for special purposes, it will be necessary to have that issued determined. The route preferred by the DPA 1998 is a stay of proceedings (s.32(4)) pending a determination by the Commissioner of the processing purpose under s.45.

DPA 1998, s.44 says:

**44. Special information notices**

(1) If the Commissioner –

(a) has received a request under section 42 in respect of any processing of personal data, or
(b) has reasonable grounds for suspecting that, in a case in which proceedings have been stayed under section 32, the personal data to which the proceedings relate –

(i) are not being processed only for the special purposes, or
(ii) are not being processed with a view to the publication by any person of any journalistic, literary or artistic material which has not previously been published by the data controller,

he may serve the data controller with a notice (in this Act referred to as a 'special information notice') requiring the data controller, within such time as is specified in the notice, to furnish the Commissioner, in such form as may be so specified, with such information as is so specified for the purpose specified in subsection (2).

(2) That purpose is the purpose of ascertaining –

(a) whether the personal data are being processed only for the special purposes, or
(b) whether they are being processed with a view to the publication by any person of any journalistic, literary or artistic material which has not previously been published by the data controller.

(3) A special information notice must contain –

(a) in a case falling within paragraph (a) of subsection (1), a statement that the Commissioner has received a request under section 42 in relation to the specified processing, or
(b) in a case falling within paragraph (b) of that subsection, a statement of the Commissioner's grounds for suspecting that the personal data are not being processed as mentioned in that paragraph.

(4) A special information notice must also contain particulars of the rights of appeal conferred by section 48.

(5) Subject to subsection (6), the time specified in a special information notice shall not expire before the end of the period within which an appeal can be brought against the notice and, if such an appeal is brought, the information need not be furnished pending the determination or withdrawal of the appeal.

(6) If by reason of special circumstances the Commissioner considers that the information is required as a matter of urgency, he may include in the notice a statement to that effect and a statement of his reasons for reaching that conclusion; and in that event subsection (5) shall not apply, but the notice shall not require the information to be furnished before the end of the period of seven days beginning with the day on which the notice is served.

(7) A person shall not be required by virtue of this section to furnish the Commissioner with any information in respect of –

(a) any communication between a professional legal adviser and his client in connection with the giving of legal advice to the client with respect to his obligations, liabilities or rights under this Act, or

(b) any communication between a professional legal adviser and his client, or between such an adviser or his client and any other person, made in connection with or in contemplation of proceedings under or arising out of this Act (including proceedings before the Tribunal) and for the purposes of such proceedings.

(8) In subsection (7) references to the client of a professional legal adviser include references to any person representing such a client.

(9) A person shall not be required by virtue of this section to furnish the Commissioner with any information if the furnishing of that information would, by revealing evidence of the commission of any offence other than an offence under this Act, expose him to proceedings for that offence.

(10) The Commissioner may cancel a special information notice by written notice to the person on whom it was served.

### 7.2.3 The Information Commissioner's power to enter premises under the DPA 1998

Under DPA 1998, Sched.9 the Information Commissioner can apply to a judge for a warrant to enter premises if he has reasonable grounds for believing that a data controller has contravened or is contravening any of the data protection principles or that an offence under the DPA 1998 has been committed and that relevant evidence will be found on the premises. If the judge is satisfied of these matters they can grant a warrant. The warrant will allow the Commissioner to enter premises and search them and inspect, examine, operate and test any equipment on the premises used for processing. The judge shall not issue a warrant unless the Commissioner has asked for and has been refused access to the premises, unless he is satisfied that a request for access would defeat the object of entry or if the case is one of urgency. Warrants cannot extend to privileged materials.

It is an offence to obstruct or warrant or to fail to provide reasonable assistance during its execution.

#### *Proposals to extend the Commissioner's powers of entry*

In December 2007 the Information Commissioner submitted to the Ministry of Justice his case for amending the DPA 1998,[2] in which he argued for new powers and new penalties. Once of the first fruits of this submission was s.144 of the Criminal Justice and Immigration Act (CJIA) 2008, which has introduced a new s.55A into the DPA 1998 that will enable the Commissioner to issue controllers with fines where he is satisfied that they are in serious contravention of the data protection principles. In July 2008 the Ministry of Justice commenced a public consultation[3] on the Commissioner's proposal for the introduction of a power to enter premises without a warrant.

### 7.2.4 The general right of access under FOIA 2000

FOIA 2000 was passed to give wide-ranging access to recorded information held by public authorities, which covers emails held by public authorities. (See FOIA 2000, s.84 for the meaning of 'information', which is 'information recorded in any form'. See Sched.1 for the list of public authorities that are subject to the Act. A public authority can also be designated under s.5 of the Act and includes publicly-owned companies as defined by s.6 (see s.4).)

The 'general right of access' is contained in FOIA 2000, s.1 and its essence is making a 'request for information'. Section 1 says:

> **1. General right of access to information held by public authorities**
>
> (1) Any person making a request for information to a public authority is entitled –
>
> (a) to be informed in writing by the public authority whether it holds information of the description specified in the request, and
> (b) if that is the case, to have that information communicated to him.
>
> (2) Subsection (1) has effect subject to the following provisions of this section and to the provisions of sections 2, 9, 12 and 14.
> (3) Where a public authority –
>
> (a) reasonably requires further information in order to identify and locate the information requested, and
> (b) has informed the applicant of that requirement,
>
> the authority is not obliged to comply with subsection (1) unless it is supplied with that further information.
> (4) The information –
>
> (a) in respect of which the applicant is to be informed under subsection (1)(a), or
> (b) which is to be communicated under subsection (1)(b),
>
> is the information in question held at the time when the request is received, except that account may be taken of any amendment or deletion made between that time and the time when the information is to be communicated under subsection (1)(b), being an amendment or deletion that would have been made regardless of the receipt of the request.
> (5) A public authority is to be taken to have complied with subsection (1)(a) in relation to any information if it has communicated the information to the applicant in accordance with subsection (1)(b).
> (6) In this Act, the duty of a public authority to comply with subsection (1)(a) is referred to as 'the duty to confirm or deny'.

*Who may make an access request?*

FOIA 2000, s.1(1) refers to 'any person'. This is unlimited in scope, in the sense that it does not refer to a person of any particular category or class.

Thus, an applicant can legitimately reside outside the UK as well as within. The applicant can be a foreign national, as well as a UK citizen.

There is no restriction on the number of requests for information that any person can make, although public authorities are able to avoid answering vexatious requests and repeated requests. Section 14 says:

> **14. Vexatious or repeated requests**
>
> (1) Section 1(1) does not oblige a public authority to comply with a request for information if the request is vexatious.
> (2) Where a public authority has previously complied with a request for information which was made by any person, it is not obliged to comply with a subsequent identical or substantially similar request from that person unless a reasonable interval has elapsed between compliance with the previous request and the making of the current request.

### *The obligations placed on the public authority*

If a public authority receives a 'valid' request for information (see below) then, subject to any exemptions, it faces four key obligations. First, it faces 'the duty to confirm or deny' (FOIA 2000, s.1(6)), which is a duty to inform the applicant, in writing, whether it holds information of the description specified in the request (s.1(1)(a)). Second, if it does hold that information then it must communicate it to the applicant (s.1(1)(b)). Third, by reason of s.16(1) it is required to provide 'advice and assistance, so far as would be reasonable to expect the authority to do so, to persons who propose to make, or have made, requests for information'. Fourth, where the applicant expresses a preference for either a copy of the information in a permanent form or in another form, or where they request a reasonable opportunity to inspect the information or where they request a digest or summary of the information the public authority should give effect to the preference in so far as it is reasonably practicable to do so (s.11).

### *'Valid' access requests – formalities, identifying information and fees*

There are no strict formalities for making access requests, but FOIA 2000, s.8(1) does require any request for information to be made in writing. Of course, a written request covers a handwritten or typed letter, but it also covers requests made by email or fax, due to the provisions of s.8(2), which says that a request will be made in writing if its text is transmitted by electronic means, is received in legible form and is capable of being used for subsequent reference. In addition to being made in writing, the request must provide the applicant's name and an address for correspondence and it should describe the information sought.

The public authority is not obliged to comply with a request for information where it reasonably requires and has requested further information to identify and locate the information sought (s.1(3)).

Public authorities are entitled to charge fees for complying with requests for information, although they are not obliged to do so. If the authority wishes to charge a fee it must calculate the fee in accordance with the formula within the Freedom of Information and Data Protection (Appropriate Limit and Fees) Regulations 2004, SI 2004/3244. However, a fee cannot be charged unless the applicant is served with a fees notice under FOIA 2000, s.9. If a fees notice is served, the public authority is not required to comply with the request until the fee is paid, which is subject to a three-month longstop provision; if the applicant does not pay the fee within this period the public authority will not be required to comply with the request even if the fee is paid after the three-month period.

FOIA 2000, s.12 provides public authorities with an exemption from the duty to confirm or deny and the duty to communicate information where the cost of complying would exceed the 'appropriate limit'. The appropriate limit for central government departments is £600 and the appropriate limit for other public authorities is £450 (see SI 2004/3244).

### *Time for complying with access request*

The time period for complying with requests for information is 20 working days commencing with the day following the date of receipt of the request (FOIA 2000, s.10). This excludes the period of time between the giving of a fees notice and the receipt of the fee.

### *Exemptions*

Despite being a legal regime designed to open up public sector information to scrutiny, FOIA 2000 contains a large number of exemptions, which are to be found at Part II of the Act. Some of these exemptions are 'absolute' exemptions, meaning that the duty to confirm or deny and the duty to communicate information do not apply. Others are 'qualified' exemptions, meaning that these duties are subject to a public interest test, which pits the public interest in maintaining secrecy against the public interest in disclosure. Some of the qualified exemptions are 'class' based, meaning that they apply to particular types of information, while some are 'prejudice' based, meaning that for the exemption to apply disclosure would have to cause prejudice to certain interests. Section 2 says:

**2. Effect of the exemptions in Part II**

(1) Where any provision of Part II states that the duty to confirm or deny does not arise in relation to any information, the effect of the provision is that where either –

- (a) the provision confers absolute exemption, or
- (b) in all the circumstances of the case, the public interest in maintaining the exclusion of the duty to confirm or deny outweighs the public interest in disclosing whether the public authority holds the information,

section 1(1)(a) does not apply.

(2) In respect of any information which is exempt information by virtue of any provision of Part II, section 1(1)(b) does not apply if or to the extent that –

- (a) the information is exempt information by virtue of a provision conferring absolute exemption, or
- (b) in all the circumstances of the case, the public interest in maintaining the exemption outweighs the public interest in disclosing the information.

(3) For the purposes of this section, the following provisions of Part II (and no others) are to be regarded as conferring absolute exemption –

- (a) section 21,
- (b) section 23,
- (c) section 32,
- (d) section 34,
- (e) section 36 so far as relating to information held by the House of Commons or the House of Lords,
- (f) in section 40 –
  - (i) subsection (1), and
  - (ii) subsection (2) so far as relating to cases where the first condition referred to in that subsection is satisfied by virtue of subsection (3)(a)(i) or (b) of that section,
- (g) section 41, and
- (h) section 44.

If the public authority considers that an exemption applies and chooses to rely upon the exemption then it must serve a 'refusal notice' on the applicant under s.17, specifying the grounds for refusal and giving details of its internal complaints procedures (s.45). After exhausting the internal complaints procedure (s.50(2)(a)) the applicant can then complain to the Information Commissioner, who will then serve a decision notice (s.50). The applicant/complainant and the public authority can both appeal to the Information Tribunal (s.57). The parties can appeal from the Information Tribunal to the High Court on points of law (s.59).

### *Case law*

The Information Commissioner has published literally hundreds of decision notices on his website. The Information Tribunal has also heard dozens of appeals and its decisions are published on its website. The decisions are too numerous to review here. Cases are now making their way to the High Court and beyond. Recent cases include *Commons Services Agency* v. *Scottish Information Commissioner* [2008] UKHL 47, a decision of the House of Lords which concerns the interplay between the Scottish Freedom of Information Act and the DPA 1998; *Corporate Officer of the House of Commons* v. *Information Commissioner* [2008] EWHC 1084, a decision of the Divisional Court concerning MPs expenses; *Office of Government Commerce* v. *Information Commissioner* [2008] EWHC 774, a decision of the Divisional Court concerning the Identity Card gateway reviews; *BBC* v. *Sugar* [2008] EWCA 191, a decision of the Court of Appeal concerning the BBC's reporting of events in the Middle East; and *R (British Union for the Abolition of Vivisection)* v. *Secretary of State for the Home Department* [2008] EWCA 417, a decision of the Court of Appeal concerning applications for licences for animal experimentation.

### *Environmental Information Regulations*

The Environmental Information Regulations 2004, SI 2004/3391 give effect to Environmental Information Directive 2003 (Directive 2003/4/EC of the European Parliament and of the Council of 28 January 2003 on public access to environmental information and repealing Council Directive 90/313/EEC), creating a general right of access to 'environmental information' held by public authorities. Environmental information is defined in reg.2 in the following terms:

> 'environmental information' has the same meaning as in Article 2(1) of the Directive, namely any information in written, visual, aural, electronic or any other material form on –
>
> (a) the state of the elements of the environment, such as air and atmosphere, water, soil, land, landscape and natural sites including wetlands, coastal and marine areas, biological diversity and its components, including genetically modified organisms, and the interaction among these elements;
> (b) factors, such as substances, energy, noise, radiation or waste, including radioactive waste, emissions, discharges and other releases into the environment, affecting or likely to affect the elements of the environment referred to in (a);
> (c) measures (including administrative measures), such as policies, legislation, plans, programmes, environmental agreements, and activities affecting or likely to affect the elements and factors referred to in (a) and (b) as well as measures or activities designed to protect those elements;
> (d) reports on the implementation of environmental legislation;
> (e) cost-benefit and other economic analyses and assumptions used within the framework of the measures and activities referred to in (c); and
> (f) the state of human health and safety, including the contamination of the food chain, where relevant, conditions of human life, cultural sites and built

structures inasmuch as they are or may be affected by the state of the elements of the environment referred to in (a) or, through those elements, by any of the matters referred to in (b) and (c);

The access regime within these Regulations mirrors closely that within the FOIA 2000. Thus, an applicant is entitled to request access to environmental information, which, subject to exemptions, is to be supplied within 20 working days commencing the day after the date of receipt of the request (reg.5).

## 7.3 INTERCEPTION OF COMMUNICATIONS AND ACCESS TO RETAINED COMMUNICATIONS DATA

As discussed in **Chapter 4**, the EU legal framework governing the interception of communications, the retention of communications data and the access to retained communications data is contained in the Privacy and Electronic Communications Directive 2002 (PECD) and the Communications Data Retention Directive 2006 (CDRD). In summary, PECD allows EU Member States to engage in interception of communications, provided that the interception is a 'necessary, appropriate and proportionate measure within a democratic society' (PECD, Article 15(1)) and CDRD requires Member States to pass laws requiring the retention of communications data (CDRD refers to 'data') by providers of publicly available electronic communications services and networks (CDRD, Article 3) so that it can be accessible to 'competent national authorities' (CDRD, Article 3(1)).

This part discusses the domestic rules on interception pursuant to warrant, the monitoring of business communications and the rules governing the retention of and access to communications data. For the meaning of 'interception' and 'communications data', see **Chapter 4**.

### 7.3.1 Interception pursuant to warrant issued under Regulation of Investigatory Powers Act 2000, s.5

Section 1 of the Regulation of Investigatory Powers Act (RIPA) 2000 makes it an offence for a person to intercept electronic communications in the course of their transmission without lawful authority. RIPA 2000, ss.3, 4 and 5 identify the circumstances in which interception will be with lawful authority. As discussed in **Chapter 4**, ss.3 and 4 are both concerned with interception without warrant, while s.5 is concerned with interception pursuant to warrant.

### *Code of Practice for interception*

RIPA 2000, s.71 requires the Secretary of State to issue a code of practice governing interception. The current code, issued under s.71(5), is the 'Interception of Communications: Code of Practice 2002' (Regulation of Investigatory Powers (Interception of Communications: Code of Practice) Order 2002, SI 2002/1693). Section 71(2) requires any person exercising or performing any power or duty in relation to interception to have regard to the provisions of the Code, but any failure to do so will not 'render him liable to any criminal or civil proceedings' (s.72(2)). The Code is admissible in evidence in any criminal or civil proceedings (s.72(3)).

### *The power to issue interception warrants*

RIPA 2000, s.5(1) permits the Secretary of State to issue an interception warrant. It says:

> (1) Subject to the following provisions of this Chapter, the Secretary of State may issue a warrant authorising or requiring the person to whom it is addressed, by any such conduct as may be described in the warrant, to secure any one or more of the following –
>
> (a) the interception in the course of their transmission by means of a postal service or telecommunication system of the communications described in the warrant;
>
> (b) the making, in accordance with an international mutual assistance agreement, of a request for the provision of such assistance in connection with, or in the form of, an interception of communications as may be so described;
>
> (c) the provision, in accordance with an international mutual assistance agreement, to the competent authorities of a country or territory outside the United Kingdom of any such assistance in connection with, or in the form of, an interception of communications as may be so described;
>
> (d) the disclosure, in such manner as may be so described, of intercepted material obtained by any interception authorised or required by the warrant, and of related communications data.

There are two kinds of interception warrants, which are both identified in s.8. The first kind of warrant requires either the identification of the 'interception subject' or 'the premises in relation to which the interception is to take place'. The second kind of warrant is often called a 'certified warrant'. Certified warrants apply in respect of 'external communications' and they do not require the identification of a person or premises.

### *Grounds for issue of a warrant*

An interception warrant can only be issued where it is necessary on prescribed grounds and where the conduct it authorises is proportionate (s.5(2)), but before issuing a warrant the Secretary of State must always consider whether the information can be reasonably obtained in another manner (s.5(4)). The Code of Practice says:

> 2.4 Obtaining a warrant under the Act will only ensure that the interception authorised is a justifiable interference with an individual's rights under Article 8 of the European Convention of Human Rights (the right to privacy) if it is necessary and proportionate for the interception to take place. The Act recognises this by first requiring that the Secretary of State believes that the authorisation is necessary on one or more of the statutory grounds set out in section 5(3) of the Act. This requires him to believe that it is necessary to undertake the interception which is to be authorised for a particular purpose falling within the relevant statutory ground.
>
> 2.5 Then, if the interception is necessary, the Secretary of State must also believe that it is proportionate to what is sought to be achieved by carrying it out. This involves balancing the intrusiveness of the interference, against the need for it in operational terms. Interception of communications will not be proportionate if it is excessive in the circumstances of the case or if the information which is sought could reasonably be obtained by other means. Further, all interception should be carefully managed to meet the objective in question and must not be arbitrary or unfair.

The grounds for issuing a warrant are identified in s.5(3). These are:

- national security (s.5(3)(a));
- the prevention or detection of serious crime (s.5(3)(b)). In these cases an interception warrant will only be considered necessary if it relates to the acts or intentions of people outside the British Isles (s.5(5));
- safeguarding the economic well-being of the United Kingdom (see s.5(3)(c); see also s.5(3)(d), which concerns international mutual assistance agreements: where such an agreement is in place the Secretary of State may issue a warrant for the purposes of prevention or detection of serious crime overseas).

Although it is necessary for the warrant to describe the communications that are to be intercepted, s.5(6) acts to substantially extend the permitted conduct, saying:

> (6) The conduct authorised by an interception warrant shall be taken to include –
>
> (a) all such conduct (including the interception of communications not identified by the warrant) as it is necessary to undertake in order to do what is expressly authorised or required by the warrant;
>
> (b) conduct for obtaining related communications data; and

(c) conduct by any person which is conduct in pursuance of a requirement imposed by or on behalf of the person to whom the warrant is addressed to be provided with assistance with giving effect to the warrant.

### *Applying for warrants and the right to issue*

RIPA 2000, s.6 identifies the people who may apply for interception warrants, while s.7 identifies the people who may authorise the issuing of a warrant. The persons who may apply for a warrant include the heads of the intelligence services, the Director General of the Serious Organised Crime Agency, all chief constables including the Metropolitan Police Commissioner, the Commissioners of Revenue and Customs, the Chief of Defence Intelligence and the competent authority of any foreign country that is party to an international mutual assistance agreement.

Warrants can only be issued 'under the hand of' a limited number of people, meaning that they must be signed by the relevant person. The people with the power to issue warrants are:

- the Secretary of State (s.7(1)(a));
- a member of the Scottish Executive (s.7(1)(a));
- a 'senior official' in either urgent cases where the Secretary of State has expressly authorised the issue of the warrant or in cases where the warrant is for the purposes of a request for assistance made under an international mutual assistance agreement and either the interception subject or the premises concerned are outside the United Kingdom (see s.7(1)(b) and (2)(a) and (b));
- a member of the Senior Civil Service of the Scottish Administration in urgent cases where the Scottish Ministers have expressly authorised the issue of the warrant (see s.7(1)(c) and (2)(aa)).

### *Contents of warrants*

RIPA 2000, s.7(3) says that warrants must be addressed to the person who made the application and where the warrant is issued under the hand of a senior official it must also state (s.7(3)(b)) that the case is either:

- an urgent one where the Secretary of State has expressly authorised the issue of the warrant (s.7(4)(a)); or
- the case is one concerning a request for assistance made by a competent authority of a foreign country under an international mutual assistance agreement (s.7(4)(b)).

In the latter case the warrant must also state either that:

- the interception subject appears to be outside the United Kingdom (s.7(5)(a)); or

- the interception is to take place in relation only to premises outside the United Kingdom (s.7(5)(b)).

RIPA 2000, s.8(1) goes on to state that a warrant must name or describe either one person as the interception subject or a single set of premises as the premises in relation to which the interception is to take place. This means that where the warrant names a person the interception can take place at any number of places, but where the warrant does not name a person the interception can only take place at one, named place. The warrant must also provide sufficient information to enable the identification of the communications that fall within its scope (s.8(2)). This identifying information is to be contained in a schedule, or schedules, to the warrant and can include addresses, numbers, apparatus 'or other factors, or combination of factors'.

### *Certified warrants under s.8(4)*

RIPA 2000, s.8(4) says that the preceding provisions do not apply if the warrant is confined to 'external communications' (s.8(4)(a) and (5)(a)) and at the time of its issue the Secretary of State certifies both the descriptions of materials that he considers need to be examined and that the material needs to be examined in the interests of national security, for preventing or detecting serious crime or for safeguarding the country's economic well-being. This kind of warrant is sometimes called a certified warrant. External communications are defined in s.20 as communications sent or received outside the British Isles.

### *Duration, cancellation and renewal of warrants*

RIPA 2000, s.9 deals with the duration of warrants, their cancellation and renewal. Warrants have a fixed initial lifespan, but they can be renewed before they expire (s.9(1)(b)). The lifespan of a warrant is called the 'relevant period' (s.9(1)(a)) and there are three relevant periods, which are:

- five working days for warrants issued under the hands of senior officials in cases of urgency (s.9(6)(a));
- six months if they are issued under the hand of the Secretary of State in the interest of national security or the economic well-being of the country (s.9(6)(ab)); if these warrants are renewed this will trigger another six-month relevant period (s.9(6)(b));
- three months in all other cases (s.9(6)(c)).

Although interception warrants can be renewed before their expiry 'by an instrument under the hand of' the Secretary of State, a member of the Scottish Executive or a senior official (s.9(1)(b)) (as appropriate: s.7(1)), they shall only be renewed if the Secretary of State believes that they continue to be necessary in the interest of national security, preventing or detecting serious crime, safeguarding the economic well-being of the country or giving effect to an international mutual assistance agreement (s.9(2)).

Conversely, the Secretary of State is required to cancel an interception warrant if he is satisfied that it is no longer necessary in any of these interests (s.9(3)). The Secretary of State is also required to cancel a warrant issued or renewed under the hand of a senior official for the purposes of an international mutual assistance agreement if he is satisfied that the interception subject is now in the UK (s.9(4)).

### *Modification of warrants and certificates*

RIPA 2000, s.10(1) gives the Secretary of State the power to modify the provisions of an interception warrant and the power to modify the certificate of a s.8(4) certified warrant. If the Secretary is minded to modify a certified warrant so as to include new material, they may only do so where they consider that an examination of the new material is necessary in the interests of national security, the prevention or detection of serious crime or the safeguarding of the economic well-being of the country (s.10(1)(b)).

The Secretary of State is also under a positive obligation to delete any information contained in a schedule to a warrant where that information is no longer relevant for the purposes of identifying a communication to be intercepted (s.10(2)). Similarly, they are under a positive duty to exclude materials certified in a certified warrant where the examination of that material is no longer necessary in the interest of national security, the prevention or detection of serious crime or the safeguarding of the economic well-being of the country (s.10(3)).

The instrument modifying a warrant must be under the hand of the Secretary of State or under the hand of a senior official (s.10(4)), although there are limits on the competency of senior officials. For example, the unscheduled parts of a warrant cannot be modified by a senior official except in urgent cases where the Secretary of State has expressly authorised the modification (see s.10(5); see also s.10(5A), which concerns similar provisions for Scotland) whereas the scheduled parts (see s.10(10) for the meaning of 'scheduled parts') can only be modified by a senior official where they are the person to whom the warrant is addressed and the warrant is endorsed with a statement that it is issued in the interests of national security (s.10(6)).

### *Implementation of warrants and the provision of reasonable assistance*

RIPA 2000, s.11 is concerned with the implementation of interception warrants. In order to achieve its implementation the person to whom the warrant is addressed may serve it on the provider of a public telecommunications system or on the controller of a private telecommunications system, whereupon it becomes the duty of the recipient to 'take all such steps for giving effect to the warrant as are notified to him by the person to whom the warrant is addressed' (s.11(4)), but this duty is limited to steps that are reasonably practicable for them to take (s.11(5)). A failure to provide the necessary level of assistance is a criminal offence (s.11(7)).

The Code of Practice says the following on the provision of reasonable assistance:

> 2.7 Any postal or telecommunications operator (referred to as communications service providers) in the United Kingdom may be required to provide assistance in giving effect to an interception. The Act places a requirement on postal and telecommunications operators to take all such steps for giving effect to the warrant as are notified to them (section 11(4) of the Act). But the steps which may be required are limited to those which it is reasonably practicable to take (section 11(5)). What is reasonably practicable should be agreed after consultation between the postal or telecommunications operator and the Government. If no agreement can be reached it will be for the Secretary of State to decide whether to press forward with civil proceedings. Criminal proceedings may also be instituted by or with the consent of the Director of Public Prosecutions.

### *Maintenance of interception capability*

The obligation to provide assistance with interception that is placed on the providers of public telecommunications systems extends much further than s.11; an Order made under s.12 of RIPA 2000 also obliges them to maintain an 'interception capability'. The main parts of s.12 say:

> **12. Maintenance of interception capability**
>
> (1) The Secretary of State may by order provide for the imposition by him on persons who –
>
> (a) are providing public postal services or public telecommunications services, or
>
> (b) are proposing to do so,
>
> of such obligations as it appears to him reasonable to impose for the purpose of securing that it is and remains practicable for requirements to provide assistance in relation to interception warrants to be imposed and complied with.
>
> (2) The Secretary of State's power to impose the obligations provided for by an order under this section shall be exercisable by the giving, in accordance with the order, of a notice requiring the person who is to be subject to the obligations to take all such steps as may be specified or described in the notice.
>
> (3) Subject to subsection (11), the only steps that may be specified or described in a notice given to a person under subsection (2) are steps appearing to the Secretary of State to be necessary for securing that that person has the

practical capability of providing any assistance which he may be required to provide in relation to relevant interception warrants.

. . .

(7) It shall be the duty of a person to whom a notice is given under subsection (2) to comply with the notice; and that duty shall be enforceable by civil proceedings by the Secretary of State for an injunction, or for specific performance of a statutory duty under section 45 of the Court of Session Act 1988, or for any other appropriate relief.

The Regulation of Investigatory Powers (Maintenance of Interception Capability) Order 2002, SI 2002/1931 is the Order made under s.12(1). It applies to 'service providers', who are defined in Article 1(2) of the Order as persons 'providing a public postal service or a public telecommunications service, or proposing to do so'. Article 2 says:

**2. Interception capability**

(1) The Schedule to this Order sets out those obligations which appear to the Secretary of State reasonable to impose on service providers for the purpose of securing that it is and remains practicable for requirements to provide assistance in relation to interception warrants to be imposed and complied with.

(2) Subject to paragraph (3) the obligations in –

 (a) Part I of the Schedule only apply to service providers who provide, or propose to provide, a public postal service; and
 (b) Part II of the Schedule only apply to service providers who provide, or propose to provide, a public telecommunications service.

(3) The obligations in Part II of the Schedule shall not apply to service providers who –

 (a) do not intend to provide a public telecommunications service to more than 10,000 persons in any one or more parts of the United Kingdom and do not do so; or
 (b) only provide, or propose to provide, a public telecommunications service in relation to the provision of banking, insurance, investment or other financial services.

However, the obligation to maintain an interception capability only arises upon service of an interception capability notice. Article 3 says:

**3. Interception capability notices**

(1) The Secretary of State may give a service provider a notice requiring him to take all such steps falling within paragraph (2) as may be specified or described in the notice.

(2) Those steps are ones appearing to the Secretary of State to be necessary for securing that the service provider has the practical capability of meeting the obligations set out in the Schedule to this Order.

The Schedule to the Order identifies the obligations that are placed on providers of public telecommunications services following the service of an interception capability notice. Key provisions are:

- Under para.5 service providers are required to provide a mechanism for implementing interceptions within one working day of them being informed that the interception has been appropriately authorised.
- Under para.6 they are required to ensure the interception, in their entirety, of all communications and related communications data authorised by the interception warrant and to ensure their simultaneous (i.e. in near real time) transmission to a handover point within the service provider's network as agreed with the person on whose application the interception warrant was issued.
- Under para.7 they are required to ensure that the intercepted communication and the related communications data will be transmitted so that they can be unambiguously correlated.
- Under para.8 they are required to ensure that the handover interface complies with any requirements communicated by the Secretary of State to the service provider, which, where practicable and appropriate, will be in line with agreed industry standards (such as those of the European Telecommunications Standards Institute).
- Under para.9 they are required to ensure filtering to provide only the traffic data associated with the warranted telecommunications identifier, where reasonable.
- Under para.10 they are required to ensure that the person on whose application the interception warrant was issued is able to remove any electronic protection applied by the service provider to the intercepted communication and the related communications data.
- Under para.11 they are required to enable the simultaneous interception of the communications of up to 1 in 10,000 of the persons to whom the service provider provides the public telecommunications service, provided that those persons number more than 10,000.
- Under para.12 they are required to ensure that the reliability of the interception capability is at least equal to the reliability of the public telecommunications service carrying the communication which is being intercepted.
- Under para.13 they are required to ensure that the intercept capability may be audited so that it is possible to confirm that the intercepted communications and related communications data are from or intended for the interception subject, or originate from or are intended for transmission to, the premises named in the interception warrant.

- Under para.14 they are required to comply with their obligations in such a manner that the chance of the interception subject or other unauthorised persons becoming aware of any interception is minimised.

### *Exclusion of interception evidence*

In order to protect the confidentiality and integrity of intelligence sources, RIPA 2000, s.17 excludes interception evidence from all legal proceedings. Section 17 says:

**17. Exclusion of matters from legal proceedings**

(1) Subject to section 18, no evidence shall be adduced, question asked, assertion or disclosure made or other thing done in, for the purposes of or in connection with any legal proceedings or Inquiries Act proceedings which (in any manner) –

(a) discloses, in circumstances from which its origin in anything falling within subsection (2) may be inferred, any of the contents of an intercepted communication or any related communications data; or
(b) tends (apart from any such disclosure) to suggest that anything falling within subsection (2) has or may have occurred or be going to occur.

(2) The following fall within this subsection –

(a) conduct by a person falling within subsection (3) that was or would be an offence under section 1(1) or (2) of this Act or under section 1 of the Interception of Communications Act 1985;
(b) a breach by the Secretary of State of his duty under section 1(4) of this Act;
(c) the issue of an interception warrant or of a warrant under the Interception of Communications Act 1985;
(d) the making of an application by any person for an interception warrant, or for a warrant under that Act;
(e) the imposition of any requirement on any person to provide assistance with giving effect to an interception warrant.

(3) The persons referred to in subsection (2)(a) are –

(a) any person to whom a warrant under this Chapter may be addressed;
(b) any person holding office under the Crown;
(c) any member of the staff of the Serious Organised Crime Agency;
(ca) any member of the Scottish Crime and Drug Enforcement Agency;
(e) any person employed by or for the purposes of a police force;
(f) any person providing a postal service or employed for the purposes of any business of providing such a service; and
(g) any person providing a public telecommunications service or employed for the purposes of any business of providing such a service.

(4) In this section –

'Inquiries Act proceedings' means proceedings of an inquiry under the Inquiries Act 2005;'intercepted communications' means any communication intercepted in the course of its transmission by means of a postal service or telecommunication system.

The Code of Practice says:

> 7.3 The general rule is that neither the possibility of interception nor intercepted material itself plays any part in legal proceedings. This rule is set out in section 17 of the Act, which excludes evidence, questioning, assertion or disclosure in legal proceedings likely to reveal the existence (or the absence) of a warrant issued under this Act (or the Interception of Communications Act 1985). This rule means that the intercepted material cannot be used either by the prosecution or the defence. This preserves 'equality of arms' which is a requirement under Article 6 of the European Convention on Human Rights.

However, while interception evidence is not admissible within legal proceedings, its existence can be brought to the attention of the Crown prosecutor and the judge (s.18(7)).

### 7.3.2 Monitoring of business communications

RIPA 2000, s.4 permits the Secretary of State to make regulations authorising the monitoring, keeping of records of, and interception of business communications over private systems and apparatus. Where material, s.4 provides:

> **4. Power to provide for lawful interception**
>
> . . .
>
> (2) Subject to subsection (3), the Secretary of State may by regulations authorise any such conduct described in the regulations as appears to him to constitute a legitimate practice reasonably required for the purpose, in connection with the carrying on of any business, of monitoring or keeping a record of –
>
> (a) communications by means of which transactions are entered into in the course of that business; or
>
> (b) other communications relating to that business or taking place in the course of its being carried on.
>
> (3) Nothing in any regulations under subsection (2) shall authorise the interception of any communication except in the course of its transmission using apparatus or services provided by or to the person carrying on the business for use wholly or partly in connection with that business.

The Telecommunications (Lawful Business Practice) (Interception of Communications) Regulations 2000, SI 2000/2699 were made under s.4(2) and as envisaged by that section they are concerned with the monitoring of business communications and, where appropriate, the keeping of records of business communications (reg.3(2)(a)). For these purposes 'references to a business include references to activities of a government department, of any public authority or of any person or office holder on whom functions are conferred by or under an enactment' (reg.2(a)). They permit interception of business communications transmitted by means of a telecommunication system where the system is for use wholly or partly in connection with the business (reg.3(2)(b)), provided that the system controller has 'made all reasonable efforts to inform every person who may use the telecommunication system in question that communications transmitted by means thereof may be intercepted' (reg.3(2)(c)). The interception must be 'effected by or with the express or implied consent of the system controller' (reg.3(1)).

The interception must be performed for one of the legitimate purposes described in the regulations. The first legitimate purpose is monitoring or keeping a record of business communications:

- in order to establish the existence of facts (reg.3(1)(a)(i)(aa));
- in order to ascertain compliance with regulatory or self-regulatory practices (see reg.2(c) for meaning; regulatory and self-regulatory practices include those prescribed by law and those published by bodies whose objectives include the publication of standards or codes of practice for the conduct of the business) or procedures that are either applicable to the system controller's business or applicable to another person's business where the system controller acts in a supervisory capacity (reg.3(1)(a)(i)(bb));
- in order to ascertain or demonstrate the standards that are achieved, or ought to be achieved, by users of the system in the course of their duties (reg.3(1)(a)(i)(bb));
- in the interests of national security (see reg.3(1)(a)(ii); in cases of national security the interception must be effected on behalf of a person falling within RIPA 2000, s.6(2)(a)–(i); see reg.3(2)(d)(i));
- for the purpose of preventing or detecting crime (reg.3(1)(a)(iii));
- for the purpose of investigating or detecting the unauthorised use of the system or any other system (reg.3(1)(a)(iv));
- where that is done as an inherent part of, or to secure, the effective operation of the system (reg.3(1)(a)(v)).

The second legitimate purpose is monitoring communications for the purpose of determining whether they are ones that are relevant to the system controller's business (reg.3(1)(b)). (See also reg.2(b), which identifies when a communication is relevant to a business. Communications are relevant to a business if they are the means by which a business transaction is entered into, or if they otherwise relate to the business, or if they otherwise take place in the course of carrying on the business. The interception must be in respect of only those communications that were intended for a person using the business system; see reg.3(2)(d)(ii).)

The third legitimate purpose is monitoring communications made to free, confidential voice-telephony counselling or support services where the users may choose to remain anonymous (reg.3(1)(c)).

### 7.3.3 Access to retained communications data

While the purpose of interception is to gain access to the content of communications, it will already be appreciated that the evidential value of communications data to law enforcement agencies is considerable. Since the terrorist atrocities of 9/11 and the subsequent ones in Madrid and London, there has been a considerable acceleration in the creation of a legal framework through which retained communications data can be accessed.

Of course, the creation of a legal framework that gives law enforcement agencies sufficient rights of access to retained communications data is only part of the picture; there is also the goal of ensuring that communications service providers retain sufficient volumes and types of communications data for sufficient periods of time, which, of course, was recognised before 9/11, as the G8's 'Principles and Action Plan to Combat High-Tech Crime' illustrate; these say that 'legal systems should permit the preservation of and quick access to electronic data, which are often critical to the successful investigation of crime'.[4] The Council of Europe's Cybercrime Convention recognises the same objective, saying at Article 16:

> **Article 16 – Expedited preservation of stored computer data**
>
> 1 Each Party shall adopt such legislative and other measures as may be necessary to enable its competent authorities to order or similarly obtain the expeditious preservation of specified computer data, including traffic data, that has been stored by means of a computer system, in particular where there are grounds to believe that the computer data is particularly vulnerable to loss or modification.

#### *Retention of communications data under the Data Retention (EC Directive) Regulations 2007*

The retention issue has been addressed by the Communications Data Retention Directive 2006 (CDRD) (Directive 2006/24/EC of the European Parliament and of the Council of 15 March 2006 on the retention of data generated or processed in connection with the provision of publicly available electronic communications services or of public communications networks and amending Directive 2002/58/EC), which has been transposed into domestic law by the Data Retention (EC Directive) Regulations 2007, SI 2007/2199. The Directive amends the Privacy and Electronic Communications

Directive 2002 (PECD), to harmonise EU laws on the retention of communications data; the effect of CDRD is to harmonise national provisions made under Article 15 of PECD, which, it will be recalled, permits Member States to restrict the operation of PECD's rules on the confidentiality of communications, the deletion of traffic and location data and the restriction of calling line identification where such restrictions constitute necessary, appropriate and proportionate measures within a democratic society for the purpose of national security and the prevention and detection of crime, etc. CDRD still allows Member States significant margins for manoeuvre of retention periods however; while Article 6 prescribes a minimum retention period of 6 months, it allows a maximum retention period of two years.

The Regulations apply to publication communications providers, provided that they have received written notice from the Secretary of State. Regulation 3 says:

**3. Application**

(1) Subject to paragraph (2), these Regulations shall apply to all public communications providers.
(2) These Regulations shall not apply, except where written notice has been given by the Secretary of State, to a public communications provider whose data are retained in the United Kingdom in accordance with these Regulations by another public communications provider.
(3) If only a part of that data is so retained by another public communications provider, these Regulations apply to the public communications provider only with respect to the data not so retained.
(4) A written notice must be given or published in such a manner as the Secretary of State considers appropriate for bringing it to the attention of the public communications provider or the category of providers to whom it applies and must specify the extent to which and the date from which these Regulations are to apply.

The obligation to retain data is contained within reg.4, which sets a 12-month retention period, but it will be noticed that the obligation does not extend to emails. Regulation 4 says:

**4. Obligation to retain data**

(1) Subject to paragraphs (4) and (5), the data specified in regulation 5 must be retained to the extent that those data are generated or processed by a public communications provider in the process of supplying the communications services concerned.
(2) The data specified in regulation 5 are to be retained by the public communications provider for a period of 12 months from the date of the communication.
(3) The duty to retain data under paragraph (1) includes the retention of the data specified in regulation 5 relating to an unsuccessful call attempt where those data are generated or processed, and stored, in the United Kingdom

by a public communications provider in the process of supplying the communication services concerned.

(4) These Regulations do not require data relating to unconnected calls to be retained.

(5) These Regulations do not require data derived from Internet access, Internet e-mail or Internet telephony to be retained.

For completeness, reg.5 provides:

**5. Data to be retained**

(1) The following data concerning fixed network telephony and mobile telephony generated in the United Kingdom must be retained in accordance with regulation 4(1):

- (a) the telephone number from which the telephone call was made and the name and address of the subscriber and registered user of that telephone;
- (b) the telephone number dialled and, in cases involving supplementary services such as call forwarding or call transfer, any telephone number to which the call is forwarded or transferred, and the name and address of the subscriber and registered user of such telephone;
- (c) the date and time of the start and end of the call; and
- (d) the telephone service used.

(2) The following data concerning mobile telephony must be retained in accordance with regulation 4(1):

- (a) the International Mobile Subscriber Identity (IMSI) and the International Mobile Equipment Identity (IMEI) of the telephone from which a telephone call is made;
- (b) the IMSI and the IMEI of the telephone dialled;
- (c) in the case of pre-paid anonymous services, the date and time of the initial activation of the service and the cell ID from which the service was activated;
- (d) the cell ID at the start of the communication; and
- (e) data identifying the geographic location of cells by reference to their cell ID.

The exception that is made for email is not a permanent one, due to the provisions of Article 15 of CDRD, which renders the exception a mere postponement, which lasts until 15 March 2009. From that date the full retention obligations within CDRD will apply to email, but the Regulations will require amendments, to identify the data to be retained; reg.5, which identifies the data to be retained for telephony, cannot extend to email without extensive amendments. However, it is not difficult to predict the nature of the amendments, as Article 5 of CDRD is highly prescriptive of the categories of data to be retained. Where it pertains to email Article 5 provides:

**Article 5**

**Categories of data to be retained**

1. Member States shall ensure that the following categories of data are retained under this Directive:

(a) data necessary to trace and identify the source of a communication:

. . .

(2) concerning Internet access, Internet e-mail and Internet telephony:

(i) the user ID(s) allocated;
(ii) the user ID and telephone number allocated to any communication entering the public telephone network;
(iii) the name and address of the subscriber or registered user to whom an Internet Protocol (IP) address, user ID or telephone number was allocated at the time of the communication;

(b) data necessary to identify the destination of a communication:

. . .

(2) concerning Internet e-mail and Internet telephony:

. . .

(ii) the name(s) and address(es) of the subscriber(s) or registered user(s) and user ID of the intended recipient of the communication;

(c) data necessary to identify the date, time and duration of a communication:

. . .

(2) concerning Internet access, Internet e-mail and Internet telephony:

(i) the date and time of the log-in and log-off of the Internet access service, based on a certain time zone, together with the IP address, whether dynamic or static, allocated by the Internet access service provider to a communication, and the user ID of the subscriber or registered user;
(ii) the date and time of the log-in and log-off of the Internet e-mail service or Internet telephony service, based on a certain time zone;

(d) data necessary to identify the type of communication:

. . .

(2) concerning Internet e-mail and Internet telephony: the Internet service used;

(e) data necessary to identify users' communication equipment or what purports to be their equipment:

. . .

(3) concerning Internet access, Internet e-mail and Internet telephony:

(i) the calling telephone number for dial-up access;
(ii) the digital subscriber line (DSL) or other end point of the originator of the communication;

(f) data necessary to identify the location of mobile communication equipment:

  (1) the location label (Cell ID) at the start of the communication;
  (2) data identifying the geographic location of cells by reference to their location labels (Cell ID) during the period for which communications data are retained.

### *Retention of communications data under the Anti-Terrorism, Crime and Security Act 2001*

Recital 5 to CDRD observes that 'several Member States have adopted legislation providing for the retention of data by service providers for the prevention, investigation, detection, and prosecution of criminal offences. Those national provisions vary considerably'. The UK was one of the countries that had introduced rules on the retention of data; Part 11 of the Anti-Terrorism, Crime and Security Act (ATCSA) 2001 is titled 'Retention of Communications Data'.

The approach to the retention of communication data that is preferred by the ATCSA 2001 is code-based, as s.102 reveals:

**102. Codes and agreements about the retention of communications data**

(1) The Secretary of State shall issue, and may from time to time revise, a code of practice relating to the retention by communications providers of communications data obtained by or held by them.
(2) The Secretary of State may enter into such agreements as he considers appropriate with any communications provider about the practice to be followed by that provider in relation to the retention of communications data obtained by or held by that provider.
(3) A code of practice or agreement under this section may contain any such provision as appears to the Secretary of State to be necessary –

  (a) for the purpose of safeguarding national security; or
  (b) for the purposes of prevention or detection of crime or the prosecution of offenders which may relate directly or indirectly to national security.

(4) A failure by any person to comply with a code of practice or agreement under this section which is for the time being in force shall not of itself render him liable to any criminal or civil proceedings.
(5) A code of practice or agreement under this section which is for the time being in force shall be admissible in evidence in any legal proceedings in which the question arises whether or not the retention of any communications data is justified on the grounds that a failure to retain the data would be likely to prejudice national security, the prevention or detection of crime or the prosecution of offenders.

The current Code (the Voluntary Code of Practice on the retention of communications data under Part 11 of the ATCSA 2001)[5] was brought into effect by the Retention of Communications Data (Code of Practice) Order 2003, SI 2003/3175 (as amended by Regulation of Investigatory Powers

(Communications Data) (Amendment) Order 2005, SI 2005/1083), but it is voluntary in nature. The purpose of the Code is to 'outline how communication service providers can assist in the fight against terrorism by meeting agreed time periods for retention of communications data that may be extended beyond those periods for which their individual company currently retains data for business purposes'.

Pending the introduction of new regulations under CDRD the domestic regime for the retention of communications data relating to email is the one within the Voluntary Code. The Code prescribes retention periods of six months and 12 months for email data (ATCSA Voluntary Code of Practice, Appendix A).

### *Accessing communications data under RIPA 2000*

The domestic regime for gaining access to communications data is contained in RIPA 2000, Part 1, Chapter II, which is titled 'acquisition and disclosure of communications data'.

In summary, this gives a designated person the power to authorise 'any conduct' in relation to a telecommunications system for obtaining communications data, other than interception (RIPA 2000, s.21(1)), provided that such conduct is necessary for the obtaining of that data for one or more prescribed grounds (s.22(2)). (For the meaning of 'designated', see s.25. This covers senior personnel within any police force, the Serious Organised Crime Agency, the Commissioners of HM Revenue and Customs, the intelligence services and many prescribed public authorities. See also the Regulation of Investigatory Powers (Communications Data) Order 2003, SI 2003/3172 which designates other public authorities. See also the Regulation of Investigatory Powers (Communications Data) (Amendment) Order 2005, SI 2005/1083 and the Regulation of Investigatory Powers (Additional Functions and Amendment) Order 2006, SI 2006/1878.)

The effect of an authorisation is to render the conduct lawful for all purposes (s.21(2)). Furthermore, there is an exclusion from civil liability for any incidental, unforeseeable conduct (s.21(3)).

Telecommunications operators are obliged to provide assistance to designated persons by giving disclosure of communications data (s.22(4)(b)). This duty also extends to obtaining communications data (s.22(4)(a)). However, the obligation to provide assistance is limited to reasonably practicable assistance (s.22(7)).

RIPA 2000, ss.21 and 22 provide:

**21. Lawful acquisition and disclosure of communications data**

(1) This Chapter applies to –

(a) any conduct in relation to a postal service or telecommunication system for obtaining communications data, other than conduct consisting in the interception of communications in the course of their transmission by means of such a service or system; and
(b) the disclosure to any person of communications data.

(2) Conduct to which this Chapter applies shall be lawful for all purposes if –

(a) it is conduct in which any person is authorised or required to engage by an authorisation or notice granted or given under this Chapter; and
(b) the conduct is in accordance with, or in pursuance of, the authorisation or requirement.

(3) A person shall not be subject to any civil liability in respect of any conduct of his which –

(a) is incidental to any conduct that is lawful by virtue of subsection (2); and
(b) is not itself conduct an authorisation or warrant for which is capable of being granted under a relevant enactment and might reasonably have been expected to have been sought in the case in question.

(4) In this Chapter 'communications data' means any of the following –

(a) any traffic data comprised in or attached to a communication (whether by the sender or otherwise) for the purposes of any postal service or telecommunication system by means of which it is being or may be transmitted;
(b) any information which includes none of the contents of a communication (apart from any information falling within paragraph (a)) and is about the use made by any person –

(i) of any postal service or telecommunications service; or
(ii) in connection with the provision to or use by any person of any telecommunications service, of any part of a telecommunication system;

(c) any information not falling within paragraph (a) or (b) that is held or obtained, in relation to persons to whom he provides the service, by a person providing a postal service or telecommunications service.

(5) In this section 'relevant enactment' means –

(a) an enactment contained in this Act;
(b) section 5 of the Intelligence Services Act 1994 (warrants for the intelligence services); or
(c) an enactment contained in Part III of the Police Act 1997 (powers of the police and of officers of Revenue and Customs).

(6) In this section 'traffic data', in relation to any communication, means –

(a) any data identifying, or purporting to identify, any person, apparatus or location to or from which the communication is or may be transmitted,
(b) any data identifying or selecting, or purporting to identify or select, apparatus through which, or by means of which, the communication is or may be transmitted,

(c) any data comprising signals for the actuation of apparatus used for the purposes of a telecommunication system for effecting (in whole or in part) the transmission of any communication, and
(d) any data identifying the data or other data as data comprised in or attached to a particular communication.

but that expression includes data identifying a computer file or computer program access to which is obtained, or which is run, by means of the communication to the extent only that the file or program is identified by reference to the apparatus in which it is stored.

(7) In this section –

(a) references, in relation to traffic data comprising signals for the actuation of apparatus, to a telecommunication system by means of which a communication is being or may be transmitted include references to any telecommunication system in which that apparatus is comprised; and
(b) references to traffic data being attached to a communication include references to the data and the communication being logically associated with each other;

and in this section 'data', in relation to a postal item, means anything written on the outside of the item.

**22. Obtaining and disclosing communications data**

(1) This section applies where a person designated for the purposes of this Chapter believes that it is necessary on grounds falling within subsection (2) to obtain any communications data.
(2) It is necessary on grounds falling within this subsection to obtain communications data if it is necessary –

(a) in the interests of national security;
(b) for the purpose of preventing or detecting crime or of preventing disorder;
(c) in the interests of the economic well-being of the United Kingdom;
(d) in the interests of public safety;
(e) for the purpose of protecting public health;
(f) for the purpose of assessing or collecting any tax, duty, levy or other imposition, contribution or charge payable to a government department;
(g) for the purpose, in an emergency, of preventing death or injury or any damage to a person's physical or mental health, or of mitigating any injury or damage to a person's physical or mental health; or
(h) for any purpose (not falling within paragraphs (a) to (g)) which is specified for the purposes of this subsection by an order made by the Secretary of State.

(3) Subject to subsection (5), the designated person may grant an authorisation for persons holding offices, ranks or positions with the same relevant public authority as the designated person to engage in any conduct to which this Chapter applies.
(4) Subject to subsection (5), where it appears to the designated person that a postal or telecommunications operator is or may be in possession of, or be capable of obtaining, any communications data, the designated person may, by notice to the postal or telecommunications operator, require the operator –

(a) if the operator is not already in possession of the data, to obtain the data; and
(b) in any case, to disclose all of the data in his possession or subsequently obtained by him.

(5) The designated person shall not grant an authorisation under subsection (3), or give a notice under subsection (4), unless he believes that obtaining the data in question by the conduct authorised or required by the authorisation or notice is proportionate to what is sought to be achieved by so obtaining the data.
(6) It shall be the duty of the postal or telecommunications operator to comply with the requirements of any notice given to him under subsection (4).
(7) A person who is under a duty by virtue of subsection (6) shall not be required to do anything in pursuance of that duty which it is not reasonably practicable for him to do.
(8) The duty imposed by subsection (6) shall be enforceable by civil proceedings by the Secretary of State for an injunction, or for specific performance of a statutory duty under section 45 of the Court of Session Act 1988, or for any other appropriate relief.
(9) The Secretary of State shall not make an order under subsection (2)(h) unless a draft of the order has been laid before Parliament and approved by a resolution of each House.

The procedure governing the acquisition and disclosure of communications data is also subject to a code of practice made under RIPA 2000, s.71,[6] which was brought into effect by the Regulation of Investigatory Powers (Acquisition and Disclosure of Communications Data: Code of Practice) Order 2007, SI 2007/2197. Again, the Code identifies the dual interests of necessity and proportionality:

2.1 The acquisition of communications data under the Act will be a justifiable interference with an individual's human rights under Article 8 of the European Convention on Human Rights only if the conduct being authorised or required to take place is both necessary and proportionate and in accordance with law.

### *Accessing protected information*

A common problem for law enforcement agencies is that electronic data may be protected by encryption, rendering it difficult, if not impossible, to access it in an intelligible form. This problem is addressed by Part III of RIPA 2000, which is titled 'investigation of electronic data protected by encryption etc.'. In summary, Part III enables a 'person with the appropriate permission' (RIPA 2000, s.49(2)) to serve notices (s.49) on persons holding the keys to encryption, requiring their disclosure. Failure to comply with a disclosure notice is an offence (s.53) and there is also a related tipping-off offence (s.54). A person with the appropriate permission is any person identified in RIPA 2000, Sched.2. This includes persons with the written permission of a Circuit

Judge, or a District Judge of the Magistrates' Court, to serve disclosure notices.

'Protected information' is defined in s.56 in the following terms:

> 'protected information' means any electronic data which, without the key to the data –
>
> (a) cannot, or cannot readily, be accessed, or
> (b) cannot, or cannot readily, be put into an intelligible form;

'Key' is defined in the following terms:

> 'key', in relation to any electronic data, means any key, code, password, algorithm or other data the use of which (with or without other keys) –
>
> (a) allows access to the electronic data, or
> (b) facilitates the putting of the data into an intelligible form;

A disclosure notice can only be served if the person with the appropriate permission reasonably believes that:

- the key is in the possession of the person upon whom the notice is to be served (RIPA 2000, s.49(2)(a));
- disclosure of the key is necessary on prescribed grounds (s.49(2)(b)), which includes the interests of national security, the purpose of preventing or detecting crime and the interests of the economic well-being of the country (s.49(3); see also s.49(2)(b)(ii));
- the requirement to give disclosure is proportionate to what is sought to be achieved by its imposition (s.49(2)(c));
- it would not be reasonably practicable for them to obtain possession of the protected information in an intelligible form without the giving of the notice (s.49(2)(d)).

RIPA 2000, s.49 says:

> **49. Notices requiring disclosure**
>
> (1) This section applies where any protected information –
>
> (a) has come into the possession of any person by means of the exercise of a statutory power to seize, detain, inspect, search or otherwise to interfere with documents or other property, or is likely to do so;
> (b) has come into the possession of any person by means of the exercise of any statutory power to intercept communications, or is likely to do so;
> (c) has come into the possession of any person by means of the exercise of any power conferred by an authorisation under section 22(3) or under Part II, or as a result of the giving of a notice under section 22(4), or is likely to do so;

(d) has come into the possession of any person as a result of having been provided or disclosed in pursuance of any statutory duty (whether or not one arising as a result of a request for information), or is likely to do so; or
(e) has, by any other lawful means not involving the exercise of statutory powers, come into the possession of any of the intelligence services, the police, SOCA, SCDEA or , or is likely so to come into the possession of any of those services, the police, SOCA, SCDEA or Her Majesty's Revenue and Customs.

(2) If any person with the appropriate permission under Schedule 2 believes, on reasonable grounds –

(a) that a key to the protected information is in the possession of any person,
(b) that the imposition of a disclosure requirement in respect of the protected information is –

(i) necessary on grounds falling within subsection (3), or
(ii) necessary for the purpose of securing the effective exercise or proper performance by any public authority of any statutory power or statutory duty,

(c) that the imposition of such a requirement is proportionate to what is sought to be achieved by its imposition, and
(d) that it is not reasonably practicable for the person with the appropriate permission to obtain possession of the protected information in an intelligible form without the giving of a notice under this section,

the person with that permission may, by notice to the person whom he believes to have possession of the key, impose a disclosure requirement in respect of the protected information.

(3) A disclosure requirement in respect of any protected information is necessary on grounds falling within this subsection if it is necessary –

(a) in the interests of national security;
(b) for the purpose of preventing or detecting crime; or
(c) in the interests of the economic well-being of the United Kingdom.

(4) A notice under this section imposing a disclosure requirement in respect of any protected information –

(a) must be given in writing or (if not in writing) must be given in a manner that produces a record of its having been given;
(b) must describe the protected information to which the notice relates;
(c) must specify the matters falling within subsection (2)(b)(i) or (ii) by reference to which the notice is given;
(d) must specify the office, rank or position held by the person giving it;
(e) must specify the office, rank or position of the person who for the purposes of Schedule 2 granted permission for the giving of the notice or (if the person giving the notice was entitled to give it without another person's permission) must set out the circumstances in which that entitlement arose;
(f) must specify the time by which the notice is to be complied with; and
(g) must set out the disclosure that is required by the notice and the form and manner in which it is to be made;

and the time specified for the purposes of paragraph (f) must allow a period for compliance which is reasonable in all the circumstances.

(5) Where it appears to a person with the appropriate permission –

(a) that more than one person is in possession of the key to any protected information,
(b) that any of those persons is in possession of that key in his capacity as an officer or employee of any body corporate, and
(c) that another of those persons is the body corporate itself or another officer or employee of the body corporate,

a notice under this section shall not be given, by reference to his possession of the key, to any officer or employee of the body corporate unless he is a senior officer of the body corporate or it appears to the person giving the notice that there is no senior officer of the body corporate and (in the case of an employee) no more senior employee of the body corporate to whom it is reasonably practicable to give the notice.

(6) Where it appears to a person with the appropriate permission –

(a) that more than one person is in possession of the key to any protected information,
(b) that any of those persons is in possession of that key in his capacity as an employee of a firm, and
(c) that another of those persons is the firm itself or a partner of the firm,

a notice under this section shall not be given, by reference to his possession of the key, to any employee of the firm unless it appears to the person giving the notice that there is neither a partner of the firm nor a more senior employee of the firm to whom it is reasonably practicable to give the notice.

(7) Subsections (5) and (6) shall not apply to the extent that there are special circumstances of the case that mean that the purposes for which the notice is given would be defeated, in whole or in part, if the notice were given to the person to whom it would otherwise be required to be given by those subsections.

(8) A notice under this section shall not require the making of any disclosure to any person other than –

(a) the person giving the notice; or
(b) such other person as may be specified in or otherwise identified by, or in accordance with, the provisions of the notice.

(9) A notice under this section shall not require the disclosure of any key which –

(a) is intended to be used for the purpose only of generating electronic signatures; and
(b) has not in fact been used for any other purpose.

(10) In this section 'senior officer', in relation to a body corporate, means a director, manager, secretary or other similar officer of the body corporate; and for this purpose 'director', in relation to a body corporate whose affairs are managed by its members, means a member of the body corporate.

(11) Schedule 2 (definition of the appropriate permission) shall have effect.

## 7.4 SEARCH AND SEIZURE IN CRIMINAL CASES

Part II of the Police and Criminal Evidence Act (PACE) 1984 codifies police powers of entry, search and seizure. The powers within Part II can enable the police to enter premises to look for and take possession of emails, whether in hard copy form or contained in a computer or communication network. PACE is supplemented by the Criminal Justice and Police Act 2001.

The Serious Organised Crime and Police Act 2005 also contains an important regime by which law enforcement agencies can obtain access to emails.

### 7.4.1 Police and Criminal Evidence Act 1984

PACE, s.66 requires the Secretary of State to issue codes of practice for the exercise of the powers of search and seizure. The codes are admissible in evidence under s.67. The code of practice for search and seizure is Code B, 'Code of Practice for searches of premises by police officers and the seizure of property found by police officers on persons or premises',[7] the latest version of which was laid before Parliament in December 2007 (Police and Criminal Evidence Act 1984 (Codes of Practice) Order 2008, SI 2008/167).

*Warrant authorising entry and search*

PACE, s.8 contains the general power for magistrates to issue warrants to the police to enable them to enter and search premises. The power to issue a warrant arises in the following circumstances.

- Where there are reasonable grounds for believing that an indictable offence has been committed.
- Where there are reasonable grounds for believing that there is material located on the premises that would be of substantial value to the investigation and that material would be 'relevant evidence', which is evidence that would be admissible at trial.
- Where there are reasonable grounds for believing that the material is not legally privileged, or 'excluded material' (PACE, s.11: excluded material covers certain kinds of confidential personal records acquired or created in the course of a business and confidential journalistic material) or 'special procedure material' (PACE, s.14: special procedure material covers other kinds of confidential business records and certain kinds of journalistic material).
- Where there are reasonable grounds for believing that it is not practicable to communicate with any person entitled to grant entry to the premises, or it is not practicable to communicate with any person entitled to grant access to the evidence, or that entry will be denied without a warrant, or

the purpose of the search would be frustrated or seriously prejudiced unless a constable arriving at the premises can gain immediate entry to them.

There are two kinds of warrants that can be issued under s.8. These are 'specific premises' warrants and 'all premises' warrants. In the first kind the application for the warrant will specify one or more sets of premises to be entered and searched, whereas in the second kind the application will focus on premises occupied or controlled by a specified person. Before issuing an all premises warrant the magistrate has to be satisfied that in light of the particulars of the offence it is necessary to search premises of the specified person that are not specified in the application and that it is not reasonably practicable to specify all the premises. The warrant may authorise multiple entries and searches, although the magistrate can set a maximum number.

PACE, s.8 says:

**8. Power of justice of the peace to authorise entry and search of premises**

(1) If on an application made by a constable a justice of the peace is satisfied that there are reasonable grounds for believing –

(a) that an indictable offence has been committed; and
(b) that there is material on premises mentioned in subsection (1A) below which is likely to be of substantial value (whether by itself or together with other material) to the investigation of the offence; and
(c) that the material is likely to be relevant evidence; and
(d) that it does not consist of or include items subject to legal privilege, excluded material or special procedure material; and
(e) that any of the conditions specified in subsection (3) below applies in relation to each set of premises specified in the application,

he may issue a warrant authorising a constable to enter and search the premises.

(1A) The premises referred to in subsection (1)(b) above are –

(a) one or more sets of premises specified in the application (in which case the application is for a 'specific premises warrant'); or
(b) any premises occupied or controlled by a person specified in the application, including such sets of premises as are so specified (in which case the application is for an 'all premises warrant').

(1B) If the application is for an all premises warrant, the justice of the peace must also be satisfied –

(a) that because of the particulars of the offence referred to in paragraph (a) of subsection (1) above, there are reasonable grounds for believing that it is necessary to search premises occupied or controlled by the person in question which are not specified in the application in order to find the material referred to in paragraph (b) of that subsection; and
(b) that it is not reasonably practicable to specify in the application all the premises which he occupies or controls and which might need to be searched.

(1C) The warrant may authorise entry to and search of premises on more than one occasion if, on the application, the justice of the peace is satisfied that it is necessary to authorise multiple entries in order to achieve the purpose for which he issues the warrant.

(1D) If it authorises multiple entries, the number of entries authorised may be unlimited, or limited to a maximum.

(2) A constable may seize and retain anything for which a search has been authorised under subsection (1) above.

(3) The conditions mentioned in subsection (1)(e) above are –

(a) that it is not practicable to communicate with any person entitled to grant entry to the premises;
(b) that it is practicable to communicate with a person entitled to grant entry to the premises but it is not practicable to communicate with any person entitled to grant access to the evidence;
(c) that entry to the premises will not be granted unless a warrant is produced;
(d) that the purpose of a search may be frustrated or seriously prejudiced unless a constable arriving at the premises can secure immediate entry to them.

(4) In this Act 'relevant evidence', in relation to an offence, means anything that would be admissible in evidence at a trial for the offence.

(5) The power to issue a warrant conferred by this section is in addition to any such power otherwise conferred.

(6) This section applies in relation to a relevant offence (as defined in section 28D(4) of the Immigration Act 1971) as it applies in relation to an indictable offence.

(7) Section 4 of the Summary Jurisdiction (Process) Act 1881 (execution of process of English courts in Scotland) shall apply to a warrant issued on the application of an officer of Revenue and Customs under this section by virtue of section 114 below.

### *Seizure of items*

PACE, s.8 is concerned only with entry and search, not seizure; seizure is dealt with by PACE, ss.19 and 20. Section 19 applies where the constable is lawfully on the premises, which can be pursued to a warrant issued under s.8 or pursuant to some other lawful ground, such as by invitation of the person entitled to grant access. Once on the premises the constable can seize anything if he has reasonable grounds for believing that the thing has been obtained in consequence of the commission of any offence, or that it is necessary to seize it to prevent its concealment, etc. or that it would be relevant evidence and it is necessary to seize it to prevent its concealment, etc. However, the constable is not entitled to seize anything for which he has reasonable grounds for believing is subject to legal privilege (see *R.* v. *Chesterfield Justices ex p. Bramley* [2000] QB 576; the seizure of privileged material is not unlawful unless the constable had reasonable grounds for believing it was privileged at the time of seizure). PACE, s.19(4) also contains interesting provisions in relation to electronic stored information; the constable 'may require' the information to produced in a visible and legible form that enables it to be taken away. Section 19 says:

**19. General power of seizure etc.**

(1) The powers conferred by subsections (2), (3) and (4) below are exercisable by a constable who is lawfully on any premises.
(2) The constable may seize anything which is on the premises if he has reasonable grounds for believing –

 (a) that it has been obtained in consequence of the commission of an offence; and
 (b) that it is necessary to seize it in order to prevent it being concealed, lost, damaged, altered or destroyed.

(3) The constable may seize anything which is on the premises if he has reasonable grounds for believing –

 (a) that it is evidence in relation to an offence which he is investigating or any other offence; and
 (b) that it is necessary to seize it in order to prevent the evidence being concealed, lost, altered or destroyed.

(4) The constable may require any information which is stored in any electronic form and is accessible from the premises to be produced in a form in which it can be taken away and in which it is visible and legible or from which it can readily be produced in a visible and legible form if he has reasonable grounds for believing –

 (a) that –

  (i) it is evidence in relation to an offence which he is investigating or any other offence; or
  (ii) it has been obtained in consequence of the commission of an offence; and

 (b) that it is necessary to do so in order to prevent it being concealed, lost, tampered with or destroyed.

(5) The powers conferred by this section are in addition to any power otherwise conferred.
(6) No power of seizure conferred on a constable under any enactment (including an enactment contained in an Act passed after this Act) is to be taken to authorise the seizure of an item which the constable exercising the power has reasonable grounds for believing to be subject to legal privilege.

Section 19(4) is bolstered by s.20, which is also concerned with the production of visible and legible forms of electronically stored information. The distinction between s.19(4) and s.20 lies in the fact that s.19(4) is concerned with situations where the constable has reasonable grounds for believing that the data are evidence, or have been obtained in consequence of the commission of an offence or that it will be concealed, etc. Section 20 does not have these limitations; rather it is designed to equip constables with the power to seize hard copies of any data.

PACE, s.20 says:

**20. Extension of powers of seizure to computerised information**

(1) Every power of seizure which is conferred by an enactment to which this section applies on a constable who has entered premises in the exercise of a power conferred by an enactment shall be construed as including a power to require any information stored in any electronic form and accessible from the premises to be produced in a form in which it can be taken away and in which it is visible and legible or from which it can readily be produced in a visible and legible form.

(2) This section applies –

(a) to any enactment contained in an Act passed before this Act;
(b) to sections 8 and 18 above;
(c) to paragraph 13 of Schedule 1 to this Act; and
(d) to any enactment contained in an Act passed after this Act.

### *Extended seizure powers under the Criminal Justice and Police Act 2001*

The seizure powers within PACE have been greatly extended by the seizure powers within Part 2 of the Criminal Justice and Police Act (CJPA) 2001. Section 50 allows a constable conducting a lawful search to seize and remove anything on the premises for later sorting in order to see whether it is or contains anything that would be liable for seizure (see CJPA 2001, Sched.1, Part 1 for the powers to which s.50 applies; para.1 covers Part 2 of PACE). This power therefore allows the police to remove computer equipment for later forensic examination, even if the equipment contains privileged materials. Section 50 says:

**50. Additional powers of seizure from premises**

(1) Where –

(a) a person who is lawfully on any premises finds anything on those premises that he has reasonable grounds for believing may be or may contain something for which he is authorised to search on those premises,
(b) a power of seizure to which this section applies or the power conferred by subsection (2) would entitle him, if he found it, to seize whatever it is that he has grounds for believing that thing to be or to contain, and
(c) in all the circumstances, it is not reasonably practicable for it to be determined, on those premises –

(i) whether what he has found is something that he is entitled to seize, or
(ii) the extent to which what he has found contains something that he is entitled to seize,

that person's powers of seizure shall include power under this section to seize so much of what he has found as it is necessary to remove from the premises to enable that to be determined.

(2) Where –

(a) a person who is lawfully on any premises finds anything on those premises ('the seizable property') which he would be entitled to seize but for its being comprised in something else that he has (apart from this subsection) no power to seize,
(b) the power under which that person would have power to seize the seizable property is a power to which this section applies, and
(c) in all the circumstances it is not reasonably practicable for the seizable property to be separated, on those premises, from that in which it is comprised,

that person's powers of seizure shall include power under this section to seize both the seizable property and that from which it is not reasonably practicable to separate it.

(3) The factors to be taken into account in considering, for the purposes of this section, whether or not it is reasonably practicable on particular premises for something to be determined, or for something to be separated from something else, shall be confined to the following –

(a) how long it would take to carry out the determination or separation on those premises;
(b) the number of persons that would be required to carry out that determination or separation on those premises within a reasonable period;
(c) whether the determination or separation would (or would if carried out on those premises) involve damage to property;
(d) the apparatus or equipment that it would be necessary or appropriate to use for the carrying out of the determination or separation; and
(e) in the case of separation, whether the separation –

(i) would be likely, or
(ii) if carried out by the only means that are reasonably practicable on those premises, would be likely,

to prejudice the use of some or all of the separated seizable property for a purpose for which something seized under the power in question is capable of being used.

(4) Section 19(6) of the 1984 Act and Article 21(6) of the Police and Criminal Evidence (Northern Ireland) Order 1989 (S.I. 1989/1341 (N.I. 12)) (powers of seizure not to include power to seize anything that a person has reasonable grounds for believing is legally privileged) shall not apply to the power of seizure conferred by subsection (2).

(5) This section applies to each of the powers of seizure specified in Part 1 of Schedule 1.

(6) Without prejudice to any power conferred by this section to take a copy of any document, nothing in this section, so far as it has effect by reference to the power to take copies of documents under section 28(2)(b) of the Competition Act 1998 (c. 41), shall be taken to confer any power to seize any document.

The Code of Practice says the following about the extended power within section 50:

> The Criminal Justice and Police Act 2001, Part 2 gives officers limited powers to seize property from premises or persons so they can sift or examine it elsewhere. Officers must be careful they only exercise these powers when it is essential and they do not remove any more material than necessary. The removal of large volumes of material, much of which may not ultimately be retainable, may have serious implications for the owners, particularly when they are involved in business or activities such as journalism or the provision of medical services. Officers must carefully consider if removing copies or images of relevant material or data would be a satisfactory alternative to removing originals. When originals are taken, officers must be prepared to facilitate the provision of copies or images for the owners when reasonably practicable.

### *Exclusion of evidence*

PACE, s.78 gives the court the power to exclude unfair evidence. Section 78 says:

> **78. Exclusion of unfair evidence**
>
> (1) In any proceedings the court may refuse to allow evidence on which the prosecution proposes to rely to be given if it appears to the court that, having regard to all the circumstances, including the circumstances in which the evidence was obtained, the admission of the evidence would have such an adverse effect on the fairness of the proceedings that the court ought not to admit it.
>
> (2) Nothing in this section shall prejudice any rule of law requiring a court to exclude evidence.

Significant and substantial breaches (see *R.* v. *Absolom* (1988) 88 CrAppR 332) of the Code of Practice can lead to the exclusion of evidence obtained through a search, although the exclusion of evidence is not automatic (*R.* v. *Delaney* (1988) 88 CrAppR 338), but discretionary (*R.* v. *Absolom*).

## 7.4.2 Serious Organised Crime and Police Act 2005

Part 2, Chapter 1 of the Serious Organised Crime and Police Act (SOCPA) 2005 confers important investigatory powers on the Director of Public Prosecutions, the Director of Revenue and Customs Prosecutions and the Lord Advocate in relation to the giving of disclosure notices in connection with certain listed offences (these include 'lifestyle offences' under the Proceeds of Crime Act 2002, such as arms trafficking, counterfeiting, intellectual property offences, pimping and brothels) and in connection with terrorist investigations (see SOCPA 2005, s.60). The investigatory powers can be delegated to 'appropriate' persons, which includes police constables, designated staff members of the Serious Organised Crime Agency and officers of HM Revenue and Customs.

*Disclosure notices*

Under SOCPA 2005, s.2 the investigating authorities can serve disclosure notices on any person where they have reasonable grounds for believing that a relevant offence has been committed, that the person has information (documentary or otherwise) relating to a matter that is relevant to the investigation and that the information will be of substantial value to the investigation. Disclosure notices can require the person to answer questions, provide specified information and produce documents. Section 62 says:

**62. Disclosure notices**

(1) If it appears to the Investigating Authority –

(a) that there are reasonable grounds for suspecting that an offence to which this Chapter applies has been committed,
(b) that any person has information (whether or not contained in a document) which relates to a matter relevant to the investigation of that offence, and
(c) that there are reasonable grounds for believing that information which may be provided by that person in compliance with a disclosure notice is likely to be of substantial value (whether or not by itself) to that investigation,

he may give, or authorise an appropriate person to give, a disclosure notice to that person.

(1A) If it appears to the Investigating Authority –

(a) that any person has information (whether or not contained in a document) which relates to a matter relevant to a terrorist investigation, and
(b) that there are reasonable grounds for believing that information which may be provided by that person in compliance with a disclosure notice is likely to be of substantial value (whether or not by itself) to that investigation,

he may give, or authorise an appropriate person to give, a disclosure notice to that person.

(2) In this Chapter 'appropriate person' means –

(a) a constable,
(b) a member of the staff of SOCA who is for the time being designated under section 43, or
(c) an officer of Revenue and Customs.

(3) In this Chapter 'disclosure notice' means a notice in writing requiring the person to whom it is given to do all or any of the following things in accordance with the specified requirements, namely –

(a) answer questions with respect to any matter relevant to the investigation;
(b) provide information with respect to any such matter as is specified in the notice;
(c) produce such documents, or documents of such descriptions, relevant to the investigation as are specified in the notice.

(4) In subsection (3) 'the specified requirements' means such requirements specified in the disclosure notice as relate to –

(a) the time at or by which,
(b) the place at which, or
(c) the manner in which,

the person to whom the notice is given is to do any of the things mentioned in paragraphs (a) to (c) of that subsection; and those requirements may include a requirement to do any of those things at once.

(5) A disclosure notice must be signed or counter-signed by the Investigating Authority.

(6) This section has effect subject to section 64 (restrictions on requiring information etc.).

Where a disclosure notice requires a person to produce documents, the investigating authority can take copies or extracts and can require that person to provide an explanation for them. If they are missing, the person can be required to explain their whereabouts. The investigating authority may also retain the original documents for the length of the investigation and any proceedings. Section 63 says:

**63. Production of documents**

(1) This section applies where a disclosure notice has been given under section 62.

(2) An authorised person may –

(a) take copies of or extracts from any documents produced in compliance with the notice, and
(b) require the person producing them to provide an explanation of any of them.

(3) Documents so produced may be retained for so long as the Investigating Authority considers that it is necessary to retain them (rather than copies of them) in connection with the investigation for the purposes of which the disclosure notice was given.

(4) If the Investigating Authority has reasonable grounds for believing –

(a) that any such documents may have to be produced for the purposes of any legal proceedings, and
(b) that they might otherwise be unavailable for those purposes,

they may be retained until the proceedings are concluded.

(5) If a person who is required by a disclosure notice to produce any documents does not produce the documents in compliance with the notice, an authorised person may require that person to state, to the best of his knowledge and belief, where they are.

(6) In this section 'authorised person' means any appropriate person who either –

(a) is the person by whom the notice was given, or
(b) is authorised by the Investigating Authority for the purposes of this section.

(7) This section has effect subject to section 64 (restrictions on requiring information etc.).

However, s.64 provides protections for legal privilege:

**64. Restrictions on requiring information etc.**

(1) A person may not be required under section 62 or 63 –

(a) to answer any privileged question,
(b) to provide any privileged information, or
(c) to produce any privileged document,

except that a lawyer may be required to provide the name and address of a client of his.

(2) A 'privileged question' is a question which the person would be entitled to refuse to answer on grounds of legal professional privilege in proceedings in the High Court.

(3) 'Privileged information' is information which the person would be entitled to refuse to provide on grounds of legal professional privilege in such proceedings.

(4) A 'privileged document' is a document which the person would be entitled to refuse to produce on grounds of legal professional privilege in such proceedings.

(5) A person may not be required under section 62 to produce any excluded material (as defined by section 11 of the Police and Criminal Evidence Act 1984 (c. 60)).

(6) In the application of this section to Scotland –

(a) subsections (1) to (5) do not have effect, but
(b) a person may not be required under section 62 or 63 to answer any question, provide any information or produce any document which he would be entitled, on grounds of legal privilege, to refuse to answer or (as the case may be) provide or produce.

(7) In subsection (6)(b), 'legal privilege' has the meaning given by section 412 of the Proceeds of Crime Act 2002 (c. 29).

(8) A person may not be required under section 62 or 63 to disclose any information or produce any document in respect of which he owes an obligation of confidence by virtue of carrying on any banking business, unless –

(a) the person to whom the obligation of confidence is owed consents to the disclosure or production, or
(b) the requirement is made by, or in accordance with a specific authorisation given by, the Investigating Authority.

(9) Subject to the preceding provisions, any requirement under section 62 or 63 has effect despite any restriction on disclosure (however imposed).

Section 65 places restrictions on the use that can be made of a statement provided under s.62 or s.63. In summary, these statements cannot be used against the person unless they are being prosecuted for perjury, or unless they make an inconsistent statement in unrelated proceedings, or unless they are being prosecuted under s.67 for making a false or misleading statement or obstructing a warrant issued under s.66.

## *Search warrants*

Section 66 gives magistrates the power to issue warrants in respect of documents, which allow the investigating authority to enter and search premises, using reasonable force if necessary. Before issuing a warrant the magistrate has to be satisfied that either a person served with a disclosure notice to produce documents has failed to produce them, or that it is not practicable to give a disclosure notice or the giving of a notice would seriously prejudice the investigation. The warrant also authorises the investigating authority to seize computer disks and other forms of electronic storage and to take steps to preserve electronic data. Section 66 says:

**66. Power to enter and seize documents**

(1) A justice of the peace may issue a warrant under this section if, on an information on oath laid by the Investigating Authority, he is satisfied –

- (a) that any of the conditions mentioned in subsection (2) is met in relation to any documents of a description specified in the information, and
- (b) that the documents are on premises so specified.

(2) The conditions are –

- (a) that a person has been required by a disclosure notice to produce the documents but has not done so;
- (b) that it is not practicable to give a disclosure notice requiring their production;
- (c) that giving such a notice might seriously prejudice the investigation of an offence to which this Chapter applies.

(3) A warrant under this section is a warrant authorising an appropriate person named in it –

- (a) to enter and search the premises, using such force as is reasonably necessary;
- (b) to take possession of any documents appearing to be documents of a description specified in the information, or to take any other steps which appear to be necessary for preserving, or preventing interference with, any such documents;
- (c) in the case of any such documents consisting of information recorded otherwise than in legible form, to take possession of any computer disk or other electronic storage device which appears to contain the information in question, or to take any other steps which appear to be necessary for preserving, or preventing interference with, that information;
- (d) to take copies of or extracts from any documents or information falling within paragraph (b) or (c);
- (e) to require any person on the premises to provide an explanation of any such documents or information or to state where any such documents or information may be found;

(f) to require any such person to give the appropriate person such assistance as he may reasonably require for the taking of copies or extracts as mentioned in paragraph (d).

(4) A person executing a warrant under this section may take other persons with him, if it appears to him to be necessary to do so.

(5) A warrant under this section must, if so required, be produced for inspection by the owner or occupier of the premises or anyone acting on his behalf.

(6) If the premises are unoccupied or the occupier is temporarily absent, a person entering the premises under the authority of a warrant under this section must leave the premises as effectively secured against trespassers as he found them.

(7) Where possession of any document or device is taken under this section –

(a) the document may be retained for so long as the Investigating Authority considers that it is necessary to retain it (rather than a copy of it) in connection with the investigation for the purposes of which the warrant was sought, or

(b) the device may be retained for so long as he considers that it is necessary to retain it in connection with that investigation,

as the case may be.

(8) If the Investigating Authority has reasonable grounds for believing –

(a) that any such document or device may have to be produced for the purposes of any legal proceedings, and

(b) that it might otherwise be unavailable for those purposes,

it may be retained until the proceedings are concluded.

(9) Nothing in this section authorises a person to take possession of, or make copies of or take extracts from, any document or information which, by virtue of section 64, could not be required to be produced or disclosed under section 62 or 63.

(10) In the application of this section to Scotland –

(a) subsection (1) has effect as if, for the words from the beginning to 'satisfied', there were substituted 'A sheriff may issue a warrant under this section, on the application of a procurator fiscal, if he is satisfied';

(b) subsections (1)(a) and (3)(b) have effect as if, for 'in the information', there were substituted 'in the application'; and

(c) subsections (4) to (6) do not have effect.

## 7.5 SEARCH ORDERS UNDER THE CIVIL PROCEDURE ACT 1997

The most famous case on civil search orders is *Anton Piller KG* v. *Manufacturing Processes Ltd* [1976] Ch55, which led directly to the introduction of the power within s.7 of the Civil Procedure Act 1997. Under s.7 litigants in civil cases also have powers to search and seize materials. Section 7 says:

**7. Power of courts to make orders for preserving evidence, etc.**

(1) The court may make an order under this section for the purpose of securing, in the case of any existing or proposed proceedings in the court –

(a) the preservation of evidence which is or may be relevant, or
(b) the preservation of property which is or may be the subject-matter of the proceedings or as to which any question arises or may arise in the proceedings.

(2) A person who is, or appears to the court likely to be, a party to proceedings in the court may make an application for such an order.
(3) Such an order may direct any person to permit any person described in the order, or secure that any person so described is permitted –

(a) to enter premises in England and Wales, and
(b) while on the premises, to take in accordance with the terms of the order any of the following steps.

(4) Those steps are –

(a) to carry out a search for or inspection of anything described in the order, and
(b) to make or obtain a copy, photograph, sample or other record of anything so described.

(5) The order may also direct the person concerned –

(a) to provide any person described in the order, or secure that any person so described is provided, with any information or article described in the order, and
(b) to allow any person described in the order, or secure that any person so described is allowed, to retain for safe keeping anything described in the order, and

(6) An order under this section is to have effect subject to such conditions as are specified in the order.
(7) This section does not affect any right of a person to refuse to do anything on the ground that to do so might tend to expose him or his spouse [or civil partner] to proceedings for an offence or for the recovery of a penalty.
(8) In this section –

'court' means the High Court, and
'premises' includes any vehicle;

and an order under this section may describe anything generally, whether by reference to a class or otherwise.

### 7.5.1 Civil Procedure Rules 1998

Search orders are governed by Part 25 of the Civil Procedures Rules 1998 (CPR). CPR 25.1 says:

**25.1 Orders for interim remedies**

(1) The court may grant the following interim remedies –

. . .

(h) an order (referred to as a 'search order') under section 7 of the Civil Procedure Act 1997 (order requiring a party to admit another party to premises for the purpose of preserving evidence etc.);

The accompanying Practice Direction to Part 25 provides the following assistance on the making of applications for search orders:

7.1 The following provisions apply to search orders in addition to those listed above.

7.2 The Supervising Solicitor

The Supervising Solicitor must be experienced in the operation of search orders. A Supervising Solicitor may be contacted either through the Law Society or, for the London area, through the London Solicitors Litigation Association.

7.3 Evidence:

(1) the affidavit must state the name, firm and its address, and experience of the Supervising Solicitor, also the address of the premises and whether it is a private or business address, and
(2) the affidavit must disclose very fully the reason the order is sought, including the probability that relevant material would disappear if the order were not made.

7.4 Service:

(1) the order must be served personally by the Supervising Solicitor, unless the court otherwise orders, and must be accompanied by the evidence in support and any documents capable of being copied,
(2) confidential exhibits need not be served but they must be made available for inspection by the respondent in the presence of the applicant's solicitors while the order is carried out and afterwards be retained by the respondent's solicitors on their undertaking not to permit the respondent –

    (a) to see them or copies of them except in their presence, and
    (b) to make or take away any note or record of them,

(3) the Supervising Solicitor may be accompanied only by the persons mentioned in the order,
(4) the Supervising Solicitor must explain the terms and effect of the order to the respondent in everyday language and advise him –

    (a) of his right to take legal advice and to apply to vary or discharge the order; and
    (b) that he may be entitled to avail himself of –

        (i) legal professional privilege; and
        (ii) the privilege against self-incrimination.

(5) where the Supervising Solicitor is a man and the respondent is likely to be an unaccompanied woman, at least one other person named in the order must be a woman and must accompany the Supervising Solicitor, and
(6) the order may only be served between 9.30 a.m. and 5.30 p.m. Monday to Friday unless the court otherwise orders.

7.5 Search and custody of materials:

(1) no material shall be removed unless clearly covered by the terms of the order,
(2) the premises must not be searched and no items shall be removed from them except in the presence of the respondent or a person who appears to be a responsible employee of the respondent,
(3) where copies of documents are sought, the documents should be retained for no more than 2 days before return to the owner,
(4) where material in dispute is removed pending trial, the applicant's solicitors should place it in the custody of the respondent's solicitors on their undertaking to retain it in safekeeping and to produce it to the court when required,
(5) in appropriate cases the applicant should insure the material retained in the respondent's solicitors' custody,
(6) the Supervising Solicitor must make a list of all material removed from the premises and supply a copy of the list to the respondent,
(7) no material shall be removed from the premises until the respondent has had reasonable time to check the list,
(8) if any of the listed items exists only in computer readable form, the respondent must immediately give the applicant's solicitors effective access to the computers, with all necessary passwords, to enable them to be searched, and cause the listed items to be printed out,
(9) the applicant must take all reasonable steps to ensure that no damage is done to any computer or data,
(10) the applicant and his representatives may not themselves search the respondent's computers unless they have sufficient expertise to do so without damaging the respondent's system,
(11) the Supervising Solicitor shall provide a report on the carrying out of the order to the applicant's solicitors,
(12) as soon as the report is received the applicant's solicitors shall –

(a) serve a copy of it on the respondent, and
(b) file a copy of it with the court, and

(13) where the Supervising Solicitor is satisfied that full compliance with paragraph 7.5(7) and (8) above is impracticable, he may permit the search to proceed and items to be removed without compliance with the impracticable requirements.

7.6 General

The Supervising Solicitor must not be an employee or member of the applicant's firm of solicitors.

7.7 If the court orders that the order need not be served by the Supervising Solicitor, the reason for so ordering must be set out in the order.

7.8 The search order must not be carried out at the same time as a police search warrant.
7.9 There is no privilege against self incrimination in:

(1) Intellectual Property cases in respect of a 'related offence' or for the recovery of a 'related penalty' as defined in section 72 Supreme Court Act 1981;
(2) proceedings for the recovery or administration of any property, for the execution of a trust or for an account of any property or dealings with property, in relation to –
    (a) an offence under the Theft Act 1968 (see section 31 of the Theft Act 1968); or
    (b) an offence under the Fraud Act 2006 (see section 13 of the Fraud Act 2006) or a related offence within the meaning given by section 13(4) of that Act – that is, conspiracy to defraud or any other offence involving any form of fraudulent conduct or purpose; or
(3) proceedings in which a court is hearing an application for an order under Part IV or Part V of the Children Act 1989 (see section 98 Children Act 1989).

However, the privilege may still be claimed in relation to material or information required to be disclosed by an order, as regards potential criminal proceedings outside those statutory provisions.

7.10 Applications in intellectual property cases should be made in the Chancery Division.
7.11 An example of a Search Order is annexed to this Practice Direction. This example may be modified as appropriate in any particular case.

## 7.6 THE EVIDENCE ACTS AND HEARSAY

Emails that have been obtained through any of the routes discussed above may become evidence in court proceedings, subject to the rules on hearsay and the peculiarities of RIPA 2000, s.17 (which prevents the admission of interception evidence in proceedings). In this section the main rules on admissibility of hearsay evidence are discussed. These rules are additional to the rules on admissibility within the E-Signatures Directive and the E-Commerce Directive discussed in **Chapter 2**.

### 7.6.1 Evidence in criminal cases

In criminal cases the scope for adducing hearsay evidence is considerably less than in civil cases; whereas the Civil Evidence Act 1995 renders hearsay generally admissible in evidence in civil proceedings, the corresponding provisions for criminal cases, contained within the Criminal Justice Act (CJA) 2003, act to exclude hearsay, unless one of the narrow gateways to admissibility is satisfied. Thus, in criminal cases it is more important to determine whether evidence is hearsay in nature, or is 'real' or 'direct' evidence. This turns on the purpose for which the evidence is being adduced.

### *Hearsay and the Criminal Justice Act 2003*

Hearsay is not specifically defined in the CJA 2003, but s.114(1) makes it clear that hearsay is a statement that is tendered to prove its contents where the maker is not called to give evidence and for these purposes a statement is any representation of fact or opinion, as CJA 2003, s.115 makes clear:

> **115. Statements and matters stated**
>
> (1) In this Chapter references to a statement or to a matter stated are to be read as follows.
> (2) A statement is any representation of fact or opinion made by a person by whatever means; and it includes a representation made in a sketch, photofit or other pictorial form.
> (3) A matter stated is one to which this Chapter applies if (and only if) the purpose, or one of the purposes, of the person making the statement appears to the court to have been –
>
> (a) to cause another person to believe the matter, or
> (b) to cause another person to act or a machine to operate on the basis that the matter is as stated.

This definition of hearsay clearly has the capacity to cover email. So, if a party to criminal proceedings attempts to adduce an email in evidence without calling the writer of it to give evidence they will engage the hearsay rule if their purpose in adducing the email is to prove that its contents are true. If this is the party's purpose, then the gateways to admissibility are those identified in CJA 2003, s.114:

> **114. Admissibility of hearsay evidence**
>
> (1) In criminal proceedings a statement not made in oral evidence in the proceedings is admissible as evidence of any matter stated if, but only if –
>
> (a) any provision of this Chapter or any other statutory provision makes it admissible,
> (b) any rule of law preserved by section 118 makes it admissible,
> (c) all parties to the proceedings agree to it being admissible, or
> (d) the court is satisfied that it is in the interests of justice for it to be admissible.
>
> (2) In deciding whether a statement not made in oral evidence should be admitted under subsection (1)(d), the court must have regard to the following factors (and to any others it considers relevant) –

(a) how much probative value the statement has (assuming it to be true) in relation to a matter in issue in the proceedings, or how valuable it is for the understanding of other evidence in the case;
(b) what other evidence has been, or can be, given on the matter or evidence mentioned in paragraph (a);
(c) how important the matter or evidence mentioned in paragraph (a) is in the context of the case as a whole;
(d) the circumstances in which the statement was made;
(e) how reliable the maker of the statement appears to be;
(f) how reliable the evidence of the making of the statement appears to be;
(g) whether oral evidence of the matter stated can be given and, if not, why it cannot;
(h) the amount of difficulty involved in challenging the statement;
(i) the extent to which that difficulty would be likely to prejudice the party facing it.

(3) Nothing in this Chapter affects the exclusion of evidence of a statement on grounds other than the fact that it is a statement not made in oral evidence in the proceedings.

However, if the party's purpose is not to prove the truth of the contents of the statement, then it will not be hearsay. For example, in the well-known Privy Council case of *Subramaniam* v. *Public Prosecutor* [1956] 1 WLR 956 a distinction was made between a statement that is adduced to prove its contents and a statement that is adduced to prove the fact that the statement was made; in the former situation the statement will not be hearsay, but real evidence. Similarly, if the statement does not contain any representation of fact or opinion it will not be hearsay (see *R.* v. *Chapman* [1969] 2 QB 436; see also *Ratten* v. *R.* [1972] AC 378 PC).

If the email is hearsay then the two most likely grounds for its admission will be those contained in CJA 2003, ss.116 and 117. Section 116, which deals with the situation where the witness is unavailable, says:

**116. Cases where a witness is unavailable**

(1) In criminal proceedings a statement not made in oral evidence in the proceedings is admissible as evidence of any matter stated if –

(a) oral evidence given in the proceedings by the person who made the statement would be admissible as evidence of that matter,
(b) the person who made the statement (the relevant person) is identified to the court's satisfaction, and
(c) any of the five conditions mentioned in subsection (2) is satisfied.

(2) The conditions are –

(a) that the relevant person is dead;
(b) that the relevant person is unfit to be a witness because of his bodily or mental condition;
(c) that the relevant person is outside the United Kingdom and it is not reasonably practicable to secure his attendance;

(d) that the relevant person cannot be found although such steps as it is reasonably practicable to take to find him have been taken;
(e) that through fear the relevant person does not give (or does not continue to give) oral evidence in the proceedings, either at all or in connection with the subject matter of the statement, and the court gives leave for the statement to be given in evidence.

(3) For the purposes of subsection (2)(e) 'fear' is to be widely construed and (for example) includes fear of the death or injury of another person or of financial loss.
(4) Leave may be given under subsection (2)(e) only if the court considers that the statement ought to be admitted in the interests of justice, having regard –

(a) to the statement's contents,
(b) to any risk that its admission or exclusion will result in unfairness to any party to the proceedings (and in particular to how difficult it will be to challenge the statement if the relevant person does not give oral evidence),
(c) in appropriate cases, to the fact that a direction under section 19 of the Youth Justice and Criminal Evidence Act 1999 (c. 23) (special measures for the giving of evidence by fearful witnesses etc) could be made in relation to the relevant person, and
(d) to any other relevant circumstances.

(5) A condition set out in any paragraph of subsection (2) which is in fact satisfied is to be treated as not satisfied if it is shown that the circumstances described in that paragraph are caused –

(a) by the person in support of whose case it is sought to give the statement in evidence, or
(b) by a person acting on his behalf,

in order to prevent the relevant person giving oral evidence in the proceedings (whether at all or in connection with the subject matter of the statement).

Section 117 is concerned with business and similar documents:

**117. Business and other documents**

(1) In criminal proceedings a statement contained in a document is admissible as evidence of any matter stated if –

(a) oral evidence given in the proceedings would be admissible as evidence of that matter,
(b) the requirements of subsection (2) are satisfied, and
(c) the requirements of subsection (5) are satisfied, in a case where subsection (4) requires them to be.

(2) The requirements of this subsection are satisfied if –

(a) the document or the part containing the statement was created or received by a person in the course of a trade, business, profession or other occupation, or as the holder of a paid or unpaid office,
(b) the person who supplied the information contained in the statement (the relevant person) had or may reasonably be supposed to have had personal knowledge of the matters dealt with, and

(c) each person (if any) through whom the information was supplied from the relevant person to the person mentioned in paragraph (a) received the information in the course of a trade, business, profession or other occupation, or as the holder of a paid or unpaid office.

(3) The persons mentioned in paragraphs (a) and (b) of subsection (2) may be the same person.

(4) The additional requirements of subsection (5) must be satisfied if the statement –

(a) was prepared for the purposes of pending or contemplated criminal proceedings, or for a criminal investigation, but

(b) was not obtained pursuant to a request under section 7 of the Crime (International Co-operation) Act 2003 (c. 32) or an order under paragraph 6 of Schedule 13 to the Criminal Justice Act 1988 (c. 33) (which relate to overseas evidence).

(5) The requirements of this subsection are satisfied if –

(a) any of the five conditions mentioned in section 116(2) is satisfied (absence of relevant person etc), or

(b) the relevant person cannot reasonably be expected to have any recollection of the matters dealt with in the statement (having regard to the length of time since he supplied the information and all other circumstances).

(6) A statement is not admissible under this section if the court makes a direction to that effect under subsection (7).

(7) The court may make a direction under this subsection if satisfied that the statement's reliability as evidence for the purpose for which it is tendered is doubtful in view of –

(a) its contents,

(b) the source of the information contained in it,

(c) the way in which or the circumstances in which the information was supplied or received, or

(d) the way in which or the circumstances in which the document concerned was created or received.

Even if a gateway to the admissibility of hearsay is established, the court may still order its exclusion from evidence, due to its powers contained in CJA 2003, s.126, which says:

**126. Court's general discretion to exclude evidence**

(1) In criminal proceedings the court may refuse to admit a statement as evidence of a matter stated if –

(a) the statement was made otherwise than in oral evidence in the proceedings, and

(b) the court is satisfied that the case for excluding the statement, taking account of the danger that to admit it would result in undue waste of time, substantially outweighs the case for admitting it, taking account of the value of the evidence.

(2) Nothing in this Chapter prejudices –

(a) any power of a court to exclude evidence under section 78 of the Police and Criminal Evidence Act 1984 (c. 60) (exclusion of unfair evidence), or
(b) any other power of a court to exclude evidence at its discretion (whether by preventing questions from being put or otherwise).

Once an email containing hearsay is ruled to be admissible, it is proved by producing the original email, or a copy, or a copy of a part, subject to the court's approval as to the method of authenticating it. Of course, as an email is electronic information, the parties to criminal litigation will produce copies for use in evidence. Consequently, the copy will need authenticating. CJA 2003, s.133 says:

**133. Proof of statements in documents**

Where a statement in a document is admissible as evidence in criminal proceedings, the statement may be proved by producing either –

(a) the document, or
(b) (whether or not the document exists) a copy of the document or of the material part of it,

authenticated in whatever way the court may approve.

For these purposes an email will be a document, due to the definitions within CJA 2003, s.134. This says that a document 'means anything in which information of any description is recorded'. A copy of a document is defined as 'anything on to which information recorded in the document has been copied, by whatever means and whether directly or indirectly'. In the case of *R.* v. *Nazeer* [1998] CrimLR 750 it was held that a computer is a document for these purposes.

There is a healthy body of case law that concerns information obtained from computers and whether that information is hearsay or real evidence. This case law divides computer-derived information into three broad categories.

- Information obtained from a computer that has been used by an operator as a calculator to process information. Where the operator-controlled computer is used as a calculator is a mere tool, as would be scales, a slide rule or an abacus, and such information will not be hearsay, but real evidence, although the user of the computer will need to be called.
- Information obtained from a computer which the computer has been programmed to record and in respect of which there is no human intervention. If tendered to prove the truth of its contents it will be hearsay, but it will not be admissible under CJA 2003, s.116 or s.117 as there is no human maker of the statements within the evidence. However, the

evidence could be admissible if, for example, the purpose is not to prove the truth of its contents, but something different, such as to prove the fact or existence of the information (*R.* v. *Governor of Brixton Prison ex p. Levin* [1997] AC 741, HL).

- Information obtained from a computer which has been entered by a person. This will be hearsay, if adduced to prove the truth of its contents, and is the clearest category of relevance to email.

In *R.* v. *Stanley William Wood* (1983) 76 CrAppR 23 the Court of Appeal considered the first category of information, in a case that arose from the theft of a consignment of metals. In summary, scientists employed by the Crown tested samples of the metals and processed the results by computer. The computer output was then relied upon in evidence by the scientists, but the defendant argued that the output was hearsay. See also *R.* v. *Coventry Justices ex p. Bullard* (1992) 95 CrAppR 175; *R.* v. *Skinner (Philip)* [2005] EWCA Crim 1439; *Sophocleous* v. *Ringer* [1988] RTR 52.

The leading judgment was given by the Lord Chief Justice, whose summary of the key facts was as follows:

> These three categories of material were submitted to Dr. Ranson of L.S.M. who was assisted by a team of scientists. Dr. Ranson and his team then analysed the retained samples and the recovered samples and compared the results both with each other and the figures for various melts given in the are furnace log sheet and the stock book. The process of analysis used by Dr. Ranson in 1980 did not differ materially from that used at the time of manufacture to derive the figures recorded in the above-mentioned documents. The material elements for which analyses were done were nickel, cobalt and copper, and where relevant boron. For this purpose the samples were subjected to an X-ray spectrometer and, for boron, to a neutron transmission monitor. But these devices do not themselves give the percentages of the metals in the samples. The X-ray spectrometer for example merely measures the X-rays given off by the samples at various wavelengths and compares them with certain other criteria and measurements and produces ratios between the sample being analysed and a standard sample of zinc. The figures thus produced then have to be subjected to a laborious mathematical process before the actual percentages of the various metals in the relevant sample can be stated as figures. The same applies to the boron analysis. This mathematical process can be expressed as a formula and can be carried out by a chemist who is prepared to spend the time to draw out the appropriate curves and graphs. But the normal thing for a chemist to do nowadays is to use a computer and this is what the L.S.M. chemists did. They had in their laboratory a computer which had been programmed by a Mr. Kellie to carry out this calculation. The computer was thus able more quickly and more accurately to carry out the calculation which otherwise would have been done by hand by the chemists.
>
> The computer was worked by the chemists. They fed into the computer the figures which they had obtained from the X-ray spectrometer and the neutron transmission monitor; they then ran the programme, which involved their giving further directions to the computer, and at the end the computer produced the results of the calculation. The computer appears to have had a visual display but it also included a printer which conveniently prints out the answers. It was these

> answers which at the time of manufacture were supplied by the chemists to Mrs. Shepherd and Mr. Allard so that they could compile their records and, in 1980, were supplied by the chemists to Dr. Ranson for the purposes of making his comparisons on the retained and recovered samples.
>
> At the trial there were called, besides Dr. Ranson, Mr. Kellie the programmer and all the chemists who had used the X-ray spectrometer, the neutron transmission monitor and the computer which the defence had required to have called. Between them they gave detailed evidence as to how the computer had been programmed and used. Before us Mr. Gale for the appellant conceded that he had no criticism to make of any of these people. The computer had been properly programmed using the right formulae and constants. The operators had used it correctly. He even conceded that the computer's answers were right. But he submitted to the trial judge and to this Court that the evidence of the computer results should be rejected as inadmissible at common law and not authorised by Statute. The trial judge rejected the submission and the evidence both documentary and oral was included in the evidence before the jury.

The court rejected the argument that the computer output was hearsay, holding that it was real evidence. The Lord Chief Justice said:

> We therefore consider the position under the common law first. The objection is that an answer provided by computer is hearsay. The breadth of the submission made by Mr. Gale was sufficient to cover virtually any conceivable computer. But we stress that our decision in this case is concerned only with the particular computer (and programme) used in this case. Doubtless, there are very many different sorts of computer and computer programme; computers may be used for very many different processes and purposes.
>
> The computer in the present case was being used as a calculator. Its programming and its use were both covered by oral evidence. But, it was argued, because the computer was interposed in the course of the production of the final figures, those figures are hearsay. In our judgment this argument cannot be accepted. Witnesses, and especially expert witnesses, frequently and properly give factual evidence of the results of a physical exercise which involves the use of some equipment, device or machine. Take a weighing machine; the witness steps on to the machine and reads a weight off the dial, receives a ticket printed with the weight or, even, hears a recorded voice saying it. None of this involves hearsay evidence. The witness may have to be cross-examined as to whether he kept one foot on the ground; the accuracy of the machine may have to be investigated. But this does not alter the character of the evidence which has been given. In the present case an earlier stage of the analysis involved the use of the X-ray spectrometer which likewise involved the derivation of figures from a device. Is it to be said that this was hearsay as well?
>
> Mr. Gale submitted that there was a difference in kind between the measuring device (even a sophisticated one) and this computer. He also suggested that there was a difference in kind between a mathematician who used a slide rule and one who used a calculating computer. We do not agree. This computer was rightly described as a tool. It did not contribute its own knowledge. It merely did a sophisticated calculation which could have been done manually by the chemist and was in fact done by the chemists using the computer programmed by Mr. Kellie whom the Crown called as a witness. The fact that the efficiency of a device is dependent on more than one person does not make any difference in kind. Virtually every

> device will involve the persons who made it, the persons who calibrated, programmed or set it up (for example with a clock the person who set it to the right time in the first place) and the person who uses or observes the device. In each particular case how many of these people it is appropriate to call must depend on the facts of, and the issues raised and concessions made in that case.

In *R.* v. *Stewart Pettigrew* (1980) 71 CrAppR 39 the Court of Appeal considered the second category of information, where it had been obtained from a computer-controller machine operated by the Bank of England. The machine automatically sorted bundles of bank notes, rejected ones that were defective in any way and recorded the serial numbers of the first and last series numbers of the notes in each bundle. The Crown contended that the computer print-out was admissible as a business record under powers equivalent to those in CJA 2003, s.117. The Court of Appeal rejected this argument, holding that the print out was not hearsay and was inadmissible. The key facts of the case and the argument on admissibility are explained in the judgment of Lord Justice Bridge:

> The other more difficult point which is raised in support of Pettigrew's appeal relates to the evidence regarding the £5 notes. The Crown tendered, and the learned judge ruled admissible after objection had been taken by the defence, what has been referred to as a computer print-out, identifying the serial numbers of a bundle of some £5,000 worth of notes, which had been sent from the Bank of England to a bank in Newcastle, parts of which could specifically be traced through a Trustee Savings Bank at Crook into the possession of Mr. Patterson, the loser in the case of the Patterson burglary. The evidence suggested, although it did not by any means conclusively prove, that the three new £5 notes found in Pettigrew's possession after the event, could well have come from the same series of notes as had been in Mr. Patterson's possession.
>
> The computer print-out was received in evidence pursuant to the provisions of the Criminal Evidence Act 1965, s. 1, which provides, so far as material, that 'In any criminal proceedings where direct oral evidence of a fact would be admissible, any statement contained in a document and tending to establish that fact shall, on production of the document, be admissible as evidence of that fact if- (a) the document is, or forms part of, a record relating to any trade or business and compiled, in the course of that trade or business, from information supplied (whether directly or indirectly) by persons who have, or may reasonably be supposed to have, personal knowledge of the matters dealt with in the information they supply . . .'
>
> The objection to the admission of the evidence before the learned judge was made solely on the ground that the issue of bank notes by the Bank of England was not an activity forming part of any trade or business. The learned judge did not accede to that submission and that is why he ruled the evidence admissible.
>
> But in this Court Mr. McHale for the appellant Pettigrew, whilst not abandoning his point about the Bank of England not carrying on a trade or business, takes a new and much more difficult point before us, namely that the information recorded in the computer print-out was not information supplied by any person who had or could reasonably be supposed to have had personal knowledge of the matters dealt with in the information.

The court ruled that the evidence was inadmissible because it could be said that the information within the printout was within the knowledge of any person. Lord Justice Bridge said:

> Mr. McHale's perfectly short and simple submission is that, in those circumstances it cannot be said that anyone – if it were to be anyone, it would have to be the machine operator – had personal knowledge of that which emerges from the machine at the end of the day in a computer printout recording the serial numbers of every note in each bundle to which the printout relates.
>
> Mr. Williamson, in an attractive argument for the Crown, submits that the operator of the machine can fairly be said to have personal knowledge of the serial numbers of the notes in each bundle which he feeds into the machine. Although he has not mentally recorded them, he has the means of knowledge of the bundle of notes he has fed into the machine, which bear consecutive serial numbers, and he records on a card the first number of each bundle which he feeds into the machine.
>
> This is a most attractive argument, and if the machine did nothing but record the totality of the numbers of notes in each bundle fed into it, it may well be – it is not necessary for present purposes to decide the point finally – that the argument for the Crown should prevail. But what at the end of the day has convinced us that we cannot accept it is the recognition that the machine has the important dual function of separating out the defective notes and rejecting them and recording the numbers of those rejected and recording the serial numbers of the notes at the beginning and end of each bundle.
>
> The numbers of the notes which have been rejected can never be said to be in the personal knowledge of the operator or in the mind of anybody. They are recorded purely by the operation of the machine. The operator could never be said to have personal knowledge of those rejected notes, and knowledge of the numbers of the rejected notes is essential to know the serial numbers of the notes in the bundles to which the computer print-out relates.
>
> Accordingly, although the point is highly technical, and one which may be thought to expose a lacuna in the Criminal Evidence Act 1965, the point is one on which the argument for the appellant Pettigrew is entitled to prevail, and though we have considered the possibility of the application of the proviso, this is not a proviso case, because it is quite clear that the evidence relating to the £5 notes was a very important part of the case for the Crown against the appellant Pettigrew. One cannot possibly say, had that evidence never been led, that the jury would necessarily have convicted him. In the result Pettigrew's appeal against conviction succeeds and his conviction is quashed.

### *Criminal Procedure Rules 2005*

CJA 2003, s.132 envisages the making of rules of court governing the procedures for tendering of evidence. Section 132 says:

> **132. Rules of court**
>
> (1) Rules of court may make such provision as appears to the appropriate authority to be necessary or expedient for the purposes of this Chapter; and the appropriate authority is the authority entitled to make the rules.

(2) The rules may make provision about the procedure to be followed and other conditions to be fulfilled by a party proposing to tender a statement in evidence under any provision of this Chapter.
(3) The rules may require a party proposing to tender the evidence to serve on each party to the proceedings such notice, and such particulars of or relating to the evidence, as may be prescribed.
(4) The rules may provide that the evidence is to be treated as admissible by agreement of the parties if –

   (a) a notice has been served in accordance with provision made under subsection (3), and
   (b) no counter-notice in the prescribed form objecting to the admission of the evidence has been served by a party.

(5) If a party proposing to tender evidence fails to comply with a prescribed requirement applicable to it –

   (a) the evidence is not admissible except with the court's leave;
   (b) where leave is given the court or jury may draw such inferences from the failure as appear proper;
   (c) the failure may be taken into account by the court in considering the exercise of its powers with respect to costs.

(6) In considering whether or how to exercise any of its powers under subsection (5) the court shall have regard to whether there is any justification for the failure to comply with the requirement.
(7) A person shall not be convicted of an offence solely on an inference drawn under subsection (5)(b).
(8) Rules under this section may –

   (a) limit the application of any provision of the rules to prescribed circumstances;
   (b) subject any provision of the rules to prescribed exceptions;
   (c) make different provision for different cases or circumstances.

(9) Nothing in this section prejudices the generality of any enactment conferring power to make rules of court; and no particular provision of this section prejudices any general provision of it.
(10) In this section 'prescribed' means prescribed by rules of court.

Part 34 of the Criminal Procedure Rules 2005, SI 2005/384 applies to hearsay evidence:

34.1 When this Part applies

This Part applies in a magistrates' court and in the Crown Court where a party wants to introduce evidence on one or more of the grounds set out in section 114(1)(d), section 116, section 117 and section 121 of the Criminal Justice Act 2003, and in this Part that evidence is called 'hearsay evidence'.

34.2 Notice of hearsay evidence

The party who wants to introduce hearsay evidence must give notice in the form set out in the Practice Direction to the court officer and all other parties.

34.3 When the prosecutor must give notice of hearsay evidence

The prosecutor must give notice of hearsay evidence –

(a) in a magistrates' court, at the same time as he complies or purports to comply with section 3 of the Criminal Procedure and Investigations Act 1996 (disclosure by prosecutor); or
(b) in the Crown Court, not more than 14 days after –
    (i) the committal of the defendant, or
    (ii) the consent to the preferment of a bill of indictment in relation to the case, or
    (iii) the service of a notice of transfer under section 4 of the Criminal Justice Act 1987 (serious fraud cases) or under section 53 of the Criminal Justice Act 1991 (certain cases involving children), or
    (iv) where a person is sent for trial under section 51 of the Crime and Disorder Act 1998 (indictable-only offences sent for trial), the service of copies of the documents containing the evidence on which the charge or charges are based under paragraph 1 of Schedule 3 to the 1998 Act.

34.4 When a defendant must give notice of hearsay evidence

A defendant must give notice of hearsay evidence not more than 14 days after the prosecutor has complied with or purported to comply with section 3 of the Criminal Procedure and Investigations Act 1996 (disclosure by prosecutor).

34.5 Opposing the introduction of hearsay evidence

A party who receives a notice of hearsay evidence may oppose it by giving notice within 14 days in the form set out in the Practice Direction to the court officer and all other parties.

34.7 Court's power to vary requirements under this Part

The court may –

(a) dispense with the requirement to give notice of hearsay evidence;
(b) allow notice to be given in a different form, or orally; or
(c) shorten a time limit or extend it (even after it has expired).

34.8 Waiving the requirement to give a notice of hearsay evidence

A party entitled to receive a notice of hearsay evidence may waive his entitlement by so informing the court and the party who would have given the notice.

### 7.6.2 Evidence in civil cases

In civil cases the contents of emails will generally be regarded as being hearsay if the writer of the email is not called to give evidence and if they are tendered for the purpose of proving the truth of their contents. Under the Civil Evidence Act (CEA) 1995 hearsay is generally admissible as evidence in proceedings, which is a much more permissive regime than the one within the CJA 2003.

### *Hearsay and the Civil Evidence Act 1995*

CEA 1995, s.1 creates the general, permissive gateway to the receipt of hearsay evidence in civil cases. Section 1 says:

**1. Admissibility of hearsay evidence**

(1) In civil proceedings evidence shall not be excluded on the ground that it is hearsay.
(2) In this Act –

 (a) 'hearsay' means a statement made otherwise than by a person while giving oral evidence in the proceedings which is tendered as evidence of the matters stated; and
 (b) references to hearsay include hearsay of whatever degree.

(3) Nothing in this Act affects the admissibility of evidence admissible apart from this section.
(4) The provisions of sections 2 to 6 (safeguards and supplementary provisions relating to hearsay evidence) do not apply in relation to hearsay evidence admissible apart from this section, notwithstanding that it may also be admissible by virtue of this section.

The safeguards referred to at s.1(4) include the requirement placed on the person intending to adduce hearsay by s.2 to give notice of the intention to adduce hearsay evidence. However, although s.2 envisages the giving of hearsay notices it does not render their absence an automatic bar to the receipt of hearsay evidence, although the court does have the power to disallow the evidence nonetheless. Furthermore, the absence of a notice can lead to adverse findings on the weight to be attached to the evidence. Section 2 says:

**2. Notice of proposal to adduce hearsay evidence**

(1) A party proposing to adduce hearsay evidence in civil proceedings shall, subject to the following provisions of this section, give to the other party or parties to the proceedings –

 (a) such notice (if any) of the fact, and
 (b) on request, such particulars of or relating to the evidence,

 as is reasonable and practicable in the circumstances for the purpose of enabling him or them to deal with any matters arising from its being hearsay.
(2) Provision may be made by rules of court –

(a) specifying classes of proceedings or evidence in relation to which subsection (1) does not apply, and
(b) as to the manner in which (including the time within which) the duties imposed by that subsection are to be complied with in the cases where it does apply.

(3) Subsection (1) may also be excluded by agreement of the parties; and compliance with the duty to give notice may in any case be waived by the person to whom notice is required to be given.
(4) A failure to comply with subsection (1), or with rules under subsection (2)(b), does not affect the admissibility of the evidence but may be taken into account by the court –

(a) in considering the exercise of its powers with respect to the course of proceedings and costs, and
(b) as a matter adversely affecting the weight to be given to the evidence in accordance with section 4.

When considering the weight to be attached to hearsay the court is required to have regard to the considerations within s.4, which says:

**4. Considerations relevant to weighing of hearsay evidence**

(1) In estimating the weight (if any) to be given to hearsay evidence in civil proceedings the court shall have regard to any circumstances from which any inference can reasonably be drawn as to the reliability or otherwise of the evidence.
(2) Regard may be had, in particular, to the following –

(a) whether it would have been reasonable and practicable for the party by whom the evidence was adduced to have produced the maker of the original statement as a witness;
(b) whether the original statement was made contemporaneously with the occurrence or existence of the matters stated;
(c) whether the evidence involves multiple hearsay;
(d) whether any person involved had any motive to conceal or misrepresent matters;
(e) whether the original statement was an edited account, or was made in collaboration with another or for a particular purpose;
(f) whether the circumstances in which the evidence is adduced as hearsay are such as to suggest an attempt to prevent proper evaluation of its weight.

Another important safeguard is contained in s.3, which permits the drawing up of Rules of Court allowing a person to call the maker of a hearsay statement. Section 3 says:

**3. Power to call witness of cross-examination on hearsay statement**

Rules of court may provide that where a party to civil proceedings adduces hearsay evidence of a statement made by a person and does not call that person as a witness, any other party to the proceedings may, with the leave of the court, call that person as a witness and cross-examine him on the statement as if he had been called by the first-mentioned party and as if the hearsay statement were his evidence in chief.

CEA 1995, s.8 contains important provisions about proving statements contained in documents. For these purposes document means 'anything in which information of any description is recorded' (s.13). Section 8 says:

**8. Proof of statements contained in documents**

(1) Where a statement contained in a document is admissible as evidence in civil proceedings, it may be proved –

(a) by the production of that document, or
(b) whether or not that document is still in existence, by the production of a copy of that document or of the material part of it,

authenticated in such manner as the court may approve.

(2) It is immaterial for this purpose how many removes there are between a copy and the original.

When s.8 is combined with s.1, it becomes clear that there are very low barriers to the use of emails in evidence; if the writer of the email is not called to give evidence it can be adduced as hearsay under s.1 and proved by a witness producing the email in evidence. Related to this are the rules on proof of business and public authority records contained in s.9. Where emails form part of the records of a business or a public authority they are receivable in evidence without further proof. Section 9 says:

**9. Proof of records of business or public authority**

(1) A document which is shown to form part of the records of a business or public authority may be received in evidence in civil proceedings without further proof.

(2) A document shall be taken to form part of the records of a business or public authority if there is produced to the court a certificate to that effect signed by an officer of the business or authority to which the records belong. For this purpose –

(a) a document purporting to be a certificate signed by an officer of a business or public authority shall be deemed to have been duly given by such an officer and signed by him; and
(b) a certificate shall be treated as signed by a person if it purports to bear a facsimile of his signature.

(3) The absence of an entry in the records of a business or public authority may be proved in civil proceedings by affidavit of an officer of the business or authority to which the records belong.

(4) In this section –

'records' means records in whatever form;
'business' includes any activity regularly carried on over a period of time, whether for profit or not, by any body (whether corporate or not) or by an individual;
'officer' includes any person occupying a responsible position in relation to the relevant activities of the business or public authority or in relation to its records; and
'public authority' includes any public or statutory undertaking, any government department and any person holding office under Her Majesty.

(5) The court may, having regard to the circumstances of the case, direct that all or any of the above provisions of this section do not apply in relation to a particular document or record, or description of documents or records.

### *Civil Procedure Rules 1998*

Part 33 of the CPR describes the procedures for use of hearsay evidence. Rule 33.2 says:

**33.2 Notice of intention to rely on hearsay evidence**

(1) Where a party intends to rely on hearsay evidence at trial and either –

(a) that evidence is to be given by a witness giving oral evidence; or
(b) that evidence is contained in a witness statement of a person who is not being called to give oral evidence;

that party complies with section 2(1)(a) of the Civil Evidence Act 1995 by serving a witness statement on the other parties in accordance with the court's order.

(2) Where paragraph (1)(b) applies, the party intending to rely on the hearsay evidence must, when he serves the witness statement –

(a) inform the other parties that the witness is not being called to give oral evidence; and
(b) give the reason why the witness will not be called.

(3) In all other cases where a party intends to rely on hearsay evidence at trial, that party complies with section 2(1)(a) of the Civil Evidence Act 1995 by serving a notice on the other parties which –

(a) identifies the hearsay evidence;
(b) states that the party serving the notice proposes to rely on the hearsay evidence at trial; and
(c) gives the reason why the witness will not be called.

(4) The party proposing to rely on the hearsay evidence must –

(a) serve the notice no later than the latest date for serving witness statements; and
(b) if the hearsay evidence is to be in a document, supply a copy to any party who requests him to do so.

Rule 33.4 deals with the power to call a witness for examination:

**33.4 Power to call witness for cross-examination on hearsay evidence**

(1) Where a party –

(a) proposes to rely on hearsay evidence; and
(b) does not propose to call the person who made the original statement to give oral evidence,

the court may, on the application of any other party, permit that party to call the maker of the statement to be cross-examined on the contents of the statement.

(2) An application for permission to cross-examine under this rule must be made not more than 14 days after the day on which a notice of intention to rely on the hearsay evidence was served on the applicant.

## CHAPTER NOTES

1 Data Protection (Subject Access Modification) (Health) Order 2000, SI 2000/413; Data Protection (Subject Access Modification) (Education) Order 2000, SI 2000/414; Data Protection (Subject Access Modification) (Social Work) Order 2000, SI 2000/415; and Data Protection (Miscellaneous Subject Access Exemptions) Order 2000, SI 2000/419.
2 'Data Protection Powers and Penalties – The Case for Amending the Data Protection Act 1998'; **www.ico.gov.uk/upload/documents/library/corporate/detailed_specialist_guides/data_protection_powers_penalties_v1_dec07.pdf**.
3 'The Information Commissioner's inspection powers and funding arrangements under the Data Protection Act 1998', CP(L) 15/08; **www.justice.gov.uk/docs/cp1508.pdf**.
4 See **www.coe.int/t/dg1/legalcooperation/economiccrime/cybercrime/Documents/Points%20of%20Contact/24%208%20Communique_en.pdf**.
5 See **http://security.homeoffice.gov.uk**.
6 'Acquisition and Disclosure of Communications Data'; **http://security.homeoffice.gov.uk/ripa/publication-search/ripa-cop/acquisition-disclosure-cop.pdf**.
7 See **http://police.homeoffice.gov.uk//operational-policing**.

CHAPTER 8

# Litigation disclosure

This chapter discusses the extent to which emails will be disclosable in criminal and civil litigation.

## A DISCLOSURE IN CRIMINAL CASES

### 8.1 INTRODUCTION

The prosecution duty to give disclosure of materials in criminal cases is fundamental to a fair trial. The right to a fair trial is guaranteed by Article 6 of the European Convention on Human Rights (ECHR), which has been incorporated into domestic law by the Human Rights Act (HRA) 1998. Article 6 of the ECHR says:

1. In the determination of his civil rights and obligations or of any criminal charge against him, everyone is entitled to a fair and public hearing within a reasonable time by an independent and impartial tribunal established by law. Judgment shall be pronounced publicly but the press and public may be excluded from all or part of the trial in the interest of morals, public order or national security in a democratic society, where the interests of juveniles or the protection of the private life of the parties so require, or to the extent strictly necessary in the opinion of the court in special circumstances where publicity would prejudice the interests of justice.
2. Everyone charged with a criminal offence shall be presumed innocent until proved guilty according to law.
3. Everyone charged with a criminal offence has the following minimum rights:
   (a) to be informed promptly, in a language which he understands and in detail, of the nature and cause of the accusation against him;
   (b) to have adequate time and facilities for the preparation of his defence;
   (c) to defend himself in person or through legal assistance of his own choosing or, if he has not sufficient means to pay for legal assistance, to be given it free when the interests of justice so require;
   (d) to examine or have examined witnesses against him and to obtain the attendance and examination of witnesses on his behalf under the same conditions as witnesses against him;
   (e) to have the free assistance of an interpreter if he cannot understand or speak the language used in court.

The Attorney-General's Guidelines on Disclosure (2005) (see **8.3.1**) make the point in the following terms:

> Every accused person has a right to a fair trial, a right long embodied in our law and guaranteed under Article 6 of the European Convention on Human Rights (ECHR). A fair trial is the proper object and expectation of all participants in the trial process. Fair disclosure to an accused is an inseparable part of a fair trial.

In the case of *R.* v. *H and C* [2004] 2 AC 134 the House of Lords said (at 147):

> Fairness ordinarily requires that any material held by the prosecution which weakens its case or strengthens that of the defendant, if not relied on as part of its formal case against the defendant, should be disclosed to the defence. Bitter experience has shown that miscarriages of justice may occur where such material is withheld from disclosure. The golden rule is that full disclosure of such material should be made.

The right to a fair trial also covers the investigatory process leading up to a prosecution, and so it is critical that the Crown conducts a proper investigation, which means pursuing all reasonable lines of enquiry. This duty extends to gathering relevant materials during the investigatory process, which, of course, will include documents such as emails. These obligations are designed to ensure that there is 'equality of arms' between the Crown and the defence (see *Jespers* v. *Belgium* (1981) 27 DR 61). If the Crown fails to carry out a proper investigation, or fails to give full disclosure, the continuation of the case can amount to an abuse of process. If so, the court should order that the case be stayed (see *R.* v. *Feltham Magistrates' Court ex p. Ebrahim* [2001] 2 Cr App R 23), which effectively brings the case to an end.

Similarly, in cases tried in the Crown Court the defendant is required to give disclosure by way of a 'defence case statement', but in the magistrates' court, defence disclosure is entirely voluntary. The key distinction between the Crown and defence disclosure obligations is that the Crown is obliged to give disclosure of the materials it seeks to rely upon together with disclosure of 'unused materials', which are materials that the Crown does not seek to rely upon but which undermine the Crown's case or assist the defence case. The obligation placed on the defence in Crown Court cases is not synonymous with disclosure of documents. Instead the defence is required to provide a written statement of the key elements of their defence, including information about alibis and why they dispute the Crown's case. The Crown Court Protocol on the Control and Management of Unused Material (see **8.4**) says the following about defence case statements:

> Where the enhanced requirements for defence disclosure apply under section 6A of the CPIA [Criminal Procedure and Investigations Act 1996] (namely, where the case involves a criminal investigation commencing on or after 4 April 2005) the

defence statement must spell out, in detail, the nature of the defence, and particular defences relied upon; it must identify the matters of fact upon which the accused takes issue with the prosecution, and the reason why, in relation to each disputed matter of fact. It must further identify any point of law (including points as to the admissibility of evidence, or abuse of process) which the accused proposes to take, and identify authorities relied on in relation to each point of law. Where an alibi defence is relied upon, the particulars given must comply with section 6(2)(a) and (b) of the CPIA. Judges will expect to see defence case statements that contain a clear and detailed exposition of the issues of fact and law in the case.

The rules on disclosure are contained in the Criminal Procedure and Investigations Act (CPIA) 1996, which was amended by the Criminal Justice Act (CJA) 2003 for cases where the criminal investigation commenced on or after 4 April 2005. Where the investigation commenced before 4 April 2005, the unamended regime applies. However, in this section it is only the amended regime that is considered. The new regime, introduced by CJA 2003, s.32, made two very important changes. First, it moved to a single, unified regime for disclosure of prosecution unused material, with the result that a defendant is no longer required to serve a defence case statement to obtain disclosure of unused material that may assist its case. Second, it abandoned the subjective test for disclosure of prosecution unused material that might undermine the prosecution's case.

The parties to criminal litigation need to consider much more than the CPIA 1996 in order to determine their obligations. Other relevant materials include the Criminal Procedure Rules, the Code of Practice made under Part II of the CPIA 1996, the Attorney-General's guidelines on disclosure of information in criminal proceedings, the Crown Court Protocol for the Control and Management of Unused Material and the CPS Disclosure Manual.

## 8.2 CONDUCTING A FAIR INVESTIGATION AND THE STATUTORY CODE OF PRACTICE

CPIA 1996, s.23 specifies that those undertaking a criminal investigation should pursue all reasonable lines of inquiry, which extends to retaining all materials gathered in the course of the investigation. These obligations are recorded in a Code of Practice made under Part II of the Act. Section 23 says:

**23. Code of practice**

(1) The Secretary of State shall prepare a code of practice containing provisions designed to secure –

(a) that where a criminal investigation is conducted all reasonable steps are taken for the purposes of the investigation and, in particular, all reasonable lines of inquiry are pursued;
(b) that information which is obtained in the course of a criminal investigation and may be relevant to the investigation is recorded;
(c) that any record of such information is retained;
(d) that any other material which is obtained in the course of a criminal investigation and may be relevant to the investigation is retained;
(e) that information falling within paragraph (b) and material falling within paragraph (d) is revealed to a person who is involved in the prosecution of criminal proceedings arising out of or relating to the investigation and who is identified in accordance with prescribed provisions;
(f) that where such a person inspects information or other material in pursuance of a requirement that it be revealed to him, and he requests that it be disclosed to the accused, the accused is allowed to inspect it or is given a copy of it;
(g) that where such a person is given a document indicating the nature of information or other material in pursuance of a requirement that it be revealed to him, and he requests that it be disclosed to the accused, the accused is allowed to inspect it or is given a copy of it;
(h) that the person who is to allow the accused to inspect information or other material or to give him a copy of it shall decide which of those (inspecting or giving a copy) is appropriate;
(i) that where the accused is allowed to inspect material as mentioned in paragraph (f) or (g) and he requests a copy, he is given one unless the person allowing the inspection is of opinion that it is not practicable or not desirable to give him one;
(j) that a person mentioned in paragraph (e) is given a written statement that prescribed activities which the code requires have been carried out.

The current version of the Code of Practice on Disclosure under Part II of the Criminal Procedure and Investigations Act 1996 was introduced by the Criminal Procedure and Investigations Act 1996 (Code of Practice) Order 2005, SI 2005/985.[1]

Under the 'general duties' section of the Code the following is said about the obligation to pursue all reasonable lines of inquiry (at para.3.5):

> In conducting an investigation, the investigator should pursue all reasonable lines of inquiry, whether these point towards or away from the suspect. What is reasonable in each case will depend on the particular circumstances. For example, where material is held on computer, it is a matter for the investigator to decide which material on the computer it is reasonable to inquire into, and in what manner.

The Code defines 'material' and 'relevant material' in the following manner:

> material is material of any kind, including information and objects, which is obtained in the course of a criminal investigation and which may be relevant to the investigation. This includes not only material coming into the possession of the investigator (such as documents seized in the course of searching premises) but also material generated by him (such as interview records)

> material may be relevant to an investigation if it appears to an investigator, or to the officer in charge of an investigation, or to the disclosure officer, that it has some bearing on any offence under investigation or any person being investigated, or on the surrounding circumstances of the case, unless it is incapable of having any impact on the case[2]

Of course, the Code addresses the practice that should be adopted where relevant materials are held by third parties. It says (at para.3.6):

> If the officer in charge of an investigation believes that other persons may be in possession of material that may be relevant to the investigation, and if this has not been obtained under paragraph 3.5 above, he should ask the disclosure officer to inform them of the existence of the investigation and to invite them to retain the material in case they receive a request for its disclosure. The disclosure officer should inform the prosecutor that they may have such material. However, the officer in charge of an investigation is not required to make speculative enquiries of other persons; there must be some reason to believe that they may have relevant material. That reason may come from information provided to the police by the accused or from other inquiries made or from some other source.

Materials that are obtained during the course of an investigation must be retained by the investigator, which may be in the form of a copy where the original material is perishable, where it is returned to the owner or where retention of a copy is reasonable in all the circumstances. The initial retention period is until the prosecutor makes a decision to institute proceedings. If proceedings are instituted the material must be retained until the date of acquittal, conviction or discontinuance of the proceedings. If the defendant is convicted and imprisoned, or committed to a hospital, the materials must be retained until the defendant's release. For convictions that do not result in imprisonment, materials must be retained for six months from the date of the conviction. If an appeal is underway at the date of release or at the expiry of the six-month period for non-custodial cases they must be retained until the disposal of the appeal or if the case is being reviewed by the Criminal Cases Review Commission at that point they must be retained until the Commission decides not to refer the case to the Court of Appeal. These are minimum retention periods however and they do not preclude longer retention periods in appropriate cases.

The CPS Disclosure Manual[3] addresses the same issues as the Code of Practice, albeit in more detail and with supporting case law. At paragraph 21 the Disclosure Manual tackles the issue of disclosure of emails head-on saying:

> Information contained in emails may be relevant unused material, particularly if the information is not recorded elsewhere. It should be recorded, retained and revealed in the same way as other relevant material. (Where however, emails are intercepted under section 5 of the Regulation of Investigatory Powers Act 2000, revelation and disclosure is specifically prohibited.)

## 8.3 DISCLOSURE PROCESS

The disclosure process in criminal cases starts with 'advanced disclosure' then continues with disclosure of unused materials. For summary cases the rule is that the Crown's case must be revealed in sufficient detail to enable the defence to prepare their case properly. Thus, in a summary trial the defence can expect to receive the Crown's witness statements and exhibits. The Attorney-General's Guidelines on Disclosure (see **8.3.1**) say (at para.57):

> The prosecutor should, in addition to complying with the obligations under the Act, provide to the defence all evidence upon which the Crown proposes to rely in a summary trial. Such provision should allow the accused and their legal advisers sufficient time properly to consider the evidence before it is called.

For cases that are triable either way, the advance disclosure rules are contained in Part 21 of the Criminal Procedure Rules (CrimPR) 2005, SI 2005/384. The starting point under CrimPR 21.2 is that as soon as practicable after being charged or served with a summons the Crown should serve the defence with a written statement of the effect of CrimPR 21.3, explaining how the defence can exercise their rights under CrimPR 21.3 to request advanced disclosure. CrimPR 21.3 says:

> **21.3 Request for advance information**
>
> (1) If, in any proceedings in respect of which this Part applies, either before the magistrates' court considers whether the offence appears to be more suitable for summary trial or trial on indictment or, where the accused has not attained the age of 18 years when he appears or is brought before a magistrates' court, before he is asked whether he pleads guilty or not guilty, the accused or a person representing the accused requests the prosecutor to furnish him with advance information, the prosecutor shall, subject to rule 21.4, furnish him as soon as practicable with either –
>
> (a) a copy of those parts of every written statement which contain information as to the facts and matters of which the prosecutor proposes to adduce evidence in the proceedings; or
>
> (b) a summary of the facts and matters of which the prosecutor proposes to adduce evidence in the proceedings.
>
> (2) In paragraph (1) above, 'written statement' means a statement made by a person on whose evidence the prosecutor proposes to rely in the proceedings and, where such a person has made more than one written statement one of which contains information as to all the facts and matters in relation to which the prosecutor proposes to rely on the evidence of that person, only that statement is a written statement for purposes of paragraph (1) above.
>
> (3) Where in any part of a written statement or in a summary furnished under paragraph (1) above reference is made to a document on which the prosecutor proposes to rely, the prosecutor shall, subject to rule 21.4, when furnishing the part of the written statement or the summary, also furnish either a copy

of the document or such information as may be necessary to enable the person making the request under paragraph (1) above to inspect the document or a copy thereof.

It follows from the advanced disclosure rules that if the Crown is intending to rely upon any emails these should be disclosed at the outset of the case. However, the Crown can refuse to give advanced disclosure in either-way offences if they feel that this will lead to witness intimidation or other interference with the course of justice (CrimPR 21.4). If the Crown takes this position it must give the defence notice and when the case first comes before the court the validity of the Crown's position will be examined. If the court considers that advanced disclosure is being wrongfully withheld, it is obliged to adjourn the proceedings, unless it feels that the defence will not be substantially prejudiced by the Crown's non-compliance (CrimPR 21.5).

The disclosure process then continues with the Crown's disclosure of unused materials, which are the materials that it does not seek to rely upon. The starting point within this process is CPIA 1996, s.3. This obliges the Crown to disclose unused materials that might reasonably be considered to undermine the Crown's case or assist the defence case. Whether material may operate in this way is an objective issue. Section 3 says:

**3. Initial duty of prosecutor to disclose**

(1) The prosecutor must –

(a) disclose to the accused any prosecution material which has not previously been disclosed to the accused and which might reasonably be considered capable of undermining the case for the prosecution against the accused or of assisting the case for the accused, or

(b) give to the accused a written statement that there is no material of a description mentioned in paragraph (a)

(2) For the purposes of this section prosecution material is material –

(a) which is in the prosecutor's possession, and came into his possession in connection with the case for the prosecution against the accused, or

(b) which, in pursuance of a code operative under Part II, he has inspected in connection with the case for the prosecution against the accused.

(3) Where material consists of information which has been recorded in any form the prosecutor discloses it for the purposes of this section –

(a) by securing that a copy is made of it and that the copy is given to the accused, or

(b) if in the prosecutor's opinion that is not practicable or not desirable, by allowing the accused to inspect it at a reasonable time and a reasonable place or by taking steps to secure that he is allowed to do so;

and a copy may be in such form as the prosecutor thinks fit and need not be in the same form as that in which the information has already been recorded.

(4) Where material consists of information which has not been recorded the prosecutor discloses it for the purposes of this section by securing that it is recorded in such form as he thinks fit and –

(a) by securing that a copy is made of it and that the copy is given to the accused, or

(b) if in the prosecutor's opinion that is not practicable or not desirable, by allowing the accused to inspect it at a reasonable time and a reasonable place or by taking steps to secure that he is allowed to do so.

(5) Where material does not consist of information the prosecutor discloses it for the purposes of this section by allowing the accused to inspect it at a reasonable time and a reasonable place or by taking steps to secure that he is allowed to do so.

(6) Material must not be disclosed under this section to the extent that the court, on an application by the prosecutor, concludes it is not in the public interest to disclose it and orders accordingly.

(7) Material must not be disclosed under this section to the extent that it is material the disclosure of which is prohibited by section 17 of the Regulation of Investigatory Powers Act 2000.

(8) The prosecutor must act under this section during the period which, by virtue of section 12, is the relevant period for this section.

The next stage in the process is disclosure by the defence, through its defence case statement. These are compulsory in Crown Court trials (CPIA 1996, s.5) and voluntary in magistrates' court trials (CPIA 1996, s.6). CPIA 1996, s.6A identifies the contents of a defence case statement:

**6A. Contents of defence statement**

(1) For the purposes of this Part a defence statement is a written statement –

(a) setting out the nature of the accused's defence, including any particular defences on which he intends to rely,

(b) indicating the matters of fact on which he takes issue with the prosecution,

(c) setting out, in the case of each such matter, why he takes issue with the prosecution, and

(d) indicating any point of law (including any point as to the admissibility of evidence or an abuse of process) which he wishes to take, and any authority on which he intends to rely for that purpose.

(2) A defence statement that discloses an alibi must give particulars of it, including –

(a) the name, address and date of birth of any witness the accused believes is able to give evidence in support of the alibi, or as many of those details as are known to the accused when the statement is given;

(b) any information in the accused's possession which might be of material assistance in identifying or finding any such witness in whose case any of the details mentioned in paragraph (a) are not known to the accused when the statement is given.

(3) For the purposes of this section evidence in support of an alibi is evidence tending to show that by reason of the presence of the accused at a particular place or in a particular area at a particular time he was not, or was unlikely to have been, at the place where the offence is alleged to have been committed at the time of its alleged commission.
(4) The Secretary of State may by regulations make provision as to the details of the matters that, by virtue of subsection (1), are to be included in defence statements.

The defence case statement is more like a witness statement than the process of disclosure of documents. However, the alibi provisions will require the defence to give particulars of any emails that can be categorised as information that might be of material assistance in identifying or finding any relevant witnesses. The process then continues with the Crown reviewing its disclosure under s.7A. This is the continuing duty of disclosure, which continues as long as proceedings remain extant (see *R.* v. *Makin* (2004) 148 SJ 821). If the defence feels that the Crown has not given full disclosure in accordance with its duties under s.7A, it can make an application to the court for disclosure under s.8, provided that a defence case statement has been served. The procedure for making and disposing of an application for an order is contained within CrimPR 25.

### 8.3.1 Attorney-General's Guidelines on Disclosure

The current version of these Guidelines[4] were published in April 2005, coinciding with the amendments to the CPIA 1996 brought about by the CJA 2003. Although the Guidelines do not have the force of law (*R.* v. *Winston Brown* [1995] 1 CrAppR 191), they do carry weight and the courts will have regard to them (see also Crown Court Protocol on the Control and Management of Unused Materials, para.10).

The Attorney-General advises that as part of the fair trial process the rules on disclosure within the CPIA 1996 must be 'scrupulously followed' (para.4) and while they have been drafted with Crown Court trials in mind the 'spirit of the Guidelines must be followed where they apply to proceedings in the magistrates' court' (para.7). As regards the requirement for disclosure that might undermine the Crown's case or assist the defence the Guidelines say (para.8):

> Generally, material which can reasonably be considered capable of undermining the prosecution case against the accused or assisting the defence case will include anything that tends to show a fact inconsistent with the elements of the case that must be proved by the prosecution. Material can fulfil the disclosure test:
>
> (a) by the use to be made of it in cross-examination; or
> (b) by its capacity to support submissions that could lead to:

(i) the exclusion of evidence; or
(ii) a stay of proceedings; or
(iii) a court or tribunal finding that any public authority had acted incompatibly with the accused 's rights under the ECHR, or

(c) by its capacity to suggest an explanation or partial explanation of the accused's actions.

The Guidelines then go on to give examples of the kinds of materials that will fall for disclosure:

i. Any material casting doubt upon the accuracy of any prosecution evidence.
ii. Any material which may point to another person, whether charged or not (including a co-accused) having involvement in the commission of the offence.
iii. Any material which may cast doubt upon the reliability of a confession.
iv. Any material that might go the credibility of a prosecution witness.
v. Any material that might support a defence that is either raised by the defence or apparent from the prosecution papers.
vi. Any material which may have a bearing on the admissibility of any prosecution evidence.

The Guidelines also address the defence disclosure obligations within the defence case statement, the Crown's continuing duty of disclosure, the withholding of materials on the grounds of public interest, the responsibilities of investigators and disclosure officers, the responsibilities of Crown advocates and the involvement of other agencies. Regarding this final point, the Guidelines make it clear that where relevant materials are held by government departments or other Crown bodies the investigator must take reasonable steps to identify and consider these materials (para.47). Where relevant materials are held by other agencies, the Guidelines say that the investigator must 'take what steps they regard as appropriate in the particular case to obtain it' (para.51), but should apply to the court for a witness summons for production if the materials are relevant but the other agency refuses to produce them (para.52, which refers to the possibility of making applications for production under Criminal Procedure (Attendance of Witnesses) Act 1965, s.2 or Magistrates' Courts Act 1980, s.97).

## 8.4 CROWN COURT PROTOCOL FOR THE CONTROL AND MANAGEMENT OF UNUSED MATERIAL

The Crown Court Protocol for the Control and Management of Unused Material[5] came into effect on 20 February 2006. The supporting note to the Protocol[6] makes it clear that the aim of the Protocol is to ensure strict compliance with the disclosure rules:

> The Disclosure Protocol is concerned with the management of issues relating to unused material in the Crown Court. Its main feature is a requirement for strict compliance with the disclosure provisions of the Criminal Procedure and Investigations Act 1996 (the Act), and the statutory Code of Practice laid under section 23 of the Act, where they apply to the proceedings.

The introduction to the Protocol reinforces the importance of full disclosure, saying:

> Disclosure is one of the most important – as well as one of the most abused – of the procedures relating to criminal trials. There needs to be a sea-change in the approach of both judges and the parties to all aspects of the handling of the material which the prosecution do not intend to use in support of their case. For too long, a wide range of serious misunderstandings has existed, both as to the exact ambit of the unused material to which the defence is entitled, and the role to be played by the judge in ensuring that the law is properly applied. All too frequently applications by the parties and decisions by the judges in this area have been made based either on misconceptions as to the true nature of the law or a general laxity of approach (however well-intentioned). This failure properly to apply the binding provisions as regards disclosure has proved extremely and unnecessarily costly and has obstructed justice. It is, therefore, essential that disclosure obligations are properly discharged – by both the prosecution and the defence – in all criminal proceedings, and the court's careful oversight of this process is an important safeguard against the possibility of miscarriages of justice.

## 8.5 WITHHOLDING MATERIALS

As well as seeking to ensure that full disclosure is given, the law is concerned to ensure that the disclosure process does not turn into a 'fishing expedition' or a substantial drain on public resources. The law is also concerned to ensure that sensitive materials are not disclosed and that any materials that are disclosed to the defence are treated with confidence. The placing of limitations on disclosure is considered to be compatible with the right to a fair trial. In the case of *Edwards and Lewis* v. *United Kingdom* (2005) 40 EHRR 24 the European Court of Human Rights said:

> The entitlement to disclosure of relevant evidence is not, however, an absolute right. In any criminal proceedings there may be competing interests, such as national security or the need to protect witnesses at risk of reprisals or keep secret police methods of investigation of crime, which must be weighed against the rights of the accused. In some cases it may be necessary to withhold certain evidence from the defence so as to preserve the fundamental rights of another individual or to safeguard an important public interest. Nonetheless, only such measures restricting the rights of the defence which are strictly necessary are permissible under Article 6.1. Furthermore, in order to ensure that the accused receives a fair trial, any difficulties caused to the defence by a limitation on its rights must be sufficiently counterbalanced by the procedures followed by the judicial authorities (*Jasper* v. *the United Kingdom*).

### 8.5.1 Fishing expeditions

As regards 'fishing expeditions', the Attorney-General's Guidelines reiterate that 'defence practitioners should avoid fishing expeditions and where disclosure is not provided using this as an excuse for an abuse of process application'. The Guidelines then go on to say that 'disclosure must not be an open ended trawl of unused material'.

### 8.5.2 The defence obligation to keep confidence in disclosed materials

Regarding the defence obligation to keep confidence in disclosed materials, CPIA 1996, s.17 says:

**17. Confidentiality of disclosed information**

(1) If the accused is given or allowed to inspect a document or other object under –

(a) section 3, 4, 7A, 14 or 15, or
(b) an order under section 8,

then, subject to subsections (2) to (4), he must not use or disclose it or any information recorded in it.

(2) The accused may use or disclose the object or information –

(a) in connection with the proceedings for whose purposes he was given the object or allowed to inspect it,
(b) with a view to the taking of further criminal proceedings (for instance, by way of appeal) with regard to the matter giving rise to the proceedings mentioned in paragraph (a), or
(c) in connection with the proceedings first mentioned in paragraph (b).

(3) The accused may use or disclose –

(a) the object to the extent that it has been displayed to the public in open court, or
(b) the information to the extent that it has been communicated to the public in open court;

but the preceding provisions of this subsection do not apply if the object is displayed or the information is communicated in proceedings to deal with a contempt of court under section 18.

CPIA 1996, s.18 explains how a breach of s.17 is punished as a contempt of court:

**18. Confidentiality: contravention**

(1) It is a contempt of court for a person knowingly to use or disclose an object or information recorded in it if the use or disclosure is in contravention of section 17.

(2) The following courts have jurisdiction to deal with a person who is guilty of a contempt under this section –

(a) a magistrates' court, where this Part applies by virtue of section 1(1);
(b) the Crown Court, where this Part applies by virtue of section 1(2).

(3) A person who is guilty of a contempt under this section may be dealt with as follows –

(a) a magistrates' court may commit him to custody for a specified period not exceeding six months or impose on him a fine not exceeding £5,000 or both;
(b) the Crown Court may commit him to custody for a specified period not exceeding two years or impose a fine on him or both.

(4) If –

(a) a person is guilty of a contempt under this section, and
(b) the object concerned is in his possession,

the court finding him guilty may order that the object shall be forfeited and dealt with in such manner as the court may order.

(5) The power of the court under subsection (4) includes power to order the object to be destroyed or to be given to the prosecutor or to be placed in his custody for such period as the court may specify.

(6) If –

(a) the court proposes to make an order under subsection (4), and
(b) the person found guilty, or any other person claiming to have an interest in the object, applies to be heard by the court,

the court must not make the order unless the applicant has been given an opportunity to be heard.

(7) If –

(a) a person is guilty of a contempt under this section and
(b) a copy of the object concerned is in his possession,

the court finding him guilty may order that the copy shall be forfeited and dealt with in such manner as the court may order.

(8) Subsections (5) and (6) apply for the purposes of subsection (7) as they apply for the purposes of subsection (4), but as if references to the object were references to the copy.

(9) An object or information shall be inadmissible as evidence in civil proceedings if to adduce it would in the opinion of the court be likely to constitute a contempt under this section and 'the court' here means the court before which the civil proceedings are being taken.

(10) The powers of a magistrates' court under this section may be exercised either of the court's own motion or by order on complaint.

### 8.5.3 Withholding disclosure of sensitive materials

If the Crown is in possession of 'sensitive' unused materials, it may apply to the court for a Public Interest Immunity (PII) Certificate to prevent disclosure of the material. If the court is persuaded that there is a real risk of serious prejudice occurring to an important public interest, it will grant the

Certificate, but if it does it must keep the issue under constant review (see *H and C*). The essence of the public interest test is that the public interest in non-disclosure of the materials outweighs the public interest that in the proper administration of justice the court should have the fullest possible access to relevant materials. The key types of public interest that are usually at the heart of an application for a PII Certificate are national security and the prevention and detection of crime. Materials about the identity of police informers and the whereabouts of police observation posts, reports from the police to the Director of Public Prosecutions and materials relating to children are commonly the focus of PII applications.

The applications themselves fall within three kinds. The first kind is where the defence is given notice of the application and the nature of the materials that the Crown is seeking to withhold and is allowed to make submissions. The second type is where the defence is merely notified of the making of the application. The third type is where the defence is given no notice at all. In all kinds of application the materials are disclosed to the court for its consideration.

In the case of *R.* v. *H and others* [2004] AC 134 HL the House of Lords identified a series of questions that must be considered by the court when presented with an application for a PII Certificate:

> When any issue of derogation from the golden rule of full disclosure comes before it, the court must address a series of questions.
>
> (1) What is the material which the prosecution seek to withhold? This must be considered by the court in detail.
> (2) Is the material such as may weaken the prosecution case or strengthen that of the defence? If No, disclosure should not be ordered. If Yes, full disclosure should (subject to (3), (4) and (5) below) be ordered.
> (3) Is there a real risk of serious prejudice to an important public interest (and, if so, what) if full disclosure of the material is ordered? If No, full disclosure should be ordered.
> (4) If the answer to (2) and (3) is Yes, can the defendant's interest be protected without disclosure or disclosure be ordered to an extent or in a way which will give adequate protection to the public interest in question and also afford adequate protection to the interests of the defence?
> This question requires the court to consider, with specific reference to the material which the prosecution seek to withhold and the facts of the case and the defence as disclosed, whether the prosecution should formally admit what the defence seek to establish or whether disclosure short of full disclosure may be ordered. This may be done in appropriate cases by the preparation of summaries or extracts of evidence, or the provision of documents in an edited or anonymised form, provided the documents supplied are in each instance approved by the judge. In appropriate cases the appointment of special counsel may be a necessary step to ensure that the contentions of the prosecution are tested and the interests of the defendant protected (see para 22 above). In cases of exceptional difficulty the court may require the appoint-

ment of special counsel to ensure a correct answer to questions (2) and (3) as well as (4).

(5) Do the measures proposed in answer to (4) represent the minimum derogation necessary to protect the public interest in question? If No, the court should order such greater disclosure as will represent the minimum derogation from the golden rule of full disclosure.

(6) If limited disclosure is ordered pursuant to (4) or (5), may the effect be to render the trial process, viewed as a whole, unfair to the defendant? If Yes, then fuller disclosure should be ordered even if this leads or may lead the prosecution to discontinue the proceedings so as to avoid having to make disclosure.

(7) If the answer to (6) when first given is No, does that remain the correct answer as the trial unfolds, evidence is adduced and the defence advanced?
It is important that the answer to (6) should not be treated as a final, once-and-for-all, answer but as a provisional answer which the court must keep under review.

The procedure governing the making of applications for PII Certificates is contained in the Criminal Procedure Rules, Part 25.

## B DISCLOSURE IN CIVIL CASES

### 8.6 INTRODUCTION

The disclosure regime in civil litigation centres around documents, which distinguishes it from the criminal regime, which focuses upon the disclosure of material. Of course, in both regimes emails will fall within the ambit of disclosure: they are material for the purposes of the criminal regime, and documents for the purposes of the civil regime. Another distinction between the civil and criminal regimes is that in civil cases disclosure means stating whether a document exists or has existed whereas in criminal cases disclosure means actually delivering-up materials. The 'delivery-up' component within the civil regime is known as inspection. Finally, the two regimes can be distinguished by the fact that disclosure in criminal cases is automatic, in the sense that the Crown always has to give disclosure once a prosecution has commenced. In civil cases there is no longer an automatic requirement for disclosure, unlike in the regime that existed prior to the introduction of the Civil Procedure Rules (CPR) 1998, SI 1998/3132. Under the new regime it requires a court order for disclosure before the parties are under an obligation to give disclosure.

Disclosure and inspection are governed by Part 31 of the CPR, which is supplemented by a Practice Direction.[7] Generally, disclosure takes place after the commencement of proceedings, but the CPR do make provision for pre-action disclosure in specified cases. Provision is also made for disclosure from third parties.

## 8.7 DISCLOSURE AND THE OVERRIDING OBJECTIVE WITHIN CIVIL LITIGATION

A novel component within the CPR that did not exist within its predecessors (i.e. the County Court Rules 1981 and the Rules of the Supreme Court 1965) is the 'overriding objective', which is contained at Part 1. The overriding objective is expressed in the following terms:

> **1.1 The overriding objective**
>
> (1) These Rules are a new procedural code with the overriding objective of enabling the court to deal with cases justly.
> (2) Dealing with a case justly includes, so far as is practicable –
>
> (a) ensuring that the parties are on an equal footing;
> (b) saving expense;
> (c) dealing with the case in ways which are proportionate –
>
> (i) to the amount of money involved;
> (ii) to the importance of the case;
> (iii) to the complexity of the issues; and
> (iv) to the financial position of each party;
>
> (d) ensuring that it is dealt with expeditiously and fairly; and
> (e) allotting to it an appropriate share of the court's resources, while taking into account the need to allot resources to other cases.

The CPR provides that the court is required to actively manage cases (CPR 1.4) and in doing so it must apply the overriding objective at all times (CPR 1.2). The parties are also under a duty to help the court further the overriding objective (CPR 1.3). This means that the overriding objective will always be at the heart of the disclosure process within civil litigation, with the result that disclosure will only be ordered where that is necessary to do justice in the case. In other words, disclosure is not an automatic process. However, the CPR do make certain presumptions about the scope of disclosure in certain categories of cases. Thus, parties in cases that are proceeding via the 'fast track' can expect the court to order 'standard disclosure', whereas parties in cases that are proceeding via the 'multi track' may anticipate that 'full disclosure' will be ordered.

## 8.8 DISCLOSURE OF EMAILS AS DOCUMENTS

CPR 31.4 contains the meaning of document, saying:

> **31.4 Meaning of document**
>
> In this Part –
>
> 'document' means anything in which information of any description is recorded; and
>
> 'copy', in relation to a document, means anything onto which information recorded in the document has been copied, by whatever means and whether directly or indirectly.

The essence of a document is that it is a carrier, or container, for information. In other words, it is not the medium upon which information is held that matters for the purposes of disclosure, but whether the medium contains information. If the medium contains no information, such as a blank piece of paper, it is probably not a document for the purposes of disclosure (see, for example, *Re Alderton and Barry's Application* (1941) 59 RPC 56).

This approach to the definition of 'document' covers paper documents and electronic documents, and the kinds of non-paper-based documents falling within this meaning include sound recordings (see *Grant* v. *Southwestern and County Properties Ltd* [1975] Ch 185) and image recordings, both still and moving (see *Senior* v. *Holdsworth* [1976] QB 23 and *Garcin* v. *Amerindo Investment Advisors Ltd* [1991] 4 All ER 655). There is also plenty of authority concerning the disclosure of electronic information contained in computers (see *Derby & Co Ltd* v. *Weldon (No.9)* [1991] 1 WLR 652, about computer files; *Alliance & Leicester Building Society* v. *Ghahremani* [1992] RVR 198, about computer hard-drives; and *Marlton* v. *Tectronix UK Holdings* [2003] EWHC 383, about databases). As such, there is no doubt that emails fall within the meaning of documents and are within the scope of litigation disclosure in civil cases: from the perspective of disclosure, emails are containers for information in which information is recorded.

However, despite the wide scope of the definition of document contained in CPR 31.4, the rules committee in charge of developing the CPR felt that it was necessary to give further clarification to the scope of disclosure as it affects electronic documents, so in October 2005 they issued a new Practice Direction which supplements CPR 31, which says the following about the disclosure of electronic documents such as email (PD 31, para.2A.1):

> Rule 31.4 contains a broad definition of a document. This extends to electronic documents, including e-mail and other electronic communications, word processed documents and databases. In addition to documents that are readily accessible from computer systems and other electronic devices and media, the definition

covers those documents that are stored on servers and back-up systems and electronic documents that have been 'deleted'. It also extends to additional information stored and associated with electronic documents known as metadata.

## 8.9 DISCLOSURE OF DOCUMENTS IN A PARTY'S CONTROL

The disclosure regime only bites on documents that are, or were, in a party's control. CPR 31.8 says:

> **31.8 Duty of disclosure limited to documents which are or have been in party's control**
>
> (1) A party's duty to disclose documents is limited to documents which are or have been in his control.
> (2) For this purpose a party has or has had a document in his control if –
>
> (a) it is or was in his physical possession;
> (b) he has or has had a right to possession of it; or
> (c) he has or has had a right to inspect or take copies of it.

The way in which CPR 31.8 is constructed means that the duty to give disclosure extends to relevant documents that no longer exist, whether through deletion or destruction, and to documents that the party has lost physical possession of. Thus, if a party gives an agent possession of their documents they will still fall within the scope of disclosure, on the grounds that they are still under the party's control and because they have a right to take possession of them. Furthermore, as CPR 31.8 does not contain a threshold requirement to the effect that the party giving disclosure must be, or must have been, in lawful possession of documents, it follows that illegally obtained documents must be disclosed.

### 8.9.1 Deletion of emails – do they still exist?

With emails, particular care has to be taken in cases where a party maintains that they have been deleted, because deletion very often means nothing more than deletion of the reference to the email in the file allocation tables used by the computer for searching purposes. The Creswell Report observes that a 'deleted document may not be necessarily destroyed as it may continue to exist in the form of residual data'. Indeed, even where a party has taken steps to delete the email rather than to remove its reference from the file allocation tables it may still be possible to recover all or part of the data using modern software. (For an example where supposedly deleted data were retrieved during the disclosure process, see *Prism Hospital Software Ltd* v. *Hospital Medical Research Institute* [1992] 2 WWR 157, a decision of the Superior Court of British Columbia, Canada.) Furthermore, even if irrevocably deleted from one storage medium, the email might still exist on another, such as on backup tapes or on a mirror server created for disaster recovery purposes.

### 8.9.2 The Creswell Report – categories of electronic data and control

In October 2004 a Working Party of the Commercial Court Users Group chaired by Mr Justice Creswell published a report on the disclosure of electronic documents.[8] This report led directly to the publication of the amended version of Practice Direction 31 in 2005. The Creswell Report, as it has become known, provides a very accessible overview on the law of electronic disclosure, but it is most notable for the fact that it categorises different kinds of electronic data:

(1) Active or online data: this is data which is directly accessible on the desktop computer. On-line storage is used in the very active steps of an electronic record's life, when it is being created or received and processed, as well as when the access frequency is high and the required speed of access of fast. Examples of such data include material held on hard drives, filed documents and inbox and sent items in an e-mail system.

(2) Embedded data: this is data which is not normally visible when a document is printed, although can be viewed on the screen. Word programs usually store information about when data files are created, when edited, by whom, and who has accessed them. Other examples are formulae for spreadsheets and calculations which are programmed into a system, but are not visible on printed out documents.

(3) Replicant data (otherwise known as 'temporary files' or 'file clones'): this is automatically created by the desktop computer. Many programs have an automatic back up feature which creates and periodically saves copies of a file as the user works on it. These are intended to assist recovery of data caused by computer malfunction, power failure or when the computer is turned-off without the user saving the data. Examples of such data include automatic saves of draft documents, temporary copies of opened e-mail attachments and recovered files automatically available following a computer malfunction.

(4) Back-up data: this is data held in a storage system. On the most basic level it can consist of offline storage in the form of a removable optical disk or magnetic tape media, which can be labelled and stored in a shelf (in contrast with near line data which is directly accessible from the computer and is readily accessible). Most organisations use back-up data to preserve information in case of a disaster. This can take various forms ranging from copying information stored on the system to a back-up system in the form of magnetic tapes or by sending files over the internet to a third party's computer (some companies even offer computer users free storage space on their web sites). The disadvantage with back-up systems is that usually the data is compressed and can be difficult and costly to retrieve.

(5) Residual data: this is material deleted from the user's active data and stored elsewhere on the database. Deleting a file or e-mail removes it from the user's active data, instead the data is stored elsewhere on the database and can become fragmented. The data can usually be retrieved with sufficient expertise and time.

The Creswell Report's view is that active or online data will usually fall within the scope of standard disclosure, due to their being 'relatively accessible', but at the opposite end of the scale it is doubted that residual data is even within a party's control. The Report says (at para.2.19):

> Whilst active data should be relatively accessible and it is not usually difficult to carry out a key word search for relevant information, the other forms of data are less accessible. In the case of residual data it may even be argued that it is not within a party's control within the meaning of CPR r.31.8. Even if it is to be regarded as being in a party's control the cost and burden of retrieval (often with the assistance of an expert) means that an application for such disclosure needs to be properly justified and confined.

As regards disclosure of email, the Report offers the following view (at para.2.20):

> Where the issue is whether a party received an e-mail it will be appropriate for a search to be undertaken of an e-mail account. If e-mails have been deleted it may even be appropriate to expect a party to obtain expert assistance to see if any record can be traced on the hard drive. However, in a straightforward case it would be rarely appropriate to expect a party to go through the time and expense of attempting to retrieve e-mails deleted from the system. The Court may make an order requiring disclosure of electronic information containing specified words or strings and thus define the extent of an electronic search.

### 8.9.3 *Harper* v. *Information Commissioner* – deleted electronic data

In the case of *Harper* v. *Information Commissioner* (2005) EA/2005/0001 the Information Tribunal had cause to consider whether deleted electronic data are disclosable under the access regime contained in the Freedom of Information Act (FOIA) 2000. The Tribunal held that depending on the facts of the case in question deleted data could still be 'held' for the purposes of the FOIA 2000:

> 20. Against this background it is still necessary to consider the question: if a public authority has information that has been deleted from computer records is it still held? The Tribunal understands that information which is held electronically and then deleted (and even emptied later from a recycle bin or trash can) is in fact still retained in its original form on the computer system until it is subsequently and actually overwritten by other information. In other words, information may be deleted and emptied but it is not actually eliminated from the system at that point. This is the case with most computer systems today, although no two systems will be identical, in terms of their treatment of deleted material. It will thus be a matter of fact and degree, depending on the circumstances of the individual case, whether potentially recoverable information is still held, for the purposes of the Act.
> 21. In view of the Tribunal's finding on the definition of information earlier in this decision, it may be incumbent on a Public Authority to make attempts to

retrieve deleted information. Accordingly, the authority should establish whether information is completely eliminated, or merely deleted. In the latter case, the authority should consider whether the information can be recovered and if so by what means. There is computer software available that can be used to recover information that has been deleted from a computer system. If information has been deleted but can be recovered by various technical means, is that information still held by the public authority? The Tribunal finds that the answer to this question will be a matter of fact and degree depending on the circumstances of the individual case.

## 8.10 STANDARD DISCLOSURE – DISCLOSURE OF 'RELEVANT' DOCUMENTS

Although disclosure is not automatic, CPR 31.5 says that where the court orders disclosure to be given this will be limited to standard disclosure, unless the court specifies otherwise. Where standard disclosure is ordered the documents to be disclosed are those identified in CPR 31.6, which says:

**31.6 Standard disclosure – what documents are to be disclosed**

Standard disclosure requires a party to disclose only –

(a) the documents on which he relies; and
(b) the documents which –
  (i) adversely affect his own case;
  (ii) adversely affect another party's case; or
  (iii) support another party's case; and
(c) the documents which he is required to disclose by a relevant practice direction.

These categories of documents can be properly termed relevant documents. However, before it can be determined whether a document is relevant, the usual starting point is a consideration of the pleadings in the case.

The procedure for standard disclosure is described in CPR 31.10 and is by 'list'. The list must identify the documents conveniently and concisely, it must identify documents which are being withheld from inspection and it must identify documents that are no longer in the party's control stating what has happened to them. The list must contain a 'disclosure statement' which identifies the search that has been carried out and that the maker of the statement understands their duty to give disclosure and that they have complied with their duty.

## 8.11 DISCLOSURE OF COPIES

The ease at which emails can be copied is one of their benefits, but for the purposes of disclosure this has the potential to cause tremendous problems for the litigant. As such, a key question is whether the litigant is required to give disclosure of copies of documents. The answer to this question is found in CPR 31.9, which says:

> **31.9 Disclosure of copies**
>
> (1) A party need not disclose more than one copy of a document.
> (2) A copy of a document that contains a modification, obliteration or other marking or feature –
>
> (a) on which a party intends to rely; or
> (b) which adversely affects his own case or another party's case or supports another party's case;
>
> shall be treated as a separate document.
> (Rule 31.4 sets out the meaning of a copy of a document)

The rule that a party need not disclose more than one copy of a document applies to exact copies only. This means that if a copy is modified or altered in some way, the copy must be disclosed, if relevant. A modification or alteration to an email can happen in many ways; for example, people sometimes reply to an email by directly inserting their comments with the body of the text of the email they received and if this technique for replying to emails is deployed, the copy will not be exact. Of course, it is very easy to delete data from emails, both deliberately and accidentally, which renders the copies disclosable.

## 8.12 SEARCHING FOR DOCUMENTS

The obligation to give disclosure could be rendered meaningless if the parties were not under a corresponding duty to search for relevant documents. The duty of search is contained in CPR 31.7 and it requires the parties to carry out a reasonable search for adverse documents and those that support the other party's case, giving a non-exhaustive list of issues to be considered in determining reasonableness. The party is not under any duty to carry out a search for documents that they rely upon, whether reasonable or otherwise, it being a matter for the party concerned as to whether they wish to make any efforts to locate documents that support their case. CPR 31.7 says:

**31.7 Duty of search**

(1) When giving standard disclosure, a party is required to make a reasonable search for documents falling within rule 31.6(b) or (c).
(2) The factors relevant in deciding the reasonableness of a search include the following –

   (a) the number of documents involved;
   (b) the nature and complexity of the proceedings;
   (c) the ease and expense of retrieval of any particular document; and
   (d) the significance of any document which is likely to be located during the search.

(3) Where a party has not searched for a category or class of document on the grounds that to do so would be unreasonable, he must state this in his disclosure statement and identify the category or class of document.

(Rule 31.10 makes provision for a disclosure statement)

The Practice Direction supporting CPR 31 gives the following advice on the extent of the search:

> The extent of the search which must be made will depend upon the circumstances of the case including, in particular, the factors referred to in rule 31.7(2). The parties should bear in mind the overriding principle of proportionality (see rule 1.1(2)(c)). It may, for example, be reasonable to decide not to search for documents coming into existence before some particular date, or to limit the search to documents in some particular place or places, or to documents falling into particular categories.

As regard the factors identified at CPR 31.7(2)(b), ease and expense of retrieval, the Practice Direction identifies the following considerations as relevant:

(i) The accessibility of electronic documents or data including e-mail communications on computer systems, servers, back-up systems and other electronic devices or media that may contain such documents taking into account alterations or developments in hardware or software systems used by the disclosing party and/or available to enable access to such documents.
(ii) The location of relevant electronic documents, data, computer systems, servers, back-up systems and other electronic devices or media that may contain such documents.
(iii) The likelihood of locating relevant data.
(iv) The cost of recovering any electronic documents.
(v) The cost of disclosing and providing inspection of any relevant electronic documents.
(vi) The likelihood that electronic documents will be materially altered in the course of recovery, disclosure or inspection.

Finally, the Practice Direction says the following on reasonableness of search:

> It may be reasonable to search some or all of the parties' electronic storage systems. In some circumstances, it may be reasonable to search for electronic documents by means of keyword searches (agreed as far as possible between the parties) even where a full review of each and every document would be unreasonable. There may be other forms of electronic search that may be appropriate in particular circumstances.

## 8.13 SPECIFIC DISCLOSURE

There will be times in litigation where one party is dissatisfied with the adequacy of disclosure made by the other party. This might arise from concerns that specific documents have been withheld, or specific classes of documents have been withheld or concerns about the adequacy of the search undertaken. To cater for these contingencies CPR 31.12 gives the court the power to order specific disclosure:

> **31.12 Specific disclosure or inspection**
>
> (1) The court may make an order for specific disclosure or specific inspection.
> (2) An order for specific disclosure is an order that a party must do one or more of the following things –
>
> (a) disclose documents or classes of documents specified in the order;
> (b) carry out a search to the extent stated in the order;
> (c) disclose any documents located as a result of that search.
>
> (3) An order for specific inspection is an order that a party permit inspection of a document referred to in rule 31.3(2).
>
> (Rule 31.3(2) allows a party to state in his disclosure statement that he will not permit inspection of a document on the grounds that it would be disproportionate to do so)

## 8.14 PRE-ACTION DISCLOSURE

The court may also order disclosure prior to the commencement of proceedings, if satisfied that would be desirable in order to dispose fairly of the anticipated proceedings, or to assist in the resolution of the dispute without proceedings or to save costs. CPR 31.16 says:

**31.16 Disclosure before proceedings start**

(1) This rule applies where an application is made to the court under any Act for disclosure before proceedings have started.
(2) The application must be supported by evidence.
(3) The court may make an order under this rule only where –

 (a) the respondent is likely to be a party to subsequent proceedings;
 (b) the applicant is also likely to be a party to those proceedings;
 (c) if proceedings had started, the respondent's duty by way of standard disclosure, set out in rule 31.6, would extend to the documents or classes of documents of which the applicant seeks disclosure; and
 (d) disclosure before proceedings have started is desirable in order to –

  (i) dispose fairly of the anticipated proceedings;
  (ii) assist the dispute to be resolved without proceedings; or
  (iii) save costs.

(4) An order under this rule must –

 (a) specify the documents or the classes of documents which the respondent must disclose; and
 (b) require him, when making disclosure, to specify any of those documents –

  (i) which are no longer in his control; or
  (ii) in respect of which he claims a right or duty to withhold inspection.

(5) Such an order may –

 (a) require the respondent to indicate what has happened to any documents which are no longer in his control; and
 (b) specify the time and place for disclosure and inspection.

In the case of *Hands* v. *Morrison Construction Services Ltd* [2005] EWHC 2018 the High Court was required to consider an application for pre-action disclosure of electronic documents in a case concerning the design and construction of a car racetrack. The defendant asserted that their electronic documents were the equivalent of 850,000 lever arch files of paper and that it would take 50 days at a cost of £90,000 just to upload them to a database for searching purposes. Mr Briggs QC refused to order this disclosure saying 'in my judgment, any order which called for anything like a search of the magnitude described by Mr Sinclair faces the most serious costs and fairness obstacles, which would only be likely to be overcome if the desirability of pre-action disclosure were very strong indeed; indeed, if it was something amounting to a necessity, rather than a desirability'. Mr Briggs was not satisfied that the disclosure sought was necessary, and refused the order sought.

*Nikitin* v. *Richards Butler* [2007] EWHC 173 is an example of a case where an application for specific disclosure was refused because proceedings were not likely and because the applicants already had sufficient materials to enable them to commence proceedings. These considerations will be fatal to an application for specific disclosure.

## 8.15 DISCLOSURE FROM NON-PARTIES

Where relevant documents are in the possession of a non-party, the court may order disclosure against that party:

**31.17 Orders for disclosure against a person not a party**

(1) This rule applies where an application is made to the court under any Act for disclosure by a person who is not a party to the proceedings.
(2) The application must be supported by evidence.
(3) The court may make an order under this rule only where –
   (a) the documents of which disclosure is sought are likely to support the case of the applicant or adversely affect the case of one of the other parties to the proceedings; and
   (b) disclosure is necessary in order to dispose fairly of the claim or to save costs.
(4) An order under this rule must –
   (a) specify the documents or the classes of documents which the respondent must disclose; and
   (b) require the respondent, when making disclosure, to specify any of those documents –
      (i) which are no longer in his control; or
      (ii) in respect of which he claims a right or duty to withhold inspection.
(5) Such an order may –
   (a) require the respondent to indicate what has happened to any documents which are no longer in his control; and
   (b) specify the time and place for disclosure and inspection.

## 8.16 WITHHOLDING DOCUMENTS ON THE GROUNDS OF PRIVILEGE

Disclosure is given by list in accordance with CPR 31.10. The list must identify all relevant documents that are, or have been, in the party's control, which extends to cover privileged documents. However, a party in possession of privileged documents is entitled to withhold them from inspection (CPR 31.3), although such documents must still be identified in the list. There are four broad categories of privilege that may be claimed, namely (a) legal professional privilege, (b) privilege from self-incrimination, (c) communications that are privileged from disclosure in the public interest, and (d) without prejudice correspondence.

### 8.16.1 Legal professional privilege

Legal professional privilege in communications falls into two categories: legal advice privilege and litigation privilege. Legal advice privilege applies irrespective of whether litigation is contemplated, pending or commenced whereas litigation privilege can only apply in respect of communications made when litigation is contemplated, pending or commenced. In *Three Rivers District Council and Others* v. *Governor and Company of the Bank of England* [2004] UKHL 48 Lord Scott said:

> The modern case law on legal professional privilege has divided the privilege into two categories, legal advice privilege and litigation privilege. Litigation privilege covers all documents brought into being for the purposes of litigation. Legal advice privilege covers communications between lawyers and their clients whereby legal advice is sought or given.

### 8.16.2 Legal advice privilege

Legal advice privilege will apply to communications between a client and solicitor which are made in confidence for the purposes of obtaining legal advice or assistance. This distinguishes legal advice privilege from litigation privilege; litigation privilege can cover communications between the legal adviser and third parties and communications between the client and third parties. Where a lawyer receives information from a third party and they relay that information to the client during the giving of legal advice, the information will be privileged; see *Re Sarah C. Getty Trust, Getty* v. *Getty* [1985] 3 WLR 302.

The advice or assistance sought need not be in respect of contentious business; legal advice privilege also covers non-contentious business. Privilege will exist not only in respect of advice or assistance on legal rights or obligations, but in respect of what is, or is not, prudent and sensible in a 'relevant legal context'. In *Three Rivers,* which considered whether privilege attached to communications between the Bank of England and its lawyers about the content of its evidence to the Lord Bingham Inquiry into the collapse of BCCI, Lord Scott explained the policy behind the law:

> First, legal advice privilege arises out of a relationship of confidence between lawyer and client. Unless the communication or document for which privilege is sought is a confidential one, there can be no question of legal advice privilege arising. The confidential character of the communication or document is not by itself enough to enable privilege to be claimed but is an essential requirement.
>
> Second, if a communication or document qualifies for legal professional privilege, the privilege is absolute. It cannot be overridden by some supposedly greater public interest. It can be waived by the person, the client, entitled to it and it can be overridden by statute (c/f *R (Morgan Grenfell Ltd)* v *Special Commissioner of Income Tax* [2003] 1 AC 563 ), but it is otherwise absolute. There is no balancing

exercise that has to be carried out (see *B* v *Auckland District Law Society* [2003] 2 AC 736 paras.46 to 54). The Supreme Court of Canada has held that legal professional privilege although of great importance is not absolute and can be set aside if a sufficiently compelling public interest for doing so, such as public safety, can be shown (see *Jones* v *Smith* [1999] 1 SCR 455). But no other common law jurisdiction has, so far as I am aware, developed the law of privilege in this way. Certainly in this country legal professional privilege, if it is attracted by a particular communication between lawyer and client or attaches to a particular document, cannot be set aside on the ground that some other higher public interest requires that to be done.

Third, legal advice privilege gives the person entitled to it the right to decline to disclose or to allow to be disclosed the confidential communication or document in question. There has been some debate as to whether this right is a procedural right or a substantive right. In my respectful opinion the debate is sterile. Legal advice privilege is both. It may be used in legal proceedings to justify the refusal to answer certain questions or to produce for inspection certain documents. Its characterisation as procedural or substantive neither adds to nor detracts from its features.

Fourth, legal advice privilege has an undoubted relationship with litigation privilege. Legal advice is frequently sought or given in connection with current or contemplated litigation. But it may equally well be sought or given in circumstances and for purposes that have nothing to do with litigation. If it is sought or given in connection with litigation, then the advice would fall into both of the two categories. But it is long settled that a connection with litigation is not a necessary condition for privilege to be attracted (see eg. *Greenough* v *Gaskell* (1833) 1 My & K 98 per Lord Brougham at 102/3 and *Minet* v *Morgan* (1873) 8 Ch. App. 361). On the other hand it has been held that litigation privilege can extend to communications between a lawyer or the lawyer's client and a third party or to any document brought into existence for the dominant purpose of being used in litigation. The connection between legal advice sought or given and the affording of privilege to the communication has thereby been cut.

As regards the meaning of 'relevant legal context', this is intended to distinguish between advice given by lawyers on general matters of business and advice given where there is a wider legal context, such as a public inquiry. Lord Scott said:

> If a solicitor becomes the client's 'man of business', and some solicitors do, responsible for advising the client on all matters of business, including investment policy, finance policy and other business matters, the advice may lack a relevant legal context. There is, in my opinion, no way of avoiding difficulty in deciding in marginal cases whether the seeking of advice from or the giving of advice by lawyers does or does not take place in a relevant legal context so as to attract legal advice privilege. In cases of doubt the judge called upon to make the decision should ask whether the advice relates to the rights, liabilities, obligations or remedies of the client either under private law or under public law. If it does not, then, in my opinion, legal advice privilege would not apply. If it does so relate then, in my opinion, the judge should ask himself whether the communication falls within the policy underlying the justification for legal advice privilege in our law. Is the occasion on which the communication takes place and is the purpose for which it takes place such as to make it reasonable to expect the privilege to apply? The criterion must, in my opinion, be an objective one.

### 8.16.3 Litigation privilege

Communications between a lawyer and client, whether by email or otherwise, which are in respect of litigation that is either in contemplation or existence, will be privileged. However, things become more difficult where the communications are not between lawyer and client. Where a lawyer is in communication with a third party, those communications will only be privileged if they were made at a time when litigation was contemplated or in existence, with a view to such litigation. A communication will be made with a view to litigation if it is made for the purposes of giving advice in respect of the litigation or for obtaining or collecting evidence to be used in the litigation. If the client communicates with a third party when litigation is contemplated or commenced and the communication is with a view to obtaining legal advice, that communication will also be privileged.

### 8.16.4 Privilege within documents attached to emails

Of course, an email can also be used to send documents. Where these documents are brought into existence for the purpose of litigation, they will also be privileged, but if they were brought into existence for some other purpose that will not be so. Thus, the mere act of emailing a document to a lawyer will not render the document privileged. In *Wheeler* v. *Le Marchant* (1881) LR 17 ChD 675, Jessel MR said 'it has never hitherto been decided that documents are protected merely because they are produced by a third person in answer to an inquiry made by the solicitor'. In *Ventouris* v. *Mountain (The Italia Express) (No.1)* [1991] 1 WLR 607, Lord Justice Bingham, as he then was, said 'I can see no reason in principle why a pre-existing document obtained by a solicitor for purposes of litigation should be privileged from production and inspection'.

In many cases a document's character will be easy to establish, but not always.

A case where the existence of privilege was clear is *Learoyd* v. *Halifax Banking Co* [1893] 1 Ch 686. In that case a trustee in bankruptcy used his statutory powers allowing for the examination of the bankrupt. The examination was conducted by the trustee's solicitor, who was accompanied by a shorthand writer. The purpose of the examination was to assist the trustee in establishing whether to commence litigation in respect of the bankrupt's affairs. After the examination, a transcript of the shorthand writer's note was created and litigation was subsequently commenced against the bankrupt's bank. It was held in those proceedings that the transcript was privileged. Stirling J said:

> The client, then, in this case, having the power of obtaining information conferred upon him by the 27th section of the Act of 1883, goes to his solicitor and asks for his advice. The solicitor says: 'You have the power of getting information which I

> advise you to avail yourself of, so that I may have the means of advising you.' The trustee then takes out a summons, and gets leave to examine certain persons named. His solicitor personally conducts the examination and gets a transcript of the proceedings. That transcript is a private document. It is true that the Rules in Bankruptcy provide that the evidence so taken is to be filed; but they do not say that it is to be filed immediately. If that was done the main object of the examination might often be defeated. The point has often been considered both by myself and by other Judges with reference to depositions taken under sect. 115 of the Companies Act, 1862. The practice under that section in all branches of the Court is that the depositions, when taken, shall be returned to the chief Clerk for use in the liquidation; but they are not filed until the Court is satisfied, through the Chief Clerk, that no harm can be done by their publication.
>
> These depositions are accordingly regarded as private documents; and why should not a document obtained by a trustee in bankruptcy for his own information, in order to enable his solicitor to advise him as to future proceedings, be privileged? If, instead of putting the Court of Bankruptcy in motion, under sect. 27, the trustee had, at the instance of his solicitor, written to the bank manager making inquiries, and had got a letter stating the facts, that would have been a privileged communication; and I fail to see why a document such as a transcript giving the result of information obtained at an examination for the same purpose should not be privileged likewise. Here the examination was conducted by the solicitor himself, which makes the case stronger; and, according to his evidence, he stated the purpose of it to the registrar in bankruptcy. That evidence amounted to this – that the examination took place with the view of enabling the solicitor in his professional capacity to advise the trustee in bankruptcy whether this action should be brought or not. So if privilege has been sufficiently claimed, this document is one which is capable of being privileged. In my opinion, privilege has been sufficiently claimed, and the application fails, and must be refused with costs.

In *Wheeler*, a case of specific performance of an agreement for a lease, the defendant claimed privilege in all documents communicated to its solicitor by its surveyor. The court found that although all of the documents were communicated to the solicitor for the purposes of legal advice to the defendant, this was done when proceedings were not in existence or contemplated. Thus, privilege did not attach to those documents sent by the surveyor. Jessel MR said:

> So, again, a communication with a solicitor for the purpose of obtaining legal advice is protected though it relates to a dealing which is not the subject of litigation, provided it be a communication made to the solicitor in that character and for that purpose. But what we are asked to protect here is this. The solicitor, being consulted in a matter as to which no dispute has arisen, thinks he would like to know some further facts before giving his advice, and applies to a surveyor to tell him what the state of a given property is, and it is said that the information given ought to be protected because it is desired or required by the solicitor in order to enable him the better to give legal advice. It appears to me that to give such protection would not only extend the rule beyond what has been previously laid down, but beyond what necessity warrants. The idea that documents like these require protection has been started, if I may say so, for the first time to-day, and I think the best proof that the necessities of mankind have not been, supposed to require

> this protection is that it has never heretofore been asked. It seems to me we ought not to carry the rule any further than it has been carried. It is a rule established and maintained solely for the purpose of enabling a man to obtain legal advice with safety. That rule does not, in my opinion, require to be carried further, and therefore I think this appeal ought to be allowed, and an order made in the terms which will be read by Lord Justice Cotton . . .

In summary, whether there is privilege in documents sent to solicitors depends upon the purpose behind their creation. If they are created in contemplation of litigation, they will be privileged. If they are created before litigation is ever contemplated, they will not be privileged, unless they were created for the purposes of obtaining legal advice, in which case they will fall within legal advice privilege.

### 8.16.5 Privilege against self incrimination

Section 14 of the Civil Evidence Act (CEA) 1968 sets out the privilege against self incrimination. The privilege is against answering questions or producing documents that would expose the person, or their spouse or civil partner, to criminal proceedings or proceedings for the recovery of a penalty. Section 14 does not apply in criminal proceedings, however:

> **14. Privilege against incrimination of self or spouse or civil partner**
>
> (1) The right of a person in any legal proceedings other than criminal proceedings to refuse to answer any question or produce any document or thing if to do so would tend to expose that person to proceedings for an offence or for the recovery of a penalty –
>
> (a) shall apply only as regards criminal offence under the law of any part of the United Kingdom and penalties provided for by such law; and
>
> (b) shall include a like right to refuse to answer any question or produce any document or thing if to do so would tend to expose the spouse or civil partner of that person to proceedings for any such criminal offence or for the recovery of any such penalty.
>
> (2) In so far as any existing enactment conferring (in whatever words) powers of inspection or investigation confers on a person (in whatever words) any right otherwise than in criminal proceedings to refuse to answer any question or give any evidence tending to incriminate that person, subsection (1) above shall apply to that right as it applies to the right described in that subsection; and every such existing enactment shall be construed accordingly.
>
> (3) In so far as any existing enactment provides (in whatever words) that in any proceedings other than criminal proceedings a person shall not be excused from answering any question or giving any evidence on the ground that to do so may incriminate that person, that enactment shall be construed as providing also that in such proceedings a person shall not be excused from answering any question or giving any evidence on the ground that to do so may incriminate the husband or wife of that person.

(4) Where any existing enactment (however worded) that –

(a) confers powers of inspection or investigation; or
(b) provides as mentioned in subsection (3) above,

further provides (in whatever words) that any answer or evidence given by a person shall not be admissible in evidence against that person in any proceedings or class of proceedings (however described, and whether criminal or not), that enactment shall be construed as providing also that any answer or evidence given by that person shall not be admissible in evidence against the husband or wife of that person in the proceedings or class of proceedings in question.

(5) In this section 'existing enactment' means any enactment passed before this Act; and the references to giving evidence are references to giving evidence in any manner, whether by furnishing information, making discovery, producing documents or otherwise.

CEA 1968, s.14 must be read subject to Fraud Act 2006, s.13, which removes the privilege in proceedings relating to property:

**13. Evidence**

(1) A person is not to be excused from –

(a) answering any question put to him in proceedings relating to property, or
(b) complying with any order made in proceedings relating to property,

on the ground that doing so may incriminate him or his spouse or civil partner of an offence under this Act or a related offence.

(2) But, in proceedings for an offence under this Act or a related offence, a statement or admission made by the person in –

(a) answering such a question, or
(b) complying with such an order,

is not admissible in evidence against him or (unless they married or became civil partners after the making of the statement or admission) his spouse or civil partner.

(3) 'Proceedings relating to property' means any proceedings for –

(a) the recovery or administration of any property,
(b) the execution of a trust, or
(c) an account of any property or dealings with property,

and 'property' means money or other property whether real or personal (including things in action and other intangible property).

(4) 'Related offence' means –

(a) conspiracy to defraud;
(b) any other offence involving any form of fraudulent conduct or purpose.

### 8.16.6 Public interest privilege

CPR 31.19 sets out the procedure to be adopted where a party wishes to withhold a document from inspection or disclosure on public interests grounds. If they wish to withhold a document from disclosure they can apply to the court for permission on the grounds that disclosure would damage the public interest. If they are happy to disclose but wish to prevent inspection, then they should state this in their list, giving reasons. CPR 31.19 says:

> **31.19 Claim to withhold inspection or disclosure of a document**
>
> (1) A person may apply, without notice, for an order permitting him to withhold disclosure of a document on the ground that disclosure would damage the public interest.
>
> (2) Unless the court orders otherwise, an order of the court under paragraph (1) –
>
> (a) must not be served on any other person; and
>
> (b) must not be open to inspection by any person.
>
> (3) A person, who wishes to claim that he has a right or a duty to withhold inspection of a document, or part of a document, must state in writing –
>
> (a) that he has such a right or duty; and
>
> (b) the grounds on which he claims that right or duty.
>
> (4) The statement referred to in paragraph (3) must be made –
>
> (a) in the list in which the document is disclosed; or
>
> (b) if there is no list, to the person wishing to inspect the document.
>
> (5) A party may apply to the court to decide whether a claim made under paragraph (3) should be upheld.
>
> (6) For the purpose of deciding an application under paragraph (1) (application to withhold disclosure) or paragraph (3) (claim to withhold inspection) the court may –
>
> (a) require the person seeking to withhold disclosure or inspection of a document to produce that document to the court; and
>
> (b) invite any person, whether or not a party, to make representations.
>
> (7) An application under paragraph (1) or paragraph (5) must be supported by evidence.
>
> (8) This Part does not affect any rule of law which permits or requires a document to be withheld from disclosure or inspection on the ground that its disclosure or inspection would damage the public interest.

The key issue within public interest privilege is whether disclosure would be injurious to the public interest. This requires a balancing of the public interest in concealment of the documents against the public interest in the proper administration of justice.

### 8.16.7 Without prejudice communications

The without prejudice rule prevents evidence being adduced of negotiations between the parties that are genuinely aimed at settling a dispute. Where the without prejudice rule applies, relevant documents are also privileged from disclosure, whether or not they are headed 'without prejudice' (see *Chocoladefabriken Lindt & Sprungli AG* v. *Nestle Co Ltd* [1978] RPC 287). In *Cutts* v. *Head* [1984] Ch 290 Lord Justice Oliver explained the policy behind the without prejudice rules:

> That the rule rests, at least in part, upon public policy is clear from many authorities, and the convenient starting point of the inquiry is the nature of the underlying policy. It is that parties should be encouraged so far as possible to settle their disputes without resort to litigation and should not be discouraged by the knowledge that anything that is said in the course of such negotiations (and that includes, of course, as much the failure to reply to an offer as an actual reply) may be used to their prejudice in the course of the proceedings. They should, as it was expressed by Clauson J. in *Scott Paper Co.* v. *Drayton Paper Works Ltd.* (1927) 44 R.P.C. 151, 156, be encouraged fully and frankly to put their cards on the table.

The without prejudice rule protects a party making an admission in correspondence purely for the purpose of attempting to arrive at a settlement, but it is not necessary for admissions to be made for the without prejudice rule to apply. For example, in the case of *Unilever* v. *Procter & Gamble* [2000] 1 WLR 2436 it was held that a round-table meeting between the parties was protected by the without prejudice rule, although no admissions were made. The result of this holding was that Unilever could not rely upon what was said at the meeting to support a claim based on Patents Act 1977, s.70. Lord Justice Walker, referring to previous cases, held:

> They show that the protection of admissions against interest is the most important practical effect of the rule. But to dissect out identifiable admissions and withhold protection from the rest of without prejudice communications (except for a special reason) would not only create huge practical difficulties but would be contrary to the underlying objective of giving protection to the parties, in the words of Lord Griffiths in the *Rush & Tompkins* case [1989] A.C. 1280, 1300: 'to speak freely about all issues in the litigation both factual and legal when seeking compromise and, for the purpose of establishing a basis of compromise, admitting certain facts.' Parties cannot speak freely at a without prejudice meeting if they must constantly monitor every sentence, with lawyers or patent agents sitting at their shoulders as minders.

In distinction to legal professional privilege, without prejudice privilege cannot be waived unilaterally, as it is a joint privilege for the benefit of both parties to the negotiation. However, where one party utilises part of the without prejudice material the other party can refer to its contents in order to advance its own case.

## 8.17 FAILURE TO MAKE ADEQUATE DISCLOSURE

A party that fails to give adequate disclosure is exposed to a wide variety of sanctions: they may be prevented from relying upon documents that assist their case, they may be penalised by a costs order and in the most extreme cases of continued default their cases could be dismissed.

## CHAPTER NOTES

1 For a copy of the Code see **http://police.homeoffice.gov.uk/publications/operational-policing/Disclosure_code_of_practice.pdf?view=Binary**.

2 Paragraph 5.5 says that 'the duty to retain material, where it may be relevant to the investigation, also includes in particular the duty to retain material which may satisfy the test for prosecution disclosure in the Act'.

3 See **www.cps.gov.uk**.

4 See **www.attorneygeneral.gov.uk/attachments/disclosure.doc**.

5 See **www.judiciary.gov.uk/docs/judgments_guidance/protocols**.

6 See **www.judiciary.gov.uk/docs/judgments_guidance/protocols**.

7 At the date of publication of this book the CPR has been subject to more than 30 amending Statutory Instruments; see **www.justice.gov.uk**.

8 See **www.hmcourts-service.gov.uk/docs/electronic_disclosure1004.doc**.

CHAPTER 9

# Core regulatory issues

## 9.1 INTRODUCTION

This chapter focuses on two important regulatory law issues that are of fundamental importance within the day-to-day use of email, namely records keeping and data security.[1]

The obligation to keep records is a primary regulatory tool (others include licensing schemes and administrative penalties), and there are literally hundreds of laws that impose records keeping obligations. Data security is, of course, one of the 'hottest' topics within the law, consequent upon many high-profile losses of data and security breaches. This chapter is also designed to provide support and legal authority for some of the discussion on compliance issues in **Chapter 10**.

## 9.2 EMAILS AS RECORDS

Organisational records keeping very often results from a legal obligation, whether direct or indirect. Although the situations in which the law imposes a records keeping obligation cannot be fully explored here, it is safe to assume that there are literally hundreds of laws imposing records keeping obligations. These may prescribe lengthy retention periods.

This part provides examples of records keeping laws relevant to businesses, with references to other European laws being made from time to time. It is hoped that the following illustrations will help with conceptualising and understanding the size, scope and extent of records keeping obligations as they apply to electronic records, and to emails in particular.

### 9.2.1 Companies Act records

If the Companies Act 2006 is considered for illustrative purposes, it will be found that it imposes dozens of substantial records keeping obligations. These obligations cover, among other things, the provision of detailed company information to Companies House, 10 years' records keeping obligations for meetings and resolutions (ss.355–9), and three years' (for private companies: s.388(4)(a)) to six years' (for public companies: s.388(4)(b)) records keeping obligations for company accounts.

Remaining with company accounts for a moment, the obligation extends to the keeping of 'adequate accounting records' (s.386(1)), which are those that are 'sufficient to show and explain the company's transactions' (s.386(2)) so as to 'give a true and fair view of the assets, liabilities, financial position and profit or loss' (s.393(1)) of the company. These records must be kept in a manner so that they are open to inspection by the company officers at a place within the UK at all times (s.388(1)(b)).

Failure to keep adequate accounting records is a criminal offence (s.387), for which directors can be held liable (s.387(1)), punishable by up to two years' imprisonment and unlimited fines (s.387(3)). Furthermore, directors are warned at pains of committing criminal offences that they must not approve accounts 'unless they are satisfied that they give a true and fair view' (s.393(1)). If their reports contain inaccuracies that result in their companies suffering loss, directors can be held liable to pay compensation to their companies (s.463).

Heightening the importance of good records keeping, the Companies Act 2006 includes measures that effectively bar company auditors from signing-off accounts if they are unsure of the directors' degree of compliance with their records keeping obligations (s.393(2)). Furthermore, if auditors are unable to vouch for the quality of the records kept by the company they must note this within their reports (s.498).

For public companies listed on the London Stock Exchange, these records keeping obligations are further bolstered by the Financial Reporting Council's (FRC) Combined Code on Corporate Governance[2] and the supporting Turnbull Guidance.[3] The main principle of financial reporting stated within the Combined Code is that 'the board should present a balanced and understandable assessment of the company's position and prospects' (FRC Combined Code (June 2006), section C.1). The Turnbull Guidance emphasises that 'effective financial controls, including the maintenance of proper accounting records, are an important element of internal control' (Turnbull Guidance (October 2005), p.3).

### 9.2.2 Tax, pay and employee records

The fundamental records keeping obligations in the Companies Act 2006 are supplemented by many more highly detailed laws relating to tax, pay and benefits. Notable obligations include:

- Companies that are required to deliver a tax return must keep relevant records for six years following the end of the tax period to which the return relates (Finance Act 1998, Sched.18, Part III, para.21). The records which must be kept are those that are 'needed to enable it to deliver a correct and complete return for the period'.

- VAT records must be kept for six years (VAT Act 1994, Sched.11, para.6).
- Wages and salary records must be kept for six years after the end of the tax period to which they apply (Taxes Management Act 1970, s.12B).
- 'PAYE' income tax records must be kept for three years following the end of the financial year to which they relate (Income Tax (Pay As You Earn) Regulations 2003, SI 2003/2682, reg.97(8)).
- National Insurance Contributions records must be kept for three years following the end of the tax year to which they relate (Social Security (Contributions) Regulations 2001, SI 2001/1004, Sched.4, paras.7(15), 26(6)).
- Statutory Maternity Pay (SMP) records must be kept for three years following the end of the tax year in which the benefit was paid (Statutory Maternity Pay (General) Regulations 1986 SI 1986/1960, reg.26).
- Statutory Sick Pay (SSP) records must be kept for three years following the end of the tax year in which the benefit was paid (Statutory Sick Pay (General) Regulations 1982, SI 1982/894, reg.13).

Companies must also be aware that HM Revenue and Customs has the power to recover taxes for up to 20 years after they fell due.[4] For the purposes of best practice, this provides a model retention period for company records relevant to tax and accounting. In any event, as a matter of good practice companies should always seek to extend the retention periods set out above by one year, to cover the possibility of records falling into two tax years. Thus, a six-year retention period should be implemented as a seven-year period.

There are many employee records that should be kept as a matter of good practice, but for which there are no defined statutory retention periods. This absence of statutory rules leaves companies with a dilemma that many have solved by reference to the limitation periods for the commencement of legal proceedings contained in the Limitation Act 1980.

### 9.2.3 Health and safety records

The workplace can be a dangerous place and for this reason health and safety law imposes many records keeping obligations. Notable obligations include:

- Records of accidents and dangerous occurrences must be kept for three years (Reporting of Injuries, Diseases and Dangerous Occurrences Regulations 1995, SI 1995/3163, reg.7).
- Records of exposure to asbestos must be kept for at least 40 years (Control of Asbestos Regulations 2006, SI 2006/2739, reg.22).

- Records of exposure to hazardous substances and materials in the workplace must be kept for between five and at least 40 years (Control of Substances Hazardous to Health Regulations 2002, SI 2002/2677, reg.10).
- Records of exposure to lead in the workplace must be kept for at least 40 years (Control of Lead at Work Regulations 2002, SI 2002/2676, reg.11).
- Records of exposure to ionising radiation in the workplace must be kept for at least 50 years (Ionising Radiations Regulations 1999, SI 1999/3232, reg.21).

Companies should also be aware of the Corporate Manslaughter and Corporate Homicide Act 2007, which makes it a criminal offence for a corporate body and other organisations to cause a death as a result of failures in its organisational structures. This offence behoves organisations to keep proper records of its health and safety systems.

### 9.2.4 Banking and financial services records

Record keeping in the banking and financial services sectors is very highly regulated. Notable records keeping obligations arise under 'stability' regimes such as Basel II and MiFID.

*Basel II*

In 1988 the Basel Committee on Banking Supervision adopted the Basel Capital Accord (Basel I), which was aimed at strengthening the international banking system through higher capital requirements. Basel II,[5] adopted in 2004, continues this agenda with the introduction of a new focus on operational risk and a widening of disclosure rules.

A major element within operational risk is the increased reliance upon technology, which, of course, carries with it an inherent risk of data loss. This risk can be ameliorated through sound records management systems. Likewise, sound records management is fundamental to the accurate assessment and measurement of risk and for ensuring compliance with disclosure rules and the transparency principles at their heart.

The rewards for banks that reduce risk are significant; in simplistic terms they are required to hold less capital, meaning they can lend more money and thereby earn greater profits.

Within the European Union, Basel II has been implemented by the 'Capital Requirements Directive',[6] which came into force on 1 January 2007.

*MiFID*

The Market in Financial Instruments Directive (Level 1) (MiFID) (Directive 2004/39/EC of the European Parliament and of the Council of 21 April 2004 on markets in financial instruments amending Council Directives 85/611/EEC and 93/6/EEC and Directive 2000/12/EC of the European Parliament and of the Council and repealing Council Directive 93/22/EEC) is a harmonisation Directive of the European Parliament and Council, aimed at furthering the Single Market in financial instruments and related investment advice, based on home country regulation and the implementation of best execution rules, pre- and post-trade transparency rules and client reporting rules. It came into force on 1 November 2007.

MiFID contains many direct and indirect records keeping obligations, including the following:

- Article 13(6) requires investment firms to 'arrange for records to be kept of all services and transactions undertaken by it which shall be sufficient to enable the competent authority to monitor compliance with the requirements under this Directive'.
- Article 25(2) requires 'investment firms to keep at the disposal of the competent authority, for at least five years, the relevant data relating to all transactions in financial instruments which they have carried out'. These records must also comply with anti-money laundering rules.
- Article 55(1)(c) obliges auditors to report any failures of records keeping.

The MiFID Level 1 Directive is supported by two Level 2 instruments, one a Directive[7] and the other a Regulation.[8] The Level 2 Directive includes the following records keeping obligations:

- Article 5(1)(f) requires investment firms to 'maintain adequate and orderly records of their business and internal organisation'.
- Article 10 requires investment firms to 'establish, implement and maintain effective and transparent procedures for the reasonable and prompt handling of complaints received from retail clients or potential retail clients, and to keep a record of each complaint and the measures taken for its resolution'.
- In order to prevent conflicts of interest, Article 12(2)(b) requires investment firms using outsourcing services to ensure that the outsourcing provider keeps records of all personal transactions entered into by certain relevant persons.
- For the purposes of safeguarding client assets Article 16(1)(a) requires investment firms to 'keep such records and accounts as are necessary to enable them at any time and without delay to distinguish assets held for one client from assets held for any other client, and from their own assets'. Article 16(1)(f) says that 'they must introduce adequate organisational arrangements to minimise the risk of the loss or diminution of client assets, or of rights in connection with those assets, as a result of misuse of the assets, fraud, poor administration, inadequate record-keeping or negligence'.

- Article 19(2) says that 'the records of the investment firm shall include details of the client on whose instructions the use of the financial instruments has been effected, as well as the number of financial instruments used belonging to each client who has given his consent, so as to enable the correct allocation of any loss'.
- Article 23 says that investment firms must 'keep and regularly to update a record of the kinds of investment or ancillary service or investment activity carried out by or on behalf of the firm in which a conflict of interest entailing a material risk of damage to the interests of one or more clients has arisen or, in the case of an ongoing service or activity, may arise'.
- Article 47(1)(b) says that client orders must be executed promptly and 'accurately recorded and allocated'.
- Article 51 sets a minimum five-year retention period, but those records which set out the rights and obligations of the investment firm must be kept for the length of the client relationship, if longer.
- Article 51(2) prescribes the records managements standards which are (a) the competent authority must be able to access them readily and to reconstitute each key stage of the processing of each transaction; (b) it must be possible for any corrections or other amendments, and the contents of the records prior to such corrections or amendments, to be easily ascertained; and (c) it must not be possible for the records otherwise to be manipulated or altered.

The MiFID Level 2 Regulation provides even more detail about the records keeping obligations facing investment firms. Notable obligations include:

- Article 7 prescribes the information that should be recorded in respect of 'every order received from a client, and in relation to every decision to deal taken in providing the service of portfolio management'.
- Article 8 prescribes the information that should be recorded after the execution of a transaction.
- Article 24 requires investment firms to keep records of their quoted prices for no less than 12 months.

### *Financial Services Authority rules on records keeping*

The Financial Services Authority's (FSA) Handbook contains a plethora of rules which import direct and indirect records keeping obligations, including those consequent upon Basel II and MiFID. A full review of these provisions is beyond the scope of this book, but the examples below should provide a flavour of the kind of issues faced by those within the FSA's regulatory scope.

- The Senior Management Arrangements, Systems and Controls rules (SYSC) contain a very important management information rule (SYSC

3.2.11), which says that 'a firm's arrangements should be such as to furnish its governing body with the information it needs to play its part in identifying, measuring, managing and controlling risks of regulatory concern'. The records rule (SYSC 3.2.20) says 'a firm must take reasonable care to make and retain adequate records of matters and dealings (including accounting records) which are the subject of requirements and standards under the regulatory system'. It also says that 'a firm should have appropriate systems and controls in place to fulfil the firm's regulatory and statutory obligations with respect to adequacy, access, periods of retention and security of records. The general principle is that records should be retained for as long as is relevant for the purposes for which they are made' (SYSC 3.2.21). There are also indirect records keeping obligations for the purposes of business continuity (SYSC 3.2.19), for compliance with the Capital Requirements Directive (SYSC 3.2.25), for compliance with the Banking Consolidation Directive (SYSC 3.2.26) and for compliance with MiFID (SYSC 4.1.5).

- The Supervision rules (SUP) require regulated firms to keep full records on their appointed representatives (SUP 12.9.1), which must be retained for a period of three years from the date of termination of the representative's contract (SUP 12.9.2).
- The Conduct of Business (COB) rules require regulated firms to keep records of all non-real time financial promotions, for a minimum of three years and extending indefinitely in cases of promotion of pension transfers, pension opt-outs and free-standing additional voluntary contributions (COB 3.7.1). These records should be 'readily available', which means they should be capable of being retrieved within 48 hours of a request being made (COB 3.7.5).
- The Insurance: Conduct of Business rules (ICOB) impose similar records keeping rules as COB, including a two business days retrieval period (ICOB 2.8.3). Where records are kept in electronic form the firm should take 'reasonable steps' to ensure that the electronic record accurately records the original information and that the electronic record cannot be subject to unauthorised or accidental alteration (ICOB 2.8.5). A minimum retention period of three years is imposed, with a recommendation that this should be extended to cover the applicable limitation period for legal proceedings (ICOB 2.8.6).
- The Client Assets rules (CASS) on segregation and operation of client money accounts say that 'a firm must ensure that proper records, sufficient to show and explain the firm's transactions and commitments in respect of its client money, are made and retained for a period of three years after they were made' (CASS 4.3.111; see also CASS Sched.1 for detailed retention periods).
- The Prudential Sourcebook for Insurers (INSPRU) says that 'firms must ensure that long-term insurance assets are separately identified and allo-

cated to a long-term insurance fund at all times. Assets in external accounts, for example at banks, custodians, or brokers should be segregated in the firm's books and records into separate accounts for long-term insurance business and general insurance business. Where a firm has more than one long-term insurance fund, a separate accounting record must be maintained for each fund. Accounting records should clearly document the allocation' (INSPRU 1.5.24).

- The Mortgages and Home Finance: Conduct of Business (MCOB) rules say that relevant records must be 'readily accessible' by the FSA, which means within two business days (MCOB 2.8.3) and repeats the ICOB rules on electronic records (MCOB 2.8.4).
- The Building Societies Regulatory Guide (BSOG) requires a building society to keep records that explain its transactions, disclose, with reasonable accuracy and promptness, the state of its business at any time and enable the directors and the society to properly discharge their respective duties (BSOG 1.4.1). These records must include day-to-day entries of all sums received and paid by the society, day-to-day entries of every transaction which will, or may reasonably be expected to, give rise to assets or liabilities of the society, and a record of the society's assets and liabilities and, in particular, the assets and liabilities of any class specifically regulated (BSOG 1.4.2).
- The Market Conduct Sourcebook (MAR) says that 'a firm should implement appropriate systems and controls with a view to ensuring that the material terms of all transactions to which it is a party, and other material information about such transactions, are promptly and accurately recorded in its books or records. The manner in which this information may be recorded include: (1) voice recordings of transactions; (2) voice recordings of oral confirmations; (3) written trading logs or blotters; and (4) automated electronic records' (MAR 3.6.3).

It is also worth noting that in 2007 the FSA commenced a process of consultation, about the introduction of a comprehensive regime for the recording of electronic communications by MiFID and non-MiFID firms.[9] The FSA's original proposal, which was intended to replace the non-binding guidance in section 3.6 of the Market Conduct Sourcebook (MAR), was that electronic communications records should be kept for three years.[10] This consultation led to the publication on 28 February 2008 of the Conduct of Business Sourcebook (Recording of Telephone Conversations and Electronic Communications) Instrument 2008. The Instrument applies to firms who are involved in receiving client orders and negotiating, agreeing and arranging transactions across the equity, bond, financial commodity and derivatives markets.[11]

The Instrument makes amendments to the Senior Management Arrangements, Systems and Controls sourcebook (SYSC) and the Conduct of Business sourcebook (COBS), which come into effect on 6 March 2009. The policy statement which announced the new instrument explains within its overview:[12]

> Preventing, detecting and deterring market abuse is one of our key priorities. However, market abuse is one of the most difficult offences to investigate and prosecute. Good quality recordings of voice conversations and of electronic communications (taping) help firms and us detect and deter inappropriate behaviour.

As indicated by the policy statement overview, the purpose of the Instrument is to require the recording of voice conversations and electronic communications to help regulated firms and the FSA detect and deter market abuse. From 6 March 2009, para.11.8.5 of COBS will say:

> A firm must take reasonable steps to record relevant telephone conversations, and keep a copy of relevant electronic communications, made with, sent from or received on equipment:
>
> (1) provided by the firm to an employee or contractor; or
> (2) the use of which by an employee or contractor has been sanctioned or permitted by the firm;
>
> to enable that employee or contractor to carry out any of the activities referred to in COBS 11.8.1R.

For these purposes, electronic communications are defined as including 'communications made by way of facsimile, email and instant messaging devices' (see COBS 11.8.7). Relevant conversations and communications include ones between employees and contractors of the firm and the client (see COBS 11.8.8 for further details).

The retention obligations are contained in COBS 11.8.10:

> A firm must take reasonable steps to retain all records made by it under COBS 11.8.5R:
>
> (1) for a period of at least 6 months from the date the record was created;
> (2) in a medium that allows the storage of the information in a way accessible for future reference by the FSA, and so that the following conditions are met:
>     (a) the FSA must be able to access the records readily;
>     (b) it must be possible for any corrections or other amendments, and the contents of the records prior to such corrections and amendments, to be easily ascertained;
>     (c) it must not be possible for the records to be otherwise manipulated or altered.

While COBS 11.8.5 will apply to all voice and electronic communications sent or received over fixed apparatus, in the first instance it will only apply to emails where mobile telephones or other mobile handheld electronic communication devices are used (see COBS 11.8.6(1)). The reason for this limitation is explained in PS08/1; during the consultation process leading to the adoption of the Instrument, the financial services industry 'asserted that recording mobile telephones was not technically feasible so the proposals were tantamount to a ban on mobile phones which were used for relevant conversations' (PS08/1, para.2.27). The FSA received conflicting evidence from its consultants, however, and so it will review the limitation 'in 18 months' time to decide whether it is still appropriate to continue with this exemption' (PS08/1, para.2.29). This review has been planned to coincide with an EU review of the taping rules in MiFID, which is scheduled to take place before 31 December 2009.

### 9.2.5 Electronic communications sector

The electronic communications sector also faces substantial records keeping obligations under the Communications Data Retention Directive (Directive 2006/24/EC of the European Parliament and of the Council of 15 March 2006 on the retention of data generated or processed in connection with the provision of publicly available electronic communications services or of public communications networks and amending Directive 2002/58/EC), which is discussed in detail at **Chapters 4** and **7**.

To recap, this Directive amends the Privacy and Electronic Communications Directive (Directive 2002/58/EC of the European Parliament and of the Council of 12 July 2002 concerning the processing of personal data and the protection of privacy in the electronic communications sector) so as to require the providers of publicly available electronic communications services and networks to retain traffic and location data. These records are retained for the purposes of investigation, detection and prosecution of serious crime.

The records to be kept under this Directive consist of the traffic and location data necessary to trace and identify the source of a communication, those that are necessary to identify the date, time and duration of a communication, those that are necessary to identify the type of communication, those that are necessary to identify the user's communications equipment and those that are necessary to identify the location of mobile communications equipment (Article 5).

The retention period for these records ranges from six months to two years (Article 6). After the expiry of the applicable retention period the records must be destroyed, unless they have been accessed and preserved for the purposes of investigation, detection or prosecution of serious crime (Article 7(d)).

The records must be stored using technical and organisational measures so as to prevent their accidental or unlawful destruction, loss or alteration, or unauthorised or unlawful storage, processing, access or disclosure (Article 7(b)). They must also be stored in a manner so that they can be transmitted to law enforcement agencies 'without delay'.

The UK Regulations implementing the Communications Data Retention Directive came into force on 1 October 2007.

### 9.2.6 Anti-money laundering

The Money Laundering Regulations 2007, SI 2007/2157, which came into effect on 15 December 2007, give effect to the EU Third Money Laundering Directive (Directive 2005/60/EC of the European Parliament and of the Council of 26 October 2005 on the prevention of the use of the financial system for the purpose of money laundering and terrorist financing).

The 2007 Regulations apply to 'relevant persons', namely credit institutions, financial institutions, auditors, insolvency practitioners, external accountants and tax advisers, independent legal professionals, trust or company service providers, estate agents, high value dealers and casinos. These relevant persons are obliged to carry out 'customer due diligence', which means properly identifying the customer by reference to reliable information obtained from independent sources. These customer due diligence procedures must be carried out whenever the relevant person establishes a business relationship, carries out an occasional transaction, suspects money laundering or terrorist financing or doubts the veracity or adequacy of documents, data or information previously obtained for the purposes of identification or verification. Additionally, the relevant person must carry out ongoing monitoring of the customer and keep associated records.

Regulation 19 sets the records keeping obligations. Customer due diligence records must be retained for five years, commencing from the date the business relationship ends or the occasional transaction is completed. Regulation 20 requires the relevant person to establish appropriate procedures for records keeping purposes.

### 9.2.7 Disputes and litigation

The fact that businesses are exposed to litigation and other contentious matters often provides a basis for the development of records keeping policies. Two important issues are at the heart of dispute-based records management, namely limitation periods and the obligation to disclose documents within litigation.

*Limitation periods*

The Limitation Act 1980 prescribes the time periods for the commencement of litigation, with the general rule being that once a limitation period has expired litigation cannot be commenced. Thus, businesses will very often set a retention period to cover the limitation periods applicable to likely court claims against them, with the reasoning being that once the limitation period has expired there will be no requirement to call up records.

The principal limitation periods are:

- Breach of contract claims: six years from the date of accrual of the cause of action (Limitation Act 1980, s.5).
- Breach of contract claims, where the contract was made under Deed: 12 years.
- Claims in tort, such as negligence claims: six years from the date of accrual of the cause of action (s.2), or three years from the date the claimant had the 'knowledge required for bringing an action for damages in respect of the relevant damage', if later.
- Personal injury claims: three years, but the court has the power to extend this.
- Actions to recover possession of land: 12 years from the date of accrual of cause of action.
- Actions in respect of defective products: 10 years (s.11A).

*Litigation disclosure and retention*

Litigation disclosure is discussed in **Chapter 8**. To recap, in civil litigation disclosure is governed by the Civil Procedure Rules 1998 (CPR), Part 31. As a general rule, parties to litigation are required to give disclosure of relevant documents that are or were within their control.

The obligation to give disclosure also carries with it an obligation to preserve documents, which effectively imposes a records keeping obligation. This obligation comes into existence when litigation is commenced or prior to the commencement of litigation where a party makes a successful application for pre-action disclosure (CPR 31.16).

### 9.2.8 Data protection

The Data Protection Act (DPA) 1998, which regulates the processing of personal data, is discussed in **Chapter 3**. To recap, the Act was enacted to give effect to the UK's obligations under the Data Protection Directive 1995 (Directive 95/46/EC of the European Parliament and of the Council of 24 October 1995 on the protection of individuals with regard to the processing of personal data and on the free movement of such data), to protect the fundamental rights and freedoms of people, particularly the right to privacy.

The compliance 'goals' are contained within the eight data protection principles, which are:

1. Personal data must be processed fairly and lawfully.
2. Personal data must be processed pursuant to a specified purpose.
3. Personal data must be adequate, relevant and not excessive in relation to the purpose for which they are processed.
4. Personal data must be accurate and kept up to date (where necessary).
5. Personal data must not be retained for longer than necessary.
6. Personal data must be processed in accordance with the rights of the individual.
7. Personal data must be kept safe and secure.
8. Personal data must not be transferred outside of the European Economic Area to an unsafe country.

When the principles are viewed in combination, it must be concluded that they impose both direct and indirect records keeping obligations. For example, keeping data accurate and safe are both features within a records management policy. The fifth principle, which imposes both retention and delete obligations, is another key feature of a records management policy. The eighth principle requires businesses engaged in cross-border trade to keep records of all data transfers to other countries.

## 9.3 DATA SECURITY AND SYSTEMS INTEGRITY

In recent years both the Information Commissioner and the Financial Services Authority have been heavily occupied with the topic of data security, acting to move the law forward at a considerable pace. **Table 9.1** identifies key events in data security since March 2006.

**Table 9.1** Key events in data security law in the UK since March 2006

| Date | Event |
|---|---|
| March 2006 | The FSA fines Capita Financial Administrators £300,000 for data security failings. |
| April 2006 | The Information Commissioner publishes guidance encouraging data controllers to implement Privacy Enhancing Technologies (PETs). |
| May 2006 | The Information Commissioner publishes his special report to Parliament, *What price privacy?*, calling for the introduction of custodial penalties for those convicted of data theft contrary to DPA 1998, s.55. The Commissioner says that he has uncovered evidence of a 'widespread and pervasive' black market trading in stolen personal information. |

**Table 9.1** *Cont.*

| Date | Event |
|---|---|
| June 2006 | The Department for Constitutional Affairs issue public consultation on the introduction of custodial penalties, per *What price privacy?* |
| December 2006 | The Information Commissioner publishes *What price privacy now?*, outlining his case that 32 press and media companies are trading in the black market for stolen personal information. |
| February 2007 | Lord Falconer, the then Lord Chancellor, announces the government's intention to introduce custodial penalties for data theft, per *What price privacy?* |
| February 2007 | The FSA fines Nationwide Building Society £980,000 following the loss of a laptop computer. |
| March 2007 | The Information Commissioner finds 10 high street banks and the Post Office to be in breach of the DPA 1998 due to insecure disposal of confidential papers. They sign undertakings admitting breach and agreeing to implement new systems. |
| March 2007 | The Information Commissioner publishes further guidance encouraging data controllers to implement PETs. |
| April 2007 | The Information Commissioner finds Cash Generators to be in breach of the DPA 1998 due to insecure disposal of confidential papers. They sign undertakings admitting breach and agreeing to implement new systems. |
| May 2007 | The FSA fines BNPP Private Bank £350,000 for data security failings. |
| May 2007 | The European Commission publishes its Communication on 'Privacy Enhancing Technologies'. |
| May 2007 | The Information Commissioner finds Phones 4U to be in breach of the DPA 1998 due to insecure disposal of confidential papers. Phones 4U signs undertakings admitting breach and agreeing to implement new systems. |
| May 2007 | Information Commissioner finds Orange to be in breach of the Data Protection Act, for failure of call centre security. Orange signs undertakings admitting breach and agreeing to implement new systems. |
| June 2007 | The government introduces the Criminal Justice and Immigration Bill, which contains draft provisions for the introduction of custodial penalties for data theft, per *What price privacy?* |
| August 2007 | The House of Lords Science and Technology Committee publishes its report on personal internet security and recommends the introduction of breach notification laws in the UK. |
| November 2007 | HM Revenue and Customs announces that it has lost two data disks containing the child benefit database for the UK. Over 7,000,000 UK families are affected. |
| November 2007 | Sir Gus O'Donnell commences his inquiry into data handling in government, as part of the official response to HMRC. |
| November 2007 | The Information Commissioner publishes his new enforcement strategy for unencrypted laptop computers, 'Our approach to encryption'. |

**Table 9.1** *Cont.*

| Date | Event |
|---|---|
| November 2007 | The Information Commissioner finds the Foreign and Commonwealth Office to be in breach of the DPA 1998 due to failures of website security. They sign undertakings admitting breach and agreeing to implement new systems. |
| November 2007 | The European Commission publishes a draft Directive containing a breach notification law for the electronic communications sector. |
| December 2007 | The Information Commissioner publishes his case for amending the DPA 1998, requesting new powers to fine organisations that breach the data protection principles, a new criminal offence of failing to comply with the principles and enhanced enforcement powers to allow him to enter premises and order the cessation of data processing activities. |
| December 2007 | The Information Commissioner finds the Department of Health to be in breach of the DPA 1998 due to failures of website security. They sign undertakings admitting breach and agreeing to implement new systems. |
| December 2007 | The House of Commons Justice Committee convenes to examine the HMRC data loss and to assess whether the DPA 1998 needs to be amended to ensure stiffer penalties for those organisations that fail to keep data safe. The Information Commissioner gives evidence supporting his case for amending the DPA 1998. |
| December 2007 | The FSA fines Norwich Union £1,260,000 for failure of call centre security. |
| December 2007 | The O'Donnell Interim Report is published. |
| January 2008 | The House of Commons Justice Committee issues its first report, 'Protection of Private Data', which recommends wholesale amendment of the DPA 1998, per the Information Commissioner's case for amendment. |
| January 2008 | The Ministry of Defence loses an unencrypted laptop containing personal data on 600,000 navy personnel. |
| January 2008 | The Information Commissioner serves an enforcement notice on Marks & Spencer ordering completion of a programme of laptop encryption. |
| January 2008 | The Information Commissioner finds Carphone Warehouse and Talk Talk to be in breach of the DPA 1998 due to failures of call centre security. They sign undertakings admitting breach and agreeing to implement new systems. |
| February 2008 | The Information Commissioner finds Skipton Financial Services to be in breach of the DPA 1998 following the loss of an unencrypted laptop. They sign undertakings admitting breach and agreeing to implement new systems. |
| March 2008 | The Information Commissioner introduces new rules on handling data security breaches. |
| March 2008 | The Information Commissioner introduces new rules on breach notification. |
| April 2008 | The FSA publishes its report on data security, requiring firms to implement stronger security controls. |

**Table 9.1** *Cont.*

| Date | Event |
|---|---|
| May 2008 | The Criminal Justice and Immigration Act 2008 introduces a power for the Information Commissioner to fine organisations that fail to comply with the DPA 1998. A power to introduce custodial penalties, per *What price privacy?*, is enacted. |
| June 2008 | The FSA fines a small firm of stockbrokers, Merchant Securities, £77,000 for various security breaches. |
| June 2008 | The Poynter Report and the IPCC Report into HMRC are published, revealing systematic failures in security. The O'Donnell Report is published identifying the remedial measures that will be implemented across government to ensure data security. The Burton Report into the loss of Ministry of Defence laptops reveals systematic failures in security. |
| June 2008 | The Information Commissioner announces that he will serve enforcement notices on HMRC and the Ministry of Defence requiring improved security and three years of reviews. He says he will commence criminal prosecutions if they fail to comply. |
| July 2008 | The Information Commissioner cancels the Marks & Spencer enforcement notice. |
| July 2008 | The Information Commissioner serves enforcement notices on HMRC and MoD. |
| July 2008 | The Ministry of Justice opens public consultation on the Information Commissioner's inspection powers. |

## 9.4 FINANCIAL SERVICES AUTHORITY

The FSA's interest in data security arises from its regulatory objectives, which are contained in the Financial Services and Markets Act (FSMA) 2000. Section 2 says:

**2. The Authority's general duties**

(1) In discharging its general functions the Authority must, so far as is reasonably possible, act in a way –

(a) which is compatible with the regulatory objectives; and
(b) which the Authority considers most appropriate for the purpose of meeting those objectives.

(2) The regulatory objectives are –

(a) market confidence;
(b) public awareness;
(c) the protection of consumers; and
(d) the reduction of financial crime.

(3) In discharging its general functions the Authority must have regard to –

(a) the need to use its resources in the most efficient and economic way;
(b) the responsibilities of those who manage the affairs of authorised persons;
(c) the principle that a burden or restriction which is imposed on a person, or on the carrying on of an activity, should be proportionate to the benefits, considered in general terms, which are expected to result from the imposition of that burden or restriction;
(d) the desirability of facilitating innovation in connection with regulated activities;
(e) the international character of financial services and markets and the desirability of maintaining the competitive position of the United Kingdom;
(f) the need to minimise the adverse effects on competition that may arise from anything done in the discharge of those functions;
(g) the desirability of facilitating competition between those who are subject to any form of regulation by the Authority.

(4) The Authority's general functions are –

(a) its function of making rules under this Act (considered as a whole);
(b) its function of preparing and issuing codes under this Act (considered as a whole);
(c) its functions in relation to the giving of general guidance (considered as a whole); and
(d) its function of determining the general policy and principles by reference to which it performs particular functions.

(5) 'General guidance' has the meaning given in section 158(5).

The FSA has expanded upon its regulatory objectives within its Handbook, particularly its Principles for Business. For the purposes of data security within the financial services sector, it is Principles 2 and 3 that are the most relevant. Principle 2 says that a regulated firm must conduct its business with due skill, care and diligence. Principle 3 says that a regulated firm must take reasonable care to organise and control its affairs responsibly and effectively, with adequate risk management systems. In its most recent activities in the field of data security the FSA has relied upon its Principles for Business, generally Principle 3 but occasionally Principle 2, and its obligation to prevent financial crime to justify regulatory action in the form of fines. Regarding financial crime, it is also worth noting the provisions of FSMA 2000, s.6, which says:

**6. The reduction of financial crime**

(1) The reduction of financial crime objective is: reducing the extent to which it is possible for a business carried on –

(a) by a regulated person, or
(b) in contravention of the general prohibition,

to be used for a purpose connected with financial crime.

(2) In considering that objective the Authority must, in particular, have regard to the desirability of –

(a) regulated persons being aware of the risk of their businesses being used in connection with the commission of financial crime;
(b) regulated persons taking appropriate measures (in relation to their administration and employment practices, the conduct of transactions by them and otherwise) to prevent financial crime, facilitate its detection and monitor its incidence;
(c) regulated persons devoting adequate resources to the matters mentioned in paragraph (b).

(3) 'Financial crime' includes any offence involving –

(a) fraud or dishonesty;
(b) misconduct in, or misuse of information relating to, a financial market; or
(c) handling the proceeds of crime.

(4) 'Offence' includes an act or omission which would be an offence if it had taken place in the United Kingdom.
(5) 'Regulated person' means an authorised person, a recognised investment exchange or a recognised clearing house.

### 9.4.1 Systems integrity in the financial services sector

The integrity of electronic systems is fundamental to a properly functioning financial services sector. Indeed, it is very hard to envisage a situation whereby the regulatory objectives of the FSMA 2000 could be achieved absent systems integrity within the regulated firms. Similarly MiFID also focuses on systems integrity and the following provisions should be noted:

- Article 13(5) of the Level 1 Directive requires investment firms to 'have sound administrative and accounting procedures, internal control mechanisms, effective procedures for risk assessment, and effective control and safeguard arrangements for information processing systems'.
- Article 5(2) of the Level 2 Directive requires investment firms to 'establish, implement and maintain systems and procedures that are adequate to safeguard the security, integrity and confidentiality of information, taking into account the nature of the information in question'.

Principle 3 of the FSA's Principles for Business is expanded upon by the Senior Management Arrangements, Systems and Controls sourcebook (SYSC). SYSC 3.2.6 says:

> A firm must take reasonable care to establish and maintain effective systems and controls for compliance with applicable requirements and standards under the regulatory system and for countering the risk that the firm might be used to further financial crime.

SYSC 13.7.6 says the following about firms' IT systems:

> A firm should establish and maintain appropriate systems and controls for the management of its IT system risks, having regard to:
>
> (1) its organisation and reporting structure for technology operations (including the adequacy of senior management oversight);
> (2) the extent to which technology requirements are addressed in its business strategy;
> (3) the appropriateness of its systems acquisition, development and maintenance activities (including the allocation of responsibilities between IT development and operational areas, processes for embedding security requirements into systems); and
> (4) the appropriateness of its activities supporting the operation of IT systems (including the allocation of responsibilities between business and technology areas).

SYSC 13.7.7 says the following about information security:

> Failures in processing information (whether physical, electronic or known by employees but not recorded) or of the security of the systems that maintain it can lead to significant operational losses. A firm should establish and maintain appropriate systems and controls to manage its information security risks. In doing so, a firm should have regard to:
>
> (1) confidentiality: information should be accessible only to persons or systems with appropriate authority, which may require firewalls within a system, as well as entry restrictions;
> (2) integrity: safeguarding the accuracy and completeness of information and its processing;
> (3) availability and authentication: ensuring that appropriately authorised persons or systems have access to the information when required and that their identity is verified;
> (4) non-repudiation and accountability: ensuring that the person or system that processed the information cannot deny their actions.

SYSC 13.7.8 says the following about information security standards:

> A firm should ensure the adequacy of the systems and controls used to protect the processing and security of its information, and should have regard to established security standards such as ISO17799 (Information Security Management).

Since early 2007 the FSA has been engaged in very high-profile regulatory action to enforce the rules on systems integrity which are required to achieve the objectives of Principle 3. Indicative actions are:

- In February 2007 the FSA fined Nationwide Building Society £980,000 for breach of Principle 3, following the loss of a laptop computer containing client data, which the FSA considered breached the rules on information security risks. The press release[13] informs:

> during its investigation, the FSA found that the building society did not have adequate information security procedures and controls in place, potentially exposing its customers to an increased risk of financial crime. The FSA also discovered that Nationwide was not aware that the laptop contained confidential customer information and did not start an investigation until three weeks after the theft. Nationwide's failings occurred at a time of heightened awareness of information security issues as a result of government initiatives, increasing media coverage and an FSA campaign about the importance of information security.

- In December 2007 the FSA fined Norwich Union Life £1,260,000 for breaching Principle 3. The press release[14] informs:

> the weaknesses in Norwich Union Life's systems and controls allowed fraudsters to use publicly available information including names and dates of birth to impersonate customers and obtain sensitive customer details from its call centres. They were also, in some cases able to ask for confidential customer records such as addresses and bank account details to be altered. The fraudsters then used the information to request the surrender of 74 customers' policies totalling £3.3 million in 2006. During its investigation, the FSA found that Norwich Union Life had failed to properly assess the risks posed to its business by financial crime, including fraudsters seeking to obtain customers' confidential information. As a result, its customers were more likely to fall victim to financial crimes such as identity theft.

- In June 2008 the FSA fined a small firm of stockbrokers, Merchant Securities Group Ltd, £77,000 for breaching Principle 3. The press release[15] informs:

> Merchant Securities had inadequate procedures for verifying the identities of customers that contacted the firm by telephone. Instead, the firm relied on being able to recognise customers' voices and talking with them informally about personal matters such as holidays or hobbies. Personal account numbers which could be used, with a customer's name, to access account information were included in routine letters. Furthermore, back up tapes containing unencrypted customer information were stored overnight in a bag at the home of a member of staff. Merchant Securities did not address the risk involved in its staff being able to use instant messaging and web based email. There was no evidence, during the FSA's investigation, that customer details had been lost or stolen.

In April 2008 the FSA's position on systems integrity was considered within its report 'Data Security in Financial Services'.[16] The report concluded that 'data security in financial services firms needs to be improved significantly', which included a recommendation that firms should consider monitoring their employees' access to data (at paras.167 and 168):

> Even staff who have a legitimate need to access customer data can present risks. The most pertinent examples include corrupt staff who wish to use customer data to commit fraud themselves, staff who have been coerced by criminals to give them customer data and staff with links to criminal groups who have managed to get a job in a financial services firm. For these reasons, it is good practice for firms to take a risk-based approach to monitoring employees' access to customer data to ensure that access is for genuine business reasons.

The report also said the following about email (at para.188):

> We would strongly encourage firms to consider whether there is a genuine business need for staff to have access to the internet and email and whether the benefits of giving internet access to staff handling large amounts of customer data outweigh the data security risks.

## 9.5 THE INFORMATION COMMISSIONER

The Information Commissioner's interest arises directly from the seventh data protection principle within the DPA 1998, which gives effect to Article 17 of the Data Protection Directive. **Table 9.2** shows these provisions side-by-side.

**Table 9.2** Data security within the Directive and the Data Protection Act 1998

| Data Protection Directive | Data Protection Act 1998 |
|---|---|
| **Article 17**<br>1. Member States shall provide that the controller must implement appropriate technical and organisational measures to protect personal data against accidental or unlawful destruction or accidental loss, alteration, unauthorised disclosure or access, in particular where the processing involves the transmission of data over a network, and against all other unlawful forms of processing. | **Seventh principle**<br>Appropriate technical and organisational measures shall be taken against unauthorised or unlawful processing of personal data and against accidental loss or destruction of, or damage to, personal data.<br><br>**Interpretation**<br>9. Having regard to the state of technological development and the cost of implementing any measures, the measures must ensure a level of security appropriate to – |
| Having regard to the state of the art and the cost of their implementation, such measures shall ensure a level of security appropriate to the risks represented by the processing and the nature of the data to be protected. | (a) the harm that might result from such unauthorised or unlawful processing or accidental loss, destruction or damage as are mentioned in the seventh principle, and<br>(b) the nature of the data to be protected. |

**Table 9.2** *Cont.*

| Data Protection Directive | Data Protection Act 1998 |
|---|---|
| 2. The Member States shall provide that the controller must, where processing is carried out on his behalf, choose a processor providing sufficient guarantees in respect of the technical security measures and organisational measures governing the processing to be carried out, and must ensure compliance with those measures. | 10. The data controller must take reasonable steps to ensure the reliability of any employees of his who have access to the personal data.<br><br>11. Where processing of personal data is carried out by a data processor on behalf of a data controller, the data controller must in order to comply with the seventh principle – |
| 3. The carrying out of processing by way of a processor must be governed by a contract or legal act binding the processor to the controller and stipulating in particular that:<br><br>– the processor shall act only on instructions from the controller,<br>– the obligations set out in paragraph 1, as defined by the law of the Member State in which the processor is established, shall also be incumbent on the processor. | (a) choose a data processor providing sufficient guarantees in respect of the technical and organisational security measures governing the processing to be carried out, and<br>(b) take reasonable steps to ensure compliance with those measures.<br><br>12. Where processing of personal data is carried out by a data processor on behalf of a data controller, the data controller is not to be regarded as complying with the seventh principle unless – |
| 4. For the purposes of keeping proof, the parts of the contract or the legal act relating to data protection and the requirements relating to the measures referred to in paragraph 1 shall be in writing or in another equivalent form. | (a) the processing is carried out under a contract –<br>(i) which is made or evidenced in writing, and<br>(ii) under which the data processor is to act only on instructions from the data controller, and<br>(b) the contract requires the data processor to comply with obligations equivalent to those imposed on a data controller by the seventh principle. |

The current Information Commissioner's first foray in to the field of data security was represented by his special report to Parliament, *What price privacy?*, in which he called for the introduction of custodial penalties for people convicted of offences under DPA 1998, s.55 (see **Chapter 6**). In addition to 'data theft' the Commissioner has also focused on the following issues within data security:

- Privacy Enhancing Technologies (PETs);
- disposal of confidential waste;

- website security;
- amendment of the DPA 1998;
- call centre security;
- encryption technologies;
- ISO 27000 series;
- public sector security;
- management of security breaches;
- notification of security breaches.

### 9.5.1 Privacy Enhancing Technologies

In April 2006 the Information Commissioner published a press release supporting the use of PETs,[17] which he expanded upon in a Guidance Note published in March 2007. The Guidance Note gives the following definition of PETs:[18]

> The Information Commissioner, considers that privacy enhancing technologies are not limited to tools that provide a degree of anonymity for individuals but they are also any technology that exists to protect or enhance an individual's privacy, including facilitating individuals' access to their rights under the Data Protection Act 1998.

In May 2007 the European Commission of the European Union published a Communication addressed to the European Parliament and Council entitled 'on promoting data protection by Privacy Enhancing Technologies'. The Communication gives the following definition of PETs:

> There are a number of definitions of PETs used by the academic community and by pilot projects on this matter. For instance, according to the EC-funded PISA project, PET stands for a coherent system of ICT measurers that protects privacy by eliminating or reducing personal data or by preventing unnecessary and/or undesired processing of personal data, all without losing the functionality of the information system. The use of PETs can help to design information and communication systems and services in a way that minimises the collection and use of personal data and facilitate compliance with data protection rules. The Commission in its First Report on the implementation of the Data Protection Directive considers that 'the use of appropriate technological measures is an essential complement to legal means and should be an integral part in any efforts to achieve a sufficient level of privacy protection. . .'. The use of PETs should result in making breaches of certain data protection rules more difficult and/or helping to detect them.

The clear effect of these definitions is that a PET is any technology that helps to protect a person's privacy, particularly by facilitating an organisation's compliance with the 'data protection principles'. Thus, PETs have a significant role to play in the field of data security. Indeed, the Information

Commissioner has adopted a PETs strategy within his enforcement policy for data security, which is reflected by regulatory action that he has taken against data controllers, which has focused upon the need for encryption of laptop computers. Clearly, this evidences a substantial connection between PETs and email, not least for the fact that most laptops with be used to store emails.

### 9.5.2 Disposal of confidential waste data

In 2007 the Commissioner commenced regulatory action against a large group of data controllers that had failed to dispose safely of confidential waste data.[19] This action was focused upon the disposal of waste documents, which, of course, is a problem that can easily impact upon email, due to the tendency for people to print hard copies of their emails.

### 9.5.3 Website security

In 2007 the Commissioner commenced regulatory action against the Department of Health and the Foreign and Commonwealth Office, for failure of website security, which was concluded by these public authorities signing undertakings agreeing to take remedial action. Again, there is an obvious connection between websites and emails.

### 9.5.4 Amendment of the DPA 1998

In December 2007 the Commissioner submitted a report to the Ministry of Justice in which he argued his case for further amendment of the DPA 1998.[20] This submission was subsequent to the loss of two data disks by HM Revenue and Customs (HMRC). The Commissioner argued for the following amendments:

- a new criminal offence of failing to comply with the data protection principles;
- a new power of inspection of controller's premises and systems;
- a new right to call for an independent report on the controller's operations;
- enhanced enforcement powers, including a power to seek injunctions to stop processing and a right to serve information notices on any person.

In May 2008 the Criminal Justice and Immigration Act received Royal Assent, which has given the Commissioner a new power to fine controllers for breach of the principles and in July 2008 the Ministry of Justice opened a public consultation on new inspection powers for the Commissioner.[21]

### 9.5.5 Call centre security

In May 2007 the Information Commissioner concluded regulatory action against mobile and broadband provider Orange, for failures of call centre security. Orange signed undertakings effectively admitting breach of the seventh data protection principle.

### 9.5.6 Encryption

As mentioned in the context of PETs, the Commissioner is now pursuing an enforcement policy for unencrypted laptop computers. This policy, 'Our Approach to Encryption',[22] was published in November 2007 and says:

> There have been a number of reports recently of laptop computers, containing personal information which have been stolen from vehicles, dwellings or left in inappropriate places without being protected adequately. The Information Commissioner has formed the view that in future, where such losses occur and where encryption software has not been used to protect the data, enforcement action will be pursued.
>
> The ICO recommends that portable and mobile devices including magnetic media, used to store and transmit personal information, the loss of which could cause damage or distress to individuals, should be protected using approved encryption software which is designed to guard against the compromise of information.

### 9.5.7 ISO 27000 series

ISO/IEC 27000 series is the current International Standard for public and private sector organisations; it is used to establish guidelines and general principles for initiating, implementing, maintaining and improving information security management. The Commissioner has endorsed this standard in 'Our Approach to Encryption', where he says:

> Personal information, which is stored, transmitted or processed in information, communication and technical infrastructures, should also be managed and protected in accordance with the organisation's security policy and using best practice methodologies such as using the International Standard 27001.

### 9.5.8 Public sector security

The loss of two HMRC data disks in November 2007, which contained the entire child benefit database, focused the spotlight on data security in the public sector and led to much 'confessional' reporting of other public sector security breaches to the Commissioner. In January 2008 the focus increased in intensity after the theft of a Royal Navy laptop containing data relating to over 600,000 recruits or potential recruits. In July 2008 the Commissioner served enforcement notices on the Chairman of HMRC[23] and the Secretary of State for Defence[24] as a result of these incidents.

### 9.5.9 Management of security breaches

In March 2008 the Commissioner published guidance on the management of security breaches.[25] The Commissioner recommends that controllers adopt a policy on the management of security breaches, which should focus on containment and recovery, assessment of ongoing risk, notification of breach and evaluation and response.

### 9.5.10 Notification of security breaches

One of the most difficult issues facing organisations that have suffered a security breach is whether they are under an obligation to report it. At the moment the law on reporting is unclear. However, the trend of the law is certainly towards the reporting of breaches. For example, in the United States more than 50 per cent of the states have already implemented legislation that requires the reporting of security breaches to some extent.[26]

If the DPA 1998 is examined, it is possible to identify some provisions that are indicative of a reporting of security breach obligation. However, the general consensus among practitioners is that there is not, as yet, a specific obligation to report security breaches within the DPA 1998. This does not mean that the obligation does not exist. For example, when the Act is read in the context of the Human Rights Act 1998 and the law of confidence, it is very arguable that an organisation suffering a security breach should report it.

Another school of thought is that it does not really matter whether there is a specific reporting of security breach obligation within the DPA 1998. The thinking here is that if you do not report and the regulator finds out, the regulator will treat you more harshly than they would have done had you reported the breach to them in the first place. For example, there is evidence in the Nationwide case that the FSA took a dim view of the Nationwide's failure immediately to report their security breach once they found out about it.[27] It is also the writer's experience that there is a different mindset within regulators depending upon whether an organisation reports.

As regards the trend of the law, a key piece of evidence was published in late 2007 by the European Commission. To explain, the European Commission was required to review the regulatory framework for electronic communications. The Commission has proposed that a specific reporting of security breach obligation should be imported into amending legislation.[28] On the domestic front, in December 2007 the Information Commissioner gave evidence about data protection to a House of Commons enquiry.[29] The Commissioner said that he would prefer the introduction of a reporting of security breaches obligation into the DPA 1998. The Commons committee was very favourable to this proposal. In the light of the dramatic events following the loss of the disks by HMRC in November 2007, it would be unwise to rule out the possibility that new legislation will be forthcoming that will mandate organisations to report security breaches as soon as they happen.

In practical terms, it is now standard advice to organisations planning for data security that they must also plan a strategy for the reporting of security breaches. This is not to say that every security breach should be reported, but a prevailing view is that if secrecy would cause greater harm or damage to those affected than transparency, then the organisation will require a compelling reason to retain secrecy. Furthermore, when planning for the reporting of security breaches organisations should take account of the fact that it is very difficult to keep them secret, particularly in an environment that requires the involvement of the police and the interviewing of staff. Thus, many organisations work on the basis that news of security breaches may leak out. Of course, with household names, blue chips and high profile companies the chances of a leak increase exponentially.

In any event, in March 2008 the Commissioner published guidance on the notification of security breaches to his office.[30] While the guidance recognises that controllers are not under a strict legal obligation to notify the Commissioner of security breaches, the Commissioner recommends notification to his office if the breach is serious. In order to assist controllers with determining whether a breach is serious enough to warrant notification to his office, the Commissioner encourages a quantitative and qualitative assessment, asking the controller to take account of the potential harm to the data subject, the volume of data involved and the sensitivity of the data. The guidance also advances an argument that there is a presumption that incidents involving large amounts of data should be reported to the Commissioner:

> There should be a presumption to report to the ICO where a large volume of personal data is concerned and there is a real risk of individuals suffering some harm. It is difficult to be precise what constitutes a large volume of personal data. Every case must be considered on its own merits but a reasonable rule of thumb is any collection containing information about 1000 or more individuals.

## CHAPTER NOTES

1 Some parts of this chapter are reproduced with the kind permission of Field Fisher Waterhouse LLP.

2 See **www.frc.org.uk/documents/pagemanager/frc/Combined%20code%202006%20OCTOBER.pdf**.

3 See **www.frc.org.uk/documents/pagemanager/frc/Revised%20Turnbull%20Guidance%20October%202005.pdf**.

4 See **www.hmrc.gov.uk**.
5 See **www.bis.org/publ/bcbs128.pdf**.
6 The Capital Requirements Directive consists of two Directives, Directive 2006/48/EC of the European Parliament and of the Council of 14 June 2006 relating to the taking up and pursuit of the business of credit institutions (referred to as 'The Banking Consolidation Directive' by the UK's Financial Services Authority) and Directive 2006/49/EC of the European Parliament and of the Council of 14 June 2006 on the capital adequacy of investment firms and credit institutions (referred to as 'The Capital Adequacy Directive' by the UK's Financial Services Authority).
7 Commission Directive 2006/73/EC of 10 August 2006 implementing Directive 2004/39/EC of the European Parliament and of the Council as regards organisational requirements and operating conditions for investment firms and defined terms for the purposes of that Directive.
8 Commission Regulation (EC) No.1287/2006 of 10 August 2006 implementing Directive 2004/39/EC of the European Parliament and of the Council as regards recordkeeping obligations for investment firms, transaction reporting, market transparency, admission of financial instruments to trading, and defined terms for the purposes of that Directive.
9 CP 07/09 'Conduct of Business regime: non-MiFID deferred matters (including proposals for Telephone Recording)'; **www.fsa.gov.uk/pubs/cp/cp07_09.pdf**.
10 'We propose firms be required to record telephone lines used for voice conversations that involve the receipt of client orders and the negotiating, agreeing and arranging of transactions across the equity, bond and financial commodity and derivatives markets, and to retain electronic communications relevant to these activities. The term electronic communications has wide application and includes fax, e-mail, chat and instant messaging – but, obviously, is not limited to those' (CP 07/09, 19.4).
11 The Instrument proceeds on the footing of being involved in activities that relate to qualifying investments admitted to trading on a prescribed market, or in respect of which a request for admission to trading has been made and related investments, within the meaning of the Prescribed Markets and Qualifying Investments Order 2001, SI 2001/996. It does not apply to collective investment schemes, corporate finance business, corporate treasury functions, to service companies, non-directive friendly societies, non-directive insurers, UCITS qualifiers and certain discretionary investment managers.
12 'Telephone Recording: recording of voice conversations and electronic communications' (PS08/1); **www.fsa.gov.uk/pubs/policy/ps08_01.pdf**.
13 See **www.fsa.gov.uk/pages/Library/Communication/PR/2007/021.shtml**.
14 See **www.fsa.gov.uk/pages/Library/Communication/PR/2007/130.shtml**.
15 See **www.fsa.gov.uk/pages/Library/Communication/PR/2008/058.shtml**.
16 See **www.fsa.gov.uk/pubs/other/data_security.pdf**.
17 'PETs – Your New Best Friends'; **www.ico.gov.uk/upload/documents/pressreleases/2006/pets_your_new_best_friend_press_release.pdf**.
18 'Data Protection Guidance Note: Privacy enhancing technologies (PETs)'; **www.ico.gov.uk/upload/documents/library/data_protection/detailed_specialist_guides/privacy_enhancing_technologies_v2.pdf**.
19 The controllers included 10 high street banks, the Post Office, Cash Generators, Phones 4U and Orange. For further information see: **www.ico.gov.uk/what_we_cover/data_protection/enforcement.aspx**.

20 'Data Protection Powers and Penalties – The Case for Amending the Data Protection Act 1998'; **www.ico.gov.uk/upload/documents/library/corporate/detailed_specialist_guides/data_protection_powers_penalties_v1_dec07.pdf**.
21 'The Information Commissioner's inspection powers and funding arrangements under the Data Protection Act 1998'; **www.justice.gov.uk/docs/cp1508.pdf**.
22 See **www.ico.gov.uk/about_us/news_and_views/current_topics/Our%20approach%20to%20encryption.aspx**.
23 See **www.ico.gov.uk/upload/documents/library/data_protection/notices/hmrc_en_final.pdf**.
24 See **www.ico.gov.uk/upload/documents/library/data_protection/notices/mod_en_final.pdf**.
25 'Guidance on data security breach management'; **www.ico.gov.uk/upload/documents/library/data_protection/practical_application/guidance_on_data_security_breach_management.pdf**.
26 See the Privacy Rights Clearinghouse website for further information: **www.privacyrights.org/index.htm**.
27 For example, see the Financial Service Authority's final notice in the Nationwide data security breach case in February 2007; **www.fsa.gov.uk/pubs/final/nbs.pdf**.
28 Search at the link below for a copy of the European Commission's proposal for a new Directive for electronic communications, which contains the reporting of security breach obligation; **http://ec.europa.eu/information_society/policy/ecomm**.
29 See the House of Commons Justice Committee report on 'Protection of Private Data', First Session 2007–08, 3 January 2008; **www.parliament.uk**.
30 'Notification of Data Security Breaches to the Information Commissioner's Office'; **www.ico.gov.uk/upload/documents/library/data_protection/practical_application/breach_reporting.pdf**.

CHAPTER 10

# Compliance issues

## 10.1 INTRODUCTION

Most organisations wish to ensure that email is used properly, which means efficiently, for the purpose of the business mission and in compliance with the law – but, of course, proper use cannot be achieved organically; instead it requires appropriate organisational and technical structures, as well as management disciplines. An organisation that works without the appropriate structures and disciplines carries unascertained risk and is probably storing embarrassing, if not incriminating, 'smoking guns', which can be discovered via the many routes to access and disclosure of email, some of which are in **Chapters** 7 and **8**.

This chapter aims to provide organisations with practical assistance on compliance issues.[1]

## 10.2 TEN CORE PRINCIPLES FOR A LEGALLY COMPLIANT AND EFFICIENT ORGANISATION

Unfortunately, while there is no shortcut route to achieving an acceptable level of compliance with the law, in the author's experience it is possible to identify 10 core principles of good practice that will operate in most organisations. Working to put these principles in practice should speed up the journey to achieving an acceptable level of compliance with the law, while also helping the organisation to increase overall efficiency in its email use. The 10 core principles identified by the author, which form the subject matter of this chapter, are:

1. Understand how email is used within the organisation.
2. Understand the laws that apply to that use.
3. Take immediate steps to avoid serious legal wrongs.
4. Supply the correct information within email.
5. Prevent spam.
6. Implement a records management policy.

7. Implement a security policy.
8. Set rules for how email is to be used.
9. Educate the users of email as to its proper use.
10. Monitor and police the use of email.

This chapter examines core principles 1, 4, 6, 7, 8, 9 and 10; principle 2, the laws that apply to email use, form the subject matter of the previous chapters and organisations that consider these laws should be able to take all necessary, immediate steps to avoid serious legal wrongs (principle 3) and the sending of spam[2] (principle 5).

## 10.3 UNDERSTAND HOW EMAIL IS USED WITHIN THE ORGANISATION

Achieving legally compliant and efficient use of email is impossible if the organisation does not know, or does not understand, how its email is used; how can an organisation reach any informed decisions about the laws that apply to its use of email and then take decisions on the actions required to be legally compliant, if it does not understand how its email is actually used? If ignorance of use represents the state of the organisation, then this is the first problem that should be addressed.

Furthermore, once a comprehensive understanding of the use of email is acquired, the organisation should strive to keep its knowledge accurate and up to date, which means periodic, ongoing reviews of use. Support for this proposition is derived from many different places, for example, in the context of notifications to the Information Commissioner under Part III of the Data Protection Act (DPA) 1998, which requires data controllers to notify changes to their processing operations in order to avoid committing a criminal offence (s.20).

There are many options available to the organisation that wishes to understand how its email is used; for example, consultants can be retained to perform an audit and there are also technological solutions on the market which facilitate discovery of the facts about email use.

### 10.3.1 Tracing the information lifecycle

Of course, the organisation can implement its own bespoke solutions. A solution developed by the author and which has been used in many situations where there is confusion about how email is used, is called 'tracing the information lifecycle'. In its rawest sense this involves identifying the point at which information enters an organisation and then tracing its flow around the organisation, to the point of its final deletion or destruction. In particular, this process will reveal the risk areas within the organisation and critical interfaces between the organisation and the outside world.

Thus, the tracing of the information lifecycle can be regarded as an exercise in detailed evidence gathering, which provides the foundation stones for all necessary work thereafter. However, it is important to understand that its focus is not actually email use, but, rather, the events that happen within the lifecycle of information and why they happen; email use is just one component of the information lifecycle, albeit a very important one.

Once the information lifecycle is known, it will then be possible to take strategic decisions on the management and use of email, including the implementation of enabling technologies.

### *Commencing the trace*

The tracing of the information lifecycle commences with identification of the categories of information within the organisation, most of which can be assumed. Key categories will include:

- worker data;
- customer data (consumer);
- customer data (not consumer);
- transaction data;
- financial data.

Once the broad categories have been identified, the organisation can then look at the means by which the information is captured. From that starting point it is relatively easy to trace what happens to the information and why.

### *Results of the trace*

Organisations that trace the information lifecycle as part of a structured response to their discovery that they do not understand how their email is used are often disturbed to uncover the following typical results:

- There may be a blurring of the lines between business email and private email.
- Users may have an expectation that their emails are private, in the sense that they will not be accessed by the organisation without their permission, an expectation that often extends to emails pertaining to official business as well as to purely personal ones.
- Emails may reside outside of the established systems for data security and records management, for example, on the local drives of computers, in many forms of portable storage media, such as USB memory sticks, and on the personal equipment of users.
- Decisions on the storage, retention and deletion or emails may be routinely user-defined, rather than organisation-defined.
- There may be a tendency to retain too many emails.

These illustrative results clearly engage many of the issues within the 10 core principles identified earlier. For example, the common blurring of the lines between business email and private email raises serious questions about how privacy and data protection laws operate to protect the users of email within the organisation. This blurring of the lines requires the setting of rules about personal use, education of the users on these rules and, perhaps, effective monitoring and policing of use going forward.

### *Tracing of the information lifecycle in diagrammatic form*

**Figure 10.1** illustrates the kinds of information that will be learned through tracing the information lifecycle, including instances of email use. This information helps the organisation address the other core principles, for example, the implementation of a security policy. The diagram reveals key 'interfaces' between the organisation and the outside world, which pose obvious security risks, namely between:

- the consumer and the website;
- the website and the network;
- the network and the worker;
- the worker and the worker's personal equipment;
- the network and the data processor; and
- the data processor and the outside world.

Once these risk areas have been identified, it is also possible to categorise the types of risk. In broad terms the diagram reveals four main risk areas:

- Information risks – The consumer enters payment data at the website, which includes financial information. A risk rating can be applied to this data, because financial data is attractive to criminals and in the event of a security breach harm could be caused to the individuals concerned.
- People risks – There is clearly worker interaction with the data, both within the organisation and at the processor's end, which introduces the potential for human error into the system.
- Physical risks – Aside from the state of physical security within the organisation, the diagram reveals three other physical risks areas: (1) the website might be hosted on a server maintained by an external internet service provider (ISP); (2) workers' homes; and (3) the data processor's premises. The risk issue here is that these premises are beyond the day-to-day control of the organisation.
- Technology risks – The information is processed within a network and is sent by email.

The diagram may also reveal other important matters, such as the movement of data across departmental boundaries and across jurisdictions; for example, the maintenance of the website and the databases might be the preserve of the IT department, while the worker who emailed a copy of the spreadsheet to their home might be part of the customer services department; the customer and the data processor might be situated in different countries to the organisation.

The diagram also helps to reveal some of the legal issues within data security. For example, the worker who emailed the spreadsheet to their home PC might be acting without authority, which could give rise to a form of disciplinary sanction, or, even a criminal investigation under DPA 1998, s.55 or Computer Misuse Act 1990, s.1. The use of the data processor will immediately engage issues under the seventh data protection principle within the DPA 1998. The disposal of customer data in the waste-paper bin would certainly trigger an investigation by the Information Commissioner, if he were ever to find out. The fact that the customer is a consumer will also engage issues under the E-Commerce Directive.

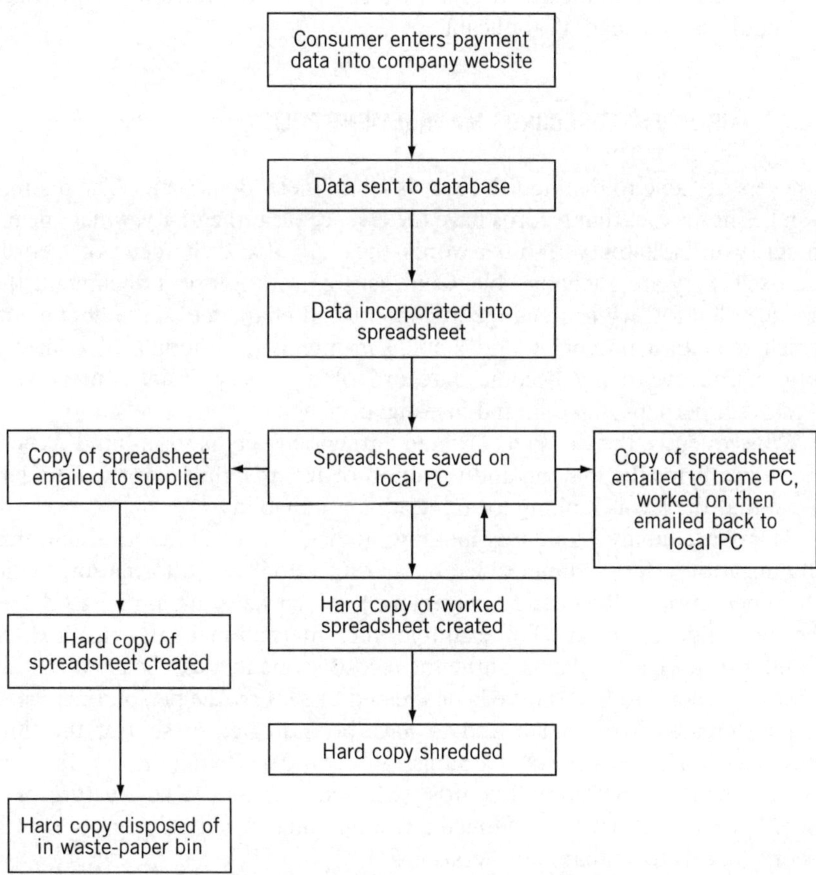


**Figure 10.1** Example of an information lifecycle

## 10.4 SUPPLY THE CORRECT INFORMATION WITHIN EMAILS

Email represents one of the most prolific forms of communication between the organisation and the outside world. This behoves the organisation to think about the messages that should be contained within the text of the email. Typical messages include:

- Business names – Companies Act legislation requires the disclosure of the company name in correspondence (see Companies Act 1985, s.349 and Companies Act 2006, s.82).
- VAT registration numbers should be displayed on invoices.
- Anti-spam legislation requires the disclosure of the organisation's true identity.
- A confidentiality notice should be included, if the information is protected by confidence.
- A notice that information is protected by legal professional privilege should be included, if applicable.

## 10.5 IMPLEMENT A RECORDS MANAGEMENT POLICY

Lawyers are able to distinguish records from 'mere' documents. The distinction lies in the fact that records have the essence of authenticity, which means integrity and reliability. In other words, the content and character of records are fixed; they are unchangeable. Contrast this with a forged document; the essence of a forgery is a change in content and character of the document, which renders it unreliable and lacking in integrity, although, of course a forgery can eventually become a record of a forgery, if its contents are preserved, perhaps in a criminal investigation!

Consequently, the words record and authenticity go hand-in-hand. Where the law calls for the making and retention of records, the lawyer will understand that the law is looking for integrity and reliability.

There are many standards-making bodies, such as the International Organization for Standardization (ISO 15489 'Information and Documentation – Records Management'), which have attempted to define the meaning of records. For example, the International Organization for Standardization says that an authentic record is one that can be proven to be what it purports to be, to have been created or sent by the person purported to have created it or sent it and to have been created or sent at the time purported. The European Commission's Model Requirements for the Management of Electronic Records[3] (MoReq) say that 'a key feature of a record is that it cannot be changed'. The National Archives' definition of a record[4] points to similar considerations:

> A record is a specific piece of information produced or received in the initiation, conduct or completion of an institutional or individual activity. It comprises sufficient content, context and structure to provide evidence of that activity. It is not ephemeral: that is to say, it contains information that is worthy of preservation in the short, medium or long term.

In the case of *R.* v. *Iqbal* [1990] 3 All ER 787 the Court of Appeal considered the meaning of records for the purposes of a criminal case. The case teaches us the following about the meaning of records:

- A book or file into which information is deliberately put in order that it may be available to others on another day is a record.
- A record is a history of events in some form which is not impermanent.
- A record is something which a historian would regard as an original or primary source.
- A record is a compilation of facts supplied by those with direct knowledge of the facts, which is preserved in writing or other permanent form in order that it is not impermanent and which will serve as an original source or memorial of those facts and thus be evidence of them.

### 10.5.1 Records management standards

There are many national and international standards that are designed to help organisations with the keeping of records. These standards are of particular value where email is concerned, as electronic documents pose far more challenges for records keeping than paper ones.

The core challenge for electronic records is how to guarantee their authenticity. The National Archives say that 'a presumption of authenticity is an inference that is drawn from known facts about the manner in which a record has been created, handled and maintained'.[5] Thus, for electronic records the key issue is the record's environment, which the National Archives refer to as its 'context':[6]

> context – the environment and web of relationships in which the document was created and used.

Fortunately, for those people responsible for the management of electronic records there is substantial guidance published by standardisation authorities that can be drawn upon to create the best possible environment for electronic records.

### *Example – British Standards DISC PD0010 and BIP 0008 (DISC PD0008)*

The British Standards Institution's (BSI) 'Principles for Good Practice for Information Management' provide an excellent benchmark for records management, having been designed to help organisations 'develop and operate new methods and technologies for managing information, and in particular, that information which is stored and managed as documents'. According to the principles, an organisation should be able to:

- recognise and understand all types of information;
- understand the legal issues and execute 'duty of care' responsibilities;
- identify and specify business processes and procedures;
- identify enabling technologies to support business processes and procedures;
- monitor and audit business processes and procedures.

These principles have been used by the BSI as the foundation of its 'Code of Practice for Legal Admissibility and Evidential Weight of Information Stored Electronically' (BSI BIP 0008 (ISBN 0 580 42774 9); this is sometimes referred to as BSI DISC PD0008). This Code of Practice 'provides a framework and guidelines that identify key areas of good practice for the implementation and operation of electronic storage systems, whether or not any information held therein is ever required as evidence in event of a dispute'. It goes on to say that 'compliance with this Code should be regarded as a demonstration of responsible business management' (failure to comply with a British Standard can be treated as evidence of negligence; *Ward* v. *Ritz Hotel* (1992)).

A detailed rehearsal of the contents of the Code of Practice is beyond the scope of this book, but it is worth drawing attention to the following passage on information security:

> Information security is key when discussing legal admissibility issues. The main discussion on this topic is likely to be the authenticity of the stored information. When the electronic information was captured by the storage system, was the process secure? Was the correct information captured, and was it complete and accurate? During storage, was the information changed in any way, either accidentally or maliciously? When responding to these questions, information security implementation and monitoring are key to demonstrating authenticity.

In amplification of these points the Code of Practice says:

> Arguments over admissibility of information as evidence can lead to an investigation into the system from which the information came, the method of storage, operation and access control, and even into the computer programs and source code. It may be necessary to satisfy the court that the information is stored in a 'proper' manner. This could be a tactic used to try to discredit the evidence and to

> make inadmissible, or reduce the evidential weight of, that evidence and any similarly stored information that is produced. Questionable hardware reliability, for example, could be used to discredit the information management system. This could call the whole system into question and cause information stored within it to be ruled inadmissible.

All of this brings into focus the issue of audit trails. The Code of Practice says:

> When preparing information for use as evidence, it is often necessary to provide further supporting information. This information may include details such as date of storage of the information, details of movement of the information from medium to medium, and evidence of the controlled operation of the system. These details are known as 'audit trail' information. This audit trail information is needed to enable the working of the system to be demonstrated, as well as the progress of information through the system, from receipt to final deletion. Audit trails need to be comprehensive and properly looked after, as without them the integrity and authenticity, and thus the evidential weight of the information stored in the systems could be called into question.

In summary, DISC PD0010 and BIP 0008 identify the following essential requirements for the technology within a sound records management policy for electronic records:

- Enabling technology must be identified.
- The hardware must be robust.
- The technology must facilitate monitoring and auditing.
- The technology must provide a high level of security.
- The technology must capture the correct information.
- The technology must capture complete information.
- The technology must have change-protection functionality.

### *Example – ISO 15489–1:2001*

ISO 15489–1 'Information and Documentation – Records Management' is designed to ensure that 'appropriate attention and protection is given to all records, and that the evidence and information they contain can be retrieved more efficiently and effectively, using standard practices and procedures'. These standards apply to public and private sector organisations. Regarding storage, these standards say:

> Records should be stored on media that ensure their usability, reliability, authenticity and preservation for as long as they are needed.

As regards electronic records these standards continue:

> Systems for electronic records should be designed so that records will remain accessible, authentic, reliable and useable through any kind of system change, for the entire period of their retention. This may include migration to different software, re-presentation in emulation formats or any other future ways of re-presenting records. Where such processes occur, evidence of these should be kept, along with details of any variation in records design and format.
>
> Information security is key when discussing legal admissibility issues. The main discussion on this topic is likely to be the authenticity of the stored information. When the electronic information was captured by the storage system, was the process secure? Was the correct information captured, and was it complete and accurate? During storage, was the information changed in any way, either accidentally or maliciously? When responding to these questions, information security implementation and monitoring are key to demonstrating authenticity.

In summary, ISO 15489–1 says that an effective records management system will be able to:

- identify which documents should be captured;
- determine retention period;
- capture the records;
- register the records;
- classify the records;
- safely store the records;
- give access to the records;
- track the movement and use of the records;
- implement disposition (destruction) of the records; and
- facilitate monitoring and auditing of the records.

### *Example – The National Archives standards*

The National Archives has published many helpful guides on the management of records. Whilst these are geared towards public sector records, they can be easily adapted for use in the private sector. For example, the 'e-Government Policy Framework for Electronic Records Management'[7] states that:

> Good electronic record-keeping requires:
>
> – a clear understanding of the nature of electronic records, and the electronic information which should be captured as records in order to document the business processes
> – that the procedures to routinely capture these records are designed into the electronic systems generating the records (for example, office systems), and are easy and understandable to use
> – electronic record-keeping systems that are designed to manage reliable and authentic records, ensuring that the integrity and reliability of electronic records is secured

- a strategy to ensure that electronic records will remain accessible and usable for as long as they are needed
- the ability to apply appropriate appraisal, scheduling and disposal procedures to managed electronic records
- a culture of best practice record-keeping among managers and end users.

Regarding the technical requirement for storage of records, the National Archives' 'generic requirements for sustaining electronic information over time'[8] provides the following guidance on selection of storage media:

> When identifying the appropriate new media format, the following factors should be considered:
>
> - longevity: the media should have a proven life span of at least 10 years. Greater longevity is not necessarily an advantage, since technological obsolescence usually precedes physical deterioration of the medium.
> - capacity: the media should provide a storage capacity appropriate for the quantity of data to be stored, and the physical size of the storage facilities available.
> - viability: the media should support robust error-detection methods for both reading and writing data. Proven data recovery techniques should also be available in case of data loss. Media should be read-only, or have a reliable write-protect mechanism, to prevent erasure and maintain the evidential integrity of the data.
> - obsolescence: the media and its supporting hardware and software should be based on mature, rather than leading-edge technology, and must be well established in the market place, widely available, and based upon open standards.
> - cost: the total cost of ownership should be affordable. This should include not only the cost of the actual media (calculated as a price per MB), but also of purchasing and maintaining the necessary hardware and software, and of any storage equipment required. susceptibility: – the media should have a low susceptibility to physical damage, and be tolerant of a wide range of environmental conditions without data loss.

In summary, the National Archives identify the following essential requirements for the technology within a sound records management policy for electronic records:

- The technology must incorporate records capture procedures.
- The technology must give ready access to the records so that the records are useable.
- The technology must facilitate monitoring and auditing.
- The hardware must be robust, with a long lifespan.
- The technology must be scaleable.
- The technology must incorporate error detection functionality.
- The technology must incorporate content protection functionality.
- The technology must have change-protection functionality.
- The technology must provide affordable cost of ownership.

### *Composite view of records management standards*

If all of records management standards are considered together, the composite view within **Table 10.1** is achieved:

**Table 10.1** Composite view of records management standards

| Records management standards | Requirements |
|---|---|
| *The technology:* | |
| 1. Robustness | The technology must display a low susceptibility to physical damage |
| 2. Longevity | The technology must prevent records degradation during the information lifecycle |
| 3. Obsolescence | The technology must be based on established, proven platforms |
| 4. Scaleability | The technology must scale to meet the organisation's requirements |
| 5. Open standards | The technology must take advantage of as many open standards as possible |
| 6. Cost | The technology must reduce the cost of records keeping by as much as possible |
| 7. Security | The technology must provide robust security |
| *Records capture:* | |
| 8. Wide capture | The technology must capture as many different file types as possible |
| 9. Complete capture | The technology must capture every new record |
| 10. Classification | The technology must allow records to be classified |
| 11. Metadata | The technology must create or support metadata |
| 12. Unique identifiers | The technology must allocate unique identifiers to each unique record |
| *Content protection:* | |
| 13. Protection against data loss or damage due to system failure | The technology must display features that go to protect the data from corruption caused by software/ hardware failure |
| 14. Protection against overwrite | The technology must display features that prevent the accidental or deliberate overwriting of records |
| 15. Protection against delete | The technology must display features that prevent the accidental or deliberate deletion of records otherwise than in accordance with a predefined schedule |
| 16. Safe delete | The technology must enable the complete and irreversible deletion of records |

**Table 10.1** *Cont.*

| Records management standards | Requirements |
|---|---|
| *Access and retrieval:* | |
| 17. Complete access and retrieval | The technology must allow access and retrieval of all records |
| 18. Speed of retrieval | The technology must facilitate quick access and retrieval of records |
| 19. Protection against unauthorised access and retrieval | The technology must facilitate controls and limitations over access and retrieval |
| 20. Search | The technology must facilitate search |
| *Monitoring and audit:* | |
| 21. Complete monitoring and audit | The technology must facilitate full monitoring and auditing |

### 10.5.2 Technologies for managing emails as records

The effective management of emails as records requires technological solutions as explained above. The key pieces of technology for these purposes are:

- Archiving technology – An email archive captures and classifies emails and sends them to storage.
- Storage technology – Where the emails are stored as records.
- Search and retrieval technology – The organisation will wish to retrieve emails from the archive.

All of these technologies must be protected by appropriate security.

## 10.6 IMPLEMENT A SECURITY POLICY

As mentioned in **Chapter 9**, both the Information Commissioner and the Financial Services Authority (FSA) have endorsed the use of the ISO 27000 series for information security management systems. The series consists of two main parts (though the series has been expanded to more parts):

- ISO/IEC 27001:2005 – Information technology – Security techniques – Information security management systems – Requirements.
- ISO/IEC 27002:2005 – Information technology – Security techniques – Code of practice for information security management.

### 10.6.1 ISO/IEC 27001

ISO/IEC 27001 is an international standard that has 'been prepared to provide a model for establishing, implementing, operating, monitoring, reviewing, maintaining an Information Security Management System (ISMS)'. An ISMS is 'designed to ensure the selection of adequate and proportionate security controls that protection information assets and give confidence to interested parties'. Organisations implementing an ISMS in accordance with 27001 can be formally 'accredited', which requires external auditing and regular reviews.

### 10.6.2 ISO/IEC 27002

ISO/IEC 27002 works differently to 27001 in that its focus is 'guidelines and general principles for initiating, implementing, maintaining, and improving information security management in an organisation'. It provides 'general guidance on the commonly accepted goals of information security management'.

ISO 27002 is a very detailed document, but its main focus is:

- Risk assessments and the treatment of risk – As a first step, organisations should identify and quantify the risks to the security of their information, following which they should take decisions on the treatment of risk. Some risks will be accepted by the organisation while others will be controlled, or eliminated.
- Security policy – The objective of the security policy is to 'provide management direction and support for information security', in the light of the needs of the organisation and the law.
- Organisation of information security – Information security needs to be properly managed within the organisation, with clear lines of responsibility.
- Asset management – The organisation needs to account for all of its assets, nominating asset owners, defining acceptable use.
- Human resources security – All people working with information, from employees to subcontractors and other third parties, need to understand their obligations, which extends to screening of workers and their training.
- Physical and environmental security – The objective is to prevent unauthorised access to the premises and the information contained within, which includes preventing damage and interference with the premises and information.
- Communications and operations management – The use of information processing facilities should be both correct and secure, which extends to the setting of appropriate management and operating procedures, with segregation of duties as necessary.

- Access controls – Access to information, information processing facilities and business processes should be properly controlled.
- Information systems, acquisition and development – The objective is to ensure that security is embedded into all information systems, particularly during design, implementation and acquisition.
- Information security incident management – Security events and weaknesses should be recorded and managed to ensure the taking of appropriate and timely corrective actions.
- Business continuity management – The organisation should implement appropriate solutions to counteract interruption to business activities consequent upon security incidents, including failures of equipment and systems.
- Compliance – All aspects of the design, operation, use and management of information systems should take account of legal requirements.

### 10.6.3 Connecting ISO 27002 to the DPA 1998

ISO 27002 has been approved by the Information Commissioner as a framework for ensuring compliance with the seventh data protection principle within the DPA 1998. All of the requirements of the seventh data protection principle are addressed by ISO 27002.

### 10.6.4 Contents of a security policy

The organisation's security policy should address all of the matters identified in ISO 27002, the seventh data protection principle and the Information Commissioner's activities in the field of data security. Necessary contents that arise from the seventh data protection principle and the Information Commissioner's activities are:

- 'Anti-blagging policies' – The Information Commissioner has drawn attention to a widespread and pervasive industry trading in stolen data.[9] One of the methodologies of those stealing data is pretexting, or 'blagging', which involves the thief pretending to be someone with a lawful right to data.
- Confidential waste – A detailed policy is required for the end of the information lifecycle, which should address issues as diverse as the destruction of confidential paper waste, 'electronic shredding', data in the possession of data processors and data stored on workers' personal equipment.
- Data processors and third parties – Again, the DPA 1998 provides a framework for the handling of relationships with data processors.[10] This provides a helpful starting point for the creation of policies, although a 'best practice' approach will require consideration of more points than are covered by the DPA 1998.

- Disaster recovery and business continuity – A security breach can be caused by, or lead to, a disaster. A disaster recovery policy needs to be considered. Disasters can be caused by fires, floods, subsidence, crime, terrorist activity, etc.
- Fraud prevention – Fraud prevention extends much further than anti-blagging policies, overlapping with many of the other disciplines identified here.
- Legal and compliance – The organisation needs to be able to identify in advance the situations where legal and compliance clearance is required.
- Identity management – The organisation should seek to verify the identity of every person coming into contact with data. Of course, the levels of verification required differ from person to person and from case to case, but they will invariably encompass some form of pre-employment verification and assignment of individual access rights post recruitment.
- Insurance – The market for insurance against security risks is likely to develop, with consequential effects on insurance policies generally. Organisations need to keep their insurance policies under review.
- Network usage – All elements of human interaction with the computer and communications network should be subject to usage policies. Key areas of interest include computer use, internet use, email use, use of portable devices, attachment and removal of devices from the network, teleworking and use of personal equipment, technology refresh and data access rights.
- Security breach – A very detailed policy is required for dealing with security breaches.
- Systems integrity – A process of ongoing testing of systems integrity is often required.
- Transparency at the point of data capture – A policy of transparency at the point of capture of data to the organisation is required in most cases for the purpose of compliance with the first data protection principle from the DPA 1998 and this stands as a model of compliance for any kind of data capture.
- Worker monitoring – If the organisation is to adopt any process of employee monitoring it is imperative that this is communicated to the employees in clear terms. Recent case law has severely sanctioned unwarranted monitoring.[11] Furthermore, the Information Commissioner has issued a Code of Practice on monitoring,[12] which promotes transparency. Of course, in cases of serious crime, monitoring without any form of prior notice may be permissible, but this will be a very rare exception.
- Worker discipline – The organisation should adopt a policy that states clearly when activity will be regarded as unauthorised so as to justify disciplinary action.

Of course, the security policy should specifically address all of the matters in ISO 27002, where they are additional to the ones listed here.

## 10.7 SET RULES FOR HOW EMAIL IS TO BE USED

Organisations should ensure that they create an email acceptable usage policy, which should be incorporated within contracts of employment and contracts of engagement of subcontractors, within company handbooks and within company disciplinary procedures. A serious breach of an acceptable usage policy can amount to gross misconduct justifying dismissal, but it is important to follow the statutory disciplinary procedure,[13] although in very serious cases a person can be suspended pending an investigation.

It is critically important that organisations state specifically within employment contracts that a breach of an acceptable usage policy will be treated as a breach of the employment contract amounting to gross misconduct (for example, see *British Telecommunications plc* v. *Rodrigues* [1995] EAT (854/92)). Failure to warn employees about the consequences of a breach of policy can inject uncertainty into the disciplinary process. Ideally, employees should be asked to sign to confirm that they have understood the organisation's rules.

## 10.8 EDUCATE THE USERS OF EMAIL AS TO ITS PROPER USE

The need for education of users of email as to its proper use is a core component of compliance, as reflected by ISO 27002, the seventh data protection principle and general principles of employment law.

## 10.9 MONITOR AND POLICE THE USE OF EMAIL

The monitoring of workers and the requirement for an assessment of the reliability of workers immediately carries with it a number of employment law concerns. These concerns arise in a number of ways:

- The assessment of an employee's reliability might infringe their reasonable expectation of privacy. It needs to be kept in mind that there has been long-standing legal recognition of the right to privacy within the workplace (see *Copland* v. *UK*).
- It might give rise to a constructive dismissal situation.
- It might be implemented in a discriminatory fashion.

- It might interfere with the employee's ability to make 'protected disclosures' under whistle-blowing legislation (see the Public Interest Disclosure Act 1998).

The difficulty for the organisation lies in balancing their obligation to assess the reliability of employees with the obligations they owe to their employees. The only way of achieving the right balance is to carry out the assessments in a proportionate, objective, non-discriminatory and transparent way. The employer should always be as open as possible with the workforce, consulting works councils, trade unions, etc. as required. The justifications for the forms of assessment should always be recorded so that they can be referred to in the event of dispute.

### 10.9.1 General principles for employee monitoring

The general principles applying to the monitoring of employees are:

- Necessity – The employer must check if any form of monitoring is absolutely necessary for a specified purpose before proceeding with that activity. Furthermore, the employer should keep the personal data collected through monitoring for no longer than is necessary for the specified purpose for the monitoring activity.
- Finality – The personal data must be collected for a specified, explicit and legitimate purpose and not further processed in a way incompatible with those purposes.
- Transparency – An employer must be clear and open about his activities. Covert monitoring is only permitted in cases where a law allows for it. The employer should provide its employees with a readily accessible, clear and accurate statement of its policy with regard to monitoring. Furthermore, the employer should, from a practical point of view, immediately inform the workers of any misuse of the electronic communications detected, unless important reasons justify continued surveillance. For instance, 'prompt information can be easily delivered by software such as warning windows, which pop up and alert the worker that the system has detected an unauthorised use of the network'.[14] Employers may also have to notify the local data protection authority before carrying out such monitoring activity and should ensure that workers have a right of access to the data collected.
- Legitimacy – Data processing operations can only take place if they are based on a legitimate purpose, e.g. preventing the transmission of confidential information to a competitor. One of the other legitimate purpose grounds is where an employer obtains the consent of employees to the monitoring. However, as a strategy this has a number of shortcomings since consent must be freely given, specific and informed. In other words, employees must be allowed to withhold their consent if they wish. If an

employee did withhold consent, then the employer would need to establish another ground upon which the processing of the data was legitimised. Furthermore, in an employer-employee context, the Article 29 Working Party has commented that 'where consent is required from a worker, and there is a real or potential relevant prejudice that arises from not consenting, the consent is not valid'.[15]

- Proportionality – Personal data must be adequate, relevant and not excessive with regard to achieving the purpose specified. The Article 29 Working Party have stated that 'the proportionality principle therefore rules out blanket monitoring of individual emails and Internet use of all staff other than where necessary for the purpose of ensuring the security of the system'.[16] In addition, if access to content of emails (or other electronic communications) is absolutely necessary, 'account should be taken of the privacy of those outside the organisation receiving them as well as those inside'.[17]
- Accuracy and retention of data – Any data legitimately stored by an employer consisting of data from a worker's email account or other electronic communication use must be accurate and up to date, and not kept for longer than necessary.
- Security – Any personal data held by an employer must be kept safe and secure from outside intrusion. In particular, the system administrator who has access to personal data about workers in the course of monitoring must be placed under a strict duty of professional secrecy with regard to the confidential information which they access.

### 10.9.2 EU framework for employee monitoring

In its Opinion on the processing of personal data in the employment context,[18] the Article 29 Working Party stated that:

- Any monitoring must be a proportionate response by an employer to the risk it faces, taking into account the legitimate privacy and other interests of workers.
- Any personal data held or used in the course of monitoring must be adequate, relevant and not excessive for the purpose for which the monitoring is justified. Any monitoring must be carried out in the least intrusive way possible. It must be targeted on the area of risk, taking into account the data protection rules and, where applicable, the principle of secrecy of correspondence.
- Monitoring must comply with the transparency requirements so that workers must be informed of the existence of the surveillance, the purposes for which personal data are to be processed and other information necessary to guarantee fair processing.

### 10.9.3 Information Commissioner's approach to monitoring

The Information Commissioner's Employment Practice Code[19] sets out recommendations on how employers can monitor employees so as to comply with the DPA 1998. A failure to comply with any particular recommendation in the Code and the Supplementary Guidance does not automatically equate to a breach of the DPA 1998, and any enforcement action by the Information Commissioner would be based on a failure to meet the requirements of the Act rather than the Code and its Supplementary Guidance. Having said that, employers should not depart from the guidance without good reason, particularly in relation to the monitoring of employees.

The Code sets out the Information Commissioner's approach to monitoring which is as follows:

- It is intrusive to monitor workers.
- Workers can expect a degree of privacy in the workplace.
- If employers wish to monitor workers they should be clear about the purpose and be satisfied that the particular monitoring arrangement is justified by the real benefits that will be delivered.
- Workers should be aware of the nature, extent and reasons for monitoring unless covert monitoring is justified. Covert monitoring will only be justified in exceptional circumstances.
- Workers' awareness will influence their expectations.

*Privacy impact assessments*

The Code advises employers wishing to undertake monitoring initially to carry out a privacy impact assessment on whether they need to process the personal information of employees in order to achieve the desired effect. The key elements of a privacy impact assessment are that the employer must:

- be clear about the purposes of the monitoring and the benefits that it is likely to deliver;
- identify the likely adverse impact of the monitoring;
- consider alternatives to monitoring or different ways in which it could be carried out;
- recognise the obligations that will arise as a result of the monitoring;
- judge whether the monitoring is justified.

Privacy impact assessments are important tools in the Information Commissioner's eyes and guidance on performing assessments has been provided through the Privacy Impact Assessment Handbook which was published in 2008.[20]

*Methods of assessing an employee's reliability*

There are many ways in which an employee's reliability can be assessed. These include:

- in the interview process of job applicants, including psychometric and other testing and the taking up of references;
- through pre-employment credit checking;
- through pre-employment vetting via the Criminal Records Bureau (see the Criminal Records Bureau website: **www.crb.gov.uk**);
- during employee induction programmes;
- through continuing education programmes;
- through the appraisal system;
- through mentoring programmes;
- through the use of CCTV;
- through the monitoring of electronic communications and related data.

When carrying out their assessments, organisations should be careful not to fall into the trap of committing an 'enforced subject access' offence: DPA 1998, s.56 makes it a criminal offence for a prospective employer to make a prospective applicant exercise their data subject rights under DPA 1998, s.7 as a condition of an offer of employment.

*Security risk detected involving employees*

Sometimes the processes used to assess an employee's reliability will reveal that they pose a security risk or that they have committed a security breach. In these situations the employer needs to gauge their reaction carefully; an employee who deliberately leaks data might be acting for a variety of reasons, ranging from the downright criminal through to public-spirited whistle-blowing. Thus a one-size-fits-all strategy cannot work. However, key points for consideration include:

- The deliberate, non-consensual leaking of data creates reasonable suspicion of the commission of a criminal offence under DPA 1998, s.55. Offences under the Computer Misuse Act 1990 might also have been committed. Furthermore, the employee might be working in a conspiracy with an outsider.
- The employer is entitled to carry out a legitimate investigation upon gaining suspicion of a security breach. This can extend to secret investigations in serious cases.
- During the investigation of a security breach, employees can also be interviewed. Third parties can be informed, such as the police and private investigators, although this will have to be justified from a data protection standpoint. (See ss.29 and 35 in particular, which justify disclosure of personal data to third parties. See also Serious Crime Act 2007, s.68,

which contains a provision that allows public bodies to share data with anti-fraud organisations.)

- A serious breach of security can amount to gross misconduct justifying dismissal. However, it is important to follow the statutory disciplinary procedure (Employment Act 2002 (Dispute Resolution) Regulations 2004, SI 2004/752). A person can be suspended pending an investigation.
- In whistle-blowing cases it is necessary to consider the Public Interest Disclosure Act 1998.
- The security breach may put the organisation in breach of contractual duties and in breach of obligations of confidence.

## CHAPTER NOTES

1 Some parts of this chapter are reproduced with kind permission of Field Fisher Waterhouse LLP.
2 Spam can be regarded as being emails where the sender's identify is withheld, concealed or disguised. There are anti-spam provisions within the Distance Selling Directive and the E-Commerce Directive (both discussed at **Chapter 3**) and within the Privacy and Electronic Communications Directive (discussed at **Chapter 4**). Readers should also consider the Consumer Protection from Unfair Trading Regulations 2008, SI 2008/1277, which came into force on 26 May 2008; these bring into force a general ban on unfair commercial practices, which includes spam.
3 See **http://ec.europa.eu/idabc/en/document/2303/5927**.
4 See 'Management, appraisal and preservation of electronic records', Vol.1, at **www.nationalarchives.gov.uk/documents/principles.pdf**.
5 See 'Generic requirements for sustaining electronic information over time: 1. Defining the characteristics for authentic records', **www.nationalarchives.gov.uk/documents/generic_reqs1.pdf**.
6 See 'Management, appraisal and preservation of electronic records', Vol.1, at **www.nationalarchives.gov.uk/documents/principles.pdf**.
7 See **www.nationalarchives.gov.uk/documents/egov_framework.pdf**.
8 See 'Generic requirements for sustaining electronic information over time: 3. Sustaining authentic and reliable records: technical requirements', **www.nationalarchives.gov.uk/documents/generic_reqs3.pdf**.
9 *What price privacy?*, May 2006; **www.ico.gov.uk/upload/documents/library/corporate/research_and_reports/what_price_privacy_low_resolution.pdf**.
10 See the seventh data protection principle. For further information see the Session 1 briefing.
11 *Copland* v. *United Kingdom*, Application No.62617/00, 3 April 2007; **http://www.bailii.org**.
12 Employment Practices Code; **www.ico.gov.uk/upload/documents/library/data_protection/detailed_specialist_guides/employment_practices_code001.pdf**.
13 Employment Act 2002 (Dispute Resolution) Regulations 2004; **http://www.opsi.gov.uk/SI/si2004/20040752**.
14 Working document on the surveillance of electronic communications in the workplace, WP55, Article 29 Working Party, para.3.13.1.
15 Opinion 8/2001, WP 48 on the processing of personal data in the employment context, para.10.

16 Working document on the surveillance of electronic communications in the workplace, WP55, Article 29 Working Party, para.3.1.5.
17 Working document on the surveillance of electronic communications in the workplace, WP55, Article 29 Working Party, para.3.1.5.
18 Article 29 Working Party Opinion 8/2001 on the processing of personal data in the employment context (WP 48).
19 See **www.ico.gov.uk/upload/documents/library/data_protection/detailed_specialist_guides/employment_practices_code.pdf**.
20 See **www.ico.gov.uk/upload/documents/library/data_protection/practical_application/pia_final.pdf**.

# Glossary

**Domain Name System (DNS)** A directory of information including the system by which the domain names we can read (such as example.com) are cross-referenced to IP addresses used by machines (currently using the IPv4 'dotted quad' format, e.g. 208.77.188.166). Name servers hold DNS records about the domains they serve, including the IP address of the relevant mail server.

**Email client** The email client can be a standalone application such as Microsoft's Outlook or Mozilla's Thunderbird. It might also be a web mail service, in which case the user will use a web browser (such as Microsoft's Internet Explorer or Apple's Safari) pointed towards the URL for the chosen web mail service. Web mail services are commonly free of charge (at least in their basic versions) and include such services as Microsoft's Hotmail (now known as Windows Live Hotmail) and Google's Googlemail (or Gmail outside Germany and the UK).

**Headers** In transmission across the internet, data blocks are preceded by small amounts of metadata that essentially explain to the machines handling the data what it is and what should be done with it. Data packets sent by TCP will have headers defining the sender and recipient and the protocol which governs the payload of the packet. Emails, in the same way, have headers. A simple email will have a header explaining the sender and recipient, the subject, and time stamps for the original and all relay mail servers before the destination. MIME headers add more information including exact details of how the message has been encoded for transfer.

**HTTP** The Hypertext Transfer Protocol governs how information (and in particular the documents which constitute as web pages) are transferred on the World Wide Web. HTTP relies on TCP to transmit information.

**IETF** The Internet Engineering TaskForce, at whose website (www.ietf.org) can be found many reference materials relating to internet standards and the protocols discussed in **Chapter 1**.

**Mail server** A mail server is a computer running a software program called a mail transfer agent, designed to transfer messages between computers.

**MIME** The set of standards known as Multipart Internet Mail Extensions, or MIME, stipulate the format in which email is most commonly sent. A MIME-formatted message consists of a number of parts, each of which tells mail servers and email clients something different about the message, and goes further than what is possible with SMTP. Where SMTP allows only the transmission of email which can be represented in a small set of Latin characters, MIME uses additional headers which describe to email programs other types of email such as that with images or other attachments. The MIME headers will also provide information as to what encoding has been used to transform a more complicated message into a character set which can be relayed by SMTP.

**MIME Base64** One of the most common forms of MIME content type encoding, by which the binary data behind any information carried in an email message, whether that be each character of each word or an attached JPEG file, is encoded to be transported by SMTP. Each bit of data is converted into a string of characters (using only those in the sets A–Z, a–z and 0–9) as required by SMTP.

**POP3** Version 3 of the Post Office Protocol, governs how email client applications retrieve messages from a mail server using the standard internet TCP/IP connection.

**SMTP** The Simple Mail Transfer Protocol, which consists of a limited number of simple commands that tell email clients and mail servers how to talk to each other (and so to exchange messages).

**TCP/IP** The Transmission Control Protocol and the Internet Protocol. Also known as the Internet Protocol Suite, TCP/IP is the core set of protocols which govern how data packets are sent across channels of communication between different computers. As well as indicating the content of the information carried in a data packet, these protocols provide the ways in which a packet's origin is identified and any errors may be detected.

**TCP ports** Any computer connected to the internet is capable of a huge number of simultaneous connections to remote computers, and each of those connections (by TCP or another transport protocol) will interface with the computer at an endpoint described as a TCP port. These are known by number and some of the most common of relevance here are port 25 (used for SMTP), port 80 (for HTTP) and port 587 (for alternative mail submission).

**URL** Uniform Resource Locator. Essentially, a domain name prefixed by the protocol command, so http://www.example.com, is really an instruction to a web browser to use the HTTP protocol to access the domain example.com.

# Index